Jock Phillips

MAKING
HISTORY

Jock Phillips

MAKING HISTORY

A New Zealand Story

AUCKLAND
UNIVERSITY
PRESS

First published 2019
Auckland University Press
University of Auckland
Private Bag 92019
Auckland 1142
New Zealand
www.press.auckland.ac.nz

© Jock Phillips, 2019

ISBN 9 781 86940 899 2

Published with the assistance of Creative New Zealand

A catalogue record for this book is available from the National Library of New Zealand

This book is copyright. Apart from fair dealing for the purpose of private study, research, criticism or review, as permitted under the Copyright Act, no part may be reproduced by any process without prior permission of the publisher. The moral rights of the author have been asserted.

All photos listed without source are by Jock Phillips or from his personal collection.

Book design by Carolyn Lewis
Jacket design by Spencer Levine

Cover photograph by Chris Maclean

Printed in China by Everbest Printing Investment Ltd

*To
Frida Susan Harper,
who has brought love and joy
to my last two decades*

Contents

Acknowledgements ix
Introduction: Out of the darkness 1

—

1 My father and the mother country 7
2 My mother and the land 43
3 Christchurch boy 67
4 America! 97
5 Discovering New Zealand 143
6 The Stout Centre 175
7 Servant of the Crown 205
8 Exhibitionist 247
9 A sojourn on the dark side 281
10 Encyclopedist 301

—

Epilogue: NZ HistoryJock 349
Notes 354
Index 362

Acknowledgements

This book grew out of a series of well-timed invitations which encouraged me to believe that telling the story of my public-history career might be of wider interest. They came from Doug Monro, who invited me to prepare a chapter for a collection on my father and World War II; from the National Museum of Australia, who requested that I speak about my experiences developing the history exhibitions at Te Papa; from Lydia Wevers and Kerry Taylor, who asked me on two separate occasions to speak about my time at the Stout Research Centre; from the Friends of the Turnbull Library, who honoured me by suggesting I give the Founder Lecture on the journey of developing Te Ara; and from Queen's University in Belfast, who invited me to give the Keith Jeffery lecture as a keynote address to a conference on public history about the trials and tribulations of taking history to a broad audience. Without that encouragement this book would never have appeared and would certainly have been longer in the gestation.

In the course of writing the book I accrued other debts. I am grateful to my mother, the late Pauline Phillips, who kept a host of family documents and photographs and also all the letters I wrote to her over thirty years. They proved essential. Jane McCartney also kept the letters I wrote to her from Harvard in 1968–70 and these were almost too revealing. My two sisters, Elizabeth Caffin and Catherine Phillips, read the text closely and, although neither agreed with every judgement, they forced me to rework matters and each picked up many significant details which needed correcting. My two children, Jesse and Hester, and my stepchildren, Laura, Eve, Julia and Lily, have put up with my absent-mindedness and encouraged me to keep writing. My good friend

Chris Maclean, who was writing his own autobiography, was consistently encouraging and urged me on at every opportunity. His close reading of the text greatly improved it; and his photographic documentation of my life made a huge contribution to the images. Geoff Norman also worked his magic on some of the photos. Good friends David Young and David Grant were helpful in the hunt for photographs. Once a full draft was completed, I had really useful comments from Malcolm McKinnon, Ben Schrader and Shaun Barnett. The members of the history reading group to which I belong (Ross Calman, Peter Clayworth, Elizabeth Cox, Mark Derby, Paul Diamond, Emma Jane Kelly, Ewan Morris, Jane Tolerton) gave excellent feedback on the chapter about my father. The readers for Auckland University Press also made crucial suggestions. I owe a special debt to Bronwyn Labrum. Sam Elworthy was enthusiastic at a vital stage and saved me from publishing the book myself; and Caren Wilton's wise and sympathetic editing improved the text greatly. The team at Auckland University Press have done a dedicated, professional job ensuring that my hopes and intentions have been fulfilled. My greatest debt, for her constant encouragement and acute reading of the manuscript, is to my wife, Frida Susan Harper, to whom this book is dedicated.

Introduction
Out of the darkness

The curtains were pulled, the lights went out, the everyday world of school and work and sport began to disappear from consciousness. We were pitched into darkness. And then the projector sprang into life. Images started to appear on the screen – of castles and country houses, Roman ruins and Renaissance paintings, the rolling manicured dales of England, all accompanied by the enthusiastic tones of my father's mellifluous voice. History was coming alive, leaving the humdrum world of Christchurch far behind.

It was 1956. The family was watching coloured slides of my parents' journey back to the Old World – to the homeland of England and the civilisations of Europe. At last we were looking at a place genuinely old, countries with long and dramatic histories. The situation may have been unusual in the New Zealand of the 1950s, where few people travelled overseas or took coloured slides when they did, but the sentiments were not. Many New Zealanders at that time considered that history was something you encountered overseas. We were a 'new country', determined to escape the crippling traditions of the old. We had simply not been around long enough to have an exciting, stirring past. The great events, such as wars, coronations and political crises, happened across the other side of the globe. If you wanted history then it was a month heading north in a boat, unless of course you were lucky enough to have a father who took a camera with him.

Those attitudes are now, thankfully, long gone in New Zealand. After years of disinterest many New Zealanders, Pākehā and Māori, began to accept that humans had been in this land for over 700 years, and that Māori had a wonderful storehouse of remarkable people and dramatic events.

We began to realise that even in the 200-odd years since Pākehā settlement in the early nineteenth century, New Zealand's history was packed with fascinating individuals and compelling stories. Slowly we started to invest our country with history – institutions like the Historic Places Trust (now Heritage New Zealand) and the Waitangi Tribunal emerged to explore and make judgements about our past; historic markers and new memorials appeared on roadsides; historians such as Keith Sinclair, Judith Binney, James Belich, Michael King and Claudia Orange were widely read; historical novels were written and television series were made about our history. Some New Zealanders even came to accept that important battles in a major civil war had taken place on the soil of this land.

This awakening of New Zealanders to their history is one of the great revolutions of my lifetime. It has been my privilege to both exemplify the change and be an actor in the story. As a child I thought of history as a kind of romantic dream which took place across the seas or in special slide-shows at home. History did not inhabit my day-to-day world. By my late twenties I had come to believe that for all countries, old and new, the past was an important path to understanding the present, and in New Zealand's case we had a fascinating multi-layered history that was central to our evolving set of identities. I felt it was a major social obligation to enrich New Zealanders' understanding of their past. While I grew up with a family background and training in academic history, a discipline which I still admire, I began, unwittingly at first, to learn how to use new techniques to talk to a wider audience than just students in the front row of my lectures or the few specialists perusing a scholarly journal. I became a 'public historian' of New Zealand, communicating to a more general non-academic audience, and I stumbled on new techniques to make this possible – a popular style of writing, the use of images, working on museum exhibitions, talking on radio and television, developing new languages of history for the web.

My life as a public historian of New Zealand, set against the context of a country discovering its own past, is the theme of this book. To understand my personal evolution we must begin with my family. There is a chapter on my father's origins, and a second on my mother's. This may seem a somewhat surprising start. Like many academically trained historians I once had little interest in family history, unthinkingly dismissing genealogists as 'granny-hunters' whose eyes were fixed on minutiae of interest only to themselves and their grandchildren (if they were lucky). But as I came to reflect upon my own career I slowly realised, as Māori have long known, that genealogy is essential to self-understanding. It was my family background that largely explained my subsequent journey as a public historian. My father was a professor of history at the University of Canterbury. He had studied for one year at Oxford before the outbreak of World War II, and he aspired to represent Oxbridge academic values in the antipodes. His greatest ambition was to contribute to scholarship on British history. He had a huge influence on me, providing a strong model of academic history focused on the Old World. The night-time slide shows were the most memorable statement of where he believed history was to be found. On the other hand, my mother came from colonial landed stock. She was the daughter of a Hawke's Bay farmer. From her and from summers spent with her family in Hawke's Bay I developed a love of the New Zealand landscape and some of its social traditions. Chapter 3 describes how I tried to navigate these different influences as I was growing up in Christchurch – caught between the intellectual life of the Old World and the physical activities of the new, between the life of the mind and daily experience.

Resolution, intellectually, came when I went to the United States in 1968 to study for a doctorate in American history. Harvard University represented the finest academic traditions. But, goaded by questions asked by my fellow students, I began to read New Zealand history and realised that New Zealand offered interesting 'New World' comparisons with American history. Furthermore, in my long-winded, unpublishable thesis, I found in the philosophy of John Dewey a mandate to bring intellectual endeavour together with the social and physical context in which I lived. In the creative cauldron of America in the late sixties I also developed a very different set of political viewpoints from the attitudes of my youth.

I returned to teach American history to university students in Wellington in 1973. It was an exciting time to be back. As a result of an invitation from Ian Cross I began to write for the *New Zealand Listener* and think about communicating to a wide audience. I rediscovered New Zealand, its landscape, its history and its culture. I became convinced that it was really important for New Zealanders to have a sense of the history which had made them. Many Māori already possessed, through oral tradition, an intense sense of their own history. It was time that Pākehā came to share this. I slowly realised that the history of the country was more intriguing than I had ever imagined. In 1987, aged forty, I published *A Man's Country?*, about the history of the Kiwi male stereotype. In its subject matter, its engaged approach and its attempt to write for a broad New Zealand audience, the book represented an intellectual homecoming and a partial rejection of the Anglophile academic traditions of history writing in which I had been brought up. This is the theme of chapter 5.

The subsequent chapters explore the different ways in which I sought to excite the interest of New Zealanders in their own history. Chapter 6 describes my establishment of the Stout Research Centre, intended to bridge the university and the wider community, partly through conferences which brought approaches from many disciplines to bear on current issues such as the land. I became interested in the place of oral history in bringing New Zealand experience to life.

Chapter 7 tells of how I left the university to take on the role of government chief historian, writing official history and war history for governments and people. My time in that role ended with a wonderful publication, the *New Zealand Historical Atlas,* in which Malcolm McKinnon and his team showed how maps could bring new questions and intriguing answers to the history of the country. The volume won prizes and sold in the thousands.

In 1993 I was lucky enough to be enticed to the new national museum, Te Papa, to take charge of the history exhibitions. This was a unique opportunity to carry New Zealand history to a very broad audience indeed. The experience taught me a huge amount about different modes of communicating history – through objects, films, interactives, computer games. I learned the value of user-testing all these modes, and of the need to cater for audiences with a range of backgrounds and diverse styles of learning.

Chapter 9 describes a short interlude when I found myself as a public-sector executive. But interestingly, in my role as a general manager I found other ways, such as the promotion of memorials, in which New Zealand history could be made meaningful.

The final major project of my working life was conceiving and then editing Te Ara, the online encyclopedia of New Zealand. Everything I had learnt up to that point about ways of communicating to diverse audiences was brought to bear on that task. With a wonderful team I set out to provide a resource of accurate information about all things New Zealand, informed by the latest scholarly research, but presented in a way that would be of value to users, whether schoolchildren wanting background information, artists looking for visual inspiration, scholars searching for a fact or foreign tourists wanting a potted introduction to our country.

The theme of this book is therefore the different styles of being a historian in the New World at a time when the country's history moved from the darkness into the light. There have been other autobiographies by New Zealand historians – indeed Keith Sinclair prefaced his with a quotation from A. J. P. Taylor: 'Every historian should, I think, write an autobiography.'[1] But unlike those by Sinclair and his fellow doyen of the post-war generation, W. H. Oliver, who interspersed descriptions of their careers as academic historians and poets with highly personal revelations in complete autobiographies, this book is a memoir with a particular focus. It is rather more like Michael King's *Being Pakeha*, where ethnic and national identity form the central theme.[2] In my case the attention falls on my life as a historian of New Zealand outside the academy. There are many aspects of my life that are barely treated, such as the pleasures I have gained from my children, stepchildren and grandchildren. There is little about the houses I have lived in, or about the holidays I have enjoyed, either around the world or here at home. My love of outdoor adventures, which have given me enormous pleasure, finds little place. There is nothing my tastes in food or music. Not much about friends. Nor have I gone into my romantic life in any detail. I have recorded such matters only where they have relevance to the larger theme. There are many possible life stories. I have chosen but one.

Yet I hope this story of 'making history' will have its own interest. I was blessed as a historian – privileged to be brought up in a home where history was in the bookshelves and the conversation, lucky to arrive back in New Zealand just as a generation of baby boomers began to articulate a new cultural nationalism, fortunate to become chief historian when there was money to spend, to be around just as a new national museum was born, and to be able to make the most of the internet while it was emerging. I have had unique opportunities to present history to New Zealanders; and the more I did so the more convinced I became that this society will only thrive and make good decisions when it has a fuller understanding of its past. I intensely share the spirit of the old whakataukī 'Ka mua, ka muri' – we move forward into the future by looking back into our past. I trust that my own adventures in pursuit of that aim will make this story worth the telling.

1
My father and the mother country

I was born in 1947. Two years later my father, Neville Phillips, became the professor of history at Canterbury University College. He provided me with the earliest and most influential model of what it was to be a historian. So this story must begin with my father's story; and his story in turn can only be understood by saying something about his father, my grandfather, Sam Phillips. In search of Sam, let's travel to the heart of the East End of London in the late nineteenth century. It was a crammed, noisy world of sweatshops, synagogues, shopkeepers selling kosher food, and desperately overcrowded housing (some fourteen people on average to a home). Yiddish was heard everywhere in the streets. In the eighteenth century the East End had been a home for respectable sea captains such as James Cook, but there had been pockets of Jewish settlement there ever since Oliver Cromwell had allowed the Jews back into Britain following their expulsion in 1290. In the eighteenth and early nineteenth centuries they made steady economic progress. Some Jews moved beyond their traditional role of peddling old clothes and rose in the social scale. A largely integrated Anglo–Jewish community emerged, and in 1858 the legal restrictions against Jews holding political office or entering the professions were abolished. Benjamin Disraeli's elevation to the position of prime minister was but one symbol of their growing acceptability. In London itself there had been no fewer than five Jewish lord mayors by 1902.

Bill Sutton's portrait of Neville Phillips as vice-chancellor of the University of Canterbury.

By then the situation had changed. The assassination of the Russian Tsar in 1881 focused Russian suspicions on the Jewish community and sparked a series of pogroms or anti-Jewish riots in western areas of the Russian Empire, especially in the areas of modern-day Poland and Ukraine. Fleeing persecution and poverty, thousands took flight, many to the United States, others to the East End of London. By 1900 there were about 100,000 in Britain, almost all crammed into the East End. These poor East European Jews, or Ashkenazim, were a considerable shock to the largely Sephardic Jews (originally from Spain and Portugal) who had been making their way successfully in England. The new arrivals usually worshipped in their own synagogues and largely worked in grimy, airless sweatshops making clothes.[1]

This was the world into which my grandfather, Sam Phillips, was born on 11 November 1887 at St Peters Road in Bethnal Green, in the very heart of the Jewish East End.[2] By 1891 the census records show that he lived with his parents on Whitechapel Rd, about a mile south but still in the Jewish East End.[3] His father, Morris Phillips, was not himself a newcomer. Phillips is an old English Jewish name and presumably the family had lived in the East End for many years, for Morris was born there. Like many Jews, he found a living in the rag trade. Morris was a tailor's cutter, the most prestigious role in a clothing factory; he was moderately successful. By 1901 he had become an employer, probably running his own sweatshop of recently arrived Jews, and he had moved house, a short way uptown out of the densest part of the ghetto, to Mile End Road (directly across the street from where James Cook had once lived). There were twelve in the house.[4] Sam's mother, Sarah Glock, was German, born in Bonn, and both her mother and sister had come to share their house when they lived on Whitechapel Road.

In the very year that Sam was born, and close to his home, the East End had become notorious for the Jack the Ripper murders. Six women, probably prostitutes, had been murdered. The event and the number of new Eastern European immigrants triggered a wave of public animosity towards the Jews of the area. By the turn of the century there were calls for the restriction of further immigration. In 1902 a parliamentary commission was established to investigate the 'alien' question, as it was called, while closer to home a British Brothers League was set up. It held a number of parades through the East End harassing Jews and stating publicly that they were unwelcome. In response to the growing numbers of newcomers and fearing that this public antagonism

Sam Phillips' home on Mile End Road in 2016. The mural shows a history of London's East End, with James Cook on the left.

would trigger a general anti-Semitism, the Jews of the East End promoted a deliberate policy of anglicisation. Hoping to encourage integration as quickly as possible, they campaigned against the continuing use of Yiddish and encouraged children to go to local schools where they would learn the English language and be taught about British civilisation. There seems little doubt that Sam went to school locally, and he must have been affected by this movement. He would have learnt the lesson that being successful in England meant learning about British culture. As part of this Anglo–Jewish movement, leaders of the community also encouraged East End Jews to leave the city and 'disperse' – perhaps to the outer suburbs of London, perhaps to English provinces, or perhaps to British possessions overseas. Leaving the East End was regarded as a positive step forward, a path to integration.

We do not know exactly why the sixteen-year-old Sam decided in 1904 to get on a boat and come to New Zealand – was he driven away by the increasing public hostility, was he encouraged to 'disperse' by Jewish leaders, or did he just dream of a land across the oceans where he could earn money and make a success of his life? He was the oldest son, and he had seen his father make a small way in the world. But conditions in the East End were hardly so comfortable as to encourage a bright, ambitious young man to stay put.

Whatever got him onto that boat, there seems little doubt he would have come with a strong commitment to an Anglo–Jewish philosophy, recognising that the path to success for Jews in the British Empire was to integrate and identify with English values. Certainly, in early 1912, just over seven years after his arrival, he married a non-Jewish woman, Clara (known as Claire) Bird, so he had clearly broken with the Jewish tradition of marrying within the race. But it is clear that he did not break entirely with tradition – Claire converted to Judaism; and indeed in a situation where there were twice as many Jewish males as females, New Zealand Jews had become tolerant of Jews marrying gentiles.[5] Neville Phillips remembered being taken as a young boy to the synagogue in Christchurch by his father, who had begun to teach him Hebrew. The family celebrated Passover. Sam was regarded as looking Jewish and never tried to hide his Semitic origins.[6] The Jewish community in New Zealand was at that stage less than 2000 people, mostly based in the North Island, while in Christchurch, where Sam began his New Zealand life, there were only 200. New Zealand Jews were almost exclusively, like Sam, of English origin and they believed strongly in ties with the British Empire. A New Zealand branch of the Anglo-Jewish Association had been established, and Jews were widely accepted in the community. They had achieved considerable prominence; merchants like Nathaniel Levin, David Nathan and Bendix Hallenstein were well-known. Julius Vogel, another migrant from the East End, had become premier.

So Sam would have felt comfortable in New Zealand, able to retain his Jewish faith but also his loyalty to his English origins. Interestingly he found his occupation within the Jewish community. Remaining in the clothing trade, he eventually became a travelling salesman of women's clothing for the van Staveren brothers, importers and exporters, who were the sons of the rabbi in Wellington.[7] Whether this was what attracted Claire Bird to him is unclear, but certainly her niece remembered that Claire had an eye for fashion and

The Christchurch synagogue on Gloucester Street at the end of the nineteenth century. The building was demolished in 1987. Burton Brothers, Museum of New Zealand Te Papa Tongarewa, C.011629

enjoyed displaying Sam's samples.[8] They must have been a slightly odd-looking couple – Claire strikingly tall and elegant, Sam a squat 5 feet, 3½ inches (161 centimetres).[9] Although Sam was often on the road, the family lived largely in Christchurch until 1922, when they moved to Whanganui.[10] Their first-born son, David, arrived in 1912, so when the Great War broke out two years later, Sam would have felt, as a married man and a father, that he was under no immediate obligation to volunteer. Conscription when it arrived in 1916 initially excluded married men. However, by 1918, by which time their second son, Neville, had arrived, the Empire's need for manpower was becoming urgent. So on 11 July 1918 while living in Christchurch, Sam Phillips decided to show his commitment to the Empire by volunteering to serve. He left for Trentham camp on 4 November 1918, a week before the armistice, but on 8 November the base records show he was admitted to the army hospital with the Spanish flu. Two weeks later he was discharged from hospital, and four days after that, on 26 November, received his formal release from military service.[11] Thus ended one of the more personally successful periods of service for a New Zealand soldier in the Great War. Sam had proved his loyalty to the Empire, been cared for during the great flu epidemic, and then received an honourable discharge.

Sadly, it was not to be the beginning of a long and happy post-war career. In December 1923, when Neville was seven, there occurred the most traumatic event of his life. The family – Sam, Claire, David and the young Neville – were living in Whanganui. While David was away at a health camp, Sam had taken Claire, Neville and some of his friends by paddle steamer for a Sunday picnic in the December sun at Hipango Park. This was a bush reserve 25 kilometres up the Whanganui River, accessible only by boat. Neville recalled later that he had boasted to his friends how long his father could swim underwater.[12] Sam dived in, along with two others, but, not surprisingly for a man brought up in the East End, it seems likely that he could not swim. Witnesses suggested that he was caught in a whirlpool which dragged him down by the head. Neville apparently said that 'Daddy's feet went round and round'. The coroner decided that he was accidentally drowned, although teetotal members of Claire's family were apparently convinced that 'strong drink was involved', an allegation not supported by the coroner. Sam's body was recovered from the river about 100 metres down river, and he was buried in the Whanganui Jewish cemetery.[13]

At the age of seven Neville Phillips was left fatherless. His mother Claire was the daughter of a policeman, Edward Punjab Bird, who, as his middle name

My granddaughter, Ocean Bloomfield, throws a feather into the Whanganui River from the wharf at Hipango Park where my grandfather, Sam Phillips, drowned in December 1923.

suggests, was born in India; he then came to New Zealand for health reasons, and became a policeman, serving in the South Island, especially Waikouaiti. He was apparently very tall (6 feet, 5 inches – 195 centimetres) and 'a frightful martinet'. Claire's mother, Helen Stewart, was from a God-fearing Baptist family, originally from Maidenhead in Berkshire (near Windsor).[14]

Following Sam's death, Claire faced tough times. It turned out that Sam had allowed his policy with the Commercial Travellers' Association's Sickness and Accident Fund to lapse, so the family never received the £500 to which they would have been entitled, and although fellow commercial travellers contributed £89 7s. 6d. that was poor compensation.[15] Claire was forced to earn her living by working as a receptionist in pubs across the lower part of the North Island. She was given accommodation in the hotels, which meant that places to live had to be found for Neville and his older brother. At one stage Neville was given a home with his grandmother Helen in Christchurch, but more often he boarded with families in the lower North Island. He was a bright child, and managed to win a gold medal as dux at a primary school in Dannevirke, and also a scholarship which provided a few pounds to help him go on to high school.

Undated photograph of Claire Phillips, née Bird.

So in 1928, not yet aged twelve, he went to Dannevirke High School in the same third-form class as his brother, David, who was over three years older. At Dannevirke he remembered especially his first classes in Latin and being encouraged in his academic interests by a master called Hogben, the son of the great secretary of education (1899–1915), George Hogben. Neville recalled being favoured by Hogben over a girl who had actually done much better in the scholarship examination. At the end of the year Claire shifted from a Dannevirke pub to one in Palmerston North, so Neville was transferred to Palmerston North to board with another family and went to the Boys' High School. His brother started work as a mechanic in a local garage.[16]

Neville was at Palmerston North Boys' High from 1929 to 1931 – from the ages of thirteen to fifteen. Most of the boys were middle-class, and Neville remembered all his life his excruciating shame that when the headmaster invited his form to a party he was the only one who did not have a suit. He also remembered that he had to give up riding his bike because he could not afford new tyres.[17] He was acutely aware of differences from his peers – he was not only much poorer and lived as a boarder in a strange house, but he was also Jewish and considerably younger than most of his classmates. His position as an outsider might have turned him into a social and even political rebel, especially since there were others at the school with a left-wing persuasion, such as Jack and Ernie Lewin.[18] It did not. Instead Neville found solace in two activities. The first was cricket. He had always been interested in sport, and in his younger years had followed closely the success of the Hawke's Bay Ranfurly Shield-winning rugby team. At Dannevirke he had distinguished himself as a long-distance runner. In Palmerston North he continued to run and play rugby, but his passion became cricket. Cricket was the 'big thing' at Palmerston North Boys' High and the classics master, W. P. Anderson, took a special interest in Neville and encouraged his ability to bowl leg-breaks.

The other focus of his life became English poetry. The English teacher was A. C. Zohrab. In his history of the school, Bruce Hamilton writes of Zohrab:

> In a school devoted to the Spartan and the sporting he had opened new windows in his teaching of English and his production of plays. Boys felt a strong affection for this gentle man who hated the thought of war, but when Hitler unleashed war on the world he believed it was his duty to go, and he was killed in action in Italy in 1944.[19]

Judging by the effusive testimonial he wrote about Neville, Zohrab took a shine to the young pupil, sometimes invited him home, and directed his attention to the great body of English literature.[20] Neville became a particular enthusiast for English pastoral poetry such as A. E. Housman's *A Shropshire Lad*. Feeling a degree of isolation because of his poverty, family situation and Jewishness, Neville came to identify with English culture – both its literary productions and its great game. In terms of ability the former was more evident in the school magazines of those years than the latter – the only mention of Neville's sporting prowess was a score of 12 in an inter-house cricket match, but he scooped many academic prizes and a poem appeared under his initials which began 'One day a-down a Devon lane'. Not much sign of New Zealand experience there. At this stage history was not a particular interest, but in his last year he did remember studying history with a good teacher. The focus was nineteenth-century Britain. This Anglophilia was not unusual among the Jewish community. The great Jewish-American lawyer Felix Frankfurter also had a passionate love of England (and had also grown up 'in less than prosperous circumstances').[21] Despite his deprived childhood, Neville aspired to the respectable middle, even upper-class, England: not its working-class traditions. It seemed he could escape reminders of his disrupted childhood by adopting a different class persona.[22]

In 1932, not yet sixteen, Neville decided to go to Canterbury University College. He had been highly successful academically, winning prizes for Latin and French. Without any support from the school, and still in the lower sixth form, he had entered the university scholarship examination and won a senior national scholarship. It gave him a few pounds to assist his time at

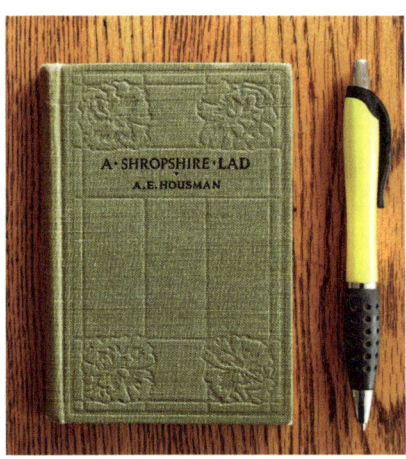

THE FLEETING YEARS.
One day a-down a Devon lane
I wandered, and the world's refrain
   Is in my memory still ;
The violet peeping from the shade
Half-hid as if it were afraid,
   The golden daffodil.

A fragrant coppice I passed by,
But there I lingered, waited nigh,
   Inhaling mead and lea
And with loth steps I turned to go,
For Nature has so much to show
   And we short time to see.

And as the sun sank in the west
And all the world prepared for rest,
   Both bird and beast did drowse.
But one thought I could not dismiss :
A sip of that, a sip of this
   Is all that life allows.
                              N.C.P. (VI).

Neville's tiny and much-thumbed copy of A Shropshire Lad, *and a highly derivative poem which appeared under his initials in the* Palmerstonian *in December 1931 (p. 57). One wonders how often he wandered 'a-down a Devon lane'.*

university. His favourite teacher, A. C. Zohrab, had wanted him to get a job with the Palmerston North daily paper, but Neville had set his heart on a university education. One reason was the influence of his father. He later remembered walking with his father in Christchurch on the way to the synagogue. His father said as they passed the university grounds, 'One day you should go to university.' Neville recalled thinking that this would become his aim. This is the strongest indication that the Jewish intellectual tradition was formative in Neville's life, although there is little other evidence to support this. Sam's major cultural interest appears to have been music, which never interested Neville. He also received strong support for a university education from non-Jewish sources, especially Claire's brother, Crompton, a favourite uncle from whom Neville had received his middle name.

Neville set off to go to university in Christchurch, partly because his grandmother, Helen, lived there and offered to board him. She had always been fond of him and he claimed later that she, rather than his actual mother, provided him with maternal support. From that time on, for the rest of his life, he had little contact with Claire or his brother David. Another uncle, Stewart, was also living in Neville's grandmother's house; Neville fell out with him, and when Stewart wanted to get married and bring his new wife home to live, Neville found himself cast out and was forced to board privately.[23] As for income, he got a job initially as a messenger for the *Sun* newspaper. He worked at the paper during the day and studied at night. Intending to study law, he enrolled in Latin and constitutional law. In the latter he came across James Hight, who enticed him from law to history. It also made a difference that the history lectures were after 4 p.m., which allowed him to go to work first. Hight was at the time professor of history and political science and also rector of Canterbury University College. Canterbury-born and -educated, Hight set out to forge a career as a serious academic historian. His standards were rigorous. Although he had researched and written on New Zealand history, especially *The Constitutional History and Law of New Zealand* with H. D. Bamford (1914), he always believed in the central importance of European history. Neville Phillips wrote of him many years later in the *Dictionary of New Zealand Biography*:

> He did not see the Old World until advanced middle age, but
> throughout his life he was the dauntless foe of insularity and saw

his own country as immovably founded on Western civilisation. It would be only a little fanciful to say that he held Richelieu and Mazarin barely less significant for New Zealand than the Maori seafarers and Edward Gibbon Wakefield.[24]

Hight's very first publication was an introduction and notes to Carlyle's *Sartor Resartus*. His second was a 300-page book, *The English as a Colonising Nation*. So where Zohrab had led Neville Phillips to English poetry, Hight led him to an appreciation of English imperial history.

The interest in poetry did not die. At the *Sun* Neville had at first been a messenger; then he worked in the reading room holding the copy while the reader corrected the proofs. But on the side he began writing a regular weekly column of light verse, 'Sunspots', which, modelled on A. P. Herbert's light verse, made witty rhyming commentary on current events. There were poems about moustaches, hot cross buns, cigarettes, cycling, racing, rugby and inevitably cricket. Many of the references were to the Old World – the cricketing poems feature W. G. Grace, Harold Larwood and the county cricketers of Kent, and the rowing poem was of course about the Oxford and Cambridge race. There was one revealing verse where 'Ol Sol' (the way Neville often identified himself in the poems) attacked George Bernard Shaw for deriding New Zealanders' use of the word 'home':

> New Zealanders, where'er they roam,
> Should have a Home away from home;
> But Mr Shaw won't have it thus,
> Describes it as ridiculous.[25]

Such light verse was, at the time, a fashionable style. When the *Sun* closed, Neville was offered a position with the *Press*; and there he shared a desk with Allen Curnow, who would himself establish a reputation as a writer of light topical verse under the pseudonym of 'Whim Wham'. At the *Press*, Neville became a subeditor on the cable page, which further developed his interest in overseas politics and news.[26] The editor described 'his clear, concise and often brilliant language', while also noting 'in manner, he is quiet and modest without being diffident'. Three years earlier the editor of the *Sun* commented that 'his only defect is a certain diffidence of manner'.[27] This was the mid-1930s, a time when the Labour government was introducing a series of progressive social and political initiatives; it was also Christchurch, a place where interesting social and cultural commentary was happening. Denis Glover had started the Caxton Press and was surrounded by a group of young poets and intellectuals; Kennaway Henderson had established the left-wing monthly *Tomorrow*.[28] But Neville was not really interested in these local cultural developments – his eyes were on the Old World. To be fair, he was apparently affected by a degree of social concern. There was a strong poem published in September 1932, in the midst of the Great Depression, about relief camps:

> Oh! it ain't all beers and skittles
> In our home away from home
> Where the fleas and bugs are many
> And the rodents love to roam
> ...
> And Mr Coates says
> 'Never mind, 'twill keep them out of harm'
> My wish is that he may receive
> 6 months on a Four A farm.[29]

And two years later came a vitriolic piece, 'Ode to Herr Hitler':

> Do you consider yourself as avatar
> Of Bonaparte or some unholy Tsar,
> Or who in Himmel do you think you are
>
> You are no Charlemagne nor Metternich
> Your historic rantings make me sick
> You're nothing but an upstart Kaiserlich![30]

Alongside these poetic doodles, Neville was throwing himself into his studies – he took units in English, Latin, economics, Greek history, art and literature, and of course history. He did honours in history and wrote a thesis under Hight entitled 'New Zealand and the Mother Country'. It provides us with an excellent sense of Neville Phillips, the historian, in 1937–38. For a start one might ask why, given his interests, the subject was New Zealand, not British or European, history. There was an obvious explanation. As Chris Hilliard explains, a thesis in history required a student to work in primary materials, and almost none were available in non-New Zealand history at that stage. So of 363 history theses completed in New Zealand universities from 1920 to 1940, only 18 were not on New Zealand subjects.[31] There were some British parliamentary papers in the General Assembly Library in Wellington, but Neville continued to hold down a part-time job so travel to Wellington for research was out of the question. In the event the primary sources he used were those available in Christchurch – the parliamentary debates, what he called parliamentary papers (also known as the *Appendices to the Journals of the House of Representatives*), and two Christchurch newspapers, the *Press* and *Lyttelton Times*. As for the subject matter, it was about New Zealand political history, but the focus was very much on New Zealand as part of the British Empire. The thesis (which is called on the spine 'New Zealand and the Mother Country, 1868–1901' and on the title page 'New Zealand's relations with Great Britain, 1868–1901') had a subtitle 'A study in Empire unionism', and the title page also includes a quote from Alfred Lord Tennyson:

> May we find, as ages run,
> The mother featured in the son.

The theme of the thesis is the move from colonial hostility towards the mother country to filial devotion. It begins at the end of the New Zealand Wars. Debate over the withdrawal of British troops and forced colonial self-reliance in defence had created a situation where, in Neville's words, 'Never before or after was mutual regard between imperial and colonial governments at so low an ebb.'[32] The thesis ended at the turn of the century, when the New Zealand government was keenly involved in providing services to the Empire in the South African War and deeply committed to membership of the Empire. It is a triumphant story of what Neville calls 'Empire unionism'. He sees this as the voluntary commitment of colonies to the Empire, creating a situation where the Empire acted as one; he contrasted it with other forms of imperialism which were essentially rule by force.

He describes the British Empire as the exemplar of international government where the colonies are allowed to develop their own identity yet remain forever British. In the first chapter of the thesis he tries to explain this unique form of imperialism. It was partly the fact that these were colonies of settlement, not exploitation, and that they were based in temperate, not tropical, areas of the world. He sees agriculture as crucial to creating happy British colonies, and he views the policy of laissez-faire in both its economic and its political guise (encouraging self-government) as crucial. But he also points to something about the racial characteristic of the British – they were descended from Anglo-Saxons and 'In their veins ran the blood of these pioneers, strongly built men, self-reliant, democratic in instinct, and laborious as well as courageous in battle'.[33] It is interesting that in discussing these characteristics he always uses the adjective 'our' – 'our success' in the Empire, 'our prowess as seamen' and so on. His identification with Britain is clear; he also expresses his sense of the importance of British cultural hegemony to the working of the Empire. 'In the arts and literature, London is still the Mecca of all Britons, and the writers of Britain are the writers of the Empire. Colonials make their pilgrimage to the Old Land, Oxford admits sons of the dominions, British statesmen meet in conference every four years and there are many British conferences of interest other than political.'[34] Interestingly, in light of Neville Phillips' future writings, the first chapter includes several quotations from the eighteenth-century political theorist of enlightened conservatism Edmund Burke.

The thesis is written with considerable literary grace and without a grammatical or spelling error in sight. It is a fine work of literature of the conventional imperial style. Neville's examiners – W. P. Morrell in Otago, W. K. Hancock, a distinguished Australian historian who was professor of history at Birmingham, and A. J. Grant, a former professor at Leeds – agreed that it was 'a very good piece of work' and, according to James Hight, regarded 'his papers and his research thesis as the best presented from New Zealand for some years'.[35] It is not really surprising that Neville Phillips' attitudes were in praise of the British Empire and British culture. New Zealand in the 1930s was a small provincial society. As John Beaglehole wrote when he travelled to London in 1926, it was excellent to be in 'a part of the earth that has really some history behind it & not just a few tuppeny-ha'penny scraps and tenth-rate politics'.[36] Expatriation was a well-recognised cultural phenomenon of the time and anyone who aspired to serious engagement with great minds was likely to want to go offshore.

On the other hand, Neville Phillips showed some interest in New Zealand nationalism. The thesis concludes with a portrait of some leading political lights of colonial New Zealand. Among these was Richard Seddon, whom Neville recognises as stimulating a national pride. But he also emphasises the limits of this national spirit – 'Seddon was the chief of those who fostered the "mother complex", the tradition of filial respect, and he, more than any other, created for New Zealand the role of the spoiled child of Britain'.[37] There is a hint here that perhaps, if only briefly, he was being affected by those stronger currents of New Zealand nationalism of the 1930s. This, after all, was a time when there was some anger at New Zealand's economic dependence on the United Kingdom and there were clear signs of cultural nationalism – not only writers outside the academy such as James Cowan but also those who had been students just before Neville Phillips and who aspired to a richer cultural life within New Zealand which would confront distinctive New Zealand issues. There were intellectuals emerging like John Mulgan, Denis Glover, Allen Curnow and Frank Sargeson. Neville offered but a brief nod in that direction. The dominant impulse of the thesis is that acceptance of Britain's culture was the logical response for a provincial culture and that political reconciliation with the mother country by 1900 was a triumph, not a tragedy. In his personal circumstances Neville Phillips had suffered economically in the 1930s and experienced a sense of being marginal. This might perhaps have turned his anger against the Empire. Instead the reverse happened and the Empire beckoned.

So in 1938 he applied for and was awarded a postgraduate scholarship to study in Britain, beating out other talented historians such as Jim Davidson. He had long held ambitions to go to Oxford University, the high academy of imperial values. But the award was only sufficient to pay for him to go to the University of London. He would have headed there, but in 1937, the year when he wrote his thesis, he had met and fallen in love with another member of the history honours class, Pauline Palmer, my mother. The daughter of a Hawke's Bay farmer, educated at the private girls' school Woodford House, she brought with her the values of the rural squattocracy. The appeal for Neville, aspiring to respectability and trying to hide his poor Jewish origins, is obvious. Pauline's sister, Patricia, had married Jim Nelson, a descendant of the early missionary Williams family. Following his schooling at Christ's College, where he had been head prefect, Jim had gone off to Merton College,

Neville in Wellington in early 1938, aged twenty-two.

Oxford, in the early 1920s. There he had studied forestry, and also rowed in the college boat. Jim looked on those years with real affection, and was determined that Neville should experience Oxford college life too. He offered to lend Neville £100 a year so he too could go to Oxford. In gratitude for this support Neville wrote every few months back to Jim and Patricia, and it is thanks to this correspondence that we know something about his Oxford and war years.

He became a devoted college sportsman, playing on the wing for the college rugby team and reporting at length (partly for Jim's benefit) on the college rowing crew's efforts to 'bump' their way up river. Pauline Palmer, who had become engaged to Neville, followed him to England and was training as a teacher in London. She came up and watched one 'division of toggers'.[38] She apparently thought 'it all savoured too much of the Old School Tie', but Neville found it exciting when a Merton boat was involved.[39]

At Christmas Pauline and Neville went off to Paris, which Neville regarded as 'infinitely more beautiful' than London, 'a wretched place'.[40] But London had its consolations. They went to four plays together there, a practice which Neville continued in Oxford. With Pauline he also discovered the 'very beautiful country' of England. They managed to meet for weekends and took walks around Oxford, such as those along the Thames with tea at 'the Trout Inn'.[41] As warm weather arrived Neville became ecstatic at how 'the spring simply changes the face of the earth in England' and savoured 'the old James II mulberry tree in the garden' where the dons played bowls.[42] There were cycling trips to villages in Berkshire and the Cotswolds, and when Pauline's parents arrived in early summer they visited gardens. Under Pauline's tutelage Neville began to learn about English cathedrals and the 'differences between Norm. and E.E. and Dec. and Perp.'.[43] Pauline's father took Neville off to a day's test cricket at Lord's. Neville looked forward to a vacation to be spent in a small village in Shropshire (no doubt inspired by A. E. Housman) where he could catch up on work.

At Oxford there were also the clubs and lectures. Neville was elected (thanks to James Hight's influence) to the Raleigh Club, an exclusive group of thirty-six which was set up in 1913 to hold discussions about Empire affairs. There were two other New Zealanders – A. G. Bogle (later professor of electrical engineering at Auckland) and W. F. Monk (later lecturer in history at Victoria).[44] Before long Neville had been made secretary and was marked

Merton College. Neville Phillips' rooms were in the building on the left overlooking the garden.

out as the next president. The club heard 'fighting imperialist speeches' from assorted aristocrats. Neville sent out invitations for the annual dinner where there were toasts to 'The King', 'The Empire of the Bretagnes' and 'The Club' and members feasted on 'Caneton roti d'Aylesbury with Sauce Pomme'. Neville was less enthusiastic about another club – 'The inevitable New Zealanders' club has been formed and I hang my head to think that I've been roped in.'[45] It was called the Pakeha Club. At the first annual dinner in the Merton senior common-room, the high commissioner, W. K. Jordan, spoke. The event ended in true Kiwi style when a Balliol man let off a fire extinguisher, and the club president was summoned to the 'Principal of the postmasters' to explain.[46]

So for all his adoration of things imperial and English, Neville could not escape his New Zealand origins. On more than one occasion in his letters, he acknowledged the presence of other New Zealanders at Oxford, and he admitted having to vote against one in Merton College politics – this may have been Harold Lusk, later a prominent lawyer, or M. K. Joseph, the noted novelist, who were the only other two New Zealanders there at the time. He also commented on New Zealand political events. The day after Nash arrived in England in May 1939 on 'a distasteful mission' of renewing a loan and placating the British, Neville wrote: 'Frankly, I'm sorry that New Zealand is so dependent on this country.'[47] There were also some signs of a slight change in his political views. He admitted to attending a meeting of the Labour Club one evening to hear G. D. H. Cole speak on trade unionism and the need for more militancy. Neville admired his 'beautifully clear mind', but could not empathise with his outlook and expressed great amusement at the 'common vocative, "Comrades", on the grounds that "Mr" is so beastly bourgeois'. He concluded: 'After listening to such talk, I conceive a profound respect for Robespierre, who, though leader of the most extreme of the French revolutionaries, insisted on wearing the buckled shoes, silk clothes and powdered wig of the ancient regime [sic].'[48] There was also in late February a meeting at the Oxford town hall, where Stafford Cripps spoke in favour of the popular front. Neville especially applauded his attacks on Chamberlain; he agreed that 'in international dealings this present government has neither honour nor acumen'. The shadows of war were lengthening, and Neville concluded his account: 'British foreign "policy" has drifted for so long that it is now next to impossible for us to get out of the present mess without dishonour or without war.'[49]

The year in Oxford had confirmed for Neville Phillips the excitement and stimulus of living in a place with real culture, tradition and history. The reality of England confirmed the dream he had had since his days as a Palmerston North schoolboy, but the outbreak of war confronted him with a tough choice. There was never much doubt where he would stand. In November 1939 he wrote to Jim Nelson that he had left Oxford and was waiting in London to be called up. He admitted that it was not 'a very enjoyable decision to have to make' and at times he considered himself 'an utter fool'. He did not relish fighting, but it was a just war, and 'it seemed unfair that, after sharing the privileges of Englishmen, as I have done at Oxford, I should shirk their responsibilities' – apart from the fact that 'New Zealand is as closely interested as England in unseating Hitler'.[50] So the loyal imperialist, the man who had always dreamed of the wonders of English culture, was forced to pay for his loyalties. Later he was quite frank that war scared him. But he decided that he could serve in as safe a way as possible. As an Oxford student, he was fairly certain of being awarded a commission as an officer, and was promised this when interviewed at Oxford within the first month of war. Further, he

Neville in officer training, early 1940.

Neville visiting his wife Pauline and young daughter Elizabeth in late 1944 or early 1945.

quickly decided to choose the artillery because this would place him far from the front, in a less exposed situation.[51] So he chose his war service – an officer in the artillery it would be.

Neville spent over three years in training all over the United Kingdom – at Gosford on the Hampshire coast, Larkhill on the Salisbury Plain, Bournemouth, Winchester, Lincolnshire and Motherwell in Scotland. He was not initially enthusiastic about army life, which he decided was 'much overrated'. He thought the food would do for 'Lord Bledisloe's pigs' but was inadequate for adult men and he found the bathing arrangements primitive.[52] In November 1940 he took leave from army training to marry Pauline Palmer, and nine months later their first child, my sister, Elizabeth, was born. In January 1943, by now a captain, he landed in Tunisia, where he was lucky to be saved from one fatal moment, which he described often in later years. On the third day of action, Neville was returning from a court martial on a motorbike and was thrown. He hurt his leg, and was unable to go forward with the infantry to serve in the Observation Post (OP) directing the guns. A replacement served instead and two days later the Germans surrounded the farmhouse where the OP was positioned. The officer and his two signalmen were found dead.[53]

But Tunisia had fallen by the end of May and Neville was able to look out on 'ruins ancient and modern' – the ancient ruins of Carthage and modern wrecks of 'Boche and Wop planes'. He celebrated by purchasing two glasses of vermouth and muscat, a fountain pen so he could write, and a volume of *Horace* with a translation in French, which at two bob he considered a bargain because no-one else was interested in the classics at this point.[54] Then it was on to Italy in November 1943. He took part in the battle for Cassino and then the long march up Italy to the end of the war when, now a major, he was briefly in charge of a camp of Polish evacuees, which he always described as one of the least pleasant periods of his life and confirmed in him a hostility to Russian communism.

The war service is of considerable interest. As an officer in command of troops for five years, Neville's experience gave him greater personal confidence and an authoritarian style of command. As early as 1941 he became aware of this effect: 'One has to be somewhat of a bully – or more than somewhat – in order to force all the necessary knowledge down eight men's throats and it's good for the cultivation of that quality which the C.O. never tires of demonstrating – "the aggressive spirit."'[55] A hint of his character in those years comes from another interesting source – a reminiscence written by a signalman in the regiment who reported to Neville. In Joe Berry's account, *Unwillingly to War*, 'Captain Phillips' comes across as quite a demanding officer with high standards. He was described as 'a scholarly man who did not smile readily' and who was in his element poring over the maps.[56] Berry also recalled meeting New Zealanders when the regiment reached Cassino in February 1944. He was impressed with the Kiwis: 'The divide between officer and other rank was much less pronounced in their army than in ours and they had an easy friendliness which, in my experience, none of our other allies were quite able to match.'[57] Neville, by contrast, had developed a rather different way of directing others than might have evolved from six years as an officer in the New Zealand forces. Yet Berry had great affection for Neville and told a lovely story about Gunner Jonah, who was in Neville's troop. He came from south Wales, where he had worked in his parents' café, and he endured much ribbing about the affinity between chips and his chunky figure. One day Neville was teaching a course in which his 'academic bent was given full rein'. But it was after lunch, it was warm and most of the class were asleep. Captain Phillips asked a question which no-one answered. He called on Jonah, who managed only a few mutterings. 'Gradually the captain's pose relaxed and a hint of a smile flickered at the corners of his mouth. In a voice with just the right amount of mock disbelief he asked, "Is this the face that launched a thousand *chips*?" There were roars of laughter.'[58]

It is also worth noting that more than five years in the British army fighting Nazism confirmed, rather than challenged, Neville's essentially conservative political values and his belief in British civilisation and respectable upper-middle-class culture – despite several potential challenges to such attitudes. During his training on the Salisbury Plain Neville consistently received good marks for the various tests, but when he received his final grade it was only a C, and the upshot was that he was not appointed to a divisional field regiment but to a position of lesser status with an army field regiment (the 140th). He was told by others that the low grade was because the marking officer had discriminated against him on the basis of his Jewish background.[59] This experience did not lead to any radical alienation, nor were his class aspirations disturbed by his observation during training that the greatest strain in his life was the behaviour of certain cadets, 'bad cases of arrested development, due, I fear, to the curbing influence of the English public school. They still get adolescent enjoyment out of drinking excessively and still more out of talking about it.'[60] On the other hand he wrote of his enjoyment of the regimental sports when the cadets all sipped tea under a marquee which savoured of a 'parish garden party', and he continued to find solace in the cultural traditions around him.[61] There were visits to Stonehenge, and Salisbury with its cathedral; at Winchester he explored the cathedral, and took an approving look at Winchester College, the oldest of the public schools.[62] In the long run he came to like his fellow soldiers, and friendships forged in the heat of war provided a long-term pull back to England. In Italy two men in particular became his lifelong friends: Roland Foxwell, later a wine merchant in the south of England, and Edward Chadwyck-Healey. Chadwyck-Healey, the grandson of a distinguished lawyer who became a baronet, was educated at Eton and decorated in World War I, and became the prime warden of the Fishmongers

Company and the Third Baronet of Wyphurst. Neville's association with Sir Edward Chadwyck-Healey was the closest he came to the English aristocracy. He treasured the relationship.

Finally, the war left Neville with an enduring love of Italy and the Italian renaissance. He learned to speak Italian and developed a taste for the local vino. He was clearly impressed by the beauty of the Umbrian and Tuscan countryside, which he recalled fondly in later years. He had two week-long holidays in Florence and Rome. In one letter to Patricia and Jim Nelson he regretted that his writing so much about Rome left no paper for 'that much more worthy city of Florence. I shall only say it is quite equal to its fame', and he confirmed this view by sending his wife Pauline a book about the city. As for Rome, he described piazzas, great churches, fountains, statues, columns and obelisks 'by the score'. He visited St Peter's and saw the Pope, but the highlight was undoubtedly a visit to a palazzo where he was shown through rooms full of paintings of the Italian Renaissance placed there for safekeeping. 'The paintings,' he wrote, 'certainly opened my eyes. I don't expect ever to see such a collection again.'[63] In later years Neville still lit up with great enthusiasm when talking about the art of the Italian Renaissance.

If the war confirmed Neville Phillips' love of the Old World, where would he live once the war was over? When the war ended Neville was a husband with a four-year-old daughter. Returning to Oxford was never a responsible option. Pauline was eager to get home, so when his old mentor James Hight offered Neville a position lecturing in history at his alma mater in Christchurch it seemed a heaven-sent opportunity. He accepted and returned to Canterbury University College. Within three years he was appointed to the chair of history and political science – at the age of thirty-two and despite stiff competition from candidates such as A. H. McLintock. From 1949 until he became the university's vice-chancellor in 1966, the years when I grew up, Neville was the god-professor of history.

I say 'god-professor' because these were the years when being a professor was not to be a chair among equal academics, but rather to be the unquestioned academic leader; and Neville took on the task as if he was still an officer in the Royal Artillery. He cared passionately about inspiring his students with the thrill of history and aimed to ensure that the best graduates would make it overseas. He was able to attract a very fine team of teachers, many of whom moved on to highly distinguished careers. They included John Owen, a historian of eighteenth-century England who became a fellow of Lincoln College, Oxford; David Fieldhouse, a much-published writer on the history of the British Empire/Commonwealth who also became an Oxford fellow, this time of Nuffield College; J. J. Saunders, a specialist on the crusades; J. G. A. Pocock, now regarded as one of the most original writers on European thought in the early modern period, whose career ended as professor at Johns Hopkins in the USA; Sam Adshead, who established an international reputation in Chinese history; and W. H. Oliver, who largely taught nineteenth-century British history at Canterbury before becoming professor at Massey and editor of the *Dictionary of New Zealand Biography*. The focus, as these men's interests suggests, was very much British and European history; Neville himself taught about the renaissance, especially the Italian renaissance, and eighteenth-century British history.

Not that there were no staff with an interest in New Zealand – Bill Oliver was writing his *The Story of New Zealand* at the time; there was also Jim Gardner, then working on his massive history of Amuri county, and a passionate advocate for local history; and later Philip Ross May, a West Coast boy, who wrote a wonderful history of the gold rushes in his home province, joined the department. But there were no courses in New Zealand history except as part of the history of the British Commonwealth, and Gardner was forced to lecture eloquently on the French Revolution instead of North Canterbury in the nineteenth century. Neville found his own necessary involvement in New Zealand history through overseeing the centennial history of Canterbury a tiresome chore. Other members of the department regarded it as a discouraging place to research New Zealand, and Neville was often somewhat resentful when they chose theses on New Zealand rather than eighteenth-century England. He seemed incredulous that a student might chose to research 'mere' New Zealand history.[64] For Neville the essence of history was to learn about the great European and English traditions and to come out of the department able to foot it with the best from Oxbridge. He also saw history as a form of fine literature, and when he was composing a piece for a public lecture or publication he would often come in from his study and recite it out loud to the assembled company. The sound of prose was almost as important as its meaning. I grew up hearing his carefully chosen words rolling off his lips. He also had high scholarly standards with an insistence on accuracy, thorough research and a logical argument. A first was never easily granted.

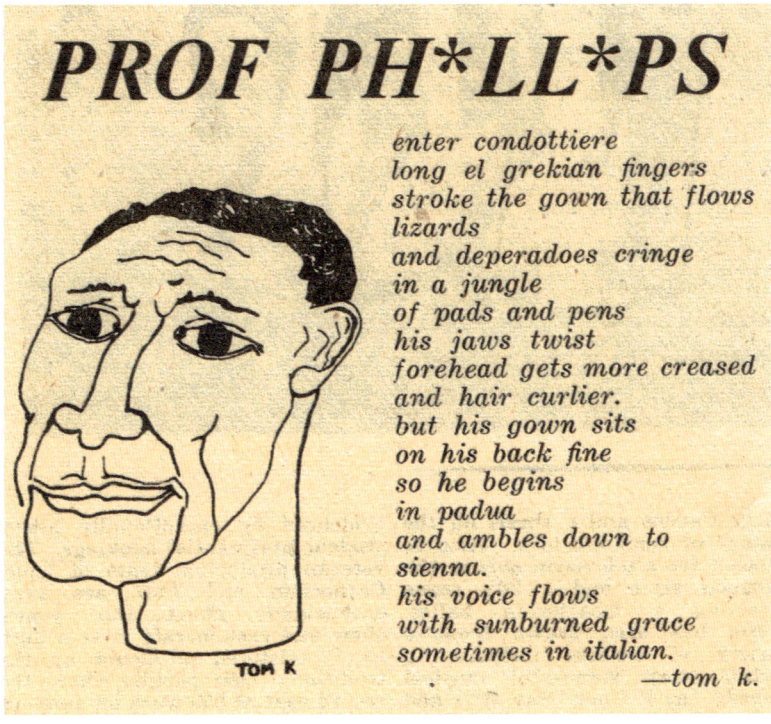

A cartoon in the student magazine Canta *of Professor Neville Phillips.*

Former students remember Neville the professor with considerable ambivalence. Some, like Mervyn Thompson, the theatre director and playwright, regarded him with awe and respect: 'A man seemingly reserved and even patrician in nature, but a lecturer who made history live for me because, while ferreting for the roots and causes of historical events, he never lost touch with their human uniqueness and idiosyncrasy . . . His lectures were formal structures of sublime eloquence and even a kind of architectural splendour.'[65] Pauline O'Regan, who won fame as a reforming nun, was less generous. She described his manner as 'distinctly cold' and recalled making her 'apprehensive way' to see him about a thesis topic. 'It was not only the church that used authoritarian methods in the 1950s. I had a few ideas for a topic for my thesis. He didn't ask me. He just told me that I was to write a history of immigration into Canterbury during the provincial period, 1853–1876.'[66] Tony Simpson, later a highly successful popular historian, agreed that

Neville was an 'authority figure' whose 'conception of history was that it was a narrow scholastic pursuit with very strict formal rules, the principal purpose of which was to produce the next generation of history teachers and scholars by imparting these. The acme of their achievement would be publication of a paper in an Oxbridge-based academic journal.'[67] Edmund Bohan, the 'singing historian', also recalled my father's authoritarian presence. He remembered Neville as 'the most intimidating man with whom I have ever had any sustained contact. Tall and saturnine, a commanding presence in the lecture room and an inhibiting, even terrifying personality in tutorials.' But even Bohan recalled that he was

> a superb teacher: a splendid prose stylist and an outstanding lecturer whose dissertations on the glories of the Italian renaissance attracted students from other faculties and even the intellectually aware public to the always packed lecture room. He was a tutor who demanded the highest standards – mere opinion, narrow ideological fixations or prejudices were not allowed, conclusions had to emerge from facts derived from reputable and quotable sources, ideally provided by Oxford men. Woolly thinking was harshly condemned and he could, and frequently did, reduce the slovenly thinker or wilfully ignorant to tears.[68]

Although most of his teaching was about the renaissance or eighteenth-century English politics, Neville's love of international ideas did lead him into interesting directions, such as initiating an interdisciplinary course on Darwinism, in which scientists unpicked the theory of evolution and Neville placed the debate about the theory in the context of nineteenth-century culture and society.

When he was appointed professor in 1949 Neville had published nothing except for leaders and light verse in the local newspapers. But it was becoming accepted that professional historians researched and wrote. What did Neville write? He was interested at the time in European political thought (he was after all professor of political science as well as history), but without contacts overseas it was difficult to find outlets for his thinking. So he turned to a vehicle close at hand, *Landfall*, which had been established in 1947 by Charles Brasch as a place to publish New Zealand short stories, poetry and reviews.

It was regarded by the young cultural nationalists as a major forum for articulating and exploring New Zealand and its culture – so it might seem surprising that Neville Phillips was found among the contributors. Neville established a good rapport with Brasch, a fellow New Zealander of Jewish background, and in the 1950s Brasch would sometimes come round to our house in Fendalton when he was in Christchurch to see *Landfall* through the Caxton Press.

Brasch accepted three substantial articles from Neville, and although two took off from local considerations, they were all in their way essays in European political thought. In September 1947 came a discussion about the British Commonwealth, in which – drawing on thinkers as diverse as Bentham, Rousseau, Karl Marx and the Webbs – he attempted to reconcile the nationalist collectivism of the state with closer and more organised Commonwealth relations. He concluded that regular gatherings of the Commonwealth were 'a preliminary essay in internationalism' and based on an appeal 'not to filial piety, but to a sense of our practical interests'.[69] Two years later he attacked the Labour government's use of the referendum on compulsory military training, on the grounds that in the British tradition of governance power descended from the centre, and political issues, as distinct from non-political matters like liquor licensing, should be determined by governments not by referenda.[70] The third essay was a nice comparison, originally presented as a public lecture, of the political philosophies of Thomas Paine, the radical, and Edmund Burke, the conservative. Not surprisingly Neville's sympathy for Edmund Burke shines through and in an interesting passage he notes that Burke 'had a deep sense of *place* . . . As soon as he could, he put down roots in English soil at Beaconsfield: he spoke of the locality of the affections', and he describes Burke's 'appeal to the historic community of the nation'.[71] One need little ask what the 'historic community of the nation' was for Neville Phillips.

Yet *Landfall* does include one fascinating review by Neville which explores the dimensions of New Zealand cultural identity. It was a review of *Infantry Brigadier* by the war hero and editor of the New Zealand war histories, Howard Kippenberger. Neville says little about the book itself, but offers a surprisingly personal reflection in response to one comment by Kippenberger. Sir Howard had written on his return to the New Zealand division in Italy: 'There was a good feeling of being home again.' This triggers Neville into an autobiographical piece which was derived from meeting the Kiwis at Cassino in

1944. He remembers the New Zealanders as being 'informal in approach but superbly disciplined on serious business'. One is immediately reminded of John Mulgan's meeting with the Kiwis in North Africa. Like Mulgan, Neville could not hide from the fact that for all his love of the English countryside and history, he had affections for the New Zealand people if not New Zealand itself.

Perhaps this was one reason why he accepted the invitation from Kippenberger to write the official history of the New Zealand soldiers in Italy. He could recount the exploits of New Zealanders amid the historic landscapes of Italy. There were other reasons. By then Neville was supporting a growing family and needed income, and the assignment would necessitate revisiting the old haunts in Italy, which he did with Pauline on extended sabbatical leave in 1955. The book that emerged was outstanding, one of the best among the fifty-odd volumes of official histories. The book has a fine architecture, beginning with the difficult crossing of the Sangro and ending with the battle for Cassino. It is beautifully written, clearly structured and always informed by his own experience. In the preface he acknowledges that he had 'shared this experience with friends from the British homeland' and that 'there are things that only soldiers know'. The book confronts two contentious political issues. The first was the question whether, once the North African campaign was won, the New Zealand forces should have returned back home like the Australians to defend the South Pacific in company with the Americans. Neville had no doubt of the answer. He denied that in choosing to remain in the Mediterranean theatre, 'New Zealand acted not boldly but traditionally', and he also denied that the act represented 'New Zealand as still the satellite of Britain'. Rather he interpreted the decision as 'one of the great maturing moments of the national life . . . never did a New Zealand parliament make a more difficult, a more adult or a less insular decision'.[72] Yet significantly, while pointing out the practical factors – the lack of available shipping, the difficulties of transferring men from North Africa into the jungles of the Pacific – Neville also emphasised the effect of pleas from General Freyberg, President Roosevelt and above all Winston Churchill, who 'addressed sentences resonant with the cadences of Gibbon and ornamented by a reminiscence of Tennyson'. Churchill's message was quoted extensively. It began with a tribute to the New Zealand Division ('there could not be any more glorious expression of the links which bind together the hearts of the people of the British and New Zealand isles') and concluded that the New Zealanders should remain in the Mediterranean on the grounds that 'it is the symbolic and historic value of our comradeship in arms that moves me'.[73]

Second, Neville discusses at length the justification for the bombing of the historical abbey of Monte Cassino. Here too there was no doubt in his mind. He certainly considers the argument that the bombing was a 'wanton act of terror and vandalism', and he concedes that the evidence of German use of the monastery for military reasons before the bombing was weak.[74] What sways him is the duty of the commanders to their troops. The men believed, rightly or wrongly, 'that "Jerry" was sitting in the "wee white house" ... it was a constant intruding presence: it looked into everything, it nagged at their nerves and became a phobia and an obsession'.[75] No doubt he wrote informed by his own personal memories of the psychological effect of the monastery watching over everything done below. When it came to the hard task of breaking through the Cassino front, then heritage and history had to give way. Neville showed himself a soldier first, a defender of heritage second.

Yet in the last paragraph of the book, Neville looked back on the scene at Cassino a decade after the war and his love for the history and traditions of Italy shone through:

> The historian of the battles of Cassino who revisits the scene finds no relief from the difficulty of commemorating them in a way that will do justice to the New Zealanders who fought there, but he is impressed anew by the need for making the attempt. For except in its boldest features, the face of the land has changed even in so short a time. To stand on the summit of Point 593 on the tenth anniversary of the peace was to be engulfed in a tranquillity made the more immense by the emphasis of a few simple sounds – the chime of a cowbell, a skylark's glee and, far below beside the new white abbey, the shouts of black-robed novices as they skirmished with a football. Earth heals her own wounds, and the husbandry of a thousand peasants has tended the growth of twelve successive springs. Ruins are dismantled and new buildings arise on the sites of the old. Men remember but their memories fade and finally die with them. And of the deeds bravely done and the hardships bravely borne, soon nothing will remain but the imperfect record itself.[76]

Italy, Volume 1 was well received. Yet Neville told New Zealand acquaintances that the task of writing the history was not enjoyable and he gave up writing the second volume when it became unbearable. He wanted to get back to the English history he loved. On his research leave to Britain in 1955, alongside visiting the Italian battlefields, he spent time collecting books on eighteenth-century English politics and researching in the archives, so he could continue his real historical love when he got back. After 1956 his historical research and publications concerned the history of the British ruling class. Edmund Burke remained an enduring interest, and he became deeply interested in the political history developed by Lewis Namier.[77] Before long he was counting late-eighteenth-century voting lists and publishing about English politics, although largely (to his disappointment) in New Zealand publications.[78] To be fair, he continued to support New Zealand history despite his own lack of interest. He was always supportive of Philip Ross May's work on the gold rushes. For *Landfall* he wrote a brilliant review of Keith Sinclair's *Penguin History of New Zealand*, in which he recognised that Sinclair presented a closely reasoned interpretation which favoured 'environment at the expense of heredity'. He suggested that 'the exploration of what it is to be a New Zealander is exhilarating and provocative. Many shrewd thrusts are made at the South Island "regional myth" of a New Zealand more British than Britain', and he concluded: 'Dr Sinclair could not adduce better proof of our cultural maturity than his own book.'[79] No wonder that Sinclair himself later told me that Neville's was the only review that really understood the point of his book.

Yet British history and British life remained his true love, so on refresher leave in London in 1963 Neville spent much energy unsuccessfully applying for professorial positions in English universities. He received several interviews but no job. Perhaps it was partly this failure which led him in 1965 to apply for the position of vice-chancellor of the University of Canterbury. This time he was successful and Neville, abandoning ambitions as a historian, threw himself into the task. These were years of student protest and Neville was forced to negotiate tricky issues such as contraceptive-vending machines, student mixed flatting, and the link between the university's observatory at Mt John and the US military machine. There were various controversies where Neville's right-wing sympathies conflicted with his commitment to freedom of opinion, such as his refusal to host the former

The abbey at Monte Cassino, Italy, 2017.

communist Frank Milner. He had visited the United States on a state department trip in 1966 and encouraged American studies at the very time when the US alliance was coming under scrutiny as a result of the Vietnam War. He put a huge amount of time and energy into ensuring that the university celebrated its centennial in an appropriate way, including overseeing the writing of a history. His major challenge as VC, however, was to complete the move of the university from its central site on Rolleston Avenue to Ilam. This was achieved and he was often seen at the weekends inspecting the planting of exotic trees at the new campus. He also came up with the idea of turning the old campus into the arts centre, so that the Gothic revival buildings, which he always loved, might continue to have a cultural life. As an administrator, Neville was often seen as cold and distant – his nickname was 'Old Frosty' – and he did not find the burdens of decision-making easy. Undoubtedly the strain of the position contributed to a major heart-attack in 1976 which, soon after, led to his retirement from the position.

Neville Phillips as vice-chancellor: the efficient administrator (above) and gracious host of Margaret Thatcher (below).

The question then became: how would he spend his retirement? One day about this time, my mother asked Neville what he would do if she died. He replied that he would move to England. He then returned the question, and she responded with the same answer. So they decided there was no point waiting until the other had died. With retirement Neville and Pauline flew back to the old country. There they bought a house just outside Canterbury. Neville occupied his time chairing the Canterbury Archaeological Trust, watching the Kent cricket team, and with Pauline making frequent visits across the Channel to France and their beloved Italy, and enjoying weekly walks in the 'garden of England'. Until his death in 2001, although he still supported the All Blacks when they played England, Neville never returned to visit New Zealand. A cultured life in the home counties of England was satisfaction enough.

2
My mother and the land

My father provided a model of European high culture, a view of history as the study of the Old World, and upper-class, or perhaps upper-middle-class, aspirations. The background of my mother, Pauline Palmer, reinforced the English gentry ideal. More important, my mother's family brought a tradition of the ownership and exploitation of colonial land through the farming of exotic animals, and developed in me a deep love for the New Zealand landscape.

Had I been writing in 2014 I would have begun this story in the small Bedfordshire village of Goldington, where there is a line of Palmer graves obligatorily visited by New Zealand descendants of the Palmers on their trips 'home'. Goldington was long believed by family members to be the birthplace and home of my mother's grandfather and the family's first male settler in New Zealand, Joseph Palmer. But, as we shall see, I discovered in 2015 that Joseph Palmer's background was not quite what I had expected. Then later that year I visited Adelaide to watch New Zealand play Australia in the first ever day–night cricket test. Predictably, the cricket finished early (with an Aussie win!), so I had time to find out a little more about Joseph's father-in-law, Sir James Hurtle Fisher. Family lore had told me that he was a lord mayor of Adelaide – that is all I knew. But it did not take long walking round the city to discover that Sir James had left his mark all over Adelaide. There

A young Pauline Palmer on a hill at her family's Hawke's Bay farm, Te Aratipi, in the late 1930s.

was a major square, Hurtle Square, named after him (presumably because it was a more colourful name than Fisher Square); I found a large marble plaque to the memory of him and his family in the original Anglican Church, Trinity Church; there was a plaque at the site of his first house; and in the art gallery, museum and parliament buildings I discovered portraits of the man. Clearly he was a big shot in South Australia; and I slowly realised that Sir James was where the cultural traditions of my mother's family began. So let us start my mother's story not in Goldington, but on board the HMS *Buffalo* in 1836, on the voyage which brought James from Portsmouth to South Australia.

The *Buffalo* had been built in India in 1813 and was primarily a ship for carrying stores. By 1836 it had already been used to transport convicts to Sydney and naval stores from New Zealand, but in that year it was fitted out to carry the first group of migrants to the new 'paradise of dissent', the colony of South Australia. James Hurtle Fisher, accompanied by eight children and his wife Elizabeth, pregnant with my great-grandmother, was on board as the colony's 'resident commissioner'. It was very far from a happy voyage, and the roots of the problem go back to the origins of South Australia as a British colony. The idea of the colony arose among a group of reformers who were keen to find a solution to the increasing poverty of the growing English population. Sending migrants to the southern hemisphere became a live option once Edward Gibbon Wakefield had penned his famous tract from Newgate prison, *A Letter from Sydney*. Wakefield's idea was that if land could be sold for 'a sufficient price', then the land revenue would pay for the migration of working families, and once there the working population would not disperse in pursuit of cheap land and descend into frontier barbarism. Instead the concentration of people would preserve a civilised society complete with the Old World's social orders. As Wakefield wrote, the colonies 'would no longer be new societies, strictly speaking. They would be so many extensions of an old society.'[1] The South Australian Association pushed for a charter to carry out their vision free from government interference, but the Colonial Office was unwilling to grant them independent power. The resulting act of 1834 was a compromise doomed to failure. The Colonial Office appointed a governor and his officials, while the Association set up a board of commissioners with authority over land sales, migration and financial matters.[2]

Conflict between the two centres of power was inevitable and it began on board ship. On one side was the resident commissioner, my great-great-grandfather James Hurtle Fisher. Born in 1790, Fisher was the son of a London architect. He had become a lawyer and as a result of work for the board of commissioners was invited to become the resident commissioner to represent the interests of the Association in South Australia. Why he decided to migrate is not clear. It may have been because he had a large family to support and his legal career had been mixed. He also had a brother in New South Wales 'who was supposed to be making a fortune'.[3] On the other side was the man appointed governor, John Hindmarsh. He was a naval captain, and he used that experience to score first points by demanding to be appointed captain of the *Buffalo* as well as governor, so on the voyage out no-one could question his authority. Hindmarsh was not used to caring for the welfare of the 176 civilians on board. Ironically it was the exotic animals (the future source of my family's wealth) that caused the major issues. The governor had obviously imagined that animals would be the key to the colony's success, so he insisted on bringing them along. On both sides of the main deck he had built pens of filthy hogs, and the migrants, who were housed in a fetid dormitory below deck, had no access to unpolluted air when they climbed up. Then their water rations were reduced to ensure the governor's guinea-fowls, geese and poultry did not suffer from thirst. The governor's dogs ran loose and bit people at their pleasure. And at one point the sail was reefed so that his cow and mules wouldn't suffer from wind draughts. No wonder the voyage lasted an unusually long time – over five months. Fisher was particularly unhappy. He suffered from epilepsy and the conditions created frequent seizures, and his family had their own complaints about Hindmarsh – above their cabin there was continual hammering as a 'hothouse, doghouses and other sorts of houses' were built for the governor.[4] Hindmarsh also excluded two of Fisher's children from the wardroom mess because the table was not big enough. Fisher saw this as a personal slight. There was also a fierce argument when Hindmarsh could not decide whether to land at Rio or the Cape and kept changing direction.

By the time the *Buffalo* reached South Australia on 28 December 1836 (the ship was eventually wrecked at Mercury Bay in the Coromandel two years later) and the weary voyagers landed to proclaim the new settlement, Resident Commissioner Fisher and Governor Hindmarsh were at loggerheads. Fisher immediately asserted his authority by refusing to allow the governor's chattels to be carried in his bullock wagons.[5] Things did not

Engraving of Sir James Hurtle Fisher as an old colonist.
THE ILLUSTRATED AUSTRALIAN NEWS, 24 FEBRUARY 1875

improve. Each had sufficient power to thwart the other but not to achieve anything themselves. Hindmarsh, backed by his government officials, suspended Fisher's supporters from the council; Fisher in turn, controlling the finances, refused to agree to the governor's requests.[6] The resident magistrate was forced to bind the two to keep the peace toward each other. It is true that Hindmarsh was a stubborn, dictatorial man, but my great-great-grandfather did not win universal approval either. The resident judge, Sir John Jeffcott, described him as 'a wily attorney, the very worst class of person that could have been selected for the office; who, by dint of writing and special pleading and splitting hairs upon every insignificant point, wished to put the governor, a bluff straightforward but not very prudent sailor, into a false position'.⁷ Eventually the conflict became unsustainable. Fisher sent an envoy to London and had Hindmarsh recalled in 1838, and the next governor combined the roles of governor and resident commissioner. But Hindmarsh also had revenge by accusing Fisher of corruption in allocating bullocks and stores. He was charged by the next governor and not finally cleared until 1845, when the young George Grey was governor. Whether or not the charges were fair is hard to determine at this distance, but it seems likely. From the start Fisher and his officials were specifically allowed to combine their official roles and their private mercantile interests, and it is said that Fisher spent most of his time and energy on those private commercial interests rather than the public accounts.⁸

I must also admit that my forebear's role as resident commissioner in distributing land was not without unfortunate consequences. For a start he gave in to the pressures of settlers and allowed the survey and sale of lands distant from Adelaide for pastoral purposes – quite contrary to Wakefield's principles of concentrated settlement – and he did so with a total blindness to the rights of Aboriginal people. In the original South Australia Act of 1834 the territory had been described as 'waste and unoccupied Lands which are supposed to be fit for the Purposes of Colonization'. But then the Colonial Office became concerned about the rights of Aboriginal people, and in the Letters Patent of 1836, which were intended to govern the actions of the Commission and Fisher in particular, there was a provision making it mandatory for all to safeguard 'the rights of any Aboriginal native of the said Province to the actual occupation or enjoyment in their own persons of their descendants of any Lands therein now actually occupied or enjoyed by such Natives'.⁹ There is not the slightest evidence that Fisher took such provisions seriously. Further, he quickly became convinced that the future economic growth of the colony and of his own family's prosperity depended on turning South Australia into an Old World farm. Within six months of arrival he wrote that 'the colonists would be able to indulge in agriculture to any extent, when they obtained possession of the land, owing to the superior soil, which was admirably adapted to all agricultural as well as pastoral purposes'.¹⁰ It was perhaps not coincidental that close members of Sir James's family quickly became owners of huge pastoral estates. Indeed his two oldest sons, James and Charles, became by the mid-1870s among the richest men and largest pastoralists in Australia.¹¹

Despite the accusations of financial skulduggery and the loss of his position as resident commissioner, Fisher did not appear to lose popularity or withdraw from public life. When a municipal corporation for Adelaide was established in 1840, Fisher topped the poll, and was elected the first mayor by his peers. The position did not last long, partly because the autocratic George Grey tried to thwart its operation. Fisher resigned and the experiment ended; but when a city council was re-established in 1852, Fisher again became mayor for two years.[12] He was also elected onto the South Australian Legislative Council in 1853, became speaker two years later, and when responsible government arrived in 1857 he became president of the Legislative Council. His instincts and actions were consistently conservative.[13] By the time he was knighted in 1860, the first resident South Australian to be so honoured, Fisher was widely regarded as the foremost representative of 'the founding fathers'; he was asked to lay the foundation stone for the statue of the pioneering surveyor, Colonel Light, and presided at Old Colonists' dinners.[14]

Two other aspects of Sir James Hurtle Fisher's life are important. One was his founding role as one of the three original trustees of the Trinity Anglican Church; the second was his social aspiration to remain, as one obituary put it, 'a fine old English gentleman'.[15] One of his triumphs in the battle with Governor Hindmarsh came when he heard that the governor had entertained a naval officer with ship's pork and bad sherry, while his table had 'stewed kangaroo, roast emu, quails, chicken, claret and champagne'. He also liked to display his crest – three square feet of 'lion rampant and his initials on top in the form of Tudor Gothic'.[16] Consistent with the style of the English rural squire, he was active in horse racing, becoming president of the local jockey club while his son Hurtle became among the country's most prominent horse-breeders. One of Hurtle's horses won the Melbourne Cup. Sir James's other son, Charles, had the C. B. Fisher Plate named after him. It was a well-known Flemington race held the week after the Melbourne Cup for over a hundred years until 1978.[17]

So Sir James Hurtle Fisher turns out to have been rather more important to our story than I had ever believed. He it was who really established in my mother's family an interest in pastoral farming, and a lifestyle in the New World as a proper English gentleman.

These aspects of Hurtle Fisher's career become important as we unravel the mystery of Joseph Palmer, my grandfather's father, who, along with his wife Emily, was the first in my mother's family to settle in New Zealand. Descendants of Joseph long believed that he was from a family of non-conformist landowners from the small Bedfordshire village of Goldington. It is true that Joseph's death certificate, presumably on the basis of information supplied by Emily, stated that he was born in Bedfordshire; his obituary in the Christchurch *Press* claimed that he was from 'an old Bedfordshire family'; and in an unpublished memoir my grandfather Selby Palmer repeated this idea.[18] Yet the documentation is not convincing. For a start there is considerable uncertainty about Joseph's date of birth – 1827 in the death register and on his tombstone, 1829 in the *Press*, but the date given by Joseph himself when he joined the Union Bank was 6 April 1826, which seems a more convincing source and is supported by the burial register. Further, in the early 1960s my grandfather paid for a professional genealogist to document his family's family tree, and although the Goldington Palmers were well documented, the genealogist was unable to link Joseph to the family. In 1987 I spent several days at the Bedfordshire Record Office repeating the exercise and again could find no link. The most likely parent was John Palmer, a landed proprietor from Goldington, but there was no record of his having children and he sold the Goldington property in 1828, which seems a strange act if indeed he had a family on the way. The first definite evidence we have of Joseph Palmer is when he signed on in London as a clerk with the Union Bank – a somewhat unusual choice for a person allegedly from a family of landed gentlemen.

What *was* Joseph Palmer's background? The simplest way to track him down is to examine the British census for 1841. There is only one Joseph Palmer in England who fits the bill. This is a Joseph Palmer aged 15 (and so born in 1826) who lived with his parents and siblings on St John's Rd, Clerkenwell, in London and is described as a 'clerk'.[19] There are several other pieces of evidence which support this. The first is that the father of the Clerkenwell Joseph Palmer was Miles Palmer. My grandfather's second name was Miles. Secondly, some other sources give his birthplace as London, including the *Cyclopedia*, which was usually based on evidence from the person concerned, and his *Press* obituary, despite its claim that he was from a Bedfordshire family.[20] Thirdly, bank records show that when the young Joseph joined the bank in 1850 there was a surety of £500 provided by 'M. Palmer'.[21] Assuming Joseph's father was indeed Miles Palmer, who was he? He is described in the census as a 'hairdresser'. As distinct from barbers, who were associated with blood-letting and had an unsavoury reputation, hairdressers had risen in the social scale in the eighteenth century, especially in providing women with wigs. By the early nineteenth century wigs were becoming unfashionable and hairdressers were on the downward slope. Certainly Clerkenwell was by this time a highly industrial area with much brewing and had lost class since the previous century. It seems plausible that Miles Palmer's status and income as a hairdresser was falling, and he encouraged his son to become a clerk as a path to better fortune.

Where then did the idea of the Bedfordshire landed-gentry origins come from? We know from bank records that Joseph joined the Union Bank in London in October 1850, hired as a clerk for the Sydney office.[22] He sailed for Sydney and, unlike Hurtle Fisher's voyage out, this one was remarkably quick – about ninety days – but it was not without personal dramas. Joseph kept a journal, deftly illustrated with amusing caricatures, which includes accounts of fierce arguments and rude language among the passengers and many descriptions of catching wildlife such as petrels, albatrosses (hooked with a bait of pork) and sharks. As an employee of the bank Joseph travelled as a passenger, not a migrant; but there is no reference to his background. He did not last long in Sydney and was quickly transferred to become a clerk in the Adelaide branch on a salary of £200. Within two years he had become an accountant on a salary of £300. Respectable as this position was, it was hardly of the same status as the family of James Hurtle Fisher, the city's lord mayor, about to become speaker of the Legislative Council. At some point Joseph must have met and fallen in love with the mayor's youngest daughter, Emily. How could he make the match acceptable? Bank clerk would not do. The solution was to claim descent from the Palmers of Goldington. So when Joseph married Emily in Trinity Church on 10 November 1855 he is described on the marriage certificate, not as a bank clerk, but simply as a 'gentleman'. Descent from 'an old Bedfordshire family' of landed proprietors it would be. The question remains, of course, how Joseph knew about the Goldington family – perhaps, indeed, they were distant relatives. But there is little solid evidence that they were immediate family.

The young couple did not last long in Adelaide. On 7 April 1856, after a month-long voyage, Joseph arrived in Lyttelton as the manager of the local Union Bank. It was not on the surface a promising assignment. The first agent had arrived insane and had to be confined to a straitjacket, a local director

A self-portrait and a sketch of a fellow passenger from Joseph Palmer's shipboard journal.

had drowned, an assistant had died of fever, and the acting agent had resigned from all the distress.[23] However, Joseph took charge. He arranged a loan of £30,000 for the province and built permanent premises in Lyttelton, the second stone building in Canterbury. Within a year he had opened a branch in Christchurch, which he serviced by walking over the bridle path twice a week. In November 1859 he moved permanently to Christchurch as the manager. He was offered the manager's position at Adelaide, but despite the family links, decided that the South Australian sun would not be good for his health.

The Union Bank had a monopoly on banking in the Canterbury district, and Joseph quickly became a figure of considerable influence. William Moorhouse was the superintendent and Joseph, always careful with the bank's money and already identified with an Anglican group with deep suspicions of the superintendent's extravagance, began to exercise close scrutiny over the province's monies. When the province requested an extension to its overdraft in 1859 Palmer restricted new developments and examined their spending. G. R. Macdonald argued later that 'Palmer was for a time the most important man in Canterbury'.[24] The *Lyttelton Times* claimed, 'The manager of that very useful institution [the Union Bank] was in the habit of dictating to officials

Joseph and Emily Palmer.

what amount of monthly drafts would be honoured, and to what purposes they would be devolved.'[25] Such power did not last long. From 1861 prosperity returned, new banks opened and Moorhouse shifted the provincial accounts to the Bank of New Zealand. Joseph continued to have some public influence. He was responsible for the bonds which financed the Christchurch–Lyttelton railway tunnel, and he opened new branches in Timaru, Ashburton, Ōamaru and Rangiora. But his cautious attitudes meant that he won little of the West Coast gold-mining business for the bank. Eventually, in December 1871 Joseph became the first chief officer of the Union Bank of Australia in New Zealand, a position he held until his retirement in 1890. His pay rose from £1000 a year to £2000 (about $400,000 in 2017), a very considerable sum. One might ask whether he really deserved the increase, because his restrained lending policies and constant conflict with his Australian boss meant that the bank's fortunes relatively declined. By 1887 the proportion of New Zealand bank business controlled by the Union had fallen to under 12 per cent.[26]

Yet it was not in his role as a banker that Joseph had importance for my family. Rather it was in his relationship with the rural lands of Canterbury and in his gentlemanly style. During the 1860s and 1870s a central focus for his banking business was the development of pastoral farming in the Canterbury Plains and high country. Never a wild lender of money, Palmer channelled mortgages on Canterbury runs through the bank's firm, the New Zealand Trust and Loan Company, and offered advances up to the value of their wool clip to 'careful and cautious flockmasters'.[27] He was proud that 'we have the pick of the business of that class' and he noted that among the large landholders whom his bank had assisted were G. H. Moore; W. Rhodes; W. Robinson; the Studholme brothers, Malloch and Lance; Leonard Harper; C. G. Tripp; and E. Elworthy. Such names include most of the really large squatters of Canterbury. Joseph was also one of the trustees for Robinson's huge estate, Cheviot Hills, at the time of its sale to the government for breaking up. He showed support for pastoral farming by becoming a life member of the A & P Association. He also became a large landowner himself. In 1863 he purchased part of the Rakaia River property Double Hill, and over the subsequent years he added a number of adjoining runs, including Manuka Point, until his total holdings were in excess of 100,000 acres (40,400 hectares) in the Rakaia valley. Joseph's ownership of the area is still recalled in the name of the high hills to the east of the river, the Palmer Range. Joseph put a manager on his high-country estate, which he rarely visited; but much closer to Christchurch he also purchased a number of properties at Burnham which he visited regularly with his family. This not to say that Joseph did not have interests in the city of Christchurch – he became a director of the Christchurch Gas, Coal and Coke Company and was a member of the Chamber of Commerce – but, like his father-in-law, he also aspired to the status of the country squire.[28]

Like Sir James, Joseph Palmer took on the airs and interests of a respectable English gentleman. He was a member of the Canterbury Jockey Club and always attended the Christchurch races, he was a vestryman at the high Anglican church of St Michael's, and he mixed with Christchurch's Anglican gentlemanly circle, who were deeply suspicious of the boosters and aspiring capitalists. He was elected to the Christchurch Club, set up to cater for pastoralists and where, as Samuel Butler remembered, 'the conversation was purely horsey and sheepy'; he was also an original shareholder of the Canterbury Club.[29]

At home Joseph and Emily held court. After moving from Lyttelton they initially purchased a large home on the Avon, Locksleys, and then bought the property beside the Union Bank on Hereford Street. It stretched through to Worcester Street and from the back garden the spire of the neighbouring cathedral was clearly visible. My grandfather, Selby, spent the first seven years of his life there and well remembered playing in that garden.

In 1887 Joseph and Emily went 'home' to England, and three years after their return, when Joseph was about to retire, they moved to a very large house on Papanui Road called Woodford. They immediately added a large two-storey wing to turn it into a mansion suitable for entertainment. The additions included a billiard room with a table weighing 1000 kilograms for the gentlemen, four extra guest rooms, expanded servants' quarters, and an upgrade of the stables and the 4½ acres (1.8 hectares) of garden, which included two tennis courts. Here Emily and Joseph proceeded to hold musical afternoons, ladies' 'at homes', balls, garden parties (with up to 400 attending), tennis parties and special Christmas gatherings for children. In 1893 they fitted their own electrical lighting system powered by a gas engine driving a dynamo. By then Woodford was 11,000 square feet (1000 square metres) with some 40 rooms.[30]

For Joseph himself, to become such a host and his home the centre of Christchurch's respectable society must have seemed a very long way from the life of a London hairdresser. Despite the luxuries of life at Woodford, Joseph and Emily were frequently away. Summers were enjoyed out at Burnham and in the winter they took a house at Sumner to be close to the sea air and water. Indeed so dependent on seawater did Joseph become for his daily bath that family legend claims servants had to drive to Sumner each day to collect water from the sea.

This was the comfortable world into which my grandfather was born in 1880. There were many social occasions, and good food, and he would have been surrounded by the distinctive Palmer voices, of which it was said, 'Half a dozen Palmers talking together made a considerable noise. It was not so much that they talked loudly, but the Palmer voice had a particularly penetrating, vibrating timbre which once heard can never be forgotten.'[31] There were plenty of servants – four maids, a groom and a gardener according to Selby, who admitted that he never even folded up his table napkin, for that was left to the 'parlour maid'.[32] Selby was the youngest of thirteen children, of whom only nine survived to adulthood. Two of his five sisters married bankers, and two others married landowning brothers. Of his own surviving brothers, the oldest, George, joined his father at the Union Bank, but in his late thirties went to England, lived well, became heavily involved in racing and returned to New Zealand with a magnificent outfit of clothes and no money. His siblings were forced to keep him, but the second son, Jim, restored the family name by becoming Christchurch's fashionable doctor. It was said that he kept a pet monkey and retired to go farming. The third son, Ted, took a degree at Jesus College, Cambridge, and was an outstanding sportsman who in 1894 played as a fast left-arm bowler in New Zealand cricket's very first official game.[33] In sum, they were typical products of a classy colonial family.

Selby Palmer and his sister Olive playing in the garden next door to the Union Bank on Hereford Street, Christchurch, about 1885. The cathedral behind is clearly visible.

Selby was very much the baby of the family – five years younger than his sister Olive and eleven years younger than Ted. He was a rather shy, introverted person who spent many childhood hours in the bank's garden hitting balls against the brick walls.[34] Despite the affluent environment, Selby did not have an easy childhood. He suffered from migraines and would retire to bed for days with his head wrapped in a scarf.[35] He was sent off to the Cathedral Grammar School, a private Anglican preparatory school in Christchurch, but was apparently frequently punished. The headmaster would lose control somewhat when using the cane and Selby learnt that by leaning back he could take the cuts on the coat-tails. He also remembered the first occasion he was caned, when he became so nervous he peed his pants, also wetting the headmaster's trousers. Then in 1887 when his parents went 'home', Selby was sent to board at the home of G. G. Stead. Stead had worked at the Union Bank and then left to establish a prominent Christchurch firm of grain merchants and exporters. He was one of the country's leading owners of racehorses, and Selby recalled that on Sundays they would drive out to Yaldhurst to inspect the horses.[36] But he did not enjoy his time there – the family member closest to him in age was Edgar, who later became a well-known naturalist and bird specialist, but whom Selby recalled had 'a devil of a temper', and he also remembered being humiliated by being forced to share the bath with Noel, the family's daughter.[37] However, summer holidays at Burnham brought 'many happy days' and Selby recalled riding round the district giving out invitations to a summer fete on his father's estate, which included the wayward boys from the Burnham Industrial School. There were running races for cash, and dances on the lawn, and magic-lantern entertainments at night. In winter holidays the Christchurch hounds visited for hunting, and Joseph hosted a big hunt breakfast. It was truly the traditional 'noblesse oblige' of an English lord of the manor! Selby also learnt the aristocratic recreation of trout fishing in the Selwyn and Rakaia Rivers, although he did concede that sometimes the method of fishing was with the use of a muzzle loader or a 12-bore shotgun.

Selby's troubles were not over. At the age of thirteen he followed his older brothers by going off, as one would expect, to the private Anglican secondary school, Christ's College. There once again he quickly came into conflict with two headmasters. This time Selby was upset to discover that the acting head had a habit of fondling the boys' buttocks – 'bum-feeling' they called it.

And then when Selby objected to a master attempting to cane him for doing something he had not, Selby broke the cane. The upshot was that the new headmaster, now arrived, wrote to Joseph complaining about Selby's behaviour. Joseph responded by saying that he did not send his son off to school to have Selby's troubles brought to him, so Selby was promptly removed and sent to Wanganui Collegiate. There the headmaster laughed when Selby told his version of his Christ's experience and from that moment he felt at home.[38] Within a year he was in the first XI, and subsequently played in the first XV for two years and became a school prefect. He was not highly successful academically, although he did matriculate. So by the time he completed at Wanganui Selby was a successful product of elite education, a proper sports-playing gentleman.

What would Selby do now? He never had a desire to follow his father into the bank, although he did toy with the thought of going to Canterbury College to study engineering. Rather, his happy days out at Burnham called, so he went off to Orari Station in South Canterbury as a farm cadet. Selby's brother Ted was already a farmer and so were two of his brothers-in-law. Orari had been established by the Tripp family and had been one of the pastoral runs that had been funded by Joseph at the bank. Thus that interest in pastoral farming which had been in the family through both Sir James Hurtle Fisher and Selby's father finally reached fruition. Selby would be a pastoral farmer. Selby stayed four years at Orari, interrupting his work to ride 25 miles (40 kilometres) to play rugby and eventually earning a game with South Canterbury. About 1903, when he was twenty-three, Selby then followed his brother Ted to his farm at Whatatutu in Gisborne before buying his own backblocks property further inland at Hangaroa.

During these years Selby met – and eventually married in 1912 – Dorothy Wells, my grandmother. Joseph, had he been still alive (he died in 1910), would have approved of the marriage, and Emily certainly did so. Dorothy too came from very respectable stock. Her father, Charles Wells, had been a sea captain who had come to New Zealand. He tried to be a farmer near Amberley in Canterbury, but was never very successful. However, he lived in style and the family had two maids and a governess, and Charles was always a martinet for good manners. He claimed that he had an aristocratic lineage and could trace his ancestry back to Lord Nelson. Whether that was true or not, his father had certainly been an army surgeon at the siege of Lucknow in 1857 during the Indian Mutiny, and it is possible to trace the family back to the pioneering Quaker Charles Fox.

Dorothy's mother, Florence Lane, had an equally respectable background. Her father was William Hannibal Lane, who established Lane's Mill on the Avon River in the centre of Christchurch and had been an associate of Joseph Palmer in starting the Canterbury Club. Florence had been sent back 'home' to be educated at Cheltenham Ladies' College, and her sister Nell was married to George Gould, a leading farmer, businessman, racehorse owner and chairman of directors of the leading stock and station agency, Pyne, Gould and Guinness. Nell, known as 'the duchess of Christchurch', held court on the 11-acre property Avonbank, on Fendalton Road.[39] Florence's brother, Beauchamp Lane, also had a large house. Dorothy and her three sisters regularly attended balls and other social occasions at these large Christchurch mansions. As Beauchamp's name suggests, the Lanes were closely related to the Wellington Beauchamp family of Katherine Mansfield fame; they were also related to the writer Elizabeth von Arnim (originally May Annette Beauchamp), author of the well-known book *Elizabeth and her German Garden*. So Dorothy's background was impeccable. She had been educated at home by governesses and developed a passion for riding and hunting with the hounds, but had not learnt either to cook or to sew.[40]

If Dorothy's background, like Selby's, meant that both considered themselves part of the genteel class, this did come under real test during their married life together. When Dorothy married Selby he was living at Hangaroa in the far backblocks of inland Gisborne, where he had bought a grazing run. The farm was 65 kilometres from Gisborne and the last 15 kilometres were along a pack track, which my grandfather recalled became in the winter 'one foot wide and six feet deep'. Later he would give vivid descriptions of bringing everything in on horseback, from sewing machines to newborn babies. The stores had to be brought in before the winter rains began. Most of the run was in fern and bush, and Selby had to set about burning it and sowing grass seed. For some years he 'bached' in a small cottage before building a house on a new site because the hillside behind was slipping down. The wood for the house was pit-sawn by 'a very tough lot of men'. So Selby had learnt to rough it with frontier blokes, many of whom enjoyed their liquor, and when Dorothy joined him in 1912, according to Selby, she thrived on 'the hardships and vicissitudes of backblocks life', although they always had household 'help'.[41]

Selby in his twenties; Dorothy with her first-born, Mary; and their home at Hangaroa, inland from Gisborne.

After three years Selby decided the backblocks life would not make for a happy future, so he sold up and bought 2000 acres (800 hectares) with Dorothy's father, Charles Wells, at Maraetōtara some 30 kilometres from Havelock North in the Hawke's Bay. Originally the property had been the outstation of the Waimārama block (it was about 10 kilometres inland from Waimārama Beach) and eventually Selby named it Te Aratipi. About a third of the land was already cultivated and the balance in heavy bush. But the rainfall was high (since its hilly terrain attracted coastal showers from the east) and it proved a productive piece of land. By the 1950s Te Aratipi was a highly profitable enterprise and Selby began both a Romney sheep and an Aberdeen Angus stud; but before then, especially in the Depression of the early 1930s, times were tough, and the farm only remained within the family because the bank, his father's bank, continued to support him.

Yet for all the struggles of backblocks isolation and then the economic 'slump', Dorothy and Selby did not forget their genteel roots. Apart from a short period they always had servants, who inhabited a separate part of the house and had to use a tin bath in the washhouse and an outside lavatory. The maid cooked the meal, waited at table, and when Dorothy rang the bell she would come to take away the plates. For afternoon tea and dinner the maid would wear a black dress, a white apron and a white band around her head to hold her hair. There were always three courses – soup from the tureen, a main course and dessert. When children came along – three girls, Mary, Patricia and my mother Pauline, and a son, John – they were educated until secondary-school age by governesses at home. As Mary wrote later, we 'were not allowed to mix with the other children who went to the local school'. The governesses had to have the right class manners. One, Miss Gully, lost the job because, in Mary's words, 'my mother did not approve of her accent, which would be considered typical New Zealand'.[42]

Then when it was time for secondary school, the girls were sent to the refined Anglican school for young ladies, Woodford House in Havelock North, while John went off to Wanganui Collegiate. In the holidays there were dances hosted by Woodford or Wanganui parents. Selby retained an interest in gentlemanly sports – billiards, snooker and bridge at the Hastings Club, golf, tennis, shooting and fishing for trout. The family always went to Taupō in the summer to go fishing. Later Selby picked up on his family interests by getting involved in racing, and one of his horses, Amber Wine,

Pauline Palmer (left) and her sister Mary with trout caught at Lake Taupō, about 1923; and off to a garden party at Buckingham Palace in 1938 with her parents, Dorothy and Selby Palmer.

won a number of steeplechases in the 1960s. As for Dorothy, she was a keen gardener. Regarding cultural interests, both were readers of history and biography, and enjoyed illustrated magazines from Britain such as the *Sphere* and the *Illustrated London News*. 'Home' continued to call, and in 1938 they visited Britain, including a date at a Buckingham Palace garden party. There were further such trips in the 1950s.

So my mother's childhood was spent primarily out on the farm with occasional picnics down at Waimārama Beach. She must have grown up with a strong sense of the land, but also, surrounded as she was by servants and talk of distinguished relations, of her own and her family's status. From about the age of eight the girls enjoyed riding horses and before long they were riding all over the hills and knew all the paddocks and gates. They sometimes helped with stock work, and on several occasions rode at the Hawke's Bay show. Eventually they took part in hunts.[43] They also began to participate in tennis parties with landowning neighbours.

From her young days Pauline expressed an interest in learning and persuaded the governess to accept her, at the tender age of four, into class along with her older sisters. This was not to her full satisfaction, sadly, because the governess, Miss Woon, took an instant dislike to the precocious girl, a grievance which Pauline carried to the end of her days. And when Pauline went to Woodford she soon showed her academic prowess. Determined to pursue her intellectual interests, and not wanting to settle down and marry into the Hawke's Bay landowning class like her older sisters, she decided to go to Canterbury University College. By then, 1935, farm prices had improved, so Selby supported her, unlike Mary, whose earlier desire to go to university had been thwarted.

At university Pauline did well. She majored in history and was awarded a national scholarship to go on to MA honours. She wrote a thesis entitled 'The Native Ministry of Donald McLean, 1869–76'. It was an interesting choice of subject. Donald McLean, of Scots Highland background, eventually became, as the land purchase commissioner and also native secretary, the government's main agent for purchasing Māori land for Pākehā settlement in the 1850s. He was responsible for the purchase in 1851 of three huge blocks of Hawke's Bay land totalling over 250,000 hectares. He himself was able to acquire over 20,000 hectares and build up a pastoral estate around Maraekakaho, near Napier. He became the superintendent of Hawke's Bay, and then represented

Pauline in 1934, aged seventeen, about to head to Canterbury University College (left); and as a graduate aged twenty in 1937 (right).

the area in the House of Representatives. So he was a natural figure of interest for Pauline, daughter of a Hawke's Bay pastoralist. But interestingly Pauline did not focus on his role as purchase officer or his landholding ambitions, both of which at the time and in the eyes of subsequent historians have come under considerable criticism and allegations of corrupt practice.[44] Rather she examined the last stage of his career, when he was the native minister almost continuously from 1869 to 1876. At that time the McLean correspondence, which has proved such a rich source for later historians and Waitangi Tribunal researchers, was not accessible, so Pauline drew primarily on official sources – the *AJHR*s, parliamentary debates and two newspapers, the *Wellington Independent* and the *Hawke's Bay Herald*. It is significant that she did not use the other Hawke's Bay paper, Napier's *Daily Telegraph*, which very much expressed an anti-McLean point of view. Not surprisingly Pauline's portrait of McLean was largely positive – although to be fair even his critics have judged his performance in those years as the most admirable of his career.

Pauline's theme in the thesis is McLean's role in bringing about the 'pacification' of the country. She begins in 1869 with Te Kooti on the east coast of the North Island and Tītokowaru on the west coast, both threatening European settlement and renewed war, and the Māori King hidden behind the aukati (or boundary) in 'sullen isolation'.[45] She argues that McLean was able to restore peace and internal confidence, and the body of the thesis describes the mechanisms he used – his encouragement of Māori agriculture and roading; his rejection of land confiscation and refusal to enforce it on the Waimea Plains or against the Ngāti Tūwharetoa leader Horonuku Te Heuheu; his support for native schools and for Māori representation in Parliament (which McLean had sponsored in 1867 before becoming native minister); and his positive hui with King Tāwhiao and the Kīngitanga. She argues that McLean liked to work through the leadership of chiefs and gave support for measures of Māori self-rule. She explains his attitudes in terms of his Highland origins which provided 'a spiritual affinity with this tribal people', and she argues that his patience and tact with Māori were essential to his success.[46]

Obviously Pauline's judgments were perhaps more positive than modern historians might make, but she relied on official sources, and she is clear about where McLean's work created future problems. She is forthright that the Land Act 1873, which he sponsored, served to weaken the tribal system and in the long run facilitated the individualising of Māori land and its sale; and she acknowledges that for all his understanding of the Māori language and culture, McLean's long-term aim was 'Europeanisation, an ideal the logical implications of which meant not adaptation, but destruction of tribal institutions'.[47]

Pauline's political sympathies were surprisingly liberal for someone from her background. She did not praise McLean as the pastoral pioneer, and she expressed a sympathy for Māori culture and Māori aspirations for self-rule. Among the reading that may have influenced her she cited particularly I. L. G. Sutherland's *The Maori Situation* and Raymond Firth's *Primitive Economics of the New Zealand Maori*. She always had a concern for the underdog and the oppressed and a lifelong belief in the importance of conciliation rather than conflict. Also, at this stage Pauline clearly had aspirations as a serious historian. She began and ended the thesis with a theoretical discussion about the relationship between the individual and society; and the thesis itself was beautifully organised and clearly expressed. Her literary education was reflected in the fact that it opened with a quote from Shakespeare's *Othello* which pertains to McLean's ability to take time and show patience.

It is striking that Pauline's thesis of 1937 and Neville Phillips' thesis of the same year have a remarkably similar structure. Both begin with a crisis in the late 1860s – Neville's starting year is 1868, Pauline's 1869 – and both show how by the end of their study conflict has become reconciliation. In Neville's thesis the conflict is between Great Britain and New Zealand; in Pauline's case between Māori and Pākehā. Whether this was coincidental, who knows. What is clear is that over these years in the history honours class, the two became close. James Hight obviously realised what was happening, because when their papers and theses were sent off to England to be marked, the pseudonyms used for telegraphing the marks were 'Altar' for Neville and 'Also' for Pauline. The attraction between the two must have had many aspects, but one can see why it worked. For Neville, Pauline Palmer offered an entrance into an anglophile and respectable landowning family; while for Pauline, Neville offered intellectual interests and the promise of a break from the Hawke's Bay rural squattocracy. She never rejected that background, and her family remained hugely important to her. She always wanted to be, and enjoyed being, a mother, but her intellectual interests meant that marrying a Hawke's Bay farmer would have been frustrating. By the time Neville left for England in 1938, the two were engaged. They had brought together four cultural traditions – an interest in English high culture represented most strongly by my father; a tradition of pastoral farming represented by my mother's background; a shared respect for genteel class values; and a joint passion for history. This was the culture in which I was brought up, and how these attitudes impacted upon me – and fought with one another – is the subject of the next chapter.

3.
Christchurch boy

I was obviously destined to be a historian of New Zealand. The first person to welcome me into this world on 14 May 1947 was a gynaecologist and obstetrician, Leslie Averill, who had won fame at Le Quesnoy in north-eastern France in World War I. Le Quesnoy was a walled town, and in the closing week of the war the New Zealanders were tasked with capturing it. Determined to avoid ruining the historic battlements by using heavy artillery, and aware of the civilians inside, the diggers decided to capture the town by scaling the walls. Lieutenant Averill was the first person to do so, thus achieving minor celebrity. Then, my first memory was at the age of three in 1950, when I distinctly recall visiting the amusement ground at Hagley Park, where the centenary of the Canterbury settlement was being celebrated.

If each of these events were important moments in New Zealand history, they also reflected the culture in which I would be raised. Averill had been a war hero, but he was also the son of a man who became an archbishop and primate of the Anglican Church.[1] Leslie Averill was the chief executive of the Anglican hospital, aptly named St George's after the patron saint of England, and sited in Papanui, less than a kilometre from Joseph Palmer's home. This was where I was born. As for the Canterbury centenary, the commemorative events included a re-enactment of the 'Canterbury pilgrims' arriving in Lyttelton from England on 'the first four ships'; a floral procession celebrating

A Cathedral Grammar School boy beneath the cherry blossom.
NEVILLE PHILLIPS

Canterbury's pastoral and agricultural richness, featuring amid the floats a huge representation of the royal insignia; and a thanksgiving service in Cathedral Square with a choir of 1300 and a sermon by the archbishop of Canterbury.

Thus christened with the name of John ('Jock' came later), I would be brought up in Anglican, and anglophile, Christchurch – more especially, in the respectable western part of the city. For my first year or so, my parents lived in the Redcliffs home of Alice Candy, while she, a pioneering woman academic and lecturer in history, was warden of the women's hostel Helen Connon Hall.[2] I learnt to walk on Redcliffs Beach.

Then we moved west to a house built by my parents, and designed by the up-and-coming architect Paul Pascoe, on a section on Glandovey Road in the very proper suburb of Fendalton. Glandovey Road was known for its very large mansions bordering on the Waimairi Stream. Our house was not large, but it had a pleasant back garden and cherry trees on the roadside, and my parents, my father especially, enjoyed living close to the elite's mansions. In Christchurch I went off with my mother each Sunday to St Barnabas Church, either for Sunday school or the monthly 'family service'. Once old enough I went to Fendalton 'Open-air' School, then from the age of eight to the Cathedral Grammar School, a preparatory school. Its name derived from its role in educating the choristers of the Anglican cathedral. Hymn singing, along with learning English, Latin, French and British history, was well represented in the curriculum. We wore a blazer in red, embroidered with a bishop's mitre, and we learnt to write using a distinctive italic script, with a broad-tipped pen. The script had been developed in the Italian renaissance and was intended to give our writing an elegant, civilised style (although in the long term I suspect it made my handwriting even more illegible than it would otherwise have been).

Inevitably, at the age of twelve I was sent off to the private Anglican school of Christ's College. This time we had to wear stiff starched collars and boaters. Half of the school pupils were boarders, nearly all children of pastoral farmers from Canterbury or Hawke's Bay. The 'day boys', who were looked down upon as a rather inferior species, were predominantly sons of city businessmen or of urban professionals, as I was. Although students from other Christchurch schools would inevitably chant, 'Blackballs are cheap today, cheaper than yesterday . . .' in reference to the black-and-white school colours when they saw us, we were quite convinced that deep down we were superior to

John, as I was then known – a toddler holding on to the keys of life.

those 'Boys' High boys', let alone those from Shirley or Cashmere, and most definitely to the 'Beedie boys', the Catholics from St Bede's.

Christ's was modelled on the English public school, with houses and prefects and 'fagging' – which involved the younger boys doing menial tasks for the prefects. The prefects were allowed to cane younger boys, a practice that even then I revolted against and refused to participate in when I became a school prefect. Many of the teachers were English and brought the attitudes and habits of English public schools with them. Most of the others were old boys of the school – and had been well indoctrinated in the school motto, 'Bene tradita, bene servanda', which from the third form I knew to translate as 'good traditions should be well handed on'. The headmaster during most of my time at the school was Harry Hornsby, an Englishman who had served with the Gurkhas during the war, and carried the values of the British Raj. He liked nothing better than to read Rudyard Kipling. But Hornsby knew the name and interests of every boy in the school, and he had a real commitment to educational and intellectual achievement. We learnt very little about our own country, learning nothing about either the Māori language or local history; but we did receive an excellent schooling in the curriculum of the English public school – Latin, French, British history, grammar and fine writing. In my last year the school was successful in winning no fewer than six university scholarships (from about seventy in the country), which was second only to Auckland Grammar. Sport of course was taken seriously at Christ's, which I enjoyed (although I only made it to the second XI and XV), and I did make some good friends there – almost exclusively from among the day boys – so I was not unhappy at the school. I slowly began to question the class values of the place, which can be seen in a rather cynical piece I wrote for the school magazine about the quadrangular rugby tournament, and I hated cadets. I achieved the distinction of being the only prefect who was not a cadet officer – which was so embarrassing to the school that they hid me away in the quartermaster's store. But I cannot be described as a rebel; I was largely comfortable at Christ's, as I had been at Cathedral Grammar, because the values represented there – the upper-class aspirations, the Anglican and anglophile intellectual interests, and the presence of many children of sheep farmers – were the values that I learnt at home.

How did my parents' values shape my upbringing? Their class aspirations were implicit in their place of residence and their choices for our

Christ's College new boy with my sister Catherine, 1960.

education. I was a middle child with one sister, Elizabeth, six years older, and one, Catherine, three years younger than me. They were sent off to the local Anglican private girls' school, St Margaret's, the female equivalent of Christ's College. My parents' interests in English, and to some extent European, high culture (especially history) and their commitment to academic excellence were part of the daily environment which surrounded me. My father was a strong presence. At the dinner table he could be funny, playing punning word games or reciting light verse, such as Ogden Nash or A. P. Herbert. But he could also come home anguished and put his head in his hands, when university politics had got too much. His intellectual interests were all around us. The sitting room was lined with a huge bookcase – mostly British academic history, but laced with a few large art books and collections of poetry. I would go to bed hearing the tap-tap of his typewriter as he prepared a lecture or public talk. When he had a draft, he would wander into the kitchen for his morning cup of tea and recite the masterpiece. I would listen to the oratory, mystified by what it all meant but learning about the cadence of fine writing.

The life of a university historian flowed round us. Neville would talk freely about his favourite students, their successes and failures; and each year my mother would join him in welcoming the honours class home, where my father would sidle up to each in turn and tell them their results. How those who had received a pass instead of honours coped, I still ponder. Quite often I would visit my father in his university study at the top of the stairs in one of those magnificent Gothic revival buildings that are now the arts centre. I would sit in the corner, waiting for him to take me home, and listen as he instructed a quivering student in the problems of his or her thesis.

There were also frequent visits from colleagues. I remember distinguished historians from the Canterbury department coming round for a chat or Sunday afternoon family visit – there was John Owen (a fine eighteenth-century British historian) and David Fieldhouse (a brisk, highly intelligent imperial historian), both of whom ended up as Oxford dons; there were younger New Zealand historians from the department, such as Phil May and Bill Oliver, then in his Catholic phase (of which my father did not approve!), at work on his *The Story of New Zealand*. There was John Pocock, a rather forbidding man to a young boy, who went on to achieve international eminence in the history of political ideas, and also his mother, a fine school history teacher, and his father Greville, professor of classics. I distinctly remember Greville pacing up and down our back lawn explaining to my father his theory that Homer's writings were actually based in Sicily, not Greece. I trailed along behind listening to every word. As for the department's leading New Zealand historian, Jim Gardner, we used to go round to his place, but there the focus was on practising cricket in the nets he had set up on his back lawn, rather than any discussions about the past.

There were also visits from eminent historians from out of town – the learned John Beaglehole, who would tell the assembled company about James Cook; a benign, friendly Fred Wood from Victoria; and the smart, handsome Keith Sinclair, who got dragged off one Saturday afternoon to watch me play rugby. I did not participate in their conversations, but I listened closely and I jotted their visits down in my diary – 'Dr Sinclair came to dinner'; 'Prof Wood here'. Occasionally there would be overseas experts who paid a fleeting visit. I remember especially the brilliant British historian of Victorian England, Asa Briggs, and a charming American historian from Wisconsin, Merle Curti. Such visits just confirmed in my father his desire to join them at a prestigious university overseas one day. My father did not try to teach me anything about the past directly; but one year, when I was about eleven, Elizabeth was sitting university scholarship in history and my father would set aside an hour or so on a Sunday afternoon to give her a history lecture. I would sit in the corner spellbound. I was too young to understand it all, but the example was compelling. There were also occasional trips with the Canterbury Historical Association. I recall a visit to Cheviot, where Jim Gardner told us all about 'Ready Money' Robinson and the forced sale of his huge estate in the 1890s; and there was a trip to Diamond Harbour, when there was not much history talked about but I took pride in climbing to the top of Mt Herbert and emulating in my mind the achievement of Edmund Hillary at Everest. So historians and the study of history were thick in the environment. But I do recall that my father took very much a back seat on these trips to local history sites, as if it was an act of duty rather than interest.

I first became really passionate about the past not directly from my parents, but from reading children's books. While others were reading Enid Blyton, I devoured the historical novels of Henry Treece and Geoffrey Trease, which told gripping stories about the Vikings or the crusades. The non-fiction books of Eileen Power and Rosemary Sutcliffe, which also concerned the Middle Ages, were other favourites. So medieval England became vivid in my imagination; and since there was another boy along the road, a recent migrant from the UK, who was equally obsessed we would imagine ourselves as knights of King Arthur's round table. We made wooden swords, used rubbish-tin lids and pranced about on our bamboo horses smiting the enemy or fighting knightly duels. Cowboys and Indians simply could not compete for my interest. Of modern tales, only Arthur Ransome's *Swallows and Amazons*, about sailing in the Lake District in the 1920s, and the Biggles stories about an English pilot in World War I held any interest. I remember no reading about New Zealand or New Zealanders, apart from a children's account of *The Ascent of Everest*, which one of my surviving youthful letters tells me I received for Christmas in 1954, along with the *BBC Children's Hour Annual*.

My parents were also interested in art. There were plenty of books about the great European masters, either in the house or brought home from the Christchurch library, and there were sometimes prints of impressionist paintings borrowed from the library (a scheme initiated by Ron O'Reilly, the city librarian). On weekends the family would occasionally visit an art

Colin McCahon, 'Painting', 1958. THE FLETCHER TRUST

exhibition and I recall especially seeing some of The Group shows from the late 1950s with painters like Rita Angus, Colin McCahon, Doris Lusk and Bill Sutton. My parents liked their impressionist landscapes, but were less impressed by abstract art; my father was more enthusiastic about some of the shows from overseas – an exhibition of prints by the eighteenth-century English cartoonists William Hogarth and Thomas Rowlandson was a special high-point for him. So from a young age I developed a love of art (as a spectator, not a creator, I hasten to add), and I recall at the age of twelve biking to town by myself to look at Colin McCahon's work 'Painting', an abstract work which had caused some controversy when it was judged joint winner of the 1960 Hay's competition. 'Painting' was put on display in the Hay's department store window, and I remember ogling it for a long time.

There was no classical music in the house, and although visitors like Charles Brasch would often communicate an excitement about New Zealand fiction and poetry, my father was not interested in reading it (though my mother was). In 1957 it was through such visitors that I first heard about Janet Frame's *Owls do Cry* and Ian Cross's *The God Boy*, although they were not in the house for me to sample. However, when in the early 1960s another visitor became enthusiastic about Tolkien's *The Lord of the Rings*, I did pick up the three volumes lying around the house and read them from cover to cover. Medieval English fantasy still held attraction.

In 1955 my parents went off to England on sabbatical leave. My mother accompanied my father for eight months while Catherine and I were looked after by Hawke's Bay relations and Elizabeth boarded at St Margaret's. While they were in England my father bought a good camera and began to take colour slides in glorious Kodachrome. My parents took this new venture seriously. My father thought a lot about the composition of every shot – there was always a telling foreground such as hanging leaves, and when they returned from abroad the two of them spent hours transferring every slide into glass protectors and labelling them scrupulously. Then would come regular slide shows. Some of the shows were of English country houses and gardens; more often they were of their trip around the continent. I recall images of French chateaux, Italian classical ruins, cathedrals and medieval hill-top villages, Swiss lakes, and Dutch markets with pallets of cheese. We all loved these shows and they left a considerable impact on me – I began to think about photography and what makes a good image, and more importantly I learnt that culture and beauty belonged on the other side of the world amid older civilisations.

When my parents returned from this leave they continued to keep in touch with the UK scene by subscribing to the weekly newspaper *The Observer*, which, though it arrived several weeks late, I read from cover to cover. They also began to drink wine with their Sunday meal. There would be discussions about 'farewells' and 'good noses' and vintages. My father, like myself, had almost no sense of taste or smell, so I am not convinced that he was very acute in his judgement about wines; but he learnt the lingo and did an awful lot of reading on the subject. Nearly all the wine we drank was from either France or Italy, but in the early 1960s I remember that he bought a barrel of experimental wine from Te Kauwhata, which sat in the garage. He would decant it periodically to try it before bemoaning its inferiority to the Old World vintages!

My father did not entirely turn his back on the local scene. He regularly gave radio talks, often on the Sunday-night slot *Lookout* on the YA stations, in which he would usually comment on overseas politics. And he was consistently interested in cricket and even rugby. He would take me along to Lancaster Park to watch touring cricket teams humiliate the New Zealand team, and from 1953 to 1956 when Canterbury held the Ranfurly Shield I would often accompany him to the park. I remember especially a game against Otago in 1954 when Canterbury retained the Ranfurly Shield with the clock showing full-time by scoring in the corner to make it 9–9. The crowd was so enthusiastic that we were swept onto the field in a massive stampede and I held onto my father's hand in desperation in case, as a mere seven-year-old, I would fall and be crushed by the trampling feet.

But even when it came to sport, I learnt from my father that the real heroes were English cricketers. Lying spreadeagled on the carpet with my head close to the radio, I listened intently to short-wave descriptions of the MCC tour of Australia in 1954–55. When England won I was ecstatically happy and Colin Cowdrey and Peter May, the young English batsmen, became my instant heroes. Later in my secondary-school years I bought an old radio and would listen to commentaries of tests in England until deep into the night. Cricket commentator John Arlott became another hero. Someone, perhaps my father, more probably my grandfather, gave me Prince Ranjitsinhji's *The Jubilee Book of Cricket*. This included details about the school colours and records of public-school, Oxford and Cambridge universities, and county teams. I studied these intently and learnt the details off by heart – supplemented by more modern information which I gleaned from *Wisden*. When not reading about cricket and working out averages, I would endlessly hit balls against the garage wall or wander down to nearby Elmwood Park to watch the senior teams play.

So under the influence of my father I developed a love of cricket and an undoubted respect for intellectual achievement. Neither of my parents was ever explicitly pushy, but the environment gave academic success a high value,

Working on a jigsaw after I had broken a leg skiing in 1958 (above) NEVILLE PHILLIPS;
*I loved doing puzzles. I also loved cricket, and was captain of the
Cathedral Grammar School first XI (below).*

and Elizabeth's outstanding academic record at school and in the national scholarships examination (she came second in the country) provided a further example. The daily diary that I kept in 1957 and 1958 lists all my examination marks and works out both the average score and my place in the class (it also records my cricket scores and the seasonal average). I also developed a romantic affection for England, especially the England of the past. I yearned to go there one day and see what I had but read about.

Although my sense of the primacy of British culture was strong as a result of my family upbringing, this was not especially unusual in New Zealand during the 1950s and early 1960s, and was reinforced by influences from wider society. I was but an extreme case of anglophilia. After all, in the 1950s and early 1960s New Zealand was still very much a 'British country'. The Māori population was under 150,000, and over 90 per cent of the population of some two million was of English, Scots, Welsh or Irish heritage. About 200,000 people, a tenth of the population, had been born in the United Kingdom, and there was a continuing flow of new migrants from the old country.[3] The influx of large numbers of people from the Pacific or Asia was still in the future. We remained Britain's offshore farm, with over 60 per cent of our exports (predominantly meat, wool and dairy products) and over half our imports going to or from the United Kingdom. We were still very conscious of our service ten years before as part of the British Empire's fight against totalitarianism, and the cinemas were full of movies recounting that story. New Zealanders thought of themselves as Britain's most loyal dominion, and they turned out in their thousands in the summer of 1953–54 when the young Queen and Prince Philip visited these shores. About two thirds of the population went out onto the streets to wave Union Jacks. The Queen's representative here, the governor-general, was always a British aristocrat like Sir Willoughby Norrie or Lord Cobham. And the culture reflected this dominance. On the cable page of our newspapers most of the stories had London as the source; and the main radio news bulletin of the day was still the 6 p.m. BBC news. Most of the books read in the country and a high proportion of the movies had originated in England. Even the more subversive radio shows which we enjoyed, such as *The Goons*, derived from Britain. So while through family influence I was unusually well-bred in English culture, this reflected a wider cultural phenomenon.

If the culture in which I grew up in Christchurch was intellectual and anglophile, I experienced a rather different world through the influence of my

With my mother on the hills above Waimārama, Hawke's Bay, about 1961.
NEVILLE PHILLIPS

mother. It was true that she shared many of my father's passions. She enjoyed art, continued to read history and also novels, and was hugely enthusiastic about visiting England and the continent in 1955. In her files I discovered a piece she had started about their trip to Italy in 1955. It begins: 'Italy at last, I said to myself as our car bumped slowly off the train at Bardenocchia. Italy at last . . .' But she added new interests to my world. As a toddler I spent much time in the kitchen 'helping' her with the cooking (which more accurately meant licking the bowl). Even now I can make marmalade or crab-apple jelly because of her deft instruction. And in the face of my father's mechanical ineptitude, she taught me how to use a hammer and a drill and how to chop wood. One day, when I was about eleven, she announced that she and my father had decided that I should give a little more help around the house and she offered me a range of options. One was vacuuming; another was weeding the ornamental garden; the third was looking after the vegetable garden.

Reluctantly I accepted the last. It was not an easy job – our garden had once been the bed of the Waimakariri River so it was littered with heavy stones and the soil was sandy and regularly suffered from droughts. There were also early disasters, especially when we ordered some manure from the local circus and a huge truckload of elephant poo was dropped on our front lawn. But I learnt under my mother's tutelage to track down manure, make compost and enrich the soil. I learnt how to plant and thin seedlings, and how to ensure that the soil never dried out. I learnt the noble art of staking tomatoes and protecting broad beans from the wind. I began to gain immense satisfaction from the responsibility and had a sense of pride when the family fed off my newly dug potatoes or freshly picked peas. Pauline encouraged me to think about the land.

Her greatest contribution in this respect was through her family. She had a cousin who had married a sheep farmer at Little Akaloa on Banks Peninsula, and on a number of occasions, especially in the May school holidays, I would be sent over there to help around the farm. It was steep country and the weather was often bitterly cold; so I was usually quite happy to get home. Very different was the experience with Selby Palmer's family in Hawke's Bay. Every Christmas holidays, from my earliest memories until I went to university, the family would catch the inter-island ferry at Lyttelton a couple of days before Christmas, grab a quick breakfast at the Wellington railway station and then take the train up to Hastings where my grandfather would be on the platform to meet us. Then it was into the car, pick up some punnets of strawberries, and head to my grandfather's farm, Te Aratipi. The big Christmas gathering would follow a couple of days later, with the whole extended family almost filling up the tiny Waimārama Anglican church, then back for a huge Christmas lunch with the obligatory turkey off the farm and plum pudding laced with silver coins. These were the first occasions when I drank alcohol and became a little tiddly. The afternoon would be spent on the tennis court, as we all tried to work off the overindulgence. The normal routine was a couple of weeks at Te Aratipi, playing tennis, going down to Waimārama to swim or surf at the beach, helping around the farm; then a week or so at Rouncil, a lovely old home about 10 kilometres out of Havelock North, the home of my mother's sister Patricia and her husband Jim Nelson. This was followed by another week or so at the magnificent five-storey kauri mansion of Aramoana, on the coast out from Waipawa, where my mother's eldest sister Mary and her

The Christmas line-up of the Palmer cousins at Te Aratipi in 1954. I am the one with the white sunhat.

husband Douglas McHardy lived before building a new home on the land which they called Ouepoto.

I loved these summer days in Hawke's Bay. It was partly that there were plenty of cousins my age – Mary had four daughters, Patricia had two sons and two daughters, and John, who did the farming at Te Aratipi (although did not yet inhabit the homestead), had a son and two daughters. They were much our age, and we played endless outdoor games with them. My uncles and aunts were incredibly generous and welcoming and keen to make us part of the family. There was much that was familiar from my Christchurch life – a similar genteel class identity, and a similar respect for England and her traditions. My grandfather subscribed to a number of English periodicals and would talk freely about his and my grandmother's regular trips 'home'. It was as a result of my cousins' royalist enthusiasms that I actually saw the Queen and Prince Philip no fewer than ten times in the summer of 1953–54. When the Queen visited Hastings the royal party then travelled south on the railway, stopping at the main stations along the way. So my cousins took their truck, we all piled on the back and then raced the royal train on the highway beside the train tracks, and stopped at each station to see the royals parade past enthusiastic crowds.

But it was the differences from my Christchurch life which really attracted; above all, the engagement with the land. For a start there was the work around the farm. When I was young this was no more than carrying the scones over to the men at the woolshed and staying to watch them dag sheep or draft lambs to be sent off to the works. But as I grew older and stronger I would get involved, until during the last couple of years I went onto the payroll and started to mix with the shepherds. I would ride out on a horse to help with the mustering, or get up about 4.30 and spend the morning pushing the heads of sheep under the water as they swam along the dip, or assist with the drafting of sheep into the woolshed when the shearing was on, or become totally exhausted stacking bales on those hot, hot days when the hay was being made. The work was tough, but I enjoyed the combination of physical effort and mental strategy, and I would pester my uncle Douglas or the head shepherd with questions about why things were being done. I found walking or riding over the hills very beautiful; and I developed a sense of belonging to the landscape.

On days off there was time at the beach – both Waimārama and Ouepoto were magnificent beaches with miles of sand and gorgeous lines of breakers. I learnt to surf with a board and then eventually to bodysurf; the bigger the waves the better. We all got dangerously sunburnt. There was plenty of time spent around horses. Despite my nervousness I learnt to ride – after a fashion – and I would accompany Aunt Mary and the McHardy girls as we went off to hunts on Hawke's Bay farms or to the local gymkhanas. I could but watch the hunts from a distance (and never blinked an eyelid at the sight of the poor hares being caught by the hounds and the young riders being 'blooded'). At the gymkhanas I enjoyed taking part in the running races – and in fact earned my very first money (five shillings, no less!), and destroyed forever my amateur status, by winning the 75 yards at the Ongaonga sports in 1958.

In Hawke's Bay I also first encountered the bush. My grandfather had some sense of the value of indigenous trees and eventually gave me his copy of Herbert Guthrie-Smith's *Sorrows and Joys of a New Zealand Naturalist*, which became one of my most loved possessions. He had carefully protected a patch of bush on the farm, above the homestead, and we used to go up there to

Scenes from the Hawke's Bay summer holidays: on the beach at Waimārama (top left); camping with Uncle Jim and my cousins James and Christine Nelson (bottom left); my 'spindly legs', also at Waimārama (right).

picnic. Aunt Mary also took us for a holiday into the Ruahines and I recorded in my diary in 1958 how beautiful I found it. My other aunt, Patricia (or Tish as we called her), allowed me to come with Uncle Jim and her family to their bach at Lake Rotoiti, near Rotorua. Again I was struck by the physical beauty of the place and the richness of bird life, and loved going in their small boat with the tiny outboard motor on adventures round the lake or to the hot pools.

I became very close to Aunt Tish, Uncle Jim and her family because when my parents went to England in 1955 I boarded with them at Rouncil, until my mother returned in August of that year. I spent hours during my time at Rouncil wandering over the hills that surrounded their place, playing tennis on their court and eeling in the Tukituki River. I also enjoyed visits to Rotoiti. On the first trip there in January 1955 we camped the whole time (because the bach was yet to be built) and also stopped overnight in tents at Taupō, which was a major thrill. There were two boys in the Nelson family, Bill and James, both somewhat older than me. They were, like Jim, strong muscular chaps, and I recall the sense that my own body was too thin and weedy for the real outdoor Kiwi bloke that I aspired to become. I would look at my spindly legs, praying that they thicken up. During that eight months at Rouncil I went to the Havelock North primary school, where my strongest recollection is of the many hours of school time which we spent in the local swimming pool.

The Nelsons also persuaded my parents to join them on a walk of the Milford Track in 1957. It was a memorable experience. The first day the rain was torrential, so heavy in fact that we had to delay going on until the following day. But then it dawned fine and clear, and I achieved family fame by racing the party to the top of McKinnon Pass. Edmund Hillary, here I come, was my private thought! I loved the Fiordland landscape and the birds, especially kea and fantails, which inhabited it. There was also more camping on the trip there and back. So my mother's Hawke's Bay relations (not 'relatives', a term which, we were told, was a very 'common' expression) developed in me a strong love of the New Zealand landscape. When I had been very young and asked what I wanted to do with my life, I would stoutly proclaim, with the 1951 dispute in the air and showing signs of class rebellion, that I wanted to be a water-sider. But once I had spent time with my Hawke's Bay 'rellies' I firmly believed for years that my future lay as a sheep farmer. Indeed at the age of thirteen when for a school assignment we were asked to write our own obituary, mine pictured my life as a New Zealand cricketer who became a Hawke's Bay farmer and member of the Meat Board.

My Hawke's Bay sojourns were the first time I had ever met Māori; in Christchurch the only Māori I had seen were on the rugby field. But at Te Aratipi the shearers were inevitably a Māori gang and during the time they were there, the whānau would live in a whare near the woolshed. I used to go over there and talk to the kuia sitting on the verandah, despite the warnings of my family. Then for about two weeks in 1955 I was sent by Aunt Tish to stay with Aunt Mary and Uncle Douglas at Aramoana. I went off to Punawaiti School, at that time with twelve pupils the smallest school in the country. I immediately became a bosom pal of a large Māori boy in the class, and then disgraced myself – in the eyes of my aunt – by joining him to tip over the jungle gym. I was punished at school and firmly lambasted at my aunt's about the company I was keeping. However, at both Havelock North and Punawaiti we did learn several waiata and learnt to play stick games – such was about the

6th June '60   My Obituary   Preparation

The death occurred last Sunday, at his residence in Havelock North, of Mr. J.O.C. Phillips O.B.E., who was 63 years of age. Born in 1947, he was educated at Christ's College and, on leaving, took a course of on farming at Lincoln.

At this stage of his life, his studies were interrupted, as he was called upon to represent New Zealand at cricket. He had a very distinguished record career, but, unfortunately his career was cut short when he injured his left leg in a farming accident.

At the age of 27 he – Mr. Phillips, or just Jock, as his friends called him, although his real name was John, acquired a farm on the Maorotatara River in Hawkes Bay. From that stage on, his whole life was devoted to the welfare of farming in Hawkes Bay and he is famous for his administration and good work in that cause. From 1982 till 1997 he was chairman of the New Zealand Meat Board and for this long service he was awarded the O.B.E.

All who knew him will regret his loss, but his cheerful, pleasant manner will remain in their minds for years to come. He is survived by his wife, and four children and nine great grandchildren.

Ridout: Ex. 70

My 1960 obituary – an English lesson at Christ's College.

extent of Māori culture for North Island Pākehā in the 1950s, but it was significantly more than I had met in the south.

When we went back to Christchurch after the holidays, life always seemed a bit flat. Indeed, the last holiday I spent at Aramoana before going to university, I ended a letter to my mother, 'Looking forward to seeing you, if not ChCh.'[4] This was a bit unfair, for there were some outside adventures in Canterbury too. My father would take us on Sunday drives to the Port Hills, or Woodend Beach, where the rugs and thermos would come out and we would have a family picnic. And for several years in the late 1950s we spent a week staying in a house made from old beer bottles at Queenstown. On the second occasion I broke my leg skiing – the diary entry for 25 August 1958 reads: 'Warm day. Went up skiing. Broke leg. Came to hospital.' This succinct description gives little idea of the trauma of a painful and rather humiliating event. I had to spend the next few weeks reading books and doing jigsaws. In later years we spent the week at Queenstown doing walks amid that magnificent landscape. I enjoyed these trips south and they reinforced a love of the New Zealand outdoors; but they had nothing like the influence on my identity and imaginings of the future that did my time as an apprentice sheep farmer with my Hawke's Bay relations.

As a young boy I inhabited two rather different worlds – the Christchurch world of books and history and respect for English culture, and the Hawke's Bay holiday world of farming, outdoor pursuits and a love of the land. How these two influences would play out became an issue at the end of 1963. In that year, my younger sister Catherine and I accompanied my parents to England. We had not expected to go. I was fifteen and just completing School Certificate. Catherine was twelve. My father had sabbatical leave to go to the UK and work on eighteenth-century politics. Initial thoughts had been to leave us both behind; but efforts to find someone to board me in Christchurch fell through. Then the idea emerged that perhaps it would be good for both of our education to spend a year in England. My older sister Elizabeth was heading off to England too and was intending to marry her fiancé, David Caffin, who had a scholarship to Cambridge to do a PhD. If we accompanied my mother, the whole family would be there and we would be able to attend the wedding in London. My father conducted his normal scrupulous research and decided that a good option would be for me to attend Dulwich College. This had been a minor public school in south London; but with the establishment of the eleven-plus examination, most of the places at the school were reserved for London boys who had done exceptionally well in the examination. Dulwich became an educational hothouse for the smart boys of London. But they also accepted students who paid their way. Dulwich was a leafy suburb in south London, still with a toll-gate, and just four stops on the train to Victoria Station. It suited; and before long my father had found a place to rent close by. Catherine went off to another good school, a private college at Sydenham Hill, not far away. So it was all arranged. My father set off early, and Catherine and I left with my mother on the SS *Remuera* a few days after I had finished sitting the School Certificate examinations.

This first encounter with the big world beyond New Zealand was of course hugely exciting, and remains etched in my memory. Not suffering from seasickness, I relished the voyage over with the generous dinners, deck games (in which, on both trips to and from England, I won the deck-tennis singles championships), bingo and quiz competitions, dress-ups and endless sunbathing. Only an unfortunate, and for me very confusing, sexual approach one night from a steward disturbed the equilibrium. I recall my feverish excitement at landing at foreign ports – the steamy tropical air of Tahiti, made even more steamy by the dancers performing for us that night which my mother described in a letter to her mother as 'a very sexy dance I thought to myself but I suppose this did not strike my children'.[5] One day at Kingston where the beat of the steel drums stirred more passions, and another day at Miami where the huge hotels of Fort Lauderdale spoke of incredible wealth ostentatiously displayed ('a millionaire's playground' was my mother's phrase), also live in the memory.

But it was England that I had dreamed of for most of my fifteen years, and which I yearned to see and experience. At first it was more like a nightmare. The ship was a day late landing, which left us deeply frustrated. Then we discovered that England was in the throes of the worst winter of the century. The roads and pavements were thick with snow, which eventually turned to slippery ice. According to my father the thermometer did not rise above 37 degrees Fahrenheit (3°C) for twenty-five days.[6] Whether it was a bug picked up on board ship, or a first encounter with English food, or simply nervousness about having to adjust to a new school, I am unsure, but for about a month after arriving I suffered acute diarrhoea, which would catch me at most unfortunate moments. The initial adjustment to an English school was testing, and one lunchtime when my father bugged me about not getting on with my work, I picked up my plate of food and threw it at him. He was too astonished to react.

Yet there was the excitement of Elizabeth's wedding in a London church within two weeks of our arrival, and we braved the icy blasts and the delayed trains to race into the centre of London at every opportunity. I recall vividly almost shaking with excitement at actually seeing the things which I had for so long imagined – Westminster Abbey, St Paul's, Buckingham Palace, Trafalgar Square. Each of these places came encrusted with so much history and so many literary associations. After our first visit to Westminster Abbey my father recorded in the diary 'rambling round the monuments, which John found highly exciting'.[7] Within the first week we also visited the National Gallery and I saw a cartoon of virgin and child by Leonardo da Vinci and paintings by Rubens and Raphael which I had pored over in books in Christchurch. Soon after we went to the Tate Gallery to discover the Ned Kelly paintings by Sidney Nolan. Before long I was sending detailed descriptions back to my housemaster at Christ's College telling of the thrill at uncovering real history and real art. He put the letters, scratched in tiny handwriting, up on the house noticeboard.

On most weekends we would brave the English traffic to head out into the country for more cultural thrills. I have a detailed record of this because on 1 January 1963 my father began a daily diary. For the first two months he kept it up, and rather dismal descriptions of frustrated research in the Public Record Office and purchases of clothes on Regent Street are interspersed with tales in convoluted prose of these weekend jaunts. Then my mother took up the pen – hers was a much more 'meat and potatoes' account of what we did and where – and finally when she tired I recorded the weekend journeys. My entries combine an unbridled enthusiasm for the historic sites I was seeing with some rather cynical cracks about the class foibles of the English. The places we visited were obvious sites. There were country houses such as Knole, Hatfield House and the Royal Pavilion at Brighton. There were the ancient sites of Stonehenge and Avebury. There were castles such as Bodiam and Hever, where I raced up and down the circular stairs really imagining myself as Sir Galahad or Sir Lancelot. Inevitably there were many cathedrals – Canterbury, Salisbury, Chichester, Winchester, and then, on a trip north in August, York Minster, Ely, Gloucester, Hereford, Lincoln,

Peterborough. I considered myself a real expert in distinguishing and being able to date the architectural styles of Norman and Gothic.

There were several memorable tours to Cambridge, on one of which my new brother-in-law David took us punting. In the last part of the year we enjoyed even closer acquaintance with the historical monuments to be found in such places because the family took up rubbing brasses. We found a book listing the locations of brasses, and then would drive into the country, wake up the local vicar from his Sunday afternoon nap, get him to open the church and proceed to lay down our paper and copy the brass in black crayon of a fourteenth-century knight or a fifteenth-century cleric. It was face-to-face with history.

If I loved the artefacts and art of history, I also grew to love the English countryside. We often drove southwards into Kent and rambled around rolling hills and oast houses; we visited my father's friends at Oxford and headed out to walk in the Cotswolds; and in the north there was a memorable drive through the Yorkshire Dales. I loved the picturesque thatched stone cottages that harmonised so neatly with the countryside, which, I explained in letters home, was caused by the fact that they were built of the rock on which they stood. I loved the gentle rolling of the hills, which I explained were manicured by thousands of years of cultivation. Catherine had become fascinated by English wild flowers and I would join her and my mother, spending hours on picnics in rural England collecting examples. A couple of weeks after these jaunts we would have a slide evening, when my father would display his take on our weekend enjoyments. Brought up with eyes for English beauty and with my head echoing with English poetry – 'Oh to be in England now that April's here' – I felt deeply satisfied.

There were other cultural attractions in England – several times we went out to the theatre. I remember especially Paul Scofield as King Lear and Diana Rigg (Emma Peel of *Avengers* fame) as Cordelia; I recall being gripped by an Ibsen play and shocked at *Oh! What a Lovely War*. There were the English newspapers, which I devoured – this was the year of the Profumo scandal and although my father described the *Observer* as 'a paper written by adulterers for adulterers', I read every word. There were also more modern attractions – this was the time of Carnaby Street and 'swinging London'; and it was the year the world discovered the Beatles. One could not be in England without feeling the pulse. I also loved English sport – a school friend took me off several times to watch Chelsea, then a second-division side, play football at Stamford Bridge; and my father, uneasy that I might become a convert to the round ball, took me off to Twickenham. But it was my own motivation that led me to watch England play the West Indies in cricket tests at Lord's and the Oval. In fact I made sure that I went to every day of the Oval test, when the crowd, who were half West Indian from the Brixton community nearby, was as entertaining as the game. Once again I encountered steel drums.

If England lived up to all my fantasies, the high points of the year in the northern hemisphere were undoubtedly our two trips to the continent. In the April holidays we took the Dover ferry and headed through France to Italy and back through Austria, Germany and Belgium. Then in August we had another two weeks in Provence. It was a rather odd travelling ritual. Four of us, my parents, Catherine and I, squeezed into a Morris 1100 (which caused anxiety to my very unmechanical father by burning too much oil). Every nook and cranny of the vehicle was crammed – with tins of Spam in the spare-wheel compartment, which we ate for our daily picnic lunch along with French bread and patisseries bought at a local baker. We had to wait while a 'Gaz' heated up water for tea. In the afternoon we would turn up at a cheap hotel and ask for two rooms – my father and I normally shared a double bed, with the two females doing likewise. It was this experience that convinced me that my father's complaints about not sleeping were in part unfounded.

My father did all the driving and my mother the navigating, until one traumatic day when she gave a wrong direction and my father refused to speak to her for the rest of the day. From then on I was in command of the map. An enormous amount of planning had gone into the itinerary and we worked very hard. Not a historic site, a church or a famous painting escaped my father's meticulous preparation. I loved the old medieval villages of Italy and Germany, and in order to be able to explore their back streets in detail I always volunteered in the late afternoon to go searching for a suitable eating place, which sent me scurrying up romantic alleys and into deserted squares. Certain places were memorable – Rome at Easter when we saw the Pope, the Etruscan town of Volterra where my father fell off a wall in his eagerness to photograph the battlements, Florence and Siena with their striking duomos, Rothenburg in Germany and Bruges on the canals in Belgium. We visited churches and cathedrals and chateaux, but it was the art that left the strongest impression. My father's passion for Italian renaissance painting especially

Dulwich College in 1963. NEVILLE PHILLIPS

was easily shared. I had the privilege of a daily lesson about the intricacies of different Italian styles and painters. Again certain moments stick in the mind – gazing at the deep colours of the stained-glass windows in Reims cathedral, wandering around the Uffizi gallery entranced at paintings which I had only seen in reproduction or in my father's slides, studying Giotto's frescoes at Assisi and Fra Angelico's at a Florentine convent, racing the crowds into the Sistine Chapel and being awed at Michelangelo's skill. Most memorable was one hot lunchtime in Tuscany, when we navigated to the sleepy hilltop village of Monterchi and woke up the local priest from his siesta to open the doors to a tiny chapel – on the wall was a stunning fresco by Piero della Francesca of the virgin in a blue dress, one of my father's favourite images. The Ravenna mosaics were another highlight.

The August trip to Provence was also a huge success, partly because in the fifth form at Christ's College our French teacher had made us read Daudet's *Lettres de Mon Moulin* (letters from my mill). So places like Avignon, Arles, Nîmes and the Camargue were familiar from my literary imagination. Here I loved the Roman remains – the Pont du Gard and the amphitheatre at Orange. I was amazed at the evidence of Roman engineering which had lasted for

Me as a very formally dressed young man under the fountain at Villa d'Este, Tivoli, outside Rome, in April 1963. NEVILLE PHILLIPS

several millennia. I also enjoyed fossicking around these old towns and sauntering along their medieval walls. The recollection of my enjoyment on these trips is borne out by my mother's letters and my father's diary (which he resumed just for the trips to the continent). After the August trip my mother wrote, 'It has been a tremendous education for the children. John, in particular, is an indefatigable sightseer and has gone up to the top of every possible tower I think.'[8]

The year in England with these two trips to Europe had been, as my mother suggested, an education, but had also strengthened my attraction to ancient places and a civilisation that breathed history. From a distance New Zealand seemed thin by comparison. So would I decide that there was where my future lay? There were two real possibilities that England would be my future home. The first was that throughout the year my father did his best to obtain a professorship at an English university – and there were quite a number of opportunities because precisely at that time there were several new universities seeking to attract staff. We lived every hope when an advertisement appeared and he was shortlisted, and every depressed moment when the rejection letter came. I fully expected that the family would soon move permanently to England and I would have no choice but to live there. But it never happened.

The second possibility was very much my choice. I had gone to Dulwich College, which was essentially the intellectual forcing house for the bright sons of London. The school was focused on gaining as many scholarships (and exhibitions, as they called them) to Oxford or Cambridge as possible. I was a bright student who had usually come close to the top of my class at Christ's College, and actually succeeded in getting 100 per cent in School Certificate mathematics. Despite the intellectual quality of the Dulwich boys I found that I could keep up with them. I also gained second prize in a Dulwich Rotary Club essay competition on 'What I am going to do when I grow up', in which I argued that leaving your options open was the best strategy. I made good friends, including several from the London Jewish community. Unlike others in my class, I spent a lot of energy on school sports, determined to live up to my image of New Zealanders as a sporting people (especially in a year when the All Blacks were touring). I received colours for playing in the colts cricket team; I represented the school in their fourth XV. We would go on long bus journeys to play other minor English public schools, like Mill Hill or

Haileybury, and I recall being shocked that the main diversion on these school trips was a game called 'spot the wogs!', which involved claiming a point if you saw a black person on the street and attempting to 'spot' more than anyone else. Embarrassed and ashamed, I refused to play, but I did join in singing the dirty songs which also occupied time on these sporting excursions.

It was not my sporting prowess but my intellectual abilities that seemed as if they might keep me in England for life. In my last term at Dulwich the school approached me, suggesting that I stay on and board with a friend in the expectation that I might win a scholarship to Oxbridge. My father of course was enthusiastic, and wrote later to my grandmother: 'The children did pretty well at school, and in a way it seemed hard to take John away from such a good school as Dulwich, where the chief history master thought him an "almost inevitable" winner of a scholarship to Oxford or Cambridge.'[9] Despite such promises, I was clear about my preference. I wanted to go back home. I had come to love the history and cultural richness of England and the ease with which you could visit the continent. I enjoyed English sport and its civilised discourse. But there was something about the uncouth wildness of the New Zealand landscape, the bush, the beaches, the challenge of a 'new society', which still held me. The encounter with the New Zealand land, especially in my time on Hawke's Bay farms, continued to pull. There were also aspects of England which I decidedly did not like. On board ship I wrote home to my grandmother:

> Unlike the rest of the family, I was not too sorry at leaving England. Although I have had a wonderful year seeing so many famous places, enjoying so much beautiful scenery, and meeting so many interesting people, I, personally, was becoming increasingly sick of England as a place to live. One is immediately annoyed by the gross overpopulation of the country, especially around London. It was most frustrating to be continually confronted by huge crowds of completely strange people. Whether it be in a queue for a sporting match or in the tube or just in a West End Street. Such a huge population breeds also an intolerable amount of traffic. This not only imposed enormous emotional stress on everybody, but it was also a dreadful waste of time.... Attractive as the English scenery is, I longed for some large open spaces completely free of people

and not contaminated by the smoke of big cities. . . . So although England is probably unrivalled as a place to visit, I still think N.Z. is unrivalled as a place to live.[10]

So in January 1964, aged sixteen, I returned home with my parents to Christchurch. There were a few thrills on the journey back – a memorable excursion to Cairo and the pyramids from Port Said, a first taste of Asia at Colombo and Singapore, and a first taste also of Australia at Melbourne and Sydney. I also met on board a young Michael Bassett, just returning from Duke University with a PhD. We chatted about history and played deck tennis together. I little realised what an impact he would eventually have on my life. But I was happy to be home. It would be one more year at Christ's College, one more summer working on Uncle Douglas's farm in Hawke's Bay, and then off to university – in New Zealand and Cambridge, Mass., not Oxford or Cambridge, England.

4
America!

My last year at Christ's College went well. I became a school prefect and academic head of the school and had my first girlfriend. By dint of good results in the English and history examinations, I just succeeded in getting a university national scholarship – I was about seventieth in the ranking, just a few marks above the cut-off. The extra money it provided was a help because I had decided that I did not want to go to the University of Canterbury. I was interested in history, my father was still the professor of history, and it would not be very comfortable studying under him. More importantly I wanted to get away from Christchurch and was attracted to Wellington. Every time we had passed through the city on our trips north to Hawke's Bay, I had enjoyed the place. The dramatic hills and sparkling harbour appealed after the dull flatness of the Canterbury Plains, and I sensed an energy and a touch of exoticism about the city. Escaping one's father was not considered grounds for a boarding bursary, but my grandfather promised to give me a £100 a year, and if I got a job in the holidays I could just afford the £300 I needed to board at Weir House, Victoria University's male hostel, and still leave a little to spend.

Accordingly I set off for Weir House to study for a BA. I quickly found the intellectual environment sympathetic. The warden of Weir House was Tim Beaglehole, whom I had met once previously when the family called in to see

Aged seventeen and just beginning university in Wellington.

John and Elsie Beaglehole on our way back from Hawke's Bay. At the time Tim was just back from King's College, Cambridge, bubbling with enthusiasm and humour. He cooked a superb dinner, which impressed me, not used to such a facility among men. At Weir Tim set out to reform the place. Its reputation was somewhat tawdry, after *Truth* had run articles about men and women showering together 'without any clothes on'. A correspondent noted that it might have been even more questionable if they had showered with clothes on, but the damage had been done.

Tim determined to make the place more like a sophisticated Cambridge college. There were regular Sunday-evening talks from such noted luminaries as the playwright Bruce Mason and the Labour Court judge Arthur Tindall; Tim persuaded the New Zealand diplomat Frank Corner to donate prints of modernist paintings which we could hang in our rooms; and every Sunday before dinner he would ask some students up to his flat to sip sherry, listen to Bach playing politely in the background and talk about cultural or political matters in a gentlemanly manner. I was awed by his sophisticated taste. Tim surrounded himself with a group of bright young students, all a couple of years older than me, who shared his interests. I became friends with the 'family' group as they were called; and under their influence not only broadened my knowledge of art and poetry, but developed a taste for classical music. I began to go along to concerts by the NZBC Symphony Orchestra and became a member of the Chamber Music Society. Mozart became my special hero; and having purchased a cheap record player and then many of his concertos and symphonies, I began to read voraciously about him. His letters became much thumbed. As for art, Tim and his friends were fierce modernists. I quickly followed suit, going off to every exhibition in the city, and reading about modern painting and architecture. Two heroes emerged out of this experience too – the architect Le Corbusier and the painter Paul Klee. I covered my walls with prints of Klee works.

In these ways my intellectual interests went further than those of my parents, for although they were interested in art and architecture, their passions in art had never extended beyond the Impressionists, and in architecture eighteenth-century good taste was about where it ended. Music was never present in our Christchurch home – apart from the hit parade, which I had listened to religiously and a bit surreptitiously every Thursday night, and which had inspired me to paste a poster of Elvis on my bedroom wall.

A newspaper photograph of my family (Elizabeth at back left, Catherine back right) on the day in May 1966 when my father was announced as the University of Canterbury's new vice-chancellor.

With Jane McCartney at a Weir House ball.

Downtown Wellington also offered cultural attractions – I spent much time in Parsons Bookshop, and in the coffee bar upstairs ate yoghurt (covered in rosehip syrup) for the first time. Not that Wellington offered many other culinary delights at this stage. The few licensed restaurants such as the Coachman were out of my price range, so it was largely big steaks, Chinese takeaways or hamburgers. All of these provided merciful relief from the Weir House tucker, where the low point came at Sunday lunch, when the beef was inevitably sliced up with the string and wooden skewers included. I will not forget the looks of horror on the faces of Colombo Plan students from Malaysia and Indonesia as they tried to sort out the string from the meat. You could also get a reasonable meal by attending Downstage theatre. Dine and a play was the menu; and several times I enjoyed memorable performances from Martyn Sanderson, Peter Bland and Pat Evison in such modern works as Edward Albee's *The Zoo Story* and Samuel Beckett's *Happy Days*.

While Wellington expanded my cultural interests towards international modernism, it was in Auckland where I encountered some creative New Zealand culture. In my second year I had met an interesting fellow arts

A sketch of Hone Tuwhare by Joanna Paul, coloured chalks on paper, 479 x 636 mm.
HOCKEN COLLECTIONS – UARE TAOKA O HĀKENA, UNIVERSITY OF OTAGO, 76/120

student, Jane McCartney, who became my girlfriend. Jane was from Hamilton, where she had been a close friend of Charlotte Paul, daughter of Janet and Blackwood Paul. So on several occasions we set off to Auckland, where Janet Paul was now living. By this stage Blackwood had died, but Janet was trying to keep the Longman Paul publishing business alive. Paul's had established a reputation as a dedicated publisher of serious New Zealand works, and Janet introduced me to some of her current enthusiasms. She spoke particularly warmly about a Māori poet who used to ring her up at lunch break from his job as a fitter and turner and get her to write down poems. His name was Hone Tuwhare. I will never forget one Sunday evening when Hone came around to talk about his poems and another of Janet's daughters, Joanna (later a very well-known painter), sketched him repeatedly in pencil. I still have some of those sketches. Janet was herself a painter, and introduced me to some of the painters then causing a storm in select Auckland circles. I discovered the work of artists like Michael Illingworth, Ralph Hotere and Pat Hanly (whom I met at Janet's), and confirmed my adolescent enthusiasm for the work of Colin McCahon.

Weir House encouraged personal and political rebellion of a mild kind. The family group offered one circle of friends but there were other interesting people in the hostel. In my second year the newcomers included a rowdy but thoughtful Paul Callaghan, later a famous scientist; but more significant for me personally were a group across the corridor, led by a funny, charismatic Māori student from Hastings, Moana Jackson, later an influential lawyer for Māori rights. At the time such interests were far from his concerns. Playing cards, betting on the horses and drinking beer were more on the agenda for those around Moana. Despite the fact that I had a part-time job working in the bar at the Trentham racecourse and my grandfather owned a successful steeplechaser at the time, I never took to the horses. But I certainly took to the beer. There were long, frantic sessions down at the Midland and too many scenes of gross overconsumption ending with the chant 'The Weir House boys are on the piss again.' Apart from the short-term hangovers, for the first, and only, time in my life I began to put on weight. This was still the era of a drinking age of twenty-one, so, not for the last time, I embarrassed my father through the media, when in 1967 at the age of twenty I was caught by a television camera drinking and guffawing at the Midland on the last night of six o'clock closing. When the clip appeared on the year's highlights show my father was very disapproving. There was also further exploration of sex, although, judging by my letters home, at least to my parents I still held to a surprisingly prudish set of attitudes. One letter describes a Saturday night:

> We went to the Sorrento Club which was a real experience. It was pure unadulterated sex. Men with long permed hair and completely waxen characterless girls moped around in disgusting postures. It was so appallingly bestial that one could see Lear's judgement 'a man a worm' at its true value. After about an hour of disbelieving observation and desperate clutching of our wallets we retired to the dignified atmosphere of the 'Chez Paree' where there was some most attractive folk-singing.[1]

These were the normal mild rebellions of youth. More profound and long-lasting was a rebellion against my parents' political attitudes. I had grown up as the son of Tories living in Fendalton, a staunch National Party stronghold. In the 1950s I used to follow the election results hoping that the local member, Sid Holland, would get back in as prime minister. In the early 1960s I swallowed my discomfort at the pomposity of Keith Holyoake to back his election. When New Zealand agreed to send troops to Vietnam in May 1965, I found myself still spouting to those around me about the need to fight the commies on the Mekong lest we had to fight them on the Waimakariri. My brother-in-law, David Caffin, was at the time in the Department of Foreign Affairs and put much work into the government's white paper defending New Zealand's involvement. So I got reinforcement from him. But at Weir House I found myself a lonely voice. Most of the students I lived with had become highly critical of the Cold War and the naïve assumptions on which fighting communism was based. In the capping parade in 1965 we Weir House boys dressed up as Vietcong with lightshades on our heads, and when we reached the mayor's viewing stand we all sang 'God save the Vietcong' to the tune of the then national anthem. This seemed fun at the time and it inevitably got me thinking. There was a teach-in at Victoria University in which my old acquaintance from on board ship, Michael Bassett, among others, presented a compelling case against New Zealand's involvement.

I realised that I needed to read more, and picked up Bernard Falls' *The Two Vietnams*. It was one of those books that overturned my perspective on the world. Before reading it I had blithely accepted that communism was a steady rolling tide coming down from Red China. I had had no idea of the nationalist impulse behind Vietnam's communism or the deceit by the West that had created two Vietnams. I changed my mind. Before long I was writing letters to politicians and arguing with my parents. In 1966 Lyndon Johnson visited Wellington to thank the country for its support in Vietnam. Along with a small group of mates I went down to Lambton Quay holding a banner, and carrying violin cases in the strange belief that this might suggest to the CIA that we had guns. Before too long the presidential motorcade came along, and to my astonishment stopped right where we were standing. LBJ got out of the limo and immediately thrust out his hand in my direction. Well, when the most powerful man in the world invites you to shake his hand, it is a hard offer to resist, so I found myself reaching out and grabbing the president's sweaty palms. So much for my newly acquired beliefs!

That was not the end of the fun because we had heard that Lady Bird, the First Lady, was due to travel up the cable car to visit the botanical gardens. Weir House was directly above the cable car, so we shot Guy Fawkes rockets down the tunnel, and then clambered up onto the roof of the hostel carrying big signs, 'Welcome the CIA'. When the secret service turned up they were greeted with water bombs – although listening on their channel, we heard a frantic American voice shouting, 'Those bastards are throwing bags of urine on us!' Perhaps after all we did make our anti-war feelings known. Two years later, in March 1968, I attended every minute of the *Peace, Power and Politics* conference in the State Opera House and town hall, where international speakers compellingly laid out the case against western involvement in the war.

Having begun to question the Vietnam War, I inevitably began to ask other questions. Victoria University at the time was a lively environment. *Salient* was nearly always a source of ideas to debate, and once a week at lunchtime there would be an open forum in front of the Students' Union where people could spout forth. I remember listening intently to people like Alister Taylor, Helen Sutch, Michael King, Tony Ashenden and Michael Hirschfeld put forward other issues – the war, yes, but also Māori rights, social inequality, women's concerns and the level of student bursaries. The first march I joined was actually about student bursaries. I was by no means a radical activist at this stage; but along with so many of the post-war baby boomers I had begun to challenge some of the norms that had become gospel to our parents.

During those years I spent the summer holidays earning money to help support myself during the year. At a time of low unemployment there was little difficulty finding labouring jobs, and I tended to move around sampling different experiences – one year as a postman on my bike, another on a building site, a time in a grain store carting large sacks, once in the Skellerup rubber factory packing the rubber rings which farmers used to castrate lambs, and in my last year driving a big truck for a Dutchman who would buy fruit and vegetables at the market in the early morning and then deliver them to dairies around Christchurch. The work was never too onerous, but what I gained was a close acquaintance with boys and men from other social circles. Most were from the working class and I became increasingly conscious, and at times embarrassed, by my own genteel background and assumptions. I enjoyed the banter and the teasing of my workmates. At Weir House I also began to notice how much more mature and self-directed were the boys from state schools. I realised that there was another world outside Fendalton and Christ's College and Hawke's Bay landholders. Inevitably such learnings affected my political attitudes.

Two scenes from my student life in 1966 – on the way to protest LBJ's visit to Wellington in 1966 (above); and performing in a German-language play – my only ever theatrical performance (below).

If experiences out of school taught me much, what did I learn in the lecture room at Victoria? Here the effect was in many ways less radical. I decided from the start to major in two subjects – English and history. Of the two I found the teaching better in English. In an early letter home I note 'Prof. Mackenzie [sic] for poetry is quite brilliant and really inspiring. The sharpest brain I have met and he makes Prof Gordon look like a waffly old bore.'[2] Certainly in both my first and second year I was spellbound by Don McKenzie's theatrical performances, especially in his course on Shakespeare; I was also fortunate to have a stimulating tutor, Roger Savage. But the course reflected the colonialist assumptions of the university at that time. There were two English tracks – for the 'serious' students wanting to major, such as myself, you were given a chronological grounding in English literature: the renaissance the first year, eighteenth century the second, and the romantics in the third. You read nothing beyond 1850 and obviously nothing written in New Zealand, let alone the USA or Australia. I was deeply jealous of those doing the 'cabbage English' course, who were allowed to read some twentieth-century works which even included John Mulgan's *Man Alone*.

The same assumption that New Zealand content was easy and for lesser brains held sway in the history department, where again the basic outline was a chronological trot from medieval times through to the nineteenth century. At least this included some non-British European material in the medieval and renaissance coverage; but there was only one New Zealand course – and again this was not advised for majors. I did not take it, because I had no interest in New Zealand or New Zealand history at this stage – indeed in a letter home I talked of seeing a short film about the villages of England, 'which made me most itchy to be back in the dales or the lanes of Kent'.[3] But, apart from Peter Munz's spellbinding lectures in the first year, the teaching generally did not encourage much interest in British or European history – it was ponderous and dull and remained heavily focused on 'great men political history'.

What kept me motivated in my first two years were several courses outside the English and history departments. There was a first-year course in German, which I took only to satisfy the language requirement in the degree. The professor was a gentle but inspiring immigrant, Paul Hoffman. He had no hesitation in exposing us to modern literature and I became excited at reading Franz Kafka, Thomas Mann and Bertolt Brecht. The German department was a small, friendly community and I found myself taking part in a play, all in German. We practised at the weekends, and there I met some of the German–Jewish community of Wellington, all interested in music and modern art. I found intellectual stimulus here that was so much more exciting than what was being dished out in my English courses. The second centre of inspiration was two courses on economic history put on by a neatly groomed Englishman, John Gould. The classes were small, mainly economics majors, but Gould was a wonderful lecturer and led us to the very forefront of debates in the field. In the second course he decided to throw away the traditional curriculum and invite us to explore in depth the debate about the economic effects of the coming of railways in the United States, which had been sparked by a recent book by Robert Fogel. It was a marvellous introduction to a debate that was raging in the profession and, because Fogel had attempted to work out what the economic consequences would have been if canals, rather than railways, had carried America's goods in the nineteenth century, the work raised many issues about the use of hypothetical history and statistics in history. Gould made history an urgent and vital subject.

There was a third course, this one in the history department, which changed my life. The lecturer was John Salmond, whose rotund, genial appearance belied a sharp intelligence and wit. He offered a third-year course in modern American history. I had long been fascinated by the United States. In the 1950s as a youngster I had enjoyed rock 'n' roll, and had begun to associate America with youthful rebellion. I had a friend from primary school whose father was American and he used to ask me home to listen to jazz and drink home-made milk shakes. The States began to acquire an allure. At school I had to write an extra essay for a prefect for some long-forgotten misdemeanour so I decided to read and write about the Beats. From about 1960, when I was thirteen, and certainly once John Kennedy had been elected, I began to follow American politics closely by a diligent reading of *Time* magazine. My interest in the States was reinforced strongly when I got to university and found myself rooming in Weir House with Frank Stone, a funny and intelligent native of Minnesota, who had decided to spend a year in Wellington. He was enthusiastic about New Zealand, but also infectiously informative about the States. He developed close friendships with a number of New Zealanders who had just returned from American Field Scholarships, and I shared many a pizza with them. My interest in the US was also piqued by the Vietnam War. I began to wonder how and why the country had found itself fighting in jungles in distant

Asia; and, like many others, I looked to the United States for models of resistance. Even in the 1950s the civil-rights movement, the sit-ins and bus rides had provided an inspiring example. Now we followed closely the teach-ins, the marches and the other forms of political and social protest against the war which were emerging in the United States.

All this was in the back of my mind when I took John Salmond's American history course. I instantly found it enthralling. For a start it was recent history, close to my experience and memory. Second, the history was not just about the political dealings of an Oxbridge elite. American politics had for a long time been intensely democratic and attracted people from a wide range of backgrounds. People like Andrew Jackson, Abraham Lincoln, Martin Luther King or Eleanor Roosevelt were unlike the political leaders I had previously analysed. There were many topics that were primarily social rather than directly political. I became deeply interested in the experience of slavery and the effects that this had had on blacks and the American South. In addition the historiography hummed. I remember reading a book, *Manifest Destiny*, on the history of American expansionism, which suddenly seemed to explain the ideological forces that had sent the US into Asia. I read Richard Hofstadter's *The Age of Reform*, which argued that the progressive movement at the turn of the twentieth century came about because the old middle class had suffered a decline in status. I did not agree with the argument, but found it original and challenging, and in the end spent so much time and energy exploring it that I was asked to lecture to the other students about the Hofstadter thesis. In sum, US history seemed fresh, relevant and – in some way that I had not yet worked out – close to my situation as a New Zealander, the inhabitant of another 'new' colonial society.

At the end of 1967, when I had just completed the American history course and was contemplating, without much enthusiasm, going on to do history honours, I casually mentioned to John Salmond that I would like one day to go on to study US history in the States. Although I had enjoyed my year in England, the thought of returning to study there, as was expected of most successful history graduates at the time, did not appeal. I still had the overseas-experience bug, and at the end of my second year had gone on a University Students' Association working trip to New Caledonia. We had spent time in Nouméa, snorkelling and drinking in bars, and then a week or so helping to mix concrete for a new school building halfway up the island. The

In New Caledonia in early 1967, we stayed in this beautiful village inland (left) and mixed concrete in the sun (right).

work was hard in the tropical heat, but I did enjoy the visit to another overseas culture. I took endless photographs of one especially beautiful village where we stopped one night. I saw Nouméa very much through the eyes of my previous French encounter – the city, I wrote home, is 'very much colonial France without the stink of history or the classical architectural beauty of the French town, but there is the same smell of rotting food, the same tree-lined "places", the same impressive cathedral dominating the town with its own highly continental courtyard, the same dogs barking at every corner, and the same hair-raising drivers'.[4] So while I still had the travel bug, France and England were not the favoured destinations. A few years in the States, at a time when there seemed to be a feast of new ideas, plenty of good music to hear and excitingly different places to explore, began to appeal.

I thought nothing more about it, until John Salmond came to me some time after and said that there was a special scholarship for New Zealanders to go to Harvard. Would I like to apply for the Frank Knox Fellowship? Frank Knox had been Franklin Roosevelt's secretary of the navy and had married a New Zealand woman. The fellowship was his recognition of the Kiwi connection. So I did apply, and once more thought little about it. I would set to and complete a history honours degree. Then in May 1968, after I had long given up, I received a letter from Harvard, sent by surface mail, saying that I was being offered the Frank Knox. The trouble was that the news had been so long arriving that I had missed out on applying for a Fulbright travelling scholarship to help pay my airfares to Boston. The letter also said that since I was a foreign national I would need to take an English-language test. I promptly wrote to Harvard telling them that I had grown up speaking English and that because of the surface mail I was now unable to obtain the travel costs. Within a fortnight I opened a letter from Harvard, sent this time by airmail, with a cheque for $1000 inside to pay for the airfares. I was stunned by American largesse. I was off – Harvard for four-and-a-half years it would be. It was August 1968.

The United States was a rude shock. I landed in Hawaii and was immediately hustled into a back room, where I was asked to swear that I was not a communist and hand over the X-ray of my lungs which I had been carefully carrying. This was projected onto the wall while officials carefully examined my lungs for signs of tuberculosis. New Zealand, I discovered, was classified as a 'third world country'. I was not impressed by my first sight of American culture. I sent a postcard home: Hawaii 'is American in all its worst aspects – fat scaly middle class women with their painted toe-nails, loud-mouthed business men spewing forth inanities, huge ungainly cars that seem to pursue one, and everything is very expensive. No-one seems very friendly so I have spent a solitary day in the sun.'[5] Then it was on to San Francisco. I collapsed into my room at a cheap hotel. I turned on the television and there saw thugs (actually Mayor Daley's Chicago policemen) bashing the heads of protesters on the floor of the Democratic Convention. I began to ask what sort of democracy, or rather tyranny, I had found myself in. I flew to meet Frank Stone in his home town of Minneapolis. My companion on the first flight was a campaigning Buddhist; my companion on the second flight quickly pulled out a pencil and pad and with deft illustrations tried to convert me to fundamentalist Christianity. Did I really want to spend time in this strange world? Nor was this all – as Frank drove us across the Midwest to New York, I became increasingly distressed at the evident signs of gross wealth on the one hand, and decrepit hungry beggars on the other. I wrote to my girlfriend Jane McCartney back in New Zealand that I was stunned 'by the crass commercial instincts and coarse attitudes of the American middle class. Size in buildings, cars and middle-aged ladies' waist-lines were very strong impressions.'[6]

By the time I reached the east coast I would have been prepared to tell the immigration authorities that I was indeed a communist.

There were also signs of real change in the air. The TV shows and newspapers were full of searching self-criticism of the United States and its policies. Over the previous few months both Martin Luther King and Robert Kennedy had been shot and killed, Eugene McCarthy had fought a spirited, but unsuccessful, anti-war campaign, and then there had been the violence in Chicago. You simply could not escape the widespread complaint that the country was in crisis – things were seriously awry. I saw McCarthy signs everywhere, and wrote at the time, 'Indeed it is very impressive to see the whole nation look at itself and debate its problems with such honest ferocity.'[7] Wherever we travelled Frank gravitated towards hippie hang-outs. In New York we spent time among the 'besandled bearded "hippies" in Greenwich Village'[8] and went to a rock concert in Central Park where the men all had long hair and the women long, flowing, flowery dresses. There was the smell of dope in the air. I had landed in the States just as the baby boomers came to adulthood. Brought up amid the affluence of the 1950s and the tensions of both the Cold War and the civil-rights movement, they were ready to break out and challenge everything, both politically and culturally. It was a hugely exciting time, and it forced me to question everything I had grown up with. I noticed something else about the United States on the journey east. I was stunned by the physical beauty of the place and the extent to which the east coast, which I had imagined as one large urban metropolis stretching from Washington to Boston, was predominantly a landscape of trees, of oaks and maples. I wrote back home, 'I am continually surprised how treed this country still is, even very close to extensive settlement, and this gives it an unexpected feeling of the Frontier [*sic*], of raw wildness even in areas settled for 200 years.'[9]

I arrived in Cambridge and immediately felt at home, noting that 'the middle class commercialism and stubbornness are swallowed up in the beautifully treed quads, pleasant old brick halls, and the tingling vivacity of Harvard Square'.[10] I spent the first two years (from September 1968 to June 1970) living in a dingy, prison-like student hostel called Perkins Hall. My room-mate the first year was an Orthodox Jew from New York complete with a yarmulke. He prayed three times a day in the room, and insisted on cooking kosher food, which made the atmosphere distinctly unpleasant. He observed the Sabbath with scrupulous commitment – to the extent that he even emptied his pockets on Friday night because carrying keys in the pocket was regarded as work. It was a fairly intense confrontation with my Jewish heritage, but fortunately all but three of our thirteen class members (including me) were Jewish, and they provided a rather more liberal and attractive representation of the culture. I came to love their wit and humour, a combination of the Marx Brothers and Woody Allen. The two smartest teachers among our professors, Bernard Bailyn and Oscar Handlin, were also Jewish, so I learnt a new respect for their intellectual traditions. In my third year I became a resident tutor in one of the Harvard undergraduate houses, Leverett House. It was a cushy number. I did not have to pay for food or board. I had a palatial apartment with bedroom and large living-room, and all I had to do was offer intelligent guidance to the undergraduates and make polite conversation in the House's senior common-room.

For the whole time I was in the States I lived and breathed politics. I became an avid reader of the newspapers, particularly the *New York Times* (which I read religiously despite its tiny type and huge bulk) and periodicals such as the *New York Review of Books* and *New Republic*, which I subscribed to. I wrote home within the first month, 'one seems immediately to get caught up in the pressure of politics here and to begin pursuing it with a committed seriousness. This intense political earnestness is universal – in the nasty slogans covering numerous walls, in the long dispirited discussion ... and in the extraordinary enthusiasm of his supporters and the massive rumbling vicious dissent of his opponents which V-P Humphrey met as he spoke at an enormous rally in Boston.'[11] I took every opportunity to experience the political turmoil – pushing to the front of the Humphrey rally, going on every anti-war march I could, and before long regularly attending the meetings of the radical student group, Students for a Democratic Society (SDS). SDS had been founded in the early 1960s and released its famous Port Huron statement challenging the Cold War and racism in the United States in 1962. In many ways this was the proclamation of a 'New Left'. The organisation had made its name in April 1968 when it led the students at Columbia University in New York in a major action concerning its links with the defence establishment and its alleged racism. The students occupied buildings and brought the university to a halt.

Now Harvard wondered if it was next on the list. The shooting of Robert Kennedy, the defeat in the Democratic Party primaries of the anti-war

In the snow in Harvard Yard in early 1969.

candidate Eugene McCarthy by Lyndon Johnson's deputy, Hubert Humphrey, and the election of Richard Nixon made critics of the war and advocates of social change feel that change was impossible. By early October, huge banners floated in Harvard Yard, 'Revolution at Harvard?' The newspapers and periodicals I was reading had large advertisements proclaiming simply, 'Resist'.[12] The enemy was no more, nor less, than 'the system'. I found myself in fierce arguments and joining an SDS march down to the Boston State House to protest the war and civil rights. The winter was cold and snowy but when the weather warmed up in spring 1969 it was time for political action. The SDS demanded the abolition of the ROTC (Reserve Officers' Training Corps), the campus organisation for training army officers. When course credit was stripped from the ROTC but it remained on campus, the SDS occupied the University Hall at the centre of Harvard Yard. The hall contained all the financial and personnel records of the university. At 5 a.m. the next morning, the police were sent in to evict the students. Just before they arrived, fire alarms sounded in all the Harvard undergraduate houses, so most of the students were in the yard to witness the very considerable brutality of the police which left forty injured. It was an instantly radicalising experience. That morning a three-day strike of students was called, and no-one dared to go to class. Instead Harvard Yard saw clusters of serious students sitting round discussing the coming revolution and getting lessons in the gospel according to Che Guevara. It was a remarkable and unforgettable sight. Over the next week, in glorious spring weather, the tension and debates became fierce. There was a huge meeting of some six thousand students in the football stadium, called Soldiers Field and shaped like a classical amphitheatre. By a majority of about three-quarters the original six SDS demands were backed. People split into different groups and wore ribbons accordingly. For a week to ten days, none of us did any school work as we were all inevitably drawn into this class in instant revolution. Debates among the Harvard faculty were broadcast on the student radio.

So where did all this political excitement and debate leave me? By the time of my arrival at Harvard I had broken with my parents' political views to the extent that I was against western involvement in the Vietnam War and was prepared to march in the streets. Exposure to the materialism of the American middle class pushed me further left. I wrote to Jane in October 1968, 'One gets so incensed by their narrow entrenched right-wing views that America really turns me into a fervent socialist. I have somewhat changed my tune since you first knew me!'[13] But I was never a revolutionary. I found myself caught between the moderate anti-war pragmatism of many Harvard liberals, whom I found too wishy-washy, and the angry extremism of SDS. During the Harvard 'revolution' I found myself sympathetic to the SDS demands but disturbed by their methods. In letters home I drew a distinction between those in SDS who were primarily humanitarians, angry about the Vietnam War and genuinely concerned by inequality of race and class within America, and those 'self-admitted Maoists whose sole aim is revolution' and who 'condone violence'.[14] I told Jane that the country needed change, 'not the bloody mess of revolution'.[15]

I continued to get involved in anti-war activity. When the nationwide day-long moratorium protesting the Vietnam War arrived on 15 October 1969,

I rose early and knocked on doors in Revere, a poor white suburb of Boston, and handed out leaflets. Then I joined a march of 12,000 from Cambridge Common to Boston Common, where a crowd of 100,000 had gathered. I described the scene at the time: 'It was a most beautiful experience – folk groups sang in the background, planes drew the peace sign in the sky with vapour trails, and George McGovern got nicely angry over the microphone.' The day had reaffirmed my faith in democracy and people power.[16] The next month, I decided to head to Washington for the second moratorium, when half a million people gathered outside the White House to protest the war. I bought a bus ticket from the local anti-war committee, but the buses ran out of seats. So we set off for Washington by car – only to be stymied when we had a massive blow-out about 80 kilometres along the way. We then watched while the spare slowly deflated, thus also deflating my little act of protest.

The next year, 1970, while the war rumbled on, things became rather more violent. 'Men no longer whisper "Revolution", they shout it; and they no longer carry banners, but throw bricks,' I wrote home.[17] In April I joined another big demonstration against the war on Boston Common, and then returned to do some reading in Harvard's Widener Library. I heard noises outside in Harvard Square, so decided to take a look. There I saw a crowd, perhaps five hundred strong, shouting slogans and throwing burning garbage containers and rocks through the windows of the shops and banks in Harvard Square. Many were armed with helmets and chains to battle the 'pigs'. Sure enough before long I saw the 'pigs', the Boston police, arrive. They were wearing gas masks and carrying batons. I was perhaps 300 metres away, well out of the riot zone. I had just caught the whiff of tear gas when I saw a phalanx of police heading up Massachusetts Avenue in our direction. I went to the sidewalk fully expecting the police to rush on by. No such luck. Several cops, swirling batons, followed me and caught me against the stone wall of Harvard Yard. Next I knew, despite pleading innocence as a pure observer, I was being pummelled over the head. I escaped without serious injury but others did not, and I recall seeing one grey-haired and very respectable bystander being brutally beaten.

The incident had several consequences. It forced me further leftwards and I developed a deep cynicism about the American police; and it had, as we shall see, a rather strange sequel. Although the Vietnam War was the initial stimulus for student protest and lay behind my participation, by early 1969 increasing numbers of incidents on campuses across the country were led by black students and concerned issues of race. I had come to the United States relatively ignorant of such matters. Like many people overseas I had grown up reading about Martin Luther King and the fight for civil rights, but that was about where it stopped. I believed in liberal integration. I had thought little about issues of race within New Zealand. In 1968 I wrote home about 'the negro problem', as if the issue was one of black people themselves rather than white attitudes and institutions.[18] After King's assassination, a new group of black leaders emerged, who spoke in more radical terms of separate institutions and violent action. This was a challenge. I spent a couple of months in my second year house-sitting in a ghetto in Boston and this brought home the realities of life in such places. I set to and began to read about the modern black movement. I began with essays by Eldridge Cleaver, one of the leaders of the radical Black Panther party, in his book *Soul on Ice*. There he articulated the case for a black-liberation philosophy backed by violence, and described, although renouncing the practice, raping white women as insurrectionary acts. My initial response was that Cleaver was 'rather extreme and irrational', but I warmed to 'the personal sequences in between'.[19]

Two months later I picked up *The Autobiography of Malcolm X*. This time the personal sequences turned my head around. I immediately told my parents that the book was 'a quite remarkable document by a very great man, describing his rise from hoodlum and dope peddler in Harlem to the leader of the "Black Revolution". These angry oppressed black writers are certainly a remarkable breed.'[20] It was not only that the book was a gripping personal story. It convinced me of the argument for separate black institutions. To Jane I said that

> *The Autobiography of Malcolm X* has had quite an effect on my thinking. I can see now that 'liberal' integration is not the answer, for it always means integration into a white man's culture, and white man's values, and of course the blacks must therefore suffer. What one wants is a black race conscious of its independence, of its distinctive racial pride, and only then will there be an equality of sorts.... There must be 'Black Power' before black integration.[21]

Other reading during these years stimulated my thinking. I picked up Herbert Marcuse's *One-Dimensional Man* and largely accepted his argument

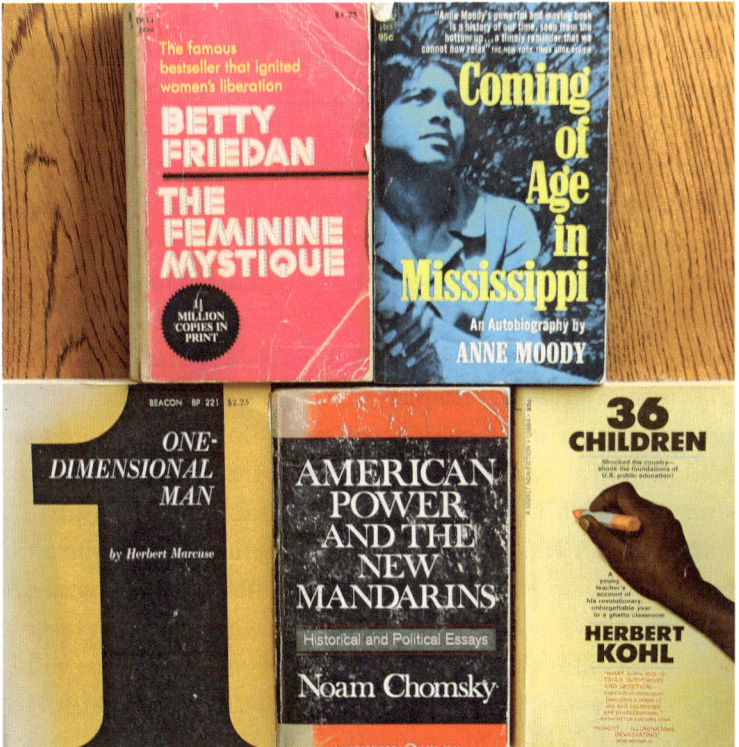

Well-thumbed copies of some of the books that turned my head around from 1968 to 1972.

that workers were co-opted into capitalism by the power of consumerism and advertising. I read Herbert Kohl's *36 Children*, which developed in me an enthusiasm for progressive education and for the need to make sure the education of the poor and minority groups was appropriate for their cultures. I toyed with the thought of breaking my PhD and 'teaching for a year in the ghettos here'.[22] I went along and heard Noam Chomsky, a professor at the Massachusetts Institute of Technology (MIT), just along the road from Harvard, lecture on American Imperialism, and became an enthusiast for his book, sparked by opposition to the Vietnam War, *American Power and the New Mandarins*. This diagnosed the role that university academics at places like Harvard had played in planning and justifying the United States' anti-communist methods.

While such reading broadened my powers of political analysis, I never became a revolutionary. I remained wedded to political change through the established system. I looked to those keen to bring about change within the system. I went and heard Eugene McCarthy, who had been the unsuccessful anti-war candidate for the Democratic nomination. I heard Edward Kennedy speak and then was lucky enough, at a subsequent reception, to have about half an hour with the man quizzing him about his relationship to Irish–Catholic politics. It was inevitable that when George McGovern put up his candidacy for the Democratic Party nomination in 1972 on an anti-war ticket, and then won the nomination, that I could not resist getting involved. Although it was technically against the law for a foreign national to be active in domestic campaigns, I went along to the McGovern headquarters in Northampton, western Massachusetts, where I was living, and began to help. There were letters to be written, press releases to pen, leaflets to distribute. At a time when I should have been hard at work on my thesis, politics called.

This was Richard Nixon's 'Watergate' election and we experienced some local examples of Watergate politics. We discovered that leaflets we had sent out to voters were being held by the post office, which was contacting the addressees to say they had been sent a letter with insufficient postage. They were invited to come along, pay the extra and receive their letter. Imagine their reaction when they discovered the letter was only a leaflet from George McGovern! In fact, of course, the letters were not overweight; it was simply that the Nixon machine was controlling the post office. Despite this, we had high hopes for McGovern's success. Our local polls suggested the tide was turning in his direction. I spent the election day in 1972 ferrying supporters to the voting booths. President McGovern it would be! Election night proved to be a very sad event – George McGovern was defeated in every state of the union, except for one: Massachusetts. Our polls had been right, but we were living in a uniquely liberal part of America. So much for my small part in American politics. It was time to go home.

Although public politics, the attempt to change 'the system', was an enduring fascination, there was another revolutionary element of the United States in the late 1960s and early 1970s, and that was people's interest in changing the self and personal identity. Here the most fundamental challenge was the politics of gender. I did not seriously contemplate the issues until 1970, partly because my own interest in the topic was very much sparked by the start of my relationship with an English woman, Phillida Bunkle. I had continued to correspond regularly with my New Zealand girlfriend, Jane McCartney, and she decided to join me in Cambridge in late 1969. But in the miserable cold of a Boston winter our relationship froze, and we decided to go separate ways. Some nine months later, in September 1970, I met Phillida when she arrived from Oxford on a Kennedy Fellowship. I was instantly dazzled by her humour and acute political insights. Phillida was interested in the history of abolitionism, the campaign to free the slaves, and was exploring how the language of abolition eventually flowed through into other liberation movements such as early feminism.

Phillida's interests reinforced wider currents that began appearing in the political environment. It had taken a while before women themselves began to confront the chauvinist culture of the radical political movements, and to question the extent of gender separation and discrimination in western society. In November 1970 I wrote home that 'the only significant activity is in the field of women's liberation. I am beginning to think this is a terribly important issue, and am at present deep in the provocative pages of Kate Millett's *Sexual Politics*.'[23] Encouraged by Phillida, I devoured other books – Betty Friedan's *The Feminine Mystique*, Germaine Greer's *The Female Eunuch*. I had always been a little uncomfortable with the expectations imposed on me as a New Zealand male, and within a few weeks of arriving at Harvard I had written to Jane of my relief that 'there is none of that ridiculous tough-man cult as in N.Z'.[24] I began to notice that, unlike in my time as a student in Wellington, I had never been in an all-male social situation at Cambridge. There were no drunken nights on the piss with the boys; most gatherings saw women and men mixing freely.

So when feminism began to attract my notice, it took on a more personal dimension and relevance. By December 1970 I was writing to my mother that I would like to 'do something on women's liberation and the cult of masculinity in New Zealand – but that can wait until I arrive'.[25] Phillida and I spent much time and energy talking through the implications of feminism for ourselves. In June 1971 we were married in a Cape Cod garden with me dressed in purple shirt and bright red floral tie to the sounds of The Beatles' 'Here comes the Sun'. Then in September 1971 we moved to Northampton in the Connecticut Valley about 100 kilometres west of Boston. We lived in this small town surrounded by trees and a number of liberal colleges (Smith

Phillida and I cut the wedding cake after being married at Cape Cod in July 1971.

College for women, Amherst for men) while Phillida taught at the University of Massachusetts at Amherst. From Northampton we would drive into Cambridge every two weeks to take part in a discussion group consciousness-raising meeting about how to develop an egalitarian marriage which respected the individuality of both men and women. The women were all strong feminists, so the issues were intense and the debates forthright. Changing the self was never easy; but we were forced to confront the politics of gender relations at the deepest personal level.

In one sense what we were doing in such groups was, in classic 1960s style, making the political personal. There were other ways in which this manifested itself in the States during those years, of which the most visible was the quiet revolution as thousands voted in their sandals by adopting a counterculture. This was a political act since it involved a rejection of the middle-class materialism of the country, but the revolt took the form of a change of lifestyle rather than demonstrations or political campaigns. As a middle-class boy who had grown up in relative material comfort, it was hardly surprising that this 'hippie' culture interested me. On landing at San Francisco I had set off for Haight-Ashbury hoping to see signs of the 'summer of love' the previous year. Apart from 'numerous bearded and moustachioed hippies' I was disappointed, but when Frank and I drove eastwards he made a beeline for sites of alternative culture, such as Greenwich Village's Washington Square.[26]

Frank became increasingly caught up in a hippie lifestyle and decided to abandon his university education to take up work making stained glass. There he was very much part of a hippie craft community. I made several trips out to Minneapolis to enjoy his hospitality. I would work in his studio, attempting to make leaded windows, listening to the folk-rock music blaring out and sharing the occasional joint. We ate wholefoods purchased at his local cooperative. Returning east, I never 'dropped out' or became a genuine hippie, but I was obviously influenced. When Phillida and I moved to Northampton in 1971 and 1972 we developed friendships with a number of hippies living out in the woods. A couple had built themselves a sauna and when the weather was really cold we would drive out there, enter the sauna and then roll in the snow in the nude before racing back into the heat once more. Inevitably too the counterculture affected my own interests and lifestyle. I grew my hair long. I wore brightly coloured floral shirts and ties. Towards the end of my time at

Northampton I became interested in meditation and would regularly sit in the corner cross-legged, reciting my personal mantra.

The counterculture naturally affected my tastes in music. One could not be young in the 1960s without being interested in popular music, and at Victoria I had enjoyed the British music explosion of the sixties – the Beatles and Rolling Stones most obviously. But in the United States I quickly discovered other traditions. I began to listen to blues, and attended a memorable B. B. King concert in Boston. Even more memorable was a concert by the legendary Texas blues singer Janis Joplin. It was midsummer 1970. The evening was still and warm. I joined thousands of others in the Harvard football stadium, Soldiers Field, where the previous year there had been those passionate debates about the Harvard strike. This time the crowd was of some twenty thousand, and the experience was rather different. Long hair and beards were prominent. As we sat in the U-shaped stadium, joints were passed along the rows, and huge balloons were released into the crowd, so that every few minutes one would descend where you were sitting and you would push it once more out into the darkening sky. Joplin was at her peak, her singing strident but also at times gentle and alluring; between numbers we could see her dive to the back for a swig of Southern Comfort. It was shaping up, for me, as one of the epic experiences of the counterculture, when to everyone's fury, including Janis's, the sound system collapsed and we eventually traipsed off home flat and disappointed. So ended Janis Joplin's very last concert, just two months before she died of an overdose.

Politics, gender, the counterculture – they all moved me and took me some distance from the background with which I had grown up. Inevitably this led me into conflict with my parents, for if the rebellions of the period were anything they were primarily a generational revolt. I was not immune. Once more my thoughts were kicked off by reading. Stimulated by Jewish friends at Harvard, I found myself reading Freud and Jung and thinking about the politics of the family. Then I read Erik Erikson's biography *Young Man Luther*, which was a study of Martin Luther's attempt to forge an identity distinct from his father's. I happened to be reading it just as my parents visited Cambridge in June 1969. They had timed their visit for the Harvard commencement. After taking them on a tour of Boston's historic sites, I found all my ambivalence about my father and his culture coming to the surface. I wrote to Jane:

I suddenly seem to despise all the "history" business, and saw in
my father's reactions and starchy good-mannered aloofness, all
that I hated in myself... my inner emotions react violently against
the stuffy polite traditionalism of my dear father... I would dearly
love to throw everything over, and live a purely existential life of
the moment – drugs, music and revolution. But behind comes
the paternal voice that long-term achievement, faithful service
of others, a social self-restraint are significant elements in life –
and they are! Luther's resolution of a similar predicament was
the protestant revolution – a kind of individual compromise.
I suppose I too will find some compromise – but moderation is
always so difficult.[27]

The next year, 1970, I received a letter from my mother asking me to give my younger sister, Catherine, then aged nineteen, 'some fatherly advice' against taking part in protests about the coming All Black tour of South Africa. I was furious, totally supportive of Catherine protesting the tour, and staggered that my parents objected. I lectured my mother about her intolerance – 'please let Cathy discover her own political attitudes, and be proud that she has the gumption to think and question for herself.'[28]

Later that year came a more serious clash, which provided a measure of how far I had moved politically from the opinions with which I had grown up. I decided to return home for four weeks over the Christmas break of 1970. I landed exhausted on the tarmac at Christchurch airport. To my astonishment I was met by a reporter and photographer from the *Press*. The reporter asked me my impressions of the United States. I proceeded to let fly about the brutality of the American police, and told two stories – I described my earlier experience of getting bashed up by the police near Harvard Square, and I also told of a scene I had witnessed when a woman on a Boston subway complained of getting her purse stolen. The police stopped the train and took off the only four blacks on the train. I then argued that marijuana should be legalised, partly because it represented a real advance over the 'virility oriented nature of alcohol'. Little did I know that just the previous week my father as the vice-chancellor of the University of Canterbury had kicked out several students for smoking dope. The *Press* was quick to make the connection, and a photograph of a long-haired Jock Phillips, described as 'son of the

U.S. police brutality "a fact of life"

Police brutality was "a fact of life" for thousands of Americans, a New Zealander who has been a student at Harvard University for the last two years and a half said in Christchurch yesterday.

He is Mr J. O. C. Phillips, son of the Vice-Chancellor of the University of Canterbury (Professor N. C. Phillips), who has returned to New Zealand for a visit of three weeks.

The anti-police element in the United States was becoming stronger among students, Mr Phillips said.

He predicted that the biggest single social issue during the next American spring would be the support American students would give to

MR PHILLIPS

the militant Black Panther movement in its attempts to control whole communities.

Describing an incident he witnessed in which a woman in a crowded subway train in Boston complained of losing her purse, Mr Phillips said that the police singled out the only four blacks in the train and arrested one of them.

"They stopped the unit and one of my friends complained of the way that the police treated the blacks. He went later to the police station to lodge his complaint formally and when he did so was arrested on a charge of inciting a riot and thrust into the cells for the night. All he had said to the policeman was 'you can't do this'."

Mr Phillips said that in another incident he was more than half a mile from a student protest march which had got out of control when he was knocked down by the police as he stepped from the pavement.

"They just descended in a platoon from the trouble area at amazing speed and laid into me with a trunchcon—they did the same to an elderly man nearby and in fact knocked over a pregnant woman," he said.

Mr Phillips said that part of the reason for the violence of the American police was that they were poorly paid and represented a white lower-middle class which objected to the pretentions of students and feared blacks.

"They prefer to deal out immediate treatment instead of waiting for the justice of courts which are often corrupt," he said.

Commenting on drugs among students in the United States, Mr Phillips said marijuana was "used very widely."

"I agree that this should be legalised. Students at Harvard have ready access to it but they know the dangers of tackling the main line drugs and in fact rarely attempt these.

"If marijuana was legalised there would not be the contacts with the criminal underground that many students have at present," he said.

To many students, Mr Phillips said, smoking "pot" represented a real advance over the virility oriented nature of alcohol drinking.

"Far too much of the aura surrounding the drug question has been blown out of proportion by the news media."

Awarded a Frank Knox Scholarship in 1968 to study at Harvard, Mr Phillips was awarded a graduate prize fellowship this year at Harvard to read for his doctorate in philosophy in American history.

He is resident tutor in history and literature at Leverett House, one of the undergraduate houses at the university.

The front-page story of Mr J. O. C. Phillips in the Christchurch Press, *23 December 1970, which so annoyed my father and a Harvard alumnus.*

Vice Chancellor of the University of Canterbury' was placed on the front page along with a story about my comments.[29] When I walked down to breakfast the next morning the front page of the paper was lying on the table, and my father was staring angrily. He did not talk to me for the next week. I realised just how far we had moved apart politically, although the moment I returned to Harvard I wrote home not to 'take my political views too seriously – I am no bomb-throwing revolutionary'.[30] Nor was that the end of the matter. Soon after settling back in Leverett House I received a 'please explain' letter from the Harvard president. He had had a letter from an alumnus who had been in Christchurch at the same time and was affronted that a Harvard student was besmirching the good name of the United States overseas. I wrote back defending my views.

If politically and culturally I had moved a long way from my parents, I continued to enjoy the high culture in which they had raised me; yet even here I went in distinct directions. True, I enjoyed regular visits to art galleries, to the Fogg in Cambridge and the Museum of Fine Arts in Boston, and on a number of hurried weekend visits to New York I inevitably raced off to the Guggenheim, the Metropolitan and the Museum of Modern Art. But I tended to gravitate to the twentieth-century art, raving about the

Josef Albers, 'Variant IV', 1966, my first American art purchase.

more recent Americans Morris Louis and Jackson Pollock rather than the French Impressionists, despite Boston's marvellous collection. After one art-filled visit to New York, when I complained to my parents that 'I felt slightly befuddled with "art-lover's constipation"', I expressed boredom with the Impressionists, which I dismissed as 'respectable art, and yet not "way out". They make a pretty scene!' I made an exception for Cézanne.[31] On a subsequent visit I was enthusiastic about an exhibition of 1940–70 New York art with 'its boldness, strident colours, and daring shapes... It was "relevant" art!'[32] My tastes were reflected in my one expensive art purchase in those years – a limited-edition abstract work by Joseph Albers.

I also went beyond my parents in a continuing discovery of music. Within a month of reaching Cambridge I had bought 'a stereogram' for $60 and found a library close by where I could borrow eight records a week, which I proceeded to do. For a time I had a passion for choral music and the sounds of sung masses would peal out of my room in Perkins Hall, to the considerable discomfort of my Jewish room-mate. With several English friends I made regular Friday-afternoon trips to the Boston Symphony Orchestra, where you could pick up cheap 'rush' tickets. But on seeing Leonard Bernstein prancing about the podium at the Lincoln Centre in New York, I decided that the New York Philharmonic had 'more fire and zip than the Boston Symphony who aptly call themselves "the aristocrat of orchestras"!!'[33] One of my English friends also dragged me, a little complaining, to my first operas – *Il Travatore* and *Der Rosenklavier*. Astonished to enjoy them, I rushed off to buy some opera records – beginning with Mozart of course. This stood me in good stead when on a later weekend visit to New York I stood in the back stalls of the Metropolitan to see Mozart's *The Magic Flute*, enriched by magnificent backdrops painted by Chagall. There were plenty of other cultural enjoyments in the buzzing communities of Cambridge and Boston. I heard readings by W. H. Auden, John Updike and Kurt Vonnegut. I went to many films, including the annual Humphrey Bogart season at the Brattle Theatre in Cambridge, when on the last showing of *Casablanca* the audience recited the dialogue! And I enjoyed some modern plays and revues. I recall especially a revue of contemporary events in a tiny underground theatre where one of the actors performed the role of a New Zealander protesting the visit of Spiro Agnew to Auckland in January 1970.

In my first year at Harvard I went to many of these events in the company of several English friends I had met there. I wrote back home that I found my fellow American students flat, hard-working, lacking a sense of humour and not interested in music or art. In November 1968 I reported that I went with an Oxford graduate, Chris Smallwood, 'to a semi-English pub and drank long pints of English beer as we systematically attacked the American character!'[34] Chris became for that year my closest friend. I described him at the time: 'tall, dark, bespectacled, a sharp Oxford nose. A mind that is clear and ordered, but great enthusiasm and sensitivity . . . very generous, and a wonderful eye for the picturesque detail'.[35] Yet as early as January 1969 I was moaning that there were too many Englishmen around, and that they stuck together and did nothing but grumble about the inferiority of Americans.[36] By the end of that year I was admitting 'How much I have come to like all the Americans here. It is strange how at first I seemed to mix constantly with the Englishmen and felt the Americans so boring and flat. Now the Englishmen seem rather stuffy and caustic, whereas the Americans are so genuinely easy and relaxed.'[37] It was true that at the end of that first year I moved rooms to share with another Oxford-educated Englishman, Constantine Brancovan; and of course the woman I met and eventually married, Phillida Bunkle, was also from England. But in the last years at Harvard my closest friends were Americans, especially Jews from the New York and New Jersey area, Bob Fishman, Carl Brauer and Barry Salkin, the last two fellow students of American history.

I experienced much the same transition in my response to the American environment. When I first arrived at Cambridge, after travelling through California and then the Midwest, I described my sense of relief to my parents: 'The fact that one is drawn so much more to the East and to the older more historic areas, is suggestive that we really yearn for what is English. Certainly it is the Englishness of Harvard that is basically responsible for my sense of elation at the moment.'[38] It was perhaps for this reason that when the summer break arrived I decided to turn down Chris Smallwood's offer of a drive around the States and instead fly to England, meet my old Victoria friend, Frank Wilson, and head off in his car around Europe. London offered some immediate excitement in the form of a Rolling Stones concert in Hyde Park, and I quickly felt at home; but I was also surprised by my own negative response to English society – the continued importance of class, the insular views, 'the stuffy contentment' and 'the scoffing superior attitude' towards America.[39] I did not find 'much evidence of a "new Britain". It is still the same eccentric old England,' I wrote.[40]

In Europe we drove through France to Switzerland, where I guided Frank to all the places that I remembered from my father's slides of my parents' 1955 trip. Then it was on to Italy – the lakes, Verona, Padua, Venice and Florence. We stayed in youth hostels, which was a new and interesting experience, but the trip left me strangely flat. I wrote back from Florence: 'It is wonderful to be in Italy again, but somehow I do feel it is a very sentimental journey – a hark back to a world that I once loved and now simply enjoy, but find it hard to become really excited. Where once a medieval street could send me into romantic imaginings, I now find I judge it according to how it works as a street. It is perhaps the passing of a youthful dream world, but the vicarious relaxation into historical fantasy is no longer easy or very attractive. America has thrown me into a world of immediate problems and basic issues, and it is strange how I miss its pressures and strife.'[41] It is significant that the Italian moment that remains freshest in the memory was one early morning in a dimly lit, noisy bar in Arezzo, where on a scratchy black-and-white television we watched Neil Armstrong land on the moon. Later we had fun in Spain, particularly in the bars laden with delicate snacks, and I felt myself drawn to the country's centre – 'a landscape that was barren and treeless, and yet magnificent in its honesty, face to the sky'.[42] We were fortunate, on arriving back in France and finding that all currency transactions had been suspended, to just make it to Frank's cousin, a Jewish psychotherapist from Brazil with a country house in the Dordogne. At first we were condemned to sleeping out under the stars, but when I began to discuss Freud and gently dropped into the conversation a mention of my Jewish heritage, we were moved inside to enjoy the marvellous food and the attentions of three Brazilian servants. Despite such luxuries, the trip cured me, at least temporarily, of the pull of England and Europe.

Instead I began to discover America. The next summer I headed west to Omaha, Nebraska, the home of Steve Rearden, a fellow graduate student. I found Omaha 'soul-destroying Nixon country', conservative middle America where the focus of interest was the local football team and meetings of Elks or Rotary.[43] But then we headed further west to Colorado and into the Rockies. Whether it was the euphoric light-headedness from being constantly above 2500 metres, or simply the sheer scale of the mountains, I was blown away by the rugged peaks, craggy gorges, sparkling lakes and vast deserted plateaus (to use just a few of the adjectives which were sprinkled liberally in my letter home).[44] I was reminded irresistibly of my August holidays at Queenstown.

When I returned east I decided to buy a car. In the company of Phillida, I spent most weekends exploring New England. There was a trip over Thanksgiving to the rocky coasts of Maine with their wooded islands and old fishing villages. Despite the age of settlement I came back thinking I had visited a harsh frontier. There were jaunts down to Cape Cod, and when the leaves turned their spectacular reds and golds in the fall we abandoned work and spent days walking amid the trees gazing at the colours.

Particularly after we moved to Northampton in 1971, we made regular trips into the rolling hills of Vermont, where a family friend of Phillida had a country home. This was an area which had been settled in the early nineteenth century, but when the railways linked the east coast with the prairie, Vermont agriculture could not compete. Farms were abandoned as families

Vermont was a place of beauty in all seasons. I took my parents to see the brilliant colours of the fall (left); and in the winter Phillida and I went cross-country skiing across frozen hillsides with the trees stark and bare (right).

headed west. The trees returned. Walking over these glorious hills coming across abandoned houses or stone fences was a delight. It was rolling country, and in the summer we would get on horses and explore the hills. Once more another old memory surfaced – of riding across the hills of Hawke's Bay in my childhood. In winter we would go up to Vermont, put on cross-country skis and head into the woods. After a half-day's skiing we would return for a kuchen or a stollen and hot coffee at the home of an old German woman who had been living there for half a century. I wrote to my mother that this was 'one of the most beautiful parts of the world'.[45]

Closer to Northampton, we also came to love western Massachusetts, where we spent many hours enjoying the old wooden churches and fascinating cemeteries, walking among the trees and soft hills in the summer and skiing in the winter. I developed a huge affection for the natural world so close at hand. After my first visit to Vermont, I wrote home, 'It is still very wild out there, and beyond the odd ancient New England village with its white colonial church and avenue of oaks, nature is supreme. After studying Emerson all last week, I can fully see how Transcendentalism found its home in New England.'[46] But it was less Ralph Waldo Emerson, the Boston intellectual of the early nineteenth century, who had an influence on me, and more his follower, Henry David Thoreau. Thoreau had followed Emerson out to Concord, the little village in the trees west of Boston, where a famous battle in the American Revolution had taken place. At Concord Thoreau decided to abandon civilisation and build a log cabin on Emerson's land at Walden Pond. When we were living in Cambridge we would often drive out to Walden Pond and either ski or walk around it. We would explore the site of Thoreau's cabin. In his famous book about his experience, *Walden*, Thoreau argued that the world of materialistic possessions imprisoned humans. If the farmer got a house, he wrote, 'he may not be the richer, but the poorer for it, and it be the house that has got him'.[47] To gain happiness and integrity then the answer was to strip off the burdens of objects and live simply off the land. It is immediately obvious why the counterculture, myself included, became so enthusiastic about the book. Thoreau recounted in loving detail the passage of the year in the trees and the animals and birds that were his neighbours.

Not that I was anti-city. Boston and New York were wonderful experiences and I loved the counterculture which flourished around Harvard Square. Cities encouraged radicalism and diversity, and were the sites of high culture. But I always found my visits to New York, although exciting, also exhausting, and I would breathe a great sigh of relief once I had left, only to realise what a wonderful forty-eight hours I had just experienced. So whether consciously or not, I found myself retreating from New York and Boston and heading west, to Northampton and then into the hills. Thoreau taught me that the civilisation and culture of the city were not essential for intellectual discovery. He described how 'instead of calling on some scholar, I paid many a visit to particular trees' and he argued for the importance of exploring the natural world around you.[48] 'Be rather the Mungo Park, the Lewis and Clark and Frobisher, of your own streams and oceans; explore your own higher latitudes – with shiploads of preserved meats to support you . . . Nay, be a Columbus to whole new continents and worlds within you, opening new channels, not of trade, but of thought.'[49] Slowly I began to realise that this model could, and should, be applied to New Zealand. The natural world of New England which had so begun to entrance me was but a model for another unspoilt nature in the South Pacific. In later years I would teach Thoreau's *Walden* alongside Herbert Guthrie-Smith's classic, *Tutira*.

Of course, like most New Zealanders on their overseas experience, I had occasionally allowed my New Zealand patriotism to show. Soon after reaching Harvard I described how 'I hunt through the turgid pages of the N.Y.Times every morning looking for "Z"s, only to find an occasional bottom-of-the-page reference to the Napier dolphins!', and I did my best to keep up with New Zealand sport.[50] I remember cheering ostentatiously amid a large group of pensive Americans as I watched the New Zealand coxed fours defeat the American crew in the Olympic rowing finals at Mexico City. I told my parents that for Christmas presents '"things New Zealand" [are] nostalgically welcomed'.[51] And I was duly very grateful when a print with 'sufficient New Zealand flavour to be distinctive' arrived.[52] I began to read New Zealand books – Janet Frame novels, Denis Glover poems. After reading Frame's *The Rainbirds* I commented that it had made me nostalgic and homesick, since she pointed out how people in New Zealand always wanted a view and sought to enjoy 'the silent company of the landscape'.[53] I was very grateful when copies of *Landfall* arrived, which I devoured cover to cover. I decided that its contents were so 'distinctive' – 'it is always concerned with the lone struggle against nature'.[54] I relished coming across little reminders of home, such as on our honeymoon at Nantucket Island, where I discovered in the local museum a large collection of Māori artefacts, gathered by the whalers who had left Nantucket for the South Pacific. I also began to draw comparisons between US and New Zealand society and decided that the occupational specialisation in America could be restricting, while in New Zealand you could live a more varied existence. I wrote back that I saw America as 'a huge white block divided vertically by thick black bars, and between two of these bars each person filled his narrow role'.[55] But what really turned me homewards was thinking about the land. I decided to return home for three weeks over the Christmas break of 1970, most obviously to see my family, but also because I had become 'homesick for that New Zealand landscape'.[56] I spent some of the time desperately recording on film the hills and the beaches, and showed them off proudly to my Harvard mates once I had returned.

If the attractions of the New England hills made me nostalgic for the hills at home, my academic studies also eventually turned me in that direction. My initial experience of the Harvard history programme was intimidating, to say the least. The welcoming professor did the old trick and invited us to turn to the fellow student on the left, then turn to the one on the right, and proceeded to say, 'Only one of you three will graduate with a PhD.' Sure enough, after the first semester ten of our class of thirteen did indeed receive letters warning them they were not up to scratch and would be sent packing in June. The quantity of work required for the first two years seemed horrendous, and I was struck by the way in which American students were quite happy to acknowledge the value of hard work. There was none of the gentlemanly pretence of lazy genius with which I had become familiar. I was also hugely impressed by the quality of discussion in my classes. Most of the students seemed very lucid and their arguments high-powered. Yet when I received my essays back, and when I read the efforts of the other students, I became more confident. I realised that the New Zealand university training in written expression was distinctly superior. From my education and my father's example, I knew how to present an argument. What I lacked were the fluent oral skills of the American students, and this was of some importance because the second year was examined wholly on one two-hour oral 'general examination' in which four Harvard professors, all world experts, quizzed you on their fields.

But the boost I received early from my written work was reassuring, and I found the material we studied immensely stimulating. In the first year there were two forms of assessment – a research seminar in each half-semester, in which we had to prepare a 10,000 word research essay; and a colloquium, in which we looked at revealing historiographical issues in American history with different members of the faculty. The colloquium was a wonderful experience. You would take a topic, such as the nature of slavery, or the origins of American involvement in the Great War; you would be asked to read about four key books or articles each week and then discuss them in a two-hour session. In the third week you wrote an essay. It was a great way to confront big issues head-on and an excellent introduction to the different faculty members. For me it was helpful because, since we all read the same books, my relative ignorance of American history was no disadvantage. I recall particularly becoming deeply fascinated by the nature of slavery, and having fierce arguments as to whether slaves, like Jews in concentration camps, had their spirits and powers of resistance broken or whether in fact resistance was widespread.

I also became enthusiastic about the possibilities of intellectual history after being exposed to Perry Miller's writing on puritanism. I discovered the 'new social history' and the importance of telling about the past from 'below'. New methodologies, such as oral history, demographic statistics, or the use of popular culture like songs or advertisements to reveal popular attitudes, were exciting. Political history as the history of elites seemed distinctly 'old hat'. After the first two meetings of the colloquium I wrote home that 'the pressure is stimulating, and I can honestly say I have thought more aggressively and more exactingly about history this week than ever before'.[57] I found the process of discovering American history alongside my discovery of the United States very exciting. I could read about the events and attitudes of the American Revolution and then wander to downtown Boston to see where they happened, and I learnt that the religious proselytising I had met followed logically from the abolition of an established church at the Revolution, which meant sects competed to attract followers. History had never felt so relevant and immediate. I began to realise that history was not just an academic exercise – it helped explain the world around you.

The seminars also seemed at first very demanding. For the first year I managed to get into Bernard Bailyn's course on England and America in the eighteenth century. Bailyn was the undoubted star of the department. He had just published a book entitled *The Ideological Origins of the American Revolution*, which had overturned accepted theories and won the Pulitzer Prize for history. I was immediately attracted to the book because it took ideas seriously and showed how they could determine political behaviour. It was brilliantly argued and beautifully presented, and the man himself was an inspiration. Alongside the colloquium and seminars we were encouraged to attend relevant undergraduate lectures to help prepare for our general examination. Harvard students could be ruthless judges and after each lecture had the habit of either clapping or booing. Bailyn always received applause, and at the end of his course a five-minute standing ovation. For clarity of argument and gripping exposition I have only ever heard one person who could compare – James Belich. In his seminar Bailyn expected us to write a hundred-page paper that was 'publishable'. He gave us no choice of topic, but simply assigned them, and perhaps because I had trained in British history I was given a crusty English peer, Lord Camden, and asked to explore his attitude towards the American Revolution. I described Camden in letters home as 'a gouty English lawyer . . .

who had hundreds of children and was a lazy old miser'.[58] It was not long before I decided that it was too English a topic and struggled to get it done.

My second seminar was with Donald Fleming, whom I described at the time as 'a wonderful tweedy bald-headed hair-lipped bachelor'.[59] He was not well-known, but was an excellent teacher. His seminar was on the New England philosopher William James, the brother of the novelist Henry James. I found the philosophy testing, but was lucky to be given a subject that interested me – William James and his father. I decided that James was influenced not by his father's ideas but by the way he lived his life. I could not help but see the relevance of this to my own family situation.

The second year at Harvard I spent reading about a book a day preparing for the dreaded general examination. I was very nervous, but fortunately the night before my oral I was tracked down by a New Zealander who was in town. It was Angus Ross, the noted professor of history at Otago. I had only met him once before and I have no idea how he knew I was there, but he insisted on taking me out that night, plying me with good red wine, and enjoying lively conversation. I came back happy and relaxed. The two-hour oral the next day was a breeze, with Bernard Bailyn and Donald Fleming particularly helping me by quizzing me on issues that I had previously discussed with them.

Several developments during these two years eventually turned me back towards New Zealand. The first was a growing sense that the life of an American history professor was just too narrow. The degree of specialisation and total commitment required to succeed seemed to restrict one's interests as a human being. I wrote, 'I cannot bring myself fully to accept this rigid professionalism of the subject here – its whole value and meaning somehow are deprived, for historical truth is not an end in itself; it is simply a means to human enjoyment.'[60] I had been amazed one day when Donald Fleming expressed his surprise that I had just come from viewing art in the Fogg Museum. I immediately wrote:

> American historians do not waste their precious time looking at pictures. No – the more I think about it, the more I want to return eventually to New Zealand, write about two really good books in my life – quietly, confidently, and in a relaxed imaginative way – and sprinkle that original work with teaching and walks in the country, and concerts, and evening sunsets, and children, and paintings...[61]

So in addition to pursuing my cultural interests, I tried to think about the wider role of the historian, rather than just the researching scholar. I was asked to teach in Bernard Bailyn's course in my second year; I followed this up with teaching my own course in my third year while a tutor at Leverett House, and also teaching tutorials for Oscar Handlin's undergraduate course. I became very involved in this challenge and began to think about novel ways of bringing history alive. I joined a seminar on teaching methods, and had one of my classes videoed. We then took the video back to the seminar and workshopped my role as teacher, minute by minute. I learnt more about teaching from this experience than from anything else. Teaching Harvard undergraduates was in fact very easy. They were bright and highly verbal, and their sheer range of backgrounds made for lively discussion. When you had sons or daughters of Chicago industrialists, Pennsylvania Italian ironworkers or black labourers from Kentucky, it was not hard to get debate going. I also became committed to the idea that teaching of history could benefit from my own range of cultural interests. Narrowness of a person would reflect itself in narrow classes. I wrote in a letter:

> ... the trouble with so much history – it is all category and no buzzing life, and I thought that when I come to teach, it might be a good idea to have a slide show of pictures, extracts from novels, photos of prominent men etc. of one period. It might capture something of the varied flavour that was life then.[62]

Consistent with this view, I widened my historical activities. I found myself leading a campaign to reform the methods of assessment in the history programme by getting rid of the authoritarian scaremongering approach and adjusting the language requirement to recognise statistical skills (to no avail, I might add). I became treasurer and social secretary of the Henry Adams History Club, in which I prepared sangria for social gatherings and organised interesting debates to widen the experience of my fellow graduate students. I also picked up a couple of jobs to enrich my experience and earn some spare cash – doing research at $4 an hour for an Italian professor on American attitudes to Italian fascism in the 1930s, and then working for the Dictionary of American Biography, which was based in Cambridge. Initially I was a checker, and then, having earned my stripes and getting on well with the editor,

The young pipe-smoking historian in his Leverett House sitting room, 1971.

Edward James, graduated to rewriting the essays that were below standard and finally being asked by James to write an entry myself. So an essay on the Boston racist Lothrop Stoddard became my first signed published academic work. I had no idea how valuable this training in ensuring a reference work was accurate would become in later years. Behind such steps was a sense that I wanted my life as a historian to be broader and more meaningful to my own and others' lives than simply becoming a research-based specialist.

If such developments were in many ways a dimly conscious preparation for the academic life in New Zealand rather than the United States, I also turned to my own country's history more directly in those years. As I discussed historiographical issues with my fellow students, they would quite often ask me when an issue arose, 'Well, how does this compare with what happened in your country?' The first couple of times this happened I laughed it off. But then I became ashamed to realise that I knew nothing about New Zealand history. One day I decided to see whether there were books of New Zealand history in Harvard's Widener Library. I found the collection. It was in the basement, four floors below the ground level – so far down that in fact the floor of the stacks was actually pounded earth! But the collection was magnificent. Harvard tries to purchase all scholarly books of any academic value from around the world. There I found a huge collection of New Zealand history, all in mint condition (for they had rarely been used). I browsed, wandering along the stacks, and before long was taking some out to read. I cannot say I made a huge dent in the collection, but I do remember reading William Pember Reeves' *The Long White Cloud* and Keith Sinclair's biography of Pember Reeves. I sensed that, despite my prejudices from childhood and undergraduate days, New Zealand history could be interesting. Carried away with such thoughts, I discovered among the regulations a provision that one of the four fields for the general examination could be Australia and New Zealand. I immediately decided to do it, despite my father's strong disapproval. It turned out to be a false hope. The department told me that sadly there was no one who could supervise the field. I would have to do medieval European history instead.

When it came for me to write a PhD thesis at the end of the two years' coursework and successful passage through the general examination, I took time to find a topic. Initially I had toyed with the idea of writing about the history of the beard. I was considering growing one myself and was thinking about the cultural meaning of such an act. I read how Abraham Lincoln had grown a beard in the 1850s as they became fashionable; and then I discovered that at the turn of the twentieth century, as the cult of professional efficiency became established in the United States, the removal of beards was regarded as one sign of the new approach. Beards became associated with old fuddy-duddies. A thesis on the subject, relating facial hair to social and cultural trends, would have been at the time a highly original study. After considerable inner debate, I decided that much as I admired him, Bernard Bailyn would not be the right supervisor because I simply did not want to work on colonial America or eighteenth-century Britain. So Donald Fleming became my choice. But when I raised the idea of a thesis on the beard he dismissed it as 'not a proper subject'. I did not have the courage to argue. Instead Fleming suggested that I do a thesis on social thinkers in Chicago at the end of the nineteenth century. It was a good topic. Chicago in the 1890s was a booming city of over two million, which had grown from almost nothing a generation before. The group included some fascinating people – John Dewey, the father of progressive education; Albion Small, who set up the first American sociology department at the University of Chicago; Jane Addams, the pioneering social worker; Frank Lloyd Wright, the revolutionary architect; and Thorstein Veblen, a highly original economist. They knew each other well and there were strong links and similarities between their ideas. If I had done what I set out to do – write a short chapter on each person, develop the links and their intellectual coherence, and relate it all to Chicago – it would have been a valuable contribution.

There were two problems. First, I simply did not know the ratio of research and writing at that stage. I began collecting material, writing quotations and my own thoughts out on index cards, which I stored in five shoeboxes. When I came to write it up, mechanically going from one index card to another, I realised that I had far, far too much material for short chapters on each person. I began writing about John Dewey, and recognised that I had enough material for a whole thesis just about him. Second, as I began to do the writing, I found that my approach was being guided by my own interests. I had begun to think, whether consciously or not, about my future role as a historian and intellectual in New Zealand. I began to interpret the development of John Dewey's ideas as his attempt to provide a philosophy for an intellectual in the new world. I argued that in nineteenth-century America, intellectuals were seen as essentially irrelevant. Their focus was on European cultural traditions, and their world of ideas was seen as having no value for tough American men of action. Intellectuals were regarded as effeminate, aristocratic dilettantes. Anti-intellectualism was rife. In response Dewey developed a psychology and philosophy that argued that the brain had evolved along Darwinian lines to ensure the survival of the fittest. Thinking was not an irrelevant cultural attribute but was intended to solve the problems of life. People were inspired to thought because they came up with a problem in their activities. To ensure that the action proceeded they needed to stop and think. I interpreted this view as originating in Dewey's own vocational aspirations to be an intellectual on the American frontier.

I then followed the argument through by showing that in his educational ideas, Dewey suggested that children should learn by explaining and interacting with the world around them. They might visit the Chicago stockyards, and then go back to school and learn maths by working out how to estimate the number of animals killed; or they might become involved in a farm attached to the school and learn botany by learning what the animals ate; or they would learn history by studying the settlement of the immediate environment – the Illinois frontier and the growth of Chicago. It was learning through, and for, doing. Intellectual life need not involve a separation between a European world of pure ideas and an American world of action. Ideas worked best when they were focused on immediate issues, problems in the near environment. I had grown up divided between the high European cultural interests of my family and the farming life of my grandparents and cousins. Dewey seemed to promise a resolution, a philosophy for a New World intellectual. Creative thinking emerged out of issues close at hand. When looking at Dewey I had simply deduced this hypothesis, but on going to Chicago and reading the letters of John Dewey's closest friend and Chicago colleague, George Mead, I found it spelled out explicitly. Mead was quite open about his own vocational crisis as an intellectual in Midwest America – and he explained Dewey's pragmatism as a solution to his dilemma. Dewey provided both a justification for the importance of intellectual life in the New World and an inspiration for action. So the thesis took a turn very different from where it had begun and was largely driven by my own personal concerns. The thesis was unfinished when I returned to New Zealand in 1973. I often found myself out of my depth dealing with the philosophy, and it was hard to keep going. I did not finally hand in the completed work until 1978. It had been a long and arduous haul, but John Dewey's pragmatism had provided me with a philosophical basis for my life work.

    I had gone to America in 1968 with every intention of becoming a historian of that country. I had little interest in the history of my own country, and I was not even sure that I wished to return home at all. I was privileged to be in the US as the 1960s generational revolt reached a crescendo; my time there was a huge learning experience, teaching me an enormous amount about political, social and cultural ideas and values. For the next thirty years I fed off that intellectual capital. Most interestingly, discovering America had led me to discover New Zealand. In the American natural world and Henry David Thoreau's interpretation of it I had found a new interest in the New Zealand landscape. Inspired by questions from fellow scholars, I had started reading

New Zealand history, and through my misconceived thesis on John Dewey I had developed a philosophy for a New World intellectual. All this turned me back home.

Despite all this, it was by no means an obvious choice to go back to New Zealand. I had married Phillida, who had been born and lived all her life in England. She had no great desire to head off to a provincial South Pacific backwater. And after almost five years in the United States I had come to enjoy much about the society – its great range of foods, its fascinating politics and the quality of political debate, the availability of high culture in the form of art and music and opera. I even found myself enjoying American sport, becoming a fan of both Boston Red Sox baseball and Boston Bruins ice hockey. On television the movement of good ice-hockey was like a soothing ballet. I had made good American friends. So I did not find the decision easy. I applied for several jobs teaching American history in Britain, and was even flown to Oxford for an interview. That was not a happy experience because the interview was accompanied by a dinner at 'high table' and my mother-in-law warned me that I would need to wear a dinner jacket for such an auspicious occasion. I hired the garb and turned up so dressed only to find that everyone else was in casual jackets. Further, my discomfort sitting at the high table was intensified when the don sitting next to me began to fondle my thigh lovingly. I beat a hasty retreat back to the States. Tim Beaglehole was keen to lure me back to Victoria and would drop enticing comments into his letters, such as that he had just returned from swimming at Mākara with a very sunburnt bottom.

After many sleepless nights and frantic international phone calls we finally accepted an offer for Phillida and myself to teach four courses of American history at Victoria. We could arrange the load however we liked. In January 1973, on the day of Richard Nixon's second inauguration, we left Boston for New Zealand. The baggage we carried, cultural and physical, was in every respect weighty.

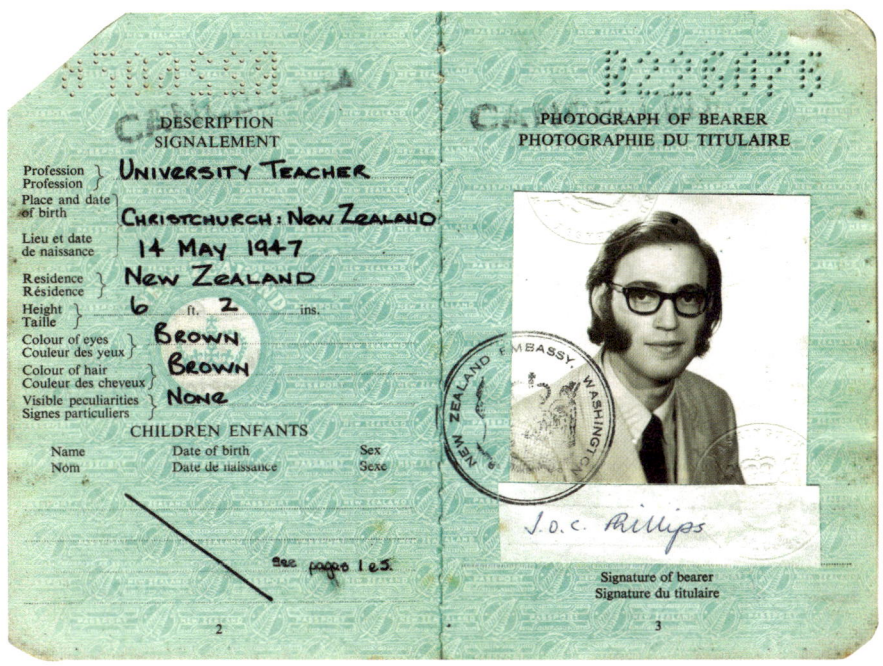

The passport on which I travelled back home to New Zealand in early 1973.

5
Discovering New Zealand

It was with some reluctance, much sadness and a good deal of nervousness that I set off back to New Zealand with Phillida. We spun out the journey as long as possible, with visits to New Orleans, where we visited the inevitable jazz bar; to Mexico City, where I was stunned by discovering a whole sequence of sophisticated civilisations in the National Museum of Anthropology and where I was cheered by the confident nationalism of the people; and to an island in Fiji, where we snorkelled in the sun.

But very quickly we felt at home. The flight from Fiji was an inaugural flight for one of Air New Zealand's new DC-10s. Flowing champagne and the Kiwi jokes in that flat nasal accent were immediately welcoming; and once we arrived and set off on the walk between Auckland's international and domestic terminals the blue skies and clarity of light were invigorating. Good to be back.

Over the next few years we found stronger reasons to make New Zealand home. A new Labour government had just taken office. The gravelly voice and silver hair of Norman Kirk, international statesman, was a welcome relief after the devious pompousness of Richard Nixon. We cheered inwardly as New Zealand recognised China, pulled out of Vietnam, stopped the Springbok

On the beach at Glenorchy, Lake Wakatipu, with Phillida in January 1974. I had just completed walking the Rees–Dart track. FELICITY GLOVER

tour and sent a frigate to Mururoa Atoll to protest French nuclear tests. The generational revolt which had become such an important part of our lives in the United States was in full flood in New Zealand, about two years behind America. The anti-war movement had spawned an articulate anti-nuclear and environmental movement; the campaign against apartheid sport had led to the establishment of HART in 1970; Ngā Tamatoa, a group of young Māori radicals with their Afro hairstyles, were just emerging on the political landscape; and a women's movement was becoming vocal. There was also a highly visible counterculture of back-to-the-land hippies. Arriving in the country with my own locks heading down to my shoulders I found many kindred spirits. Phillida's transition to New Zealand was made much easier by her previous involvement in the American women's movement. Within a year she was speaking at New Zealand's first women's convention, on her way to becoming one of the country's best-known feminists, and had discovered a lively group of friends among that community.

The land also began to call. In Wellington we had rented Tim Beaglehole's house while he was overseas, but Phillida found it forbidding and cold. Within two months, with the help of my parents and a lawyer's funds, we had bought a two-bedroom house nestled in the bush in Karori. Quickly I found myself spending hours making a vegetable garden and planting native trees on the bank. The lessons from Thoreau had been well learnt, and with the aid of several books, especially John Salmond's magnificent *Native Trees of New Zealand*, I found myself able to identify native plants on our regular weekend bush-walks. And we set out to explore the country. There were several tramps in the Tararuas, and then, having purchased an old van with a double bed in the back, we explored further. After the Christchurch Commonwealth Games in early 1974, I did a strenuous four-day tramp on the Rees–Dart track at the head of Lake Wakatipu with a mate, followed by a trip up the West Coast with Phillida – my first visit to that land of towering trees, glaciers and hard-nosed blokes. We headed north to stay with Felicity Glover in her geodesic dome amid the bush of the Coromandel, and when the van collapsed we spent several days staying at Barry Brickell's pottery. The next summer we headed off camping in the van around the East Coast, and while staying at Lake Waikaremoana conceived our first offspring, born later that year – our son, Jesse. Hester arrived fourteen months later. Parenthood put some limits on such explorations but we still managed family holidays

A view of the beach at Ouepoto, Hawke's Bay, where I used to holiday as a child, and spent much time in the 1970s bodysurfing, snorkelling along the rocks and climbing the hills.

in the Wairarapa and then, memorably, in the Bay of Islands, where, as I told my parents, 'I read furiously about Marsden, Kendall and Williams' between visiting the 'historic spots'.[1]

I also rekindled my love for pastoral Hawke's Bay with frequent trips to stay with my aunt at Ouepoto. On several such holidays I managed to get away tramping in the Ruahines, and remember vividly my first encounter with fields of yellow and white mountain flowers on the Armstrong Saddle. There were also tramps into the Richmond Range near Blenheim with my friend Chris Maclean. On such trips I developed a growing love for the landscapes of New Zealand and a deeper knowledge of the flora and fauna. Closer to home there were regular trips to the beach, especially Mākara, where I would inevitably dive for pāua to cook on an open fire. I began to record my enthusiasms with the camera – distant shots of beautiful New Zealand and close-ups of seaweed or alpine lichen. Inevitably, too, I became increasingly interested in the human history to be found in small-town New Zealand. The old wooden buildings of Ongaonga, the woolsheds of Otago, the art-deco streetscapes of Napier and the deserted dairy factories of Taranaki appeared in my slide collection.

Yet while I discovered the landscape – and slowly the physical reminders of history – in New Zealand, and while I started to thrive in the lively social and cultural scene of 1970s New Zealand, my work life remained teaching and researching American history. I still had a thesis on John Dewey to complete. So that division, which had shaped me, between my intellectual life and my New Zealand experience, remained. How did I deal with this? One way, which I fell into by accident and good fortune, was through popular writing about New Zealand. It all began with a rather ill-tempered letter I wrote to the *New Zealand Listener* in early 1975, about two years after coming back. I had read a piece by the former *Listener* editor Monte Holcroft, in which he was effusive in his praise of J. C. Beaglehole as the great New Zealand historian. I particularly objected to Holcroft's comment that Beaglehole's greatness had been cemented 'when the Queen summoned him to a private audience and appointed him to the Order of Merit'. I let fly, oozing contempt:

> Here speaks the polite tired voice of the provincial mentality. The provincial mind sees culture as defined by the forms and traditions of a larger metropolis – in our case London – and he sees his task as the defence of that culture in the provincial wilderness. He is a missionary of taste, a kind of WEA lecturer to the colonies. Success in this view does not occur when the locals begin to think creatively about their own condition in their own way, but rather when the province finally makes a mark on the metropolitan culture and is given the nod of recognition from Oxford and Buckingham Palace.[2]

I went on to say that Beaglehole's biography of Cook expressed the literary grace of English culture without a hint of Kiwi colloquialism, and while its physical setting was New Zealand the culture described was eighteenth-century English culture. The book was ultimately, I claimed, 'a tribute to the Great White Father'. I argued that the danger of the 'provincial mentality' was that it produced 'a national self-contempt' and that it led to a schism between people's culture and their experience. High English culture was 'at odds with the bush slopes and egalitarian ethos' of New Zealand. I suggested that it was new experience which germinated new ideas. Because Beaglehole's work was blind to the colonial experience, it aped the forms of Old World culture but would not produce new ideas illuminating the New Zealand condition. This broadside was both implicitly a critique of the culture I had learned from my father and a reflection of the insights I had gained from John Dewey – that new ideas derived from wrestling directly with the environment. They grew out of experience.

The letter had several interesting consequences. Tim Beaglehole, the great man's son and a close friend, was remarkably kind about it; but Ormond Wilson, the father of my good friend Frank, who had worked with John Beaglehole in the Historic Places Trust, took me aside and told me off severely. Janet Paul was appalled and my relationship with her was never restored to its former closeness. Only later, when reading Tim Beaglehole's biography of his father, did I discover that Janet had been a lover of J. C. Beaglehole's during the war years. Others were more positive. Keith Sinclair sidled up to me and slapped me on the back, confiding that he had never had the courage to say such truths. Another cultural nationalist, Ian Cross, author of the path-finding novel *The God Boy*, was by this stage editor of the *New Zealand Listener*. He contacted me, congratulated me on the letter and then asked me if I would like to write an editorial once a month for the journal. He found the burden unreasonably heavy and wanted to have a break once every four weeks.

This was an opportunity too good to turn down. Seven hundred words once a month seemed not too onerous and it would give me the chance to write about the country and its issues while my day job remained American history. At the time the *Listener* was the only really serious journal of opinion in the country. It still had a monopoly over television and radio schedules, and so had a very large audience. Ian Cross had collected around him a lively group of young writers – there was Tom Scott writing columns and drawing cartoons, Rosemary McLeod doing likewise, and interesting journalists like David Young, Gordon Campbell and Helen Paske. I was happy to join the stable. Ian Cross had only one condition. I had signed the original letter 'J. O. C. Phillips'. Cross said that someone writing for a 'people's paper' could not go under their initials. I had to come across as one of the ordinary blokes. Even Joc Phillips was too poofy. So 'Jock Phillips' I became, and since the *Listener* provided my entrance onto the New Zealand literary scene that was the name I was stuck with. Thank you, I. R. Cross.

The timing could hardly have been better. In August 1974 Norman Kirk had died and the Labour government, hit by a drastic fall in the terms of trade, was limping to its end under the desultory leadership of Wallace Rowling.

A loud-mouthed bully and former accountant, Robert Muldoon, had taken control of the National Party and in November 1975 he romped to power with a huge majority and the support of 'Rob's mob'. Very unhappy about the direction in which Muldoon promised to take the country, I had briefly joined the Labour Party and became part of the campaign team for Margaret Shields in her unsuccessful campaign for the Karori seat. Door-knocking was never my style, so once the election was over I resigned from the party but had in the *Listener* a gold-plated opportunity to say what I thought about the policies of the new Muldoon government. I did so, once a month, for the next two years (and then more occasionally under Tony Reid's editorship until 1980). Ian Cross himself was a politically conservative man, but he was committed to the cut and thrust of ideas and was happy to let me have my head. I was never once censored. Few of the editorials attacked Muldoon's policy and government directly. The notable exception was a piece entitled 'The Class of '21', which argued that Muldoon's national superannuation scheme represented an extravagant and self-interested shift of resources to older people, Muldoon's age, who believed they deserved universal super because of their struggles through Depression and war.[3] Muldoon himself was so stung that I became his target in his next *Truth* column, where he dismissed me as one of 'the half-baked trendy lefties'.[4]

More commonly I asked questions about the direction of his government by examining central New Zealand myths and beliefs. I tried to raise the debate to issues of national identity. Thus there were pieces about the death of the welfare state, the decline of an egalitarian society and, in response to Muldoon's appeal to the 'ordinary blokes', an essay on 'Unordinary Blokes' about the welcome diversity, both cultural and ethnic, which an urban society had brought to New Zealand.[5] When Muldoon attacked Colin Moyle with suggestions of homosexuality, I wrote a spirited piece about why New Zealand had been homophobic and that the country needed to move beyond this.[6] When protests erupted at the visit of a US warship, the *Truxtun*, I showed how the debate was between two national myths – New Zealanders as a warrior people, and New Zealand as an unspoilt Eden, the 'most beautiful country in the world'.[7] There were also editorials which examined New Zealanders' social behaviours and beliefs. In 'The Repressed' I suggested that we were overly keen to keep our emotions in check, only to discover six months later that Gordon McLauchlan had written a whole book on the subject, *The Passionless People*.[8]

Two of these explorations of national character led to worthwhile consequences. In 'Towards the Bush Garden' I suggested that historically 'the garden has represented "civilisation", a place to perpetuate the memories, the smells and the fruits of the old world', while the bush represented the reverse – 'savage nature, untamed wilderness, an anarchy which has to be conquered'. So native plants were kept out of the garden and criticised as unsuitable because they were slow-growing, lacked seasonal change and had boring flowers. I challenged such views as a form of 'horticultural imperialism' and suggested that the bush needed to find a home in the city garden.[9] The editorial captured the attention of a group of young landscape architects, just beginning to establish their profession. They invited me to speak at their annual conference in 1981, 'New Zealand, Where Are You?' The result was an address, subsequently published, entitled 'Fear and loathing in the New Zealand landscape'. The argument of the paper was simple. Beginning with an image of the world upside-down with New Zealand at its centre, I noted that traditional maps expressed 'northern hemisphere chauvinism' and that 'not until we stopped looking at ourselves and our land through the eyes of the northern hemisphere will we begin to live in some kind of permanent harmony with our landscape'. I quoted Robert Frost: 'The land was ours before we were the land's.' Because we took our duties, our history, our sense of beauty from Britain, we did not look upon the New Zealand landscape as a place of heritage and history but as a source of wealth and exploitation. I suggested that the land became a place to be tamed – rivers were not romantic streams but fearful places of danger; the bush was not a beautiful glade but a dark, frightening environment to be felled and transformed into English grasslands. I drew on nineteenth-century texts to illustrate this fear and loathing, and quoted Charlotte Godley: 'It is wonderful how completely the look of anything at all like home and its ways carries it here (and with nearly everyone) above novelty and actual beauty.'[10] I pointed to hopeful signs in the society, such as the bush garden, but wrote that the country faced an imminent threat to its landscape in the form of multinational businesses on the lookout for cheap resources.

It was presumably this last comment which then attracted the activists campaigning against the proposed aluminium smelter at Aramoana on Otago Harbour. I was invited down to talk at a rally at the site of the smelter. The occasion was not a roaring success for me. The numbers were not great, the wind was cold, and most people shivering on the sand could not hear a thing through the crackly sound system. I was singularly unconvincing, but I did meet some of the speakers, including a young lecturer in economics, Heather Simpson, later Helen Clark's assistant, and Molly Melhuish, the long-time energy activist. Further, my trip to Dunedin to talk about Aramoana offered an excuse on the previous afternoon to knock on the door of the artist Ralph Hotere. My companion on the trip, Chris Maclean, had heard that Hotere had erected an anti-Aramoana sculpture in his Port Chalmers garden. Sure enough, out in the garden was a huge construction in wood, which I later learned was the work of Chris Booth. Ralph, charming and welcoming, invited us to climb it, and when we reached the top there was a telescope focused on the Aramoana site – a stunning experience.

The association with the landscape architects continued. I spoke again at a subsequent conference ten years later, this time on 'Love and affection

The anti-Aramoana sculpture by Chris Booth which once stood in Ralph Hotere's garden, and is now in the Hotere Garden Oputae. SANDRA SIMPSON

in the New Zealand landscape', and I served for some years as a judge of the landscape architects' awards. My own award was to become an honorary life member of the New Zealand Institute of Landscape Architects. I treasured it at the time, and still do, for my writings about New Zealanders' attitudes to their land went to the very core of my being. They were a way of reconciling my cultural background and my experiences as a child on the land. Yet as I look at these jottings of an angry young man now, I am struck by the complete absence of any reference to Māori understandings of the land. Born to a Pākehā background I simply assumed at this stage that 'New Zealand' attitudes were represented by Pākehā attitudes.

The second *Listener* editorial which led to spin-offs was one entitled 'Gold Medals or Movies?' in 1977. The previous year at the Montreal Olympics, Australia had not won a single gold medal but New Zealand, to national delight, had won five. So my editorial began: 'Last year Australia won no Olympic gold medals, but produced a dozen full-length films. Evidence of national degeneracy perhaps . . . Whether we, sitting smugly with our gold medals but watching their films, can label it as decline is more questionable.' I went on to argue that sport was no longer a unifying symbol for a New Zealand becoming urban and diverse; and that we urgently needed to define ourselves through creative culture. I recycled my old argument that New Zealand intellectual life had turned away from the bush towards the traditions of aristocratic Europe:

> . . . our universities, the official seat of culture, were strong in the civilised graces, renaissance literature, medieval philosophy, the classical languages and pathetically weak in the sociology and history of New Zealand . . . It would be absurd to argue that such national self-consciousness should be the sole aim of every artist and writer in New Zealand. It is, however, probably true that without such a consciousness our culture will remain imitative and 'tasteful', sealed off from the dirt of experience which is the real source of inspiration.[11]

This led to an invitation to give a public address on this theme at the University of Waikato winter lectures in 1979. As early as 1974, just over a year after arriving back, I had joined Chris Wainwright, a young politics lecturer, to try to plan a conference on how to make the university and intellectual life 'more relevant to our lives'.¹² The effort at that time came to nought. Five years later speaking about the issue seemed a lot easier. So in 'Paradise by degrees', I spelled out my argument in greater detail. I claimed that in 1979 New Zealand faced two crises – a cultural crisis as the old certainties of the 1950s faced a noisy and diverse society, and an economic crisis following Britain's entry into the EEC. To respond to both crises the country needed intelligent debate and forceful analysis of the economic and social potential of New Zealand. Solutions would not come from cheap slogans but from the hard work of the intellect. The university had a central role at this juncture. In my view the university was not fitted for its task. Academia was divided between professionals like lawyers and doctors, who were keen to establish their expertise through exclusive methodologies, and the aesthetes teaching literature and the humanities, who were more focused on forms than content. Neither group, I suggested, was really capable of asking penetrating questions, and neither was primarily interested in New Zealand or its problems. They both yearned for international professional acceptance. I denied that my argument was a narrow cultural nationalism, since any study of New Zealand had to be informed by overseas scholarship and comparison, but I did ask for university scholars to start asking the big questions about their own society – about its history, its social structures, its mythologies. I called for the universities to lead a new cultural nationalism, 'one focused on the character and problems of New Zealand society, and one that does not just unearth facts, but presents usable hypotheses and broad visions'. The talk was well received, even by some in the university. It was reprinted in the Waikato student paper, was broadcast on national radio, and I received a warm letter from the director-general of education, Bill Renwick. But there was no evidence that it had much impact on the nature of academic life in New Zealand. It was as much a gospel for myself as for others.

Through the *Listener* editorials and the talks that followed from them, I began to become an engaged intellectual in New Zealand society; and there were other ways I played this role in the years after arriving back in New Zealand in 1973. Because Phillida and I had been appointed at Victoria in a shared role, this became of some public interest. The result was a number of newspaper stories and a television programme in which we were portrayed as a model of a modern 'liberated' couple who shared both occupational and domestic duties. I found myself arguing the case for men's responsibility to

An article in the Dominion, *16 June 1973, about Phillida and me sharing a job.*

make women's liberation possible. I took part in various protests on behalf of women, including one very rowdy night of placard-waving outside the site of the Miss New Zealand beauty contest.

I also became involved in fighting the extension of the motorway in Wellington and wrote a newspaper article about the importance of protecting inner-city Wellington as part of the country's urban heritage. I put energy into trying to preserve a historic building, the Skyline in Kelburn, and also led a movement to defend a university lecturer, Bob Rigg. He had been sacked from Waikato University for publicly claiming that students had died from cancer as a result of poor supervision in the university's isotope laboratory. The charges were later shown to be unfounded, but I considered it wrong for an academic's intellectual freedom to be compromised. In 1981 I inevitably got caught up in the protests against the Springbok tour, marching solemnly through the streets of Wellington on the day of every match, witnessing some

5 metres away the batoning of marchers in Molesworth Street on the night of Charles and Di's wedding, and acting as an 'under-officer' on the day of the Springbok test in Wellington.

In such ways I lived up to my emerging world view that the intellectual had a responsibility to use his or her abilities to improve and inform the society close at hand. Yet there remained an issue. In my professional academic job I was teaching and researching the history of the United States, not New Zealand. At the time this did not seem a problem. I threw myself into my teaching, attempting to make the history of the United States as exciting and meaningful to the students as possible. I would draw on the students' existing knowledge of America (I usually began my course by playing Jimi Hendrix's version of 'The Star-Spangled Banner' from Woodstock), and I would try to pull out many comparisons with New Zealand. When I came to talk about the American Revolution I would begin by describing the situation there in 1776, a description I also used in a *Listener* article on the occasion of the bicentenary in 1976:

> It was a country of about three million people, mostly Anglo-Saxon in stock. It had been settled for some 150 years, and had gradually come to conceive of itself as God's own country, a special and beautiful land free from European corruptions. It exported mainly agricultural goods and forest products, but it suffered from a perennial balance of payments problem, and its traditional trade with the mother-country, Great Britain, was faced with new and threatening restrictions.[13]

On one occasion I used the visit of a prominent American scholar to put together a two-day seminar on 'Why is there no socialism in the United States', hoping that this might tap into a question that many New Zealanders must have pondered. We did attract considerable interest, including attendance by the prominent union leader Ken Douglas.

I also tried to make my teaching lively and innovative. In place of the expected short ten-page essay and written examination, I experimented with assessing students in a face-to-face oral examination (building on my Harvard experience) and regularly assessed using longer research-based papers. In one interesting experiment I took all the honours students up to Bushy Park near Whanganui just before their final examinations. Over a residential weekend the students offered to teach each other about areas of knowledge in which they considered themselves well learned. Their final examinations were significantly improved. There were a number of highly creative colleagues who provided stimulation – Miles Fairburn then excitedly uncovering New Zealand social history, Peter Webster just completing a fascinating study of Rua Kēnana, and Colin Davis, a historian of seventeenth-century British intellectualism, but always interested in what was current in other forms of history. We had intense, often humorous, debates about history, usually New Zealand history.

Teaching and interactions with colleagues provided intellectual stimulus. But what of my own academic writing? Every summer I continued writing up my thesis on John Dewey. It was a long, pedestrian haul as I floundered with philosophical concepts at the limit of my understanding. However, I was keen to become accepted within the academic community by presenting papers at New Zealand historians' conferences and at American studies conferences held every two years. I particularly enjoyed the latter, which were held at various Australasian universities – Newcastle, Sydney, Melbourne and Christchurch. I developed close relationships with the other New Zealanders teaching American history – Erik Olssen in Otago, Jim Holt in Auckland and my old teacher John Salmond, who had moved to La Trobe in Melbourne – and also with two Aucklanders, Wystan Curnow and Roger Horrocks, who were teaching American literature at Auckland but were both intensely interested in New Zealand culture. I recall fierce discussions at these gatherings, especially at an Australian and New Zealand American Studies Association (ANZASA) conference in Sydney in 1980, where Jim Holt, by then an adviser to the shadow finance minister, Roger Douglas, presented a provocative view that the New Zealand economy had to be deregulated and freed of subsidies.

For these conferences I prepared papers on subjects which grew out of my thesis research. One on Jane Addams argued that Addams' social work in Chicago expressed a union of her father's example of public service and her mother's 'spiritual' feminine identity. It was published in the *History of Education Quarterly* as my first academic article. I also presented a provocative piece on 'Sex roles and the American intellectual'. This had grown out of my thesis on John Dewey, where I had argued that as an intellectual in the nineteenth-century United States the young Dewey had to deal with

A 1984 photo of Erik Olssen, who, like me, studied in the United States and then returned home to teach US and New Zealand history. He became professor of history at Otago University. An old friend and a fine historian.

a popular image of thinkers as 'effeminate', not hard-boiled men of action, and that his pragmatism was in part a response to this allegation. I decided to explore this idea in relation to other American writers, especially Ralph Waldo Emerson and the novelist Nathaniel Hawthorne. When I gave the paper it created considerable interest among two Australian teachers of American cultural history, Lucy Frost and Gay Fitzgerald. We decided to put together a volume on the sexual identity of American writers; and I spent one summer in Melbourne battling the incredible heat and working with them on this idea. Sadly it never came to fruition.

At the end of 1977 I went on leave to Boston with Phillida and our two young kids to finish the thesis. It was all written in longhand, and I had to then wait for it to be typed out and bound. The binding company was in central Boston and on the way back, before I went on to Cambridge to hand in the finished work by 5 p.m., I had to walk over a footbridge crossing Boston Harbour. I remember vividly, perhaps thinking of the American revolutionaries tossing tea into the same harbour in the Boston tea party, that I had an almost insatiable urge to toss the bound thesis into the water. Studying John Dewey had given me a valuable world view. It had imbued me with the vision that intellectual endeavours could not be an end in themselves; they needed to relate to the deeper problems of life in the social and cultural environment. But it had also been a long haul in which I felt too often out of my depth, and it had occupied my energies when I would rather have been investigating New Zealand's history. Soon after I returned, I went down to the university library and was glancing at the new-book section when I spied a title, *The Young John Dewey*. Shaking, I picked it up and began to leaf through the book. It had been recently published and I realised that its argument was identical to the main point of my thesis – that Dewey's philosophy had emerged as a response to his vocational crisis as a new society intellectual. Further, the key manuscript source which I had used to confirm my argument, the letters of Dewey's close friend George Mead, had been used extensively. I looked in the front of the book to scan the acknowledgements and there found the name of an American historian with whom I used to meet regularly and discuss my work while we were living in Northampton. I could never prove my suspicions of course, but I came to believe that my discovery of Mead's letters had been passed on to the author. I did try subsequently to get my thesis published but every press to whom I submitted it came back with the verdict that it essentially repeated a message that was already well covered in *The Young John Dewey*. The experience did more than anything to encourage me to draw a line on my academic life as a historian of the United States.

Further, while our leave in Boston had been fun and I had been impressed with the facilities provided for our two small children, it had also been hard work. 1977–78 was the worst winter in a century and we had two enormous snowfalls. There was also a muck-up with my pay, which had been sent by the bank to the Cambridge Trust rather than the Harvard Trust in Cambridge. We literally ran out of money, and with two small children in a ferocious winter, that was not a happy experience. We survived only by persuading a friend to lend us something. I remember a sense of resentment against American privilege and inequality made manifest one day when I was pushing the children along the road between the mounds of snow and a huge car came round the corner and drenched us all with a shower of snowy spray. I wrote back to my mother, 'America seems like a rather cruel and ruthless capitalist world.'[14]

The title illustration for my article about our time in Cambridge, Massachusetts, which appeared in the New Zealand Listener *on 27 January 1979. The piece was in effect a farewell to America.*

When I returned I wrote a piece for the *Listener*, 'Come into my Parlour, said the 70s to the 60s', which took off from a strike at Steve's ice-cream parlour in Cambridge and described how the cooperative egalitarian ideals of the 1960s had become the capitalist ambitions of the 1970s. The counterculture turned out to be just 'another turn of the Madison Avenue wheel'.[15] The United States had lost its allure.

Returning from leave, I determined to become more seriously a New Zealand historian. While on leave I had continued to toy with the possibility of an American career, but I wrote to my parents, 'Ultimately I feel that I could do more for New Zealand society by going back and in the end count for more, than by becoming a minor professional in America.'[16] In 1979 I proposed an honours course on New Zealand intellectual history, but this was turned down by the department on the grounds that I had been appointed as 'an Americanist'. I then tried to promote the idea that the comparative study of new societies should become a serious academic subject. To this end I tried to organise a seminar along these lines using comparisons between the United States, Australia and New Zealand. I wrote in the call for papers: 'The new world comparison really does provide a more coherent framework for New Zealand historians than the old imperial network; and ... is the only way to get New Zealand historiography into an international debate.'[17] The call fell on deaf ears.

Instead I looked at reshaping my third-year course on American intellectual history. Ever since I had arrived, the theme of that course had been the relationship between the ideas of American thinkers and their social role. I now refocused it onto the issue of intellectual life in new societies. The starting point was the argument, well articulated in Richard Hofstadter's book *Anti-intellectualism in American Life*, that in colonial societies where the priority was the quick exploitation of the frontier, intellectual life was seen as an unnecessary luxury, the beleaguered remnant of European culture in a new world of progress and action. We then looked at different ways in which intellectuals in new societies had tried to adjust to this situation and define a philosophy and world view for the life of the mind. We looked at the thinkers of the American Revolution, such as Thomas Jefferson and James Madison, and suggested that in framing the politics of a new society, thinkers could play a determinative role – and we drew comparisons with the place of William Pember Reeves in the Liberal government of the 1890s. We examined my old hero, Henry David Thoreau, and discussed the idea that the natural world provided a distinctive focus for cultural life in new societies. We compared Thoreau's *Walden* with Herbert Guthrie-Smith's classic *Tutira*, and we pointed to the long tradition of landscape painting in New Zealand, Australia and the United States. We studied the *Bulletin* school of writers and creative artists which emerged in Sydney in the 1890s. For these people, such as short-story writer Henry Lawson, poet Banjo Paterson and the Heidelberg school of painters, cultural nationalism took the form of an admiration for bush life in the Australian outback, summed up in the famous description of Joseph Furphy's novel *Such is Life*: 'temper democratic, bias offensively Australian'.

There were other examples – Dewey's pragmatism of course, the documentary tradition of 1930s America, and the New Zealand nationalist poets of the 1930s and 1940s.

The example that began to interest me were those writers and artists in New Zealand at the end of the nineteenth century who conceived of New Zealand culture as 'Maoriland' culture. This included historians like James Cowan, poets and novelists like Arthur Adams, composers like Alfred Hill, artists like Charles Goldie. These intellectuals argued that Māori culture was distinctive to New Zealand and could form the basis of a lively national tradition. Of course this did not mean that they learnt or spoke te reo, or looked to traditional Māori carving as the basis for modern New Zealand art. It was rather that the 'dying Māori' provided a romantic subject-matter and a picturesque addition to 'beautiful New Zealand', and the 'myths and legends' of Māori offered an instant mythology and history for a 'new' land. The more I studied this material the more interested I became. I relished the range of media and cultural forms involved – literature, art, history, opera, and eventually, with Rudall Hayward, film – and I thought that it was an unusual path to national traditions for a colonial society. I decided that there was a book to be written here. I did a trial run by putting together an article, 'Musings in Maoriland – or was there a *Bulletin* school in New Zealand?'[18] The article explored whether at the turn of the twentieth century New Zealanders had participated in the *Bulletin* school, and then decided that in fact Maoriland became, for them, far more important a focus than the bush. Interestingly I chose to publish the article not in a New Zealand journal, but in *Historical Studies*, the leading Australian history journal, because I saw the subject as having interest at a comparative level for intellectual historians of any new society. Not many Australians noticed the piece; but it was certainly picked up in New Zealand. To my thrill I received a warm letter of congratulation from the doyen of New Zealand cultural history, E. H. McCormick,[19] and over the next twenty years a number of New Zealand scholars far more versed in this tradition than myself, people like the literary historian Mark Williams and the art historian Roger Blackley, drew on the article for context. Sadly other books prevented me ever completing the planned volume of my own, but at least I had established a foothold in the writing of academic New Zealand history. Further, I examined the students in this third-year course on the basis of a research exercise in New Zealand intellectual history, using primarily the great resources of the Alexander Turnbull Library and drawing on the historiographical insights from American and Australian writing. Some of those students continued on in the area, most notably Rachel Barrowman, author of a path-breaking book on New Zealand culture in the 1930s and then biographies of R. A. K. Mason and Maurice Gee.

In the early 1980s there was another way I used my academic position to contribute to New Zealand history. The 1981 Springbok rugby tour split New Zealand society. In a remarkable series of protests, opponents of apartheid South Africa expressed their displeasure at the presence of that regime on our sporting fields. The game in Hamilton was cancelled, protesters' heads were bashed in front of my eyes at Molesworth Street, and the tour continued only because Robert Muldoon marshalled a huge police presence to ensure that rugby could be played. New Zealanders battled physically and verbally with fellow New Zealanders. It rapidly became clear that this was not simply a dispute over South Africa; it was an argument about the identity, the soul of the country. I had begun to research and write about the place of rugby in the New Zealand psyche, so I rapidly became convinced that the tour and the ritualistic protests (which remarkably caused no deaths) were a defining moment in the history of the country. I became interested in which social groups were fighting each other. On the last protest march in Wellington I gathered a group of students and we distributed questionnaires, asking people about their age, educational level, occupation and social attitudes.

In 1981 the New Zealand economy was in a sorry state, and there were few jobs available for students over the summer. The government decided to offer students temporary positions on projects of community service. Immediately I realised that this provided the possibility for research into the Springbok tour. I managed to garner the support of my colleagues in the history department, Peter McPhee, David Mackay and Malcolm McKinnon, and we applied to the Labour Department to hire a dozen students on this scheme. To my surprise the application succeeded. Over the summer the students put together an archive of materials about the tour. The topics included the membership and strategy of the Wellington anti-tour organisation COST; the roles of the media, church, unions and both major political parties; the participation of women and Māori; and the attitudes of the Rugby Union and the police. Many scrapbooks of newspaper clippings, memoranda and pamphlets, and over 100 oral histories, were collected and deposited in the university library. At the end of the project the students wrote up essays on their research which we then published under the title *Counting the Cost*.[20] I worked with a student, Peter King, to find out more about who the protesters actually were. We supplemented the survey from the last march with a second survey of those on the COST mailing list. The findings showed that the protesters were overwhelmingly under the age of 40, were tertiary-educated and, if not students, belonged to the caring or teaching professions, rather than to the world of law or business. The comments from those who had filled in the survey also showed that many people had marched as much because they were hostile to the dominance of male culture and rugby football in New Zealand identity, as out of concern about apartheid. One woman wrote: 'I have for years resented the dominance that rugby has in the homes, schools and society in general. It's time that a few other values took over from bloody rugby.' Another simply said, 'Bugger rugger'.[21] The insights gained in this research stayed with me, encouraging later work on New Zealand in the second half of the twentieth century.

While I was able to smuggle some New Zealand history research into my university teaching responsibilities, I realised that if I was to do major book-length work then this had to be done outside the academy. In the years after getting back from leave and completing my thesis until the mid-1980s, I worked on two books – one on domestic stained-glass windows and a second on Kiwi men. The stained-glass book grew indirectly out of two friendships. The first was with my former Weir House room-mate from the United States, Frank Stone, with his flourishing studio in Minneapolis making leaded windows, where I had visited him and been impressed by the lifestyle. The second was with Chris Maclean. When I returned to New Zealand and began teaching I quickly developed close relationships with my students. I was only 25 and had far more in common with a number of students than with my colleagues. Some of these friendships, such as those with Charlotte Macdonald, Jamie Belich, Kerry Taylor, Caroline Daley and Ben Schrader, primarily flourished because we talked history. They learnt from me and I learnt significantly from them. Others became close personal friends. Chris Maclean was one of these. He was a good student but I quickly found that our interests out of school drew us together. We both enjoyed tramping in the hills; we both enjoyed music; and Chris was as committed to exploring New Zealand and its history as I was. But on leaving university he drifted for a while and then set off overseas. At my suggestion he spent time with Frank Stone working in his Minneapolis studio. When Chris returned to Wellington he decided to replicate Frank's lifestyle and began a business making leaded windows. Soon afterwards we decided one night to go looking at leaded windows in Wellington. We drove down The Terrace and realised that the windows were far more interesting than we had expected. That experience convinced us that there was a book in the story of New Zealand domestic stained glass.

The project had attractions for me. It would require us to travel throughout New Zealand in the hunt for windows; it would uncover an architectural detail that had not been documented before and would teach us about the wider history of domestic architecture; it drew on Chris's glass knowledge and my historical background; and it would require us to take a lot of photos, which we both enjoyed. I also liked the fact that the study was not about traditional high culture but about one of the crafts, which had been so ignored in writings previously. Anything we did would break new ground. We did a first trial in Whanganui and quickly developed a technique. We would drive around the suburban streets at night spotting windows lit up from inside. The next day we would return to photograph them in daylight from inside the house. Normally we received a warm reception with cups of tea and scones offered by the proud owners. Only in Auckland did those answering the door breathe suspicion and assume that we were casing their joint. I applied for and we were given $2000 from the Turnbull Library for the travel expenses, so long as they received all the slides.

Every few months we hit the road to explore the windows of a region of the country. We had some marvellous moments of discovery. I recall particularly the flowing art-nouveau windows that adorned a mansion on the hill above Whanganui on that very first trip; the bizarre 'devil's window' in a Victorian mansion in Roslyn, Dunedin by the country's first glass painter, Robert Fraser; the striking clear glass art-deco windows, often using the sun motif, which we found, to our astonishment, in Hamilton. We also met some highly creative modern artists in glass, especially a very clever designer, James Walker. It became clear that few of the windows were distinctive to New Zealand. They followed international styles, and emphasised clearly the extent to which New Zealand was a colonial province when it came to domestic design. We looked long and hard to find local elements and were

My friendship with Chris Maclean began with our shared enthusiasm for New Zealand history, but we bonded on tramps and in working together on the book about New Zealand stained glass. Here Chris is about to photograph the wreck of a DC-3 on Mt Richmond, on a tramp we did together about 1976 (above); and working on a stained-glass window – in this case repairing the windows from Robert and Anna Stout's house on The Terrace, Wellington, which were subsequently installed in the Stout Centre (below).
JOCK PHILLIPS, PRIVATE COLLECTION; JIM WILSON

overjoyed when native plants or Māori designs appeared in the windows, but this was rare. In this respect my nationalistic yearnings were frustrated.

Yet the research for *In the Light of the Past*, as the book was eventually called, did foster my discovery of New Zealand in another ways. It led us to explore cityscapes and to develop a rich knowledge of domestic architecture and the history of decorative style (in which we were hugely helped by the exhaustive knowledge of a great Wellington eccentric and collector, Walter Cook), and we met an interesting cross-section of New Zealanders. While we worked hard driving the streets and interviewing former glass workers, there was time for other pursuits. Chris had a huge knowledge of New Zealand from boyhood travels with his family, and we had the guidance of Diana and Jeremy Pope's wonderful Mobil guides to the North and South Islands, which had first appeared in the mid-1970s. These magnificent volumes documented in loving detail the localities of New Zealand, with special attention to historical sites. We followed their suggestions religiously. And when there were not untouched townships to explore or old churches to visit, the land offered other options – we would take time off for a short tramp, or spend the afternoon at the beach bodysurfing. With Chris as a generous and informed companion, these journeys through New Zealand in the search for interesting windows enriched my knowledge of, and love for, New Zealand in all its cultural and regional variety.

In the Light of the Past had a somewhat fraught birth. A muck-up in the design process meant that the cover image, a detail of one of Robert Fraser's windows, was drawn from a back-up slide and was slightly out of focus. Then the photo proofs were lost, the printing press in China broke down, the ship was delayed and the very day the books finally arrived in Auckland the warehousemen went on strike. The delays meant that the bulk of the copies did not make it into the shops in time for Christmas 1983. When we finally launched the book in mid-December, it turned out to be a traumatic occasion. Several months earlier, my brother-in-law, David Caffin, who at the time was New Zealand's high commissioner to Western Samoa, had been diagnosed with stomach cancer, and by this time he was close to the end of his life. I was spending as much time as possible supporting my sister Elizabeth through the ordeal, and my mother had flown from England. I was already stressed. Then we decided to hold the event at a private house, Carrigafoyle, which turned out to be an unfortunate choice. The house had some magnificent windows we had first seen during that initial night-time foray along Wellington's The Terrace. Rex Nicholls had bought the house with our encouragement and was a willing host. But he had also become a city councillor and had just joined the majority on council voting to give money for the Miss World contest to come to Wellington. When we arrived at Carrigafoyle for the launch, there to greet us was a protest group carrying banners and chanting aggressively about Rex's attack on women's rights. It was embarrassing for me and Chris; it was even more embarrassing for Phillida, who knew many of those on the picket line. The evening was saved from disaster only by an excellent launching speech from James Mack, director of the Dowse Art Museum and a great supporter of the project, and by the fact that when Phillida and I returned home there on

The stained-glass project had its highs and lows. The windows of Carrigafoyle on The Terrace in Wellington (left) first attracted Chris Maclean and me to the idea of recording domestic windows; the house was also the site of the painful launch of the completed book. Here (right) I am trying to take a good photo of a window in the Northern Cemetery in Dunedin in June 1981 without falling flat on my back. ALEXANDER TURNBULL LIBRARY, PA12-1442_02; CHRIS MACLEAN

the doorstep was a huge bowl of flowers, a glorious apology from the feminists who had greeted us.

In the end the book sold relatively well, and was widely and positively reviewed with the notable exception of a ferocious attack in the *Listener* by a Christchurch woman who was a specialist in ecclesiastical, not domestic, windows, but still felt the need to patch-protect. It was ignored by the academic community, who regarded domestic glass as not worthy of a serious historical study. But from my perspective it was a success. With Chris I had published my first book, and I had made a contribution to uncovering a novel element of New Zealand's culture.

The second venture 'out of school' was a history of the Kiwi male stereotype. This had a long gestation. There was my initial realisation while in the United States that the extent of gender separation was so much greater at home than among my friends in Boston. Then after meeting and marrying Phillida I had read widely in contemporary feminism and thought a good deal about how men should respond to the challenge of women's claims for equality. I also found myself talking about New Zealand men and the bizarre nature of a rugby scrum on Brian Edwards' Saturday night talk-show on the new South Pacific Television. To help the two of us think about what a 'liberated' partnership might look like, we met regularly with some other Wellington couples who were also working through the issue. The 'family group', as it was called, shared childcare and we would meet once a week for a family dinner together. The members were all educated and highly talented people including Tom Scott, just beginning his cartoon career, and his partner, the union activist Christine Gillespie; Robert Beaglehole and his lively wife, Ruth Bonita, who both became prominent public-health activists; my old school friend Michael Keith, who was at the time in charge of School Publications, and his wife Gerry, a distinguished psychologist. Some of us then went on to meet as a group of men to talk through what it was to be a modern man. Another who joined us was Geoff Walker, later editor at Penguin Books. In 1982 I spent my thirty-fifth birthday at a memorable weekend at Tauhara, near Taupō, where a group of four men calling themselves 'FOR*MEN' organised two days of workshops and interactive sessions about appropriate styles of masculinity in modern New Zealand. The workshop was 'designed to support the movement of men in New Zealand away from the masculine stereotype'.[22] One of the 'FOR*MEN' collective, Garth Baker, became one of my closest friends.

Another significant friendship was Phillida's close relationship with Sandra Coney. Out of this emerged their path-breaking investigation of 'The unfortunate experiment' by Dr Herbert Green at National Women's Hospital, which caused a storm when published in *Metro* and revolutionised the relationship of doctors and patients, especially women.[23] Over several summers Sandra Coney invited the two of us to share a week on board the yacht of her partner, Peter Hosking. Sailing round the Bay of Islands and then out to the Cavalli Islands and Whangaroa Harbour, eating the scallops freshly caught by Peter, and talking to all hours was another experience that inevitably enriched my understanding of gender in New Zealand. Nor was this interest purely theoretical. On several occasions I joined women on picket lines. I also found myself leading discussions at a sexual-harassment conference in Wellington and a male-studies day held by the Auckland WEA.

This day-to-day thinking about gender obviously informed my work on Kiwi men; but what turned it in the direction of writing a book was a conversation with Phoebe Meikle. She had been for twenty-five years a school teacher and then became an editor, succeeding Janet Paul, at Longman Paul. In the 1950s she had written a piece in *Landfall* about men and women in New Zealand, in which she argued that the two genders inhabited separate spheres in the country. I had read and admired her article and was somewhat amazed that she had chosen, presumably for her own self-protection, to publish it under the pseudonym of 'Leslie Hall'. One day in the late 1970s I met her at a lunchtime social occasion. I immediately expressed my enthusiasm for her article. She shot back, 'Well, why don't you write a book about Kiwi men?' The moment she said it, I knew she was right. I had been wrestling personally for half a dozen years with my background as a New Zealand male and thinking about how to reshape it. The book would help me, as much as others. I had now completed my PhD, with its sad consequence that had turned me firmly away from American history. The stained-glass windows book was a gentle step into New Zealand history, but it would never be a major contribution. A book on Kiwi men promised to throw me into the very centre of New Zealand identity and social history. I realised that some of the obvious subjects – the place of alcohol, the social history of rugby, the experience of soldiers in war, the nature of the Kiwi family – were all big topics which at that stage were remarkably untouched by serious historians, who were more interested in either politics or race relations.

Although as an 'Americanist' I was firmly told that I could not teach such a topic in the university, I was able to explore the subject in two other ways. For about four years I taught a continuing-education course on the history of New Zealand males. The participants included several people who became good friends, such as Dave Kent, a brilliant graphic artist, and Jonathon Besser, a highly creative composer. The last year was, somewhat controversially, a class exclusively for men because I had discovered previously that women were filling up the course and I wanted to get men's feedback. I tried out my ideas, and discovered which topics worked and which did not. The classes were more enjoyable because I invited visitors to add to the discussion – Ken Gray, towering All Black front-row forward, came and talked about what went on in the back seat of the All Blacks bus; Les Cleveland, plus guitar, talked about the culture of Kiwi soldiers. During the session on rugby I would invite people in the class to pack down in a scrum, women against men. The women would inevitably lift up their heads at the end and comment 'Now I understand footie', but it was slightly embarrassing when I invited one woman in the class to be 'the hooker'!

My other source of intellectual stimulus came from my fourth-year honours course on the American family. This kept me in touch with international writing about women, and, to the extent that it was happening, on men. As I wrote in the bibliographical essay of *A Man's Country?*, 'The intellectual framework was set by feminist scholarship', and I went on to cite works by Shulamith Firestone, Kate Millett, Nancy Chodorow and Ann Douglas, all of whom were American academics. My American history training paid off in the end. I had been particularly stimulated by an article by Carol Smith-Rosenberg, 'The Female World of Love and Ritual', which used women's letters to suggest there was a nineteenth-century women's culture with its own language and set of rituals that was quite separate from the culture of men. This led me to think about the possibility that in colonial New Zealand and thereafter there might have been a separate male world of swearing, drinking and fisticuffs. So it proved.

I had planned six chapters in the book, so each year in the period between marking examinations in November and the start of the new teaching year, I would research the material for one chapter, then write it up during the year. The research was exciting – the first chapter, on colonial men, allowed me to read most nineteenth-century New Zealand novels; I also started analysing the census, discovering the major surplus of adult men compared to women, which seemed crucial in explaining the origins of the New Zealand male culture. For the chapter on alcohol I read all the debates in parliament about prohibition and realised how far the movement, and even women's suffrage, represented an attack on male frontier culture. For the chapter on rugby I relied heavily on newspaper accounts of the All Black touring teams, supplemented by players' memoirs.

When it came to the Kiwi experience at war I began reading the diaries and letters of New Zealand soldiers, which had been collected by Jim Traue, chief librarian of the Alexander Turnbull Library, in response to an early-1970s visit from Peter Liddle to obtain such material from New Zealand families and take them to Britain. The moment I encountered the diaries I was hooked. I had started reading them because I wanted to find evidence of how determinative the male stereotype had been in encouraging New Zealand men to enlist and fight. What I found stunned me. I discovered that in fact the 'official' legend had not lasted, and that many soldiers had become very cynical about the experience of war. I found this so engrossing that I ended up spending two years on that chapter and getting together material for at least one more book. I also read newspaper coverage of the South African War, and exhaustively read many files, mainly about World War I, in the National Archives, as well as many published novels and memoirs from World War II. Finally the chapter on the family led me into looking at popular magazines with their cartoons and short stories. In sum the research for the book was exciting and gave me a solid grounding in a very wide range of the sources available in Wellington.

In writing up this material, I made three decisions. First, this would be a history of the male stereotype, not male behaviour. I realised that the stereotype was what limited men's range of human possibilities. It was a model that they dare not challenge. Simply discussing the image of the male would provide relief. Further, it was much easier from literary sources, especially newspapers, to define the stereotype, whereas what Kiwi men were actually like was a much more difficult and potentially never-ending task. Second, I decided that the subject matter would be primarily the Pākehā stereotype. The history of the male role in Māori society was a huge subject. I had no background in the study of Māori society, and I could not read te reo Māori. I realised that the image of the Kiwi man had been forged primarily from Anglo-Saxon sources, particularly the traditions brought from the United Kingdom and reinforced by British writings. This was not to say that the stereotype had not affected Māori, and at the end of the book I did claim that Māori participation in the Kiwi male legend, especially in rugby and war, had been one factor in establishing the myth of great race relations in New Zealand. Michael King in his review of the book criticised me for confining my treatment to Pākehā, but in my defence, I did acknowledge this, and the subtitle became 'the image of the Pakeha male – a history'. The third decision was to introduce each chapter with a personal reminiscence. One reason for this was simply that I thought it would attract readers and bring the book to life. I also wanted readers to be aware of my own personal background so that they could judge my conclusions with this in mind. I had learnt from the feminist dictum that 'the personal is political', and had become very sceptical of historians' claim to objectivity. Behind that supposed objectivity lay hidden personal judgements and self-interest. I was keen to be quite explicit about my own point of view and thus challenge the 'objective' model. I hoped the book would not only contribute to New Zealand historiography, but would also give support to New Zealand men wanting more diverse options and would help women understand their menfolk. In the event these personal reminiscences became the most popular sections of the book.

A Man's Country? was not published until 1987 – I received the first advance copy on my fortieth birthday. There was much to-ing and fro-ing with Geoff Walker at Penguin about editorial matters and a major fight over the cover illustration, which I detested, especially since I had set my heart on a Nigel Brown image of a mournful Kiwi bloke in a black singlet. But the book was well received. I was flown from one end of the country to another to talk on radio shows and chat to newspaper reporters, and reviewers were generally kind, with two exceptions. Warwick Roger in *Metro* went to the defence of the Kiwi bloke, and the review in the *New Zealand Journal of History* was extremely critical. There were two elements here. One was that some months earlier Keith Sinclair had published his history of New Zealand identity, *A Destiny Apart*. It included some adequate material on the history of rugby and of New Zealanders at war. Annoyed that I had been gazumped, I grumpily and unwisely criticised the book in a review for the *Dominion*, pointing out that the great historian had even misspelt the famous battle of Le Quesnoy in a chapter heading. Sinclair had actually been very supportive

Kicking the Kiwi bloke about 1985 (above) CHRIS MACLEAN; *and two years later at the centre of the scrum when* A Man's Country? *was being promoted (below).*

when I had delivered a paper to the New Zealand historians' conference in 1982 on 'Rugby, war and the mythology of the New Zealand male'. He was enthusiastic at the time and made it the lead article in the journal soon after. But to criticise him in public was too much, so when my book was reviewed in his journal I was appropriately lambasted. It was tit for tat. There was another element here. For some years professional academic historians of New Zealand did not quite know what to make of the book. It opened up areas which had previously been outside the canon, and the subjective elements were disconcerting to many professional historians who still believed in the cult of objectivity. For some time the book was far more often cited by sociologists and literary critics than historians.

Although the book was not published for another three years, I essentially completed *A Man's Country?* in 1984. In the same year I became the inaugural director of the Stout Research Centre for the study of New Zealand society, history and culture. In the eleven years since I had arrived back in New Zealand I had weaned myself off American history, discovered New Zealand and begun to write about it. First through *Listener* editorials, then two books, I had gradually established a role as a well-known writer, and historian, about the country. It was now time to institutionalise this, and make it possible for others to write about New Zealand.

6
The Stout Centre

In May 1983 I wrote to my parents describing a highly successful New Zealand historians' conference in Auckland and expressing my enthusiasm at 'just what a lively field New Zealand history has suddenly become'. I went on to say, 'My next project is an effort to follow up this revival in New Zealand history by establishing a research institute based in Wellington.'[1] Ever since I had met Jim Holt in my first year at Harvard and heard about his time at Harvard's Charles Warren Center for American History I had been excited about such institutions. I was hugely impressed by the programme of seminars and the publications promoted by the centre. To be among a group of scholars all sharing a similar intellectual focus seemed like nirvana, and I longed to have my own time at such a centre. It never happened overseas. But the idea hung around. The more interested I became in the study of New Zealand, the more I saw the need to encourage scholarly research in the country's history, society and culture. I had a number of conversations with the chief librarian of the Alexander Turnbull Library, Jim Traue, and he too was frustrated at the lack of use by scholars of the library's extraordinary collections. I became convinced that Wellington, with the Turnbull Library, the National Archives and the research community spawned by government departments, was the obvious location for a centre of New Zealand studies. There were increasing numbers of overseas people, especially Americans, wanting to explore New Zealand subjects. They might find a home in such a centre. And from my journalism and public lectures I retained an instinct to reach out to the wider community.

Hard at research in the National Archives in the 1980s. CHRIS MACLEAN

I was hopeful that a new centre might bring scholars outside the university into its fold.

There were also push factors. I used to say that the main reason I started the Stout Centre was because I was scared of earthquakes and I wanted to move out of the top floor of the Rankine Brown building where the history department had its offices. It was only half a joke. More seriously, I had become increasingly demoralised by my experiences within the department. I had always been a bit of a rebel in its ranks – the long-haired critic and spawner of mad ideas. This had been fine while I was the youngest and newest lecturer, and could grumble away with Miles Fairburn, another malcontent. But by the mid-1980s I had been teaching for ten years, and I was beginning to have ambitions of leadership. I had developed reasonably intelligent and well-formed ideas about the way history should be communicated to students and I was naturally keen to try them out. I came up with a proposal for a reorientation of all the undergraduate courses, so that instead of teaching national histories we would teach problems and bring in examples from a range of cultures. The study of New Zealand's past would inform and be informed by international debates. That was far too radical for colleagues who had their store of lectures about Australian history or British history or medieval history, and did not want to rework everything and read 'outside their field'. Then, drawing on my Harvard experience, I proposed a new system of honours courses so that instead of simply offering more surveys, we should see the honours year as a way of training professional historians. Two types of skill would be developed – a self-consciousness about historiography, theory and methodology; and research methods such as how to use archives, how to organise primary material, how to write up the fruits of research in an engaging way. My scheme envisaged a core methodology course taught by all members of the department, and a series of research exercises. The idea was flatly rejected.

I also found that my aspirations to move increasingly into New Zealand history and away from US history were thwarted on the grounds that American history was very popular; so I could not afford to stop teaching it. There were a series of tense and bitter conflicts within the department over workloads and appointments; and I was nearly always one of an increasingly frustrated minority, along with Malcolm McKinnon, a young historian of New Zealand, and Peter McPhee, an Australian and a very fine historian of France. Peter was my closest colleague.

In the 1980s I was fortunate to have a few very congenial colleagues in the history department at Victoria University. They included Malcolm McKinnon and Douglas Newton, seen here with me in December 1985 (above); and I photographed Peter McPhee on a walk at Mākara Beach (below). Peter, from Melbourne and an outstanding historian of France, was my closest ally in the department.

As I noted in a submission to the university's review of the position of professor, we had a dysfunctional system of power and rewards in universities at that time. Professors were appointed for life, were given a prestigious title and paid infinitely more money, yet they no longer functioned as they once had as 'god-professors', with responsibility for administering departments and providing intellectual leadership. Instead we elected chairs of departments, usually not of professorial status, and there was a real lack of clarity as to where the intellectual leadership came from.[2] It was immensely frustrating for a young person with ideas such as myself. I also found that there was a disappointing lack of support from colleagues when it came to one's own research and writing. Rarely did they engage with you about an article or book you had published – I never once had a good conversation about *A Man's Country?*, for example. There was a real lack of clarity as to what success meant in the academic world. If you were a good teacher, this was dismissed as simply kowtowing to students; if you were a successful researcher, your lack of commitment to teaching and administration was raised; and if you spent energy administering the department or university, this was regarded as the refuge of failed scholars. So the culture of a university department began to pall. I realised that a research centre could create a community for myself and others which was supportive and committed to a sharing of learning and the process of intellectual discovery.

In addition, the more I threw myself into the study of New Zealand the more horrified I became by the lack of serious study of the subject within the university. In a submission in the mid-1980s to a review of New Zealand universities I pointed out that the university presses had made great progress in their willingness to publish scholarly monographs about the country, and there were now professional journals such as the *New Zealand Journal of History*, as well as journals of literature and educational studies. But the teaching of New Zealand material in the humanities subjects like English literature, or the social sciences like sociology and geography, remained very spotty. I commented on the striking absence of 'Maori people teaching in departments other than Maori Studies'.[3] A particular deficiency was the lack of institutional support for research into local topics. Two universities (out of six) made it almost impossible for university teachers to take their refresher/research leave within New Zealand, and others penalised them if they wanted to do so. Even if academics did want to stay in the country and research, there was no place for them to go; nor was there a suitable centre for overseas scholars to base themselves.

So the vision that lay behind the Stout Centre was well expressed in the proposal I put up to the university's Professorial Board in mid-1983. The main purpose of the new institute, I wrote, 'would be to encourage scholarly research into New Zealand society, history and culture, and to provide a centre for that personal contact and exchange of ideas which enrich the quality of research'. I pointed to the growing interest by scholars, both local and overseas, in researching New Zealand subjects and the need for 'a prestigious research institution' to provide a home for such people. I noted the obvious advantages of Wellington as the location, because of the research resources of the various archives and libraries. I also argued that the institute should be consciously interdisciplinary and attract a range of scholars 'from literary critics and historians to sociologists, educationalists and anthropologists'. I cited the models provided by the Humanities Research Centre in Canberra and the Institute for Advanced Study at Princeton. The institute, I noted, would provide scholars with a study, secretarial support and 'a locus for the exchange of ideas'. It would host seminars and conferences and sponsor publications.

With this vision in my head, I started to promote it. My first visit was to the new vice-chancellor of the university, Ian Axford. Axford, born in Dannevirke, had gone on to have a stellar academic career as a space scientist, which culminated in him becoming director of the Max Planck Institute for Solar System Research in Germany. In 1982 he decided to come back home as the new vice-chancellor at Victoria. His ambition was to turn Victoria into a research-based institution, and when I went to see him he had just moved to a remodelled office at one corner of the campus, positioned with a view down Waiteata Rd. He hoped that before long he would be able to gaze down on the road which would be lined with a series of research institutes. I knew none of this when I went to see him, but immediately when I raised the idea of a centre for research into New Zealand, his face lit up and he pointed to a house two doors up from his lookout: 'Well, you can have that house,' he said. He knew nothing about New Zealand society or history; he had little interest in the details of how my proposed centre might work, but it fulfilled his requirements. It was a research centre which would attract scholars from overseas. I walked out of the meeting stunned. I had a building. It was not perfect – it was an old residential house, and it needed about $100,000 of work, including creating a seminar room. But the promise of money for the upgrade and fit-out came with the offer of the building.

This was a remarkable, and surprising, start to my plans – and with a building secured and the support of the vice-chancellor, it was not long before others came into line. The arts faculty endorsed the idea, the Professorial Board supported it, and at the end of November 1983 the University Council gave it the go-ahead. Nor was this all. I had worried from the outset that we might find a building but how could we attract scholars without offering some support? One day I was talking over the matter with the university librarian, David Wylie, and he replied that he was a member of the Stout Trust, which had been set up from the estate of John David Stout, a research scientist and grandson of Victoria University founder Robert Stout. He suggested that I apply to the Stout Trust for support. Little did I know that my earliest supporter, Jim Traue, was also a trustee. Before long we had been offered one fully funded fellowship, available annually at a senior lecturer's level. I also wrote to the minister of internal affairs, Allan Highet, seeking support and received $15,000 from lottery funds. It had all been astonishingly easy. I wrote to my parents in July 1983, 'The N.Z. Studies proposal has taken off with quite amazing speed and enthusiasm from other people . . . It was a dream which I thought might come to fruition in about five years' time – and now it seems likely to start next year.' I decided to delay my overseas leave with the possibility of becoming director.

It was not all plain sailing. I had always assumed that any centre for New Zealand studies should have substantial Māori involvement. But I was naïve in dealing with this. What I should have done was pay a visit to Sidney Mead, professor of Māori studies, and get him and his colleagues on board from the start. I did not. Instead I decided to try to signal Māori involvement by adopting a Māori name. I turned to my old friend Michael King, who was at the time the university's writing fellow, and asked for his suggestion. He suggested that it be called a wānanga, a traditional Māori learning centre and a name being adopted at that time by Māori universities. With this in mind I invited Sid Mead to come to the new house and discuss how we might work together and what the centre might be called. In retrospect it was also somewhat of an affront on my part to invite him there rather than meeting on his turf. When we met, Professor Mead was polite. We began with the name. He initially suggested the Kumutoto Centre, referring to the stream which had once flowed down the valley close by, emptying into the harbour at Woodward Street. It may be that secretly Professor Mead enjoyed the thought that the meaning of the new centre was 'bloody anus'. I later joked about the 'flaming arseholes centre for New Zealand studies'! When I suggested the word 'wānanga' and he asked where that suggestion came from, the answer 'Michael King' did not go down at all well. Some years before I had reviewed Michael's biography of Te Puea Hērangi in the *Listener* and had praised it as elevating a new heroine into the New Zealand pantheon. Professor Mead had replied in a letter to the editor that it was time Māori, not Pākehā, historians, wrote their own history and biographies. So my continued relationship with Michael was not helpful. Mead then told me the story of the kahawai and the shark. He said that the Pākehā in the centre would be like the shark, Māori like the kahawai. Inevitably, as the larger fish, the shark would swallow the kahawai. Maori concerns and interests would disappear. He noted that before long Māori scholars in the university would set up their own Māori studies research centre. This discussion was reflected in a statement that we included in the first published hand-out about the centre – that it 'will work in partnership with a planned Centre of Maori and Polynesian Studies without affecting the autonomy of either'. So the centre would not be a bicultural institution, and the board that we established included no Māori. I was mortified and disappointed and somewhat shamefaced by this outcome. But it was a powerful lesson for the future.

Meanwhile we still did not have a name. Eventually the solution came to me. Since the Stout Trust had provided a valuable fellowship, and since Robert Stout had started Victoria University and left his papers to the university, using his name had many advantages. I hoped that it would ensure the Stout Fellowship would become a permanent part of the institution. Then, just as we were firming up on this choice, the old mansion built for Robert and Anna Stout on The Terrace burnt down. I remembered from our stained-glass explorations along The Terrace that the house had some nice windows. So the morning after the fire Chris Maclean and I raced down to the shell of the building to search through the rubble and see if we could find them. Some of them had cracked or were smashed. But enough remained to restore the three main windows, which included Anna and Robert's initials. We quickly received permission from the owners for Chris to collect the glass. Just at that very time the house on 12 Waiteata Road was being upgraded

The windows from Anna and Robert Stout's house on The Terrace given a new home in the seminar room of the Stout Research Centre. The RS in the left window refers to Robert Stout; the APS in the right one recalls his wife, Anna P. Stout.

for the institute. We persuaded the architect to provide space for the three windows in the corner of the proposed meeting room. The timing could hardly have been better. So with a long-term fellowship secured and windows about to be installed, the Stout Research Centre had its name. Not everyone approved. Some considered Robert Stout to have been a conservative old fogey. Publisher Hugh Price, who had been very helpful in encouraging the development of the centre, offered to design a letterhead, and presented the word Stout in an embarrassingly rotund shape; Peter Gibbons in Waikato always jokingly called us 'The Harry Fatt Centre' in reference to the villain of the 1930s play *Waiting for Lefty*. But the name stuck and has served the place well.

I set up a board to drive the proposal. There were seven members appointed by the Professorial Board from within the academic community. They included Tim Beaglehole from history, Don McKenzie and John Thomson from English, Michael Hill from sociology and Jim Collinge from education. There were also seven appointed by the University Council, including Jim Traue from the Turnbull, Ray Grover from the National Archives, Geraldine McDonald from the Council of Educational Research, and the prominent public-health doctor Ian Prior. Bill Oliver, who had just moved back to Wellington to lead the Dictionary of New Zealand Biography, agreed to chair the board and he soon suggested that his friend and poet Lauris Edmond should join. It was a wise and wide-ranging group who provided support and enthusiasm.

The formal opening of the Stout Centre came on the evening before the inaugural conference on 27 July 1984. In gratitude for his financial contribution to the concept and hoping for future public support, I had invited Minister of Internal Affairs Allan Highet to do the honours. But soon after, Robert Muldoon called a snap election and almost two weeks before the opening, a new David Lange-led Labour Government was elected. It was too late to bump Allan Highet, who was appropriately relaxed and enthusiastic. We had a celebratory cake, and in my rather lengthy and pompous speech, I provided a sense of the intellectual vision that had driven the idea. I began with a potted history of higher education in the country, arguing that the colonial tradition of the college was that it stood for the genteel culture of the Old World, a protection from the barbarism of the wilderness. Research in local subjects was not encouraged. Cultural nationalists, I claimed, had only emerged outside the academy, with writers like James Cowan and Elsdon Best, while within the university there was minimal study of New Zealand history, sociology or literature. But the previous twenty years had seen an upwelling of work about this country and now was the time to provide a home for it. The centre was primarily designed to encourage a base for research into New Zealand subjects by providing studies, research seminars and conferences. I noted that the traditional college with no interest in New Zealand subjects had remained isolated from the society. But New Zealand research required an engagement with the country and I hoped that the centre would provide such a bridge. I ended by answering three possible criticisms of the venture – firstly, that it was too nationalistic and would suffer isolation from the international world of learning. Far from this being so, I suggested that the centre would bring overseas scholars to New Zealand and would encourage researchers to draw on foreign theory and apply these ideas to New Zealand content. Second, I noted the absence of Māori involvement on the board, but expressed a commitment to work closely with Māori studies and politely acknowledged the help of Professor Mead. Finally I addressed the allegation that the Stout Centre was too interdisciplinary. I responded that disciplines were largely bureaucratic conveniences and that there were an increasing number of subjects that dealt with problems in an interdisciplinary fashion, such as criminology, women's studies and education. It was my hope that a focus on New Zealand studies would permit the breaking of barriers too long established.

We had a vision, a name, a building and had been formally opened. Now the challenge was to make it work. My greatest anxiety was that no one would actually come. Had I conned people that there was a bevy of scholars wanting such a centre? Then came a call from Judith Fyfe. She had developed a partnership with Hugo Manson to record oral histories of older New Zealanders and develop professional techniques of recording which would provide solid evidence of earlier social mores for future use. Judith and Hugo had developed a formal institution, the New Zealand Oral History Archive. They were looking for a place to live. In the past most academic historians had dismissed them as amateur antiquarians who had nothing to contribute to the scholarly world. Oral evidence was regarded with suspicion – historical truth could only be found in the written or printed document. But I had already a deep sympathy for oral history. In the United States I had begun to realise that if you were going to capture 'history from below', tell the stories of less literate people, then recording their memories verbally was a crucial tool. Coming back to New Zealand I had been deeply impressed by the use made by Michael King of oral history in his biography of Te Puea, and took seriously his argument in a 1976 article that because Māori were an oral people who recounted their history through spoken oratory and waiata, oral history was a crucial tool for the historian of Māori. So I responded warmly to Judith's suggestion. I was keen that the Stout Centre reach out beyond the academy, and the archive had already established a following within the wider community. Judith and Hugo were heavily involved at the time in recording the 1984 election campaign with nightly interviews of the respective leaders. It seemed like a worthwhile project. So they became our first residents.

The connection with oral history developed other elements. In 1985, the next year, Judith Binney became our second John David Stout fellow, and her project was to work editing and preparing for publication interviews with eight Māori women connected to the Ringatū faith. The book eventually became a classic, *Ngā Mōrehu*. Under these influences I decided that it was time to take on some oral history myself, and spent my leave in late 1985 doing oral histories of Sussex farm labourers in the hope of discovering the Old World origins of Kiwi male culture. The Oral History Archive also initiated a conference on oral history in April 1986 in association with the university's centre for continuing education. It was a great weekend. The pioneers were well represented – Michael King, Tony Simpson, Judith Binney – and the radio documentary-makers Alwyn Owen and Jack Perkins. I was asked to chair the final wrap-up session, and threw out the challenge – wasn't it time to establish a formal oral history organisation? Out of this call eventually grew NOHANZ, the National Oral History Association of New Zealand. The Stout Centre continued to encourage oral history – it became the site where Jane Tolerton and Nicholas Boyack got together to plan a major initiative to

Oral history was an important part of the Stout Centre's early years. The first residents (left) were Judith Fyfe and Hugo Manson, shown here flanking the administrator of the New Zealand Oral History Archive, Jean Harton. Judith Binney (right) is shown in characteristic pose. She was the second John David Stout fellow, and a highly dedicated and influential oral historian.
SARAH HUNTER; *NZ HERALD*

record oral histories with surviving veterans of World War I. The resulting archive became one of the most important collections of reminiscences in the country.

The first John David Stout fellow, in 1984, had been John Mansfield Thomson. John, originally from Blenheim, had helped edit a significant local periodical in the 1950s, *Here and Now*. He had then headed to London where he founded and edited a very distinguished journal, *Early Music*. Despite his long expatriation, interest in baroque classical music and polished gentlemanly style, John was also a deep-rooted cultural nationalist who had written a biography of Alfred Hill, the New Zealand turn-of-the-century composer. At the Stout Centre he completed a history of New Zealand music and became an ardent champion of the centre, a cause which he often lubricated with fine red wine. John also awoke the interests of the composer Douglas Lilburn in the Stout Centre. One day Lilburn contacted me offering his complete collection of New Zealand journals, like *Landfall*, for the centre. The *Landfall* run went back to issue 1. His gifts formed the beginnings of a library.

Later John David Stout fellows illustrated some of the larger goals of the centre. One was an eminent international historian, Don Akenson from Canada. He had published extensively on the history of the Irish, both at home and in the worlds they created overseas. He brought a huge historiographical knowledge and an original mind to a study of the New Zealand Irish community. When published in 1990 as *Half the World from Home*, Don's book revolutionised the understanding of migration in New Zealand by pointing up the extent to which Irish culture lived on in New Zealand history. Akenson was a perfect illustration of the kind of scholar the Stout Centre hoped to attract – international experts who wished to apply their insights to the fertile and largely untilled soil of New Zealand society and history. Another scholar with a similar mission was a returning expatriate, Peter Coleman, who applied his American work on the history of imprisonment for debt to New Zealand.

Two other Stout fellows in my time as director, Geoff Park and David Young, were non-academics who were venturing into scholarly waters, and each explored a subject dear to my heart – the cultural meaning of the land. I had first met Geoff Park at the Institute of Landscape Architects conference. At that stage Geoff was a young botanist working for the DSIR in Nelson, studying forest remnants. He had developed an original proposal to examine a number of locations on the west coasts of both islands and explore the Māori and Pākehā cultural responses to these places and how these reactions shaped the history of the land. He was a knowledgeable and passionate man whose work resulted in a classic and highly influential book, *Ngā Uruora: Ecology and History in a New Zealand Landscape*. David Young, originally from Whanganui, was writing a history of the Whanganui River. I had first met David when I was doing my stint for Ian Cross at the *Listener*. David was then a staff writer with a particular focus on environmental issues. Like Geoff, he brought to the centre a wide-ranging interest in history and in the interactions of scientific and cultural knowledge. In the mid-1990s it was my privilege to kayak down the Whanganui River in their company and be constantly enlightened by their botanical, ecological and cultural insights.

There were other very capable scholars who joined the Stout community as residents and brought other approaches. John Martin, writing a book on rural workers, and Tony Dreaver, doing a biography of the Horowhenua farmer, photographer and amateur scientist Les Adkin, added rural history and culture. Peter Franks, preparing a history of the Clerical Workers' Union, brought some labour history. Jane Tolerton doing a brilliant biography of Ettie Rout and Heather Roberts completing a book on women in New Zealand fiction brought a focus on women's history and creativity. Stevan Eldred-Grigg came to polish up his epic novel about a working-class family in Sydenham, Christchurch, which became *Oracles and Miracles*.

We also had several excellent and original initiatives in the history of creative culture. Peter Beatson, blind and usually accompanied by his guide dog and his spouse Dianne, worked on a profile of cultural life since 1940. Geoffrey Lealand examined the impact of American culture in New Zealand. Even more exciting, one day the poet Ian Wedde approached me and asked if he could use the Stout Centre as a base to create an archive of New Zealand writers reading their works. This built on the expertise of Judith and Hugo, and drew the writing community to the Stout Centre. The Stout Literary Archive, in other words Ian Wedde, recorded readings by such figures as Hone Tuwhare, Allen Curnow, Fleur Adcock, Margaret Mahy and Keri Hulme, and sponsored a great one-day seminar at Downstage Theatre on 'Why Books Happen', featuring interviews with prominent writers. Ian became an invaluable member of the Stout Centre and his wide-ranging knowledge and curiosity encouraged others' pursuits. Cultural and literary history, the meaning of the land, Māori history, oral history, the experience of the working class – these were all subjects dear to my heart and I could not really believe how quickly such able people pursuing such relevant topics had landed at our door.

The one disappointment about those who became residents of the Stout Centre was the relatively small number of scholars who came from overseas. So while on leave in Britain in late 1985 I met with the New Zealand high commissioner, Bryce Harland, to discuss a scheme, ultimately stillborn, to assist European scholars wishing to do research in New Zealand. 'If the study of New Zealand history and culture is to grow it must become part of the international debate,' I wrote at the time. 'There is no shortage of young European academics interested in New Zealand – it is now our responsibility to encourage their interests.'[4]

I believed it important that the centre functioned as a community – it could not simply be a set of studies with lonely writers working behind closed doors. So I encouraged the rich discussion and exchange of ideas that had driven the vision in the first place. Every Thursday we shared lunch, and all residents were encouraged to attend and join in. Every Wednesday afternoon the centre held a seminar, where the scholars could present their findings or listen to talks from other New Zealand researchers. As well as the residents, the audiences for these seminars included some lecturers or graduate students of the university, but more often interested members of the public, who were offered membership of the centre. Often these seminars sought to develop a theme – immigration, religion, inequality were some that I recall. That the Stout Centre provided an intellectually productive environment was nicely confirmed in Peter Beatson's sabbatical leave report to Massey University. He noted that in preparing his chronology of New Zealand culture between 1940 and 1990 he found invaluable 'the wide spectrum of people' whom he met. 'The Stout Centre,' he wrote, 'provides a relaxed but at the same time intellectually stimulating environment, both in its informal contacts and through its seminars and conferences and its members were very willing to share and exchange information and tips.'[5]

The big events for the Stout Centre were the annual conferences, which I always saw as a mechanism for raising new ideas and approaches to the study of New Zealand, and a way of establishing the wider credibility and public influence of the centre. We began with a conference on biography. This was partly because it had relevance to a range of disciplines, but even more because the Dictionary of New Zealand Biography was just beginning its labours under the editorship of Bill Oliver, who was also chair of the centre's advisory board. So with Bill, we developed a wide-ranging programme – Antony Alpers, the pioneering biographer of Katherine Mansfield on literary biography; Colin Davis, scholar of the seventeenth century, who had developed a course on theories of biography; Keith Sinclair on political biography, with comments by Michael King and Erik Olssen; a session for the sociologists on the life-history method, drawing on insights from Alison Gray, Charles Sedgwick, Anne Meade and Sue Middleton; an excellent presentation on women's biography orchestrated by Charlotte Macdonald; and one on Māori biography which included Ngahuia Te Awekotuku, Ruka Broughton and Joe Pere. Whether it was the glittering roll-call of names or the subject matter, the weekend in July 1984 attracted well over a hundred attendees, and a considerable level of enthusiasm and engagement. Colin Davis, about to be appointed to Massey as Bill Oliver's replacement, and a stern taskmaster, wrote the next day: 'The Stout Centre is off to a flying start . . . in one fell swoop you have brought the Centre beyond the threshold. It is now poised to play an influential part in the cultural life of NZ.'[6] I was deeply gratified. I collected together the essays and Bridget Williams agreed to publish the proceedings as *Biography in New Zealand*. It was the centre's first publication.

    The next year came a bigger intellectual challenge. We decided that the theme would be 'Te Whenua, Te Iwi – the Land and the People'. Obviously my own interest, sparked by the landscape architects, was partly a factor. More important was the growing relevance of the subject to the relations of Māori and Pākehā. Still embarrassed and uneasy from my interactions with Sid Mead, I was determined to signal the commitment of the centre to Māori knowledge and to bicultural approaches. So the conference was designed as a dialogue between Pākehā and Māori approaches to the land. We had some powerful Māori voices. Kicking off with a spellbinding presentation by Tipene O'Regan on the mythology of Te Whanganui a Tara (Wellington Harbour), we were privileged to hear from such prominent Māori luminaries as Aila Taylor, who had led the Te Āti Awa Waitangi Tribunal submission against the outfall from the Motunui synthetic petrol plant and whose paper was supported by Fiona Clark's powerful images of gathering kai moana on the reef; Eddie Durie, at that stage chief judge of the Māori Land Court and chair of the

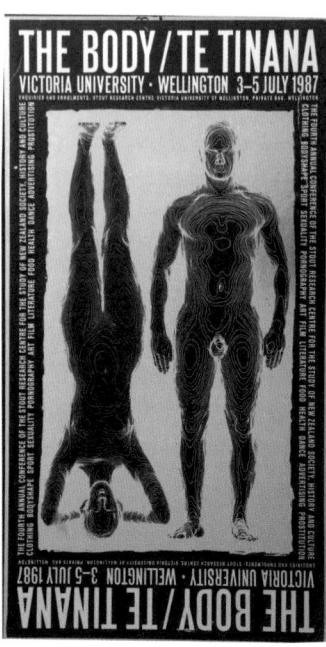

Bill Oliver was a very supportive chair of the Stout Centre advisory board. I arranged for my old friend Tom Scott to draw this cartoon of Bill (left), which we gave to him upon his retirement from the Dictionary of New Zealand Biography. At right is Dave Kent's poster for the Stout Centre's 'The Body/Te Tinana' conference in 1987.

Waitangi Tribunal; Robert Mahuta from the Kīngitanga; Ranginui Walker, the country's leading Māori historian; and Keri Hulme, who was about to receive the Booker Prize for *The Bone People*. Such a line-up guaranteed a good Māori response – and it came. People such as Hone Tuwhare travelled a long way to be there, and I will never forget the waiata which spontaneously followed the appearance of Keri Hulme at the lecturn.

On the Pākehā side there were also original thinkers – Helen Leach, anthropologist and historian of gardening; Rollo Arnold on early settlement and the land; John Thomson speaking about Douglas Lilburn; Francis Pound, Roger Horrocks, Wystan Curnow and a brilliant young poet, Leigh Davis, who all analysed cultural responses to the land. William Main presented a survey of photographic images. There was even a fascinating session with the sociologists Nick Perry and Ian Carter, looking at rural imagery on New Zealand television. By the second day the lecture theatre holding over 150 was full and people were sitting illegally in the aisles. There was an exciting buzz. The range of presentations appeared to validate the interdisciplinary intent. Geoff Park, ecologist and historian, wrote later, 'It was successful for the disciplines it brought together in a way no one had experienced in New Zealand before that event. For myself, and many others I know, it was a highlight of their learning life.'[7] This time we also published the papers and the volume *Te Whenua, Te Iwi – the Land and the People* sold out. The timing was perfect – the 1975 land march and the establishment of the Waitangi Tribunal had focused the attention of New Zealanders on conflicts over land; and as the country became increasingly urban the old rural mythology of Pākehā New Zealand seemed a strange historical oddity and anachronism, but one worth exploring. I felt by the end of the weekend in June 1985 that we had earned our stripes.

Other annual conferences followed. In the second half of 1985 I had gone on leave so J. E. P. Thomson stepped in as the acting director and orchestrated an excellent two days on 'The American Connection'. Held at a time when there was still great public excitement about the new Labour Government's anti-nuclear policy and the subsequent break with the United States alliance through ANZUS, the conference explored all aspects of the American relationship – not only foreign policy, but also language, literature, education, social movements and popular culture. As in the previous year, a range of disciplines exploring a highly relevant public issue was the essence of the weekend. In 1987 we chose to replicate the recipe of the land conference by examining Māori and Pākehā attitudes towards the body. 'The Body/Te Tinana', promoted via a striking poster by Dave Kent, began in an appropriately bicultural way with Pou Temara from Ngāi Tūhoe talking about the body in Māori culture followed by an exciting Australian scholar, Jill Matthews, setting the international western context. Over the next two days there were papers on clothing, pornography, food, sport, health care, art and literature, broken up by performances of dance, and film from the New Zealand Film Archive. Christine Cheyne from the sociology programme at Massey University wrote to me that it was 'by far the best' Stout Centre conference and 'indeed the weekend was far more interesting, enlightening and convivial than any conference I have been to for a long time'.[8] The final conferences I organised in 1988 were one on 'A War-like People', which was a little heavy with military enthusiasts, and another on Katherine Mansfield on the occasion of the hundredth anniversary of her birth, initiated by Roger Robinson.

Although the Stout Centre brought many personal rewards, including a trip to Queensland in 1987 where the Australian Studies Centre sought to build bridges by inviting me to give three public lectures, I found the energy required for organising conferences emotionally taxing and intellectually demanding. There were endless small details to follow through, and many prima donnas to satisfy – from the provision of childcare (demanded by one stroppy feminist) to the order of the programme or the identity of fellow speakers. So towards the end of 1987 I decided that I had done my stint at the Stout Centre and began to look round for a successor. I tried to enthuse a number of people about the possibilities for growth and experiment but it took a while before things fell into place and it was 1988 before I passed the baton to Jim Collinge from the school of education. Subsequently the centre has indeed benefited from the creativity of a number of thoughtful directors – notably Vincent O'Sullivan, and then from 2000 to 2017 Lydia Wevers who, with the assistance of Anna Green, Richard Hill and Jamie Belich, really made it a dynamic centre of intellectual life. Lydia did a magnificent job and ensured that the Stout not only survived but continued to flourish by exploring new issues and providing a home for eminent researchers and writers.

Even as I completed my term I could look back at some fine books which had emerged from the centre. In the 1988 New Zealand Book Awards, the winner was Claudia Orange's work on the Treaty of Waitangi, which had provided the topic for our very first seminar. The second and third places went to Stevan Eldred-Grigg's *Oracles and Miracles* and my *A Man's Country?*, both of which were completed at the centre. Other classics to be written there included Judith Binney's *Ngā Mōrehu*, Don Akenson's *Half the World from Home*, Geoff Park's *Ngā Uruora*, David Young's *Woven by Water* and John Thomson's history of New Zealand music. This was a fine validation for the idea which had created the Stout Centre in the first place.

If the Stout Centre was my major focus during the second half of the 1980s, my own research and writing continued apace. Although I had essentially completed the text of *A Man's Country?* by the time I became director, there was much cleaning up before the book was finally published in 1987. The book also provided the inspiration for further ventures. Some of these were public appearances such as keynote addresses or appearances as a

For six happy months in 1985, Phillida and I and our two children lived in this beautiful manor house at Kingston, near Lewes in Sussex. It was an enjoyable encounter with historic England.

talking head on television programmes, most notably one about the history of rugby. More important was the opportunity to explore in greater detail matters that I had briefly touched on in the book. One of the issues that I had left unresolved was how far the powerful male culture of nineteenth-century rural New Zealand was something novel, and how far an amplification of traditions begun in Britain. So in the second half of 1985 I applied for leave to go to the University of Sussex and investigate this problem. I decided to take one rural community that had sent a number of migrants to New Zealand and investigate male and female cultures. I chose the village of Alfriston, which had given its name to a location just south-east of Auckland. I was based at the University of Sussex, which was an ideal host. The department had a number of historians, most notably Alun Howkins, who were researching nineteenth-century rural society and were heavily influenced by Raphael Samuel's *History Workshop* journal which had concentrated on rural working-class history. There were regular seminars and a very lively group of young historians, many of whom were using oral history to explore the lives of working people. One of those was Alistair Thomson, an Australian, who was working on a brilliant book drawing on oral histories with Australian diggers. After our seminars we would often proceed to a local pub where I learned much about pub games and the culture of beer drinking.

Sussex was also a convenient location for family reasons. Phillida's parents were still living near Hampstead Heath, and we managed to rent a seventeenth-century manor house for six months near Lewes, close to the South Downs, which we would ramble over regularly to great enjoyment. I completed about fifteen oral histories with old-time residents of Alfriston. I never wrote this up, but I learnt enough to decide that the colonial male culture did indeed have precedents in 'those who slept rough', in the men who drifted round looking for casual work in the countryside. The difference was that their culture constituted a minority of rural males in nineteenth-century Britain, while it became an influential majority on the colonial frontier.

A Man's Country? had also, to my great surprise, stimulated my fascination with the experience of New Zealanders at war. This took me in a number of directions. One was an attempt to broaden my studies beyond simply the experience of those who had gone to the Great War, so I began to look at groups to whom I had given less attention – women, pacifists, Māori. I tried to argue that the nationalist mythology which had been built on the experiences of New Zealand soldiers obscured the meaning of war to minority groups. An essay, 'War and National Identity', articulated the argument.

But I still felt that the experiences of soldiers were too little known in New Zealand. The mythology had created an image of the heroic Kiwi male loyally defending the Empire with his mates, and had obscured the horrific experiences and bitter disillusionment which I had discovered in reading the letters and diaries of soldiers in the Great War. The subject needed more work. One day a student, Nicholas Boyack, came to see me, looking for a PhD thesis topic. I suggested that he do for New Zealand what Bill Gammage had done for Australia – tell the story of the war from the writings of the ordinary soldiers. Nicholas said that he was a pacifist, had no interest in war, but he did agree to go down to the Turnbull Library and look at a couple of collections of letters. Within a day he was back – like me he had been stunned by his discoveries and was convinced the soldiers' view of the war needed to be told. He agreed to pursue the topic, and I also convinced him that we should work together to prepare a volume of the most powerful soldiers' writings.

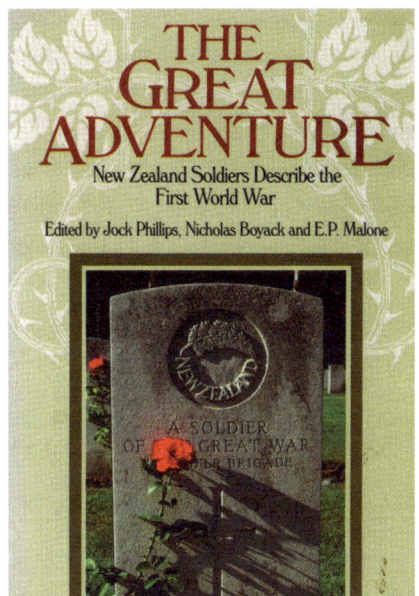 

The cover of The Great Adventure *(left), and George Bollinger, whose powerful story we were unable to include (right).*

I was keen to include the writings of William Malone, the commanding officer of the Wellington Battalion who had been killed on the summit of Chunuk Bair on 8 August 1915. Malone was a beautifully articulate writer who came across initially as a stern imperialist and martinet, but whose experiences humanised him and led him to an eloquent appreciation of the qualities of the ordinary soldiers serving under him. I then discovered that Malone's grandson, E. P. Malone, was preparing an edition of Malone's writing, so we decided to combine our efforts.

The diary of George Bollinger had also long been a favourite. Bollinger, the tallest man in the Expeditionary Force, had been a typical Kiwi bloke – playing footie and serving in the territorials. But he was the son of German migrants to Taranaki. While Bollinger was encountering the full horror of Gallipoli, the Anti-German League was campaigning against the presence of such a disloyal son of Germany in the New Zealand forces. He became deeply disillusioned by the contrast between his expectation of war and the savage reality of Gallipoli trench life, but he remained a loyal soldier. Despite this record he was withdrawn from the forces under pressure from the Anti-German League and brought back home to help train future recruits. Even this was too much for the league; and eventually, to still the whispers about his treasonous background, Bollinger offered to go back to the front, where in 1917 he was killed. George Bollinger was a fine, and at times highly cynical, writer, and I put together excerpts of his diary along with appropriate images, which with Hugo Manson's help as a narrator we presented at a number of Anzac Day events. The story worked superbly as live theatre but sat uncomfortably in our book after Malone's diary. You simply could not ask the reader to go through the Gallipoli experience twice, so in the end we dropped the Bollinger material.

We did include some other strong writings however, and in researching them had memorable meetings with the families who had presented the papers to libraries in the first place. I recall especially a visit in Te Kūiti to Athol Smith, whose father, Wilfred Collinson Smith, despite having two children, had volunteered for service. Athol, who was born after his father went to war, only got to know him later in life from the letters. Wilfred became increasingly bitter about what he discovered and increasingly sad that he had never seen his son. He too lost his life in 1917 on the Western Front. And there was Peter Howden, whose father, a Wellington College old boy, had written religiously every day to his wife. He was desperately in love and found the separation difficult. Eventually he was gassed, and in his delirium became desperate that he had not communicated with his wife or heard from her. In the end a nurse in the military hospital composed a letter purporting to be from his wife and read it to him, and he died happy. There was also an extraordinarily vivid account of the disastrous Passchendaele offensive in October 1917 by a former lighthouse-keeper, Leonard Hart.

The book worked as a series of strong short stories, vivid re-creations of the attitudes and experiences of a range of New Zealand soldiers. The theme was very much the contrast between enthusiastic enlisting and the savage disillusionment of war – hence the ironic title 'The Great Adventure', which sat on the front cover above a close-up of a New Zealand soldier's headstone. The book sold well, but it had at least one very sad consequence. One of the collections we decided to include was the writing of Robin Hamley. His style was not especially fluent; but his letters represented one not-unusual reaction to the horrors of war. Rather than confronting the dangers at the front,

Hamley would often discover a sickness or an injury that would keep him away from the fighting. It was a sane and logical response to the situation and not uncommon. In our introduction to the chapter we made the error of spelling out the nature of his response, and in effect accused him of 'malingering', which we interpreted as an understandable reaction. We had sent drafts of each chapter to relevant family members. One afternoon I was paid a visit by Professor Bob Clark of the university's geology department, who had given Robin Hamley's letters to the Turnbull Library. Clark and I had developed a warm relationship when we both served, along with the eminent lawyer Ken Keith, on the selection committee of the Fulbright Foundation. Robin Hamley was Clark's uncle, and he was furious about our interpretation of Hamley's behaviour. I was polite but insisted that our understanding followed from the content of the letters. The next day I opened the newspaper to discover that Professor Clark had suffered a major heart attack walking along Upland Road in Kelburn on the previous afternoon about 3 p.m. He had collapsed and had died later that day. I was stunned. Professor Clark had left my office about 2.30 p.m. Further, the newspaper stated that his full name was 'Robin Hamley Clark' – he had been named in honour of his fallen uncle. In writing about the Great War, it was difficult indeed to escape the reality of death.

There was a further intellectual consequence of *A Man's Country?* The interest in war spurred by that book led me to consider the many hundreds of war memorials found throughout the country. At the time Chris Maclean and I were criss-crossing the country in pursuit of stained-glass windows. We had our cameras with us, so as we passed the war memorials in small country towns we began to take photos of them, thinking that the resulting images might make a nice calendar. But when we came home and looked at them on the big screen, they took on a new interest. We began to realise that no two were exactly the same. Almost every single one had a point of interest, whether the peculiarity of an inscription, the sculptural work on the monument, the way the names were listed or the positioning of the memorial. The modern memorial halls and swimming baths built after World War II were also a fascinating architectural and community story. Before long we were hooked, suffering from what Ken Inglis described as the 'war memorial disease' – an infliction that requires the sufferer to get unreasonably excited about hunks of erect concrete. So Chris and I proceeded to explore the country systematically for memorials. Whereas for the stained-glass project we had focused on towns, the war-memorial research required us to comb the rural districts too. We would spend four to five days in each district, and became impressed by the local peculiarities of each region – war-memorial gates in Taranaki, World War II Māori obelisks in Northland. I became more aware of the country as a place of many cultures. Once again we interspersed our photography and local research with walks and bodysurfing and other enjoyable outdoor pursuits.

Ken Inglis, of the 'war memorial disease' phrase, was a great Australian historian, almost twenty years my senior and the first historian since Charles Bean to take the Anzac mythology seriously. I met him in the mid-1980s at a conference in Canberra and when he discovered our joint interest in memorials, his support and enthusiasm knew no bounds. He was carrying out a statistical survey of Australian memorials, so I decided that we would copy his form and conduct a similar survey. An army officer, Joe Bolton, who did a lot of travelling round the country for his job graciously agreed to fill out forms on his journeys. The resulting statistics provided an intriguing comparison with Inglis's Australian findings. The most notable difference was that in Australia 80 per cent of Great War memorials listed those who had served, whereas in New Zealand 80 per cent listed only those who had died for their country. Ken and I interpreted this difference as a result of the absence of conscription in Australia, which meant that the sheer act of volunteering was worthy of public honour. Ken also invited me to a fascinating conference at Les Invalides in Paris. This was the traditional hospital for wounded soldier veterans, and I will never forget the moment when the proceedings of the conference were halted to allow a veteran to be wheeled in his bed through the hall from one part of the building to another. At that conference I also met for the first time, and greatly enjoyed, the deeply original historian of World War I culture Jay Winter.

Like the stained-glass book, the war-memorial project began with the photos; but unlike that earlier project, we also discovered abundant documentary sources. Most of the memorials to the New Zealand Wars had been put up by the New Zealand government, and I discovered a wonderful series of files in the National Archives which told their story. A woman named Edith Statham was a prime mover. She had begun in the years just before the Great War as secretary of the Victoria League, with an interest in using memorials to imbue a sense of the value of service to the British Empire. She became 'inspector

Researching war memorials – using James Cowan to locate New Zealand Wars sites in May 1987 (top left); interviewing Alan Trethewey at his Mt Pleasant home in Christchurch (top right); copying the inscription on the Ashburton war memorial onto a survey form (bottom left); and photographing the Kowai Bush memorial (bottom right). CHRIS MACLEAN

of old soldiers' graves' for the Department of Internal Affairs and helped see some twenty memorials put up in the battle locations and cemeteries of the North Island. There were also abundant files about the more than 500 World War II memorials, for which the Labour Government offered subsidies if they qualified as community facilities. Chris took over the research and writing on this section of the book, while I laboured through old newspapers to tell the story of the memorials to the South African War and World War I. It was an intriguing story, which uncovered a number of sculptors until then largely ignored – most notably Richard Gross in Auckland and a Christchurch stonemason, William Trethewey, who sculpted two of the finest public memorials in the country – the Kaiapoi digger and the Christchurch memorial. We had several memorable sessions with William Trethewey's son, Alan, who showed us his father's scrapbooks and photos of the man at work. By the time we had finished researching and writing *The Sorrow and the Pride,* as the resulting book became known, I considered it the most rigorous and exhaustive piece of research I had done. I also saw it as a contribution to understanding the limits of New Zealand nationalism, since the real burden of the argument was that war memorials functioned as propaganda for the imperial cause. But the argument and indeed the book itself was largely ignored. Government Print, the publishers, decided to compromise the quality by allowing coloured images only on one face every four pages; and New Zealanders at that stage were interested neither in war nor in the popular culture represented by memorials. Although well reviewed, *The Sorrow and the Pride* sank largely without trace and sold few copies.

My role in establishing the Stout Centre, if not the publication of *A Man's Country?*, at last won me some credibility as a New Zealand historian within Victoria University. I was allowed to begin teaching New Zealand history and began to lecture on New Zealand since World War II. I became interested in the question of how and why the New Zealand value system had changed in the years from 1945 to the 1980s. This led to several interesting papers and lectures – I returned to the landscape architects and examined the question of how the recent social changes had impacted on the New Zealand landscape. At a time when the country was still working through the implications of the anti-nuclear ANZUS rift with the United States, I found myself asked to talk on several occasions about the historical origins of this development. For the foreign-policy school in Dunedin I set out to explore the relationship between

American culture and New Zealand's changing foreign policy. Paradoxically I decided that among the opinion-making elite, American intellectual influences had actually become stronger, not weaker, as New Zealand's foreign policy had become less sympathetic to the United States. I suggested that this was partly because it was America's own critics who had achieved an impact on New Zealand, and partly that the real influence behind New Zealand's more independent foreign policy was the emergence of a cultural nationalism within the country. Using the reviews of books in the *New Zealand Listener* I charted the dramatic rise, since the 1960s, in reviewed books which had been published in New Zealand and the even more dramatic decline in books published in Great Britain. I began to realise that my own discovery of New Zealand and a growing disenchantment with British cultural influences had reflected others' experience, and that the drive for an independent New Zealand was the real story of the ANZUS rift. I realised that just as I had been affected by America's own critics, so too had other New Zealanders.

It may have been partly the result of this paper that I was invited by the East–West Centre in Hawaii to prepare a paper on 'New Zealand and the ANZUS Alliance: Changing national self-perceptions 1945–88' for a conference on 'Australia–New Zealand–U.S. Relations'. The conference was held in Hawaii, and the East–West Centre put us up in a very flash hotel on the waterfront at Waikiki. At the time I initially accepted this largesse as merely American generosity; but I grew suspicious when on the evening of the first day a gentleman knocked on the door, opened a suitcase and handed out $1000 in 'spending money'. I was taken aback, clutched the gift and proceeded to spend it. But later, as I reflected on the gesture, I recalled that the East–West Centre had long been associated with the CIA; and I wondered if I had been caught in the agency's clutches.

If so, then the CIA would not have been reassured by my paper. I began with the statement that 'I am an unabashed enthusiast for New Zealand's nuclear-free policy'. I built on the implications of my earlier paper to suggest that since World War II New Zealand had become a society capable of developing its own norms. It no longer had to look to London for its moral and political guidance. I noted that the numbers of people with university degrees had risen from about 5000 in 1945 to over 200,000. These people had led a new cultural nationalism which resulted in a redefinition of New Zealand identity. That identity, I suggested, was based on the elements that made the

In 1987 I displayed in the university library an exhibition of photos of memorials to New Zealanders on the Western Front, and also included cartoons from New Zealand at the Front. *I look very pleased with the result!* CHRIS MACLEAN

country different: 'Its small size and isolation, which encourage a moral role in world affairs and feeds the utopian vision of a place free from old world diseases; its Maori inhabitants, growing in numbers and influence, which help to shake confidence about the necessary dominance of western interests; and its South Pacific location, which counterpoises romantic island dreams against superpower bombs.' I concluded in words which expressed my own process of self-discovery as much as the nation's: 'This awakening of Aotearoa to a new vision of itself has been the most challenging and exciting development of the last twenty years in New Zealand. It was the United States' misfortune to be on the receiving end.'[9] The sense of a country coming to a heroic identity mirrored the way my own discovery of New Zealand had given my life a sense of purpose and direction.

I was now thoroughly content living in New Zealand. Tramps in the hills with friends, summers on Hawke's Bay beaches with Phillida and our two children, a flourishing vegetable garden, occasional games of cricket, good friends and a city with fine foods and a lively theatre scene – life seemed good.[10] I was taking a lot of photographs and held a couple of exhibitions of these in the university library – one on the churches of Samoa and one on the memorials to New Zealanders on the Western Front. More important, I had found an intellectual direction. With the Stout Centre dedicated to exploring New Zealand culture and my own researches uncovering elements which were central to the nation's mythology, I had broken with the cultural traditions of my upbringing, and in exploring the society and culture of my own country, I had found my niche in life.

7
Servant of the Crown

Towards the end of 1988 I happened to run into Michael Bassett, at the time minister of internal affairs in the Third Labour Government. It was almost twenty-five years since I had first met Michael while coming back on board ship from England. He was returning from completing a PhD in American history on the history of the Socialist Party, at Duke University in North Carolina, and I feasted off his opinionated radicalism, which seemed a merciful relief from the prejudices of my father. By the late 1980s Michael Bassett had somewhat changed his political stripes – he had become an MP and then minister in the Lange government, and the youthful radical had become an outspoken apostle of new-right economics and one of Roger Douglas's leading advocates. He had no time for his cousin and party leader, David Lange. Despite this ideological change, Bassett remained an enthusiastic supporter of New Zealand history and was happy to use his position to advance the cause. Whatever he knew about my subsequent career, I do

Chief historian, suitably dressed in tie and jacket, standing in front of the Historical Branch library, which included a run of Appendices to the Journals of the House of Representatives *that I rescued from a government department who were about to take them to the tip.*

not know, but one day he tapped me on the shoulder and suggested that I apply to become chief historian in the Historical Branch of his ministry, the Department of Internal Affairs.

The invitation took me by surprise, and initially I rejected the idea. True, there were reasons why I might want a break from teaching American history at Victoria. I had become frustrated at my lack of influence in the history department, where my leadership ambitions were blocked; and I found teaching had lost its allure. Marking essays, which were so often an ill-digested version of one's own lectures, was an immensely dispiriting task which turned the brain to mush. A series of internal wrangles had made me somewhat disillusioned at the collegiality of university departments where

The three key people who initiated the War Histories Branch are shown here at a conference to plan the unit war histories. They are (on the left with cigarette) Eric McCormick, the army archivist; Joe Heenan, the secretary for internal affairs; and speaking on the right, Major-General Howard Kippenberger, who became the general editor of the volumes. The photo was taken by John Pascoe on 5 July 1946. ALEXANDER TURNBULL LIBRARY, PACOLL-0783-2-0339

status was uncertain and prima donnas flourished. I realised too that although my interests had moved into New Zealand history, the department needed American history to be taught, so I was likely to be stuck with that role for the foreseeable future. Leaving American history behind had a real appeal.

If there were strong push factors, the pull was much less certain. The Historical Branch had a distinguished past. The state had been involved in supporting historical research and publication as early as the 1920s, when James Cowan had been paid to write his impressive history of the New Zealand Wars. Then in 1936 a Historical Branch was established in Internal Affairs under Joe Heenan to prepare publications for New Zealand's centennial in 1940. It worked on a series of eleven overview volumes, a thirty-part periodical, *Making New Zealand*, and began a historical atlas, which never appeared. In 1946 the War Histories Branch was created under the editorship of Howard Kippenberger to write the official history of New Zealand's efforts in World War II. In the end no fewer than forty-four titles were produced, which included my father's volume on the Italian campaign. The standard of these publications was high, and, as Robin Williams wrote in his review of the Historical Publications Branch in 1986, 'The names associated with the first phase read like a roll of honour of some of the most distinguished names in New Zealand's political, administrative and academic life... Fraser, Macintosh, Beeby, Heenan, Wood, Beaglehole, Davidson, McCormick to name only some.'[1]

But in 1963, as the activities of the War History Branch wound down, it was replaced by a Historical Publications Branch with a mandate to edit and publish documents, prepare historical works based on these documents and produce administrative studies of government departments. The output since then had not been impressive – Nancy Taylor's huge two-volume study of the home front in World War II had completed the war history project; there were also an even more mammoth first volume (in two parts) of a history of the police, three volumes of diplomatic documents, a poorly received New Zealand atlas, a volume of essays to mark the Queen's silver jubilee in 1977, two works on military history and four small works on diplomatic history. None had sold many copies, and their areas of speciality – government and military history of the old kind – were hardly my style of history. Collections of documents seemed distinctly old-fashioned in a world where digital publication was becoming a possibility. I was about to publish an essay in the *New Zealand Journal of History* which specifically argued that what New Zealand history needed was cultural and social history, not areas in which the branch appeared to have any mandate.[2]

Further, the branch itself had gone through a very rocky period with personnel. After the retirement of the previous chief historian, Ian Wards, in 1982, an old friend and another American historian, Jim Holt, had been lured from the University of Auckland; but he had died suddenly from a heart attack after only five weeks in the job. Ian McGibbon, distinguished military historian, had been appointed chief historian, but his appointment had been challenged by another member of the branch, Richard Hill, a fine historian of left-wing sympathies. The appointment was overturned, and there was very bad blood between the two. The only other people in the branch were Charlotte Macdonald, an able historian but one itching to become an academic; an editor, David Green; and a newly appointed administrator. It did not seem an inviting atmosphere.

But there were several attractive aspects. The problems offered opportunities – things could only improve. I was attracted by the thought of being able to build up the branch from scratch; and also appealing was co-location alongside the Dictionary of New Zealand Biography project, with Bill Oliver as general editor and Claudia Orange as his deputy, heading a very able staff. Reluctantly I applied and was offered the position. Even then I hummed and ha'ed, and accepted it only after persuading the vice-chancellor to allow me three years' leave without pay, so that a retreat back to academia was always possible.

I began work in March 1989 after allowance had been made for the possibility of an appeal, and immediately wondered if I had made a stupid decision. I discovered that the unit was located in a scruffy, run-down old building on Molesworth Street which had once been the home of the probation service. Former probationers would periodically turn up to check in, and an old homeless man was in residence in the garden. I discovered too that none of the staff had either computer terminals or typewriters and wrote everything in longhand, which was then handed over to a typing pool. I seemed to be back in the 1950s. The endless requests for compliance memoranda coming down from head office mystified me. I was forced to wrestle with a new language of 'outputs' and 'outcomes'. In this respect I found myself very much in the late twentieth century.

A more depressing discovery was that the staff tensions were considerably worse than I had feared. Richard Hill and Ian McGibbon were not talking to one another and there was a stand-off between the two regarding the publication of Richard's next volume of police history. The book was too long for the publishers and there was a commitment to publication in 1989. I thought I had resolved this satisfactorily by dividing the book into two until I discovered that there had been a misunderstanding. I had thought we had agreed that it would be shortened by omitting an extensive bibliography; but Richard and David Green had thought that I had instructed the omission of footnotes. So the first major publication under my watch went ahead with no references, which was, to say the least, embarrassing and gave very poor messages about my commitment to scholarly standards. Another issue which confronted me even before I turned up for work was the request from the newly appointed administrator that her elderly dog, a smelly old spaniel called Grover, be allowed to come to work and sleep under her desk. I was not happy but gave permission, which was fine until two years later when on a rare visit to our offices by a new minister, Graeme Lee, he stepped out of the lift and just managed to avoid a pile of dog poo. I also discovered within the first week that I was expected to prepare ministerials – letters from the minister. I had no experience in the format and found it very difficult indeed to author text in another person's voice.

The challenges were made worse by the fact that within a year or so my personal life became distinctly unstable. One morning in 1990 I woke up early. Phillida was already awake, and she said that our marriage was at an end and she wanted me to leave the house. Obviously, like all long-term marriages, there had been difficulties and tensions, but I had always gained hugely from her engaging and highly original intellect. *A Man's Country?* would never have emerged without her insightful questioning. It was a shock when the marriage began to dissolve. I moved out of the house into a nice art-deco place several streets away, where my teenage children plus dog could easily visit. But there were inevitable difficulties and financial pressures as I struggled to pay rents and mortgages. It took several years of anguish before Phillida and I disentangled ourselves emotionally. Along the way I had an on-again, off-again liaison with a beautiful and highly intelligent Australian historian, Jan Bassett. She had written about Australian nurses in war and helped give me a greater appreciation of the place of women in the military. Then I spent three happy years with a lecturer in the English department at Victoria University, Kim Walker. She was a renaissance scholar and a theatre enthusiast, and widened my sense of cultural studies. Eventually Kim too wanted out. Again I went through torments of disentangling. Added to all this were various other family crises, the normal rocky incidents of teenagers.

These personal traumas were not easy, but they encouraged me to throw myself into my work. For the only time in my life, I dreaded the lonely weekends and felt most happy in front of a computer in the office. For the next five years I put all my creative energies into reviving the branch, increasing its output and inspiring a buzzing hive of new history. It was all-consuming, exhausting and immensely satisfying, and helped compensate for the pain at home. Soon after I began the job, a community newspaper did a profile. It included this portrait:

> If the label of Chief Historian hosts an image of an owlish, grey-haired, bespectacled, besuited senior citizen, then there are nothing but surprises in store. He seems young for a start (for an historian that is – 42), and not grey. He has glasses, but for one generation at least they are more reminiscent of Peter Fonda, than E. P. Thompson. He is neither in a suit, nor in a tie, and we are not sitting in a room wall to wall with leather-bound volumes, but in one on Molesworth street with a computer terminal in it. A 'new' historian?[3]

As I had hoped, the problems in the Historical Branch did indeed provide opportunities; and I had extraordinary luck and fortuitous timing. The staffing issues resolved themselves almost immediately. Richard Hill, frustrated with years of in-house fighting, accepted a job with the Office of Treaty Settlements. Charlotte Macdonald partially succeeded in her academic aspirations by being awarded a Claude McCarthy Fellowship for a year, and then left to replace me in the history department at Victoria University. This meant the loss of a fine historian, but she would never have been happy at the branch. Ian McGibbon was only temporarily embittered by not becoming the chief historian, and I quickly found a distinguished role for him as the managing editor of the *Historical Atlas*. Freed from the administrative burdens of the chief historian's position, he threw himself into his historical research and writing and made an outstanding contribution in completing a two-volume history of New Zealand's involvement in the Korean War.

This left me with an unparalleled opportunity to appoint people that I could work with, blessed with the strengths and skills that I desired. Within two months I decided to structure the staffing around two concepts, relative to different forms of history and types of government activity.[4] I was keen that each historian take responsibility for initiating projects and then supervising them on this basis. So Ian McGibbon took responsibility for diplomatic and military history with an overview of the ministries of defence and foreign affairs. I proposed a new historian to replace Charlotte Macdonald, with interests in social, family and women's history and with an overview of the social-welfare activities of government. We advertised and I was lucky to be able to appoint a lively and original historian, Melanie Nolan, who immediately began work on the state and women's welfare. In 1992 she followed Charlotte to the Victoria University history department, but once more we found an outstanding replacement in the person of Bronwyn Dalley.

I suggested a third historian with strengths in economic and labour history and with a portfolio which covered government activities in agriculture, commerce, energy, labour, transport and of course finance. Here too we advertised and were able to appoint a senior lecturer in sociology, John Martin, who proved a hard-working and highly proficient historian. He had previously been employed in the Ministry of Works. So when in my early days I discovered that the Electricity Department had sponsored a history from Mary Ronnie and Peter O'Connor, which proved overly long, unbalanced and therefore unpublishable, John Martin eagerly picked up the challenge and rewrote it remarkably quickly into a beautifully illustrated history which pleased both the new Electricorp and the many readers.[5] Later he wrote a definitive history of the Labour Department.[6] So, along with an editor with impeccable standards, David Green, very quickly I had the core of a great staff. I used to say that we had by far the best department of New Zealand history in the country. Every morning at 10.40 we joined the staff of the Dictionary for coffee and good conversation, and on Thursdays the branch had lunch together. The morale and sense of excitement in the branch rose, and we had a very collegial team, which expanded rapidly with additional resident historians as I won new contracts for us.

The second piece of luck and good timing was the presence of Michael Bassett as minister. These were the last years of the Fourth Labour Government, which achieved fame by introducing 'Rogernomics' and by corporatising the public sector. But while all other public servants were struggling with the new priorities, I found that the history business had in Bassett a special patron. Within a week of the announcement of my appointment I received a handwritten note inviting me to visit to discuss plans, and this was repeated subsequently. At the time I thought it was not at all strange for a third-tier public servant to have one-on-ones over lunch with the minister, but later I realised how unusual it was. I was able to talk through ideas with the minister, and he in turn would make them happen with financial support. To my astonishment I found that he had persuaded the Lottery Grants Board to offer us $250,000 for a new historical atlas, a grant repeated the following year, and finally topped off by a grant of $1 million. So we had $1.5 million to develop this exciting project. Then I discovered, when I looked

Michael Bassett, as minister of internal affairs, presents $1 million to Raewyn Dalziel, chair of the Historical Branch advisory committee, and Peter Boag, secretary of internal affairs. The money was for the New Zealand History Trust, and the presentation occurred just before I became chief historian in 1989. MICHAEL BASSETT COLLECTION

at the branch budget, that the minister had ensured it was very well provided for. In the first quarter I was amazed to discover that we had $71,000 to spend on operating expenses but the budgeted spending only amounted to $40,000. I had $31,000 for discretionary spending which, innocently unaware of the difference between capital and operating expenses, I immediately splurged on five new Macintosh personal computers, several printers and a projector. There would be no more handwritten notes for the typing pool.

There was other largesse from the minister. Several months before my arrival he had set up a New Zealand History Research Trust Fund with capital of $1.1 million to support research and writing in New Zealand history, and had given funding for bursaries to support graduate students researching New Zealand history. Then I received a note from the Lottery Grants Board one day that $200,000 had been offered to us for a new encyclopedia of New Zealand. It took me some time and anguish to work out quite how to spend this, for it seemed to me at the time that with the Dictionary of New Zealand Biography in full operation and work about to begin on the historical atlas, there was simply not the scholarly capital and human energy around to begin a new encyclopedia at that moment. Eventually the money helped fund an encyclopedia of women's organisations. Most people taking on a new government job arrive to find the coffers bare. To discover an embarrassment of riches, plus a hotline to the minister, was unusual indeed. It also helped to give me instant status among the boffins of Internal Affairs. They were a really impressive lot to work with – professional, efficient and good fun, and a far cry from *Gliding On*. To my surprise I quickly came to the judgement that working in the public service was more enjoyable than in a university, from the perspective of day-to-day interactions.

A third piece of luck and timing was that two years before, at a time when the appointment of a chief historian was on hold and the future of the branch very uncertain, a previous minister, Peter Tapsell, had invited Robin Williams, a former vice-chancellor of Otago University and former head of the State Services Commission, to prepare a report on the Historical Publications Branch, as it was then called. He was tasked with working out whether the branch still had a role, and if so, what it should do. Williams decided that indeed the branch should exist, largely because there were no more than a dozen full-time-equivalent people writing history in New Zealand universities, and 'Historical research and publication promotes a sense of national identity, has a cultural value, and is useful in policy development'.[7] Williams suggested that the time for the branch to collect and publish documents was over and that its publications should be shorter and 'written to be read'; he also argued that the branch should make a real effort to encourage Māori and oral history.[8] This report in effect gave me a strategic plan which I proceeded to follow religiously over the subsequent few years.

In addition the report recommended the setting up of an advisory committee appointed by the minister and providing advice to the chief historian. It was given a role 'in offering professional advice, maintaining standards, and monitoring performance'. In 1988 the committee had been appointed, and had held four meetings before I began work. Its existence was a huge advantage. It was a strong committee, chaired by Raewyn Dalziel from Auckland University, who was another close friend of Michael Bassett and a fine historian. Raewyn had been on the committee which appointed me. On the advisory committee of ten, there were also five other academics, all of whom I knew. The group provided a wonderful sounding board for ideas and became enthusiastic supporters of our new direction with a hotline to the minister.

I came to realise that the committee also provided great protection. There is a major problem with the role of official historians hired by governments. Because the government pays their salary, it is very easy for critics to see their work as propaganda, intended to justify the actions of government. The advisory committee provided a mechanism to protect the intellectual integrity and scholarly independence of such historians. They examined all proposals for branch work and stood ready to defend its quality and direction. As the political and departmental environment began to become rather less favourable to my kind of history over the subsequent years, I sought added protection from the committee. In mid-1991 I brought their deliberations into the Historical Branch's formal 'statement of service performance', presented to Parliament at the end of each year. I set up a system whereby every project had a cover sheet, specifying its outline, structure, approach and detailed timetable. The committee met every four months, and at each meeting the writers had to provide a formal report outlining their progress against this cover sheet. The committee then formally approved, or did not approve, progress on the project. The percentage of approvals became the formal statement of service to Parliament. This became both an effective way of monitoring the projects and an advertisement for our own efficiency.

I became convinced that the advisory committee offered a uniquely valuable system to uphold the academic freedom of official history. In other societies, such as the United States and Australia, historians of war and government were usually hired by the departments they were researching. American military historians were employees of the US defence forces. Obviously this provided little protection. If they wrote history not approved by their political masters, they could be ordered to rewrite the material. In our situation we had a group of dedicated historians located not in the department they were researching, but in the Department of Internal Affairs. What made the timing of my appointment even more fortunate was that a month before I took up my position, Cabinet, under Michael Bassett's leadership, had passed a formal minute which asserted that the development of government histories, the appointment of their historians and the monitoring of the work required the oversight of the Department of Internal Affairs, which would of course be exercised by the Historical Branch. Thus we had a branch of government which was at one remove from the subject matter of official history, and was protected by an advisory committee filled with scholars and academics and by a Cabinet minute. So convinced did I become that this was a solution to the old issue of intellectual freedom for official historians that I began to promote it overseas. I talked to people in Australia, who began to agitate for such a structure there, and in 1992 I went to Canberra to brief members of the Australian senate on our system. Then in 1995 I presented a paper to the Society for Federal Government Historians in Washington, where I outlined how our system upheld scholarly independence for official historians. Neither, it must be conceded, followed our lead.

It was not long before the political situation changed and I found the advisory committee did indeed provide protection. For in October 1990 the Labour Government was defeated and a National Government came to power. Michael Bassett had retired from the role as minister of internal affairs even before the election, with Margaret Austin becoming our minister. She was an educated woman and fully supportive of our work. But Jim Bolger, head of the new National government, decided that Internal Affairs should be the responsibility of Graeme Lee, member for Coromandel. Lee was a fundamentalist Christian with little background in New Zealand history. My relationship with him did not get off to a good start. In December 1990 I was asked to give the keynote address to the New Zealand sociology conference in Christchurch. Given that it was 1990, the sesquicentenary of the Treaty of Waitangi, I decided to look at how New Zealand had commemorated the centennial of the Treaty fifty years before, in 1940. In the course of my remarks I briefly compared the 1940 celebrations with what had happened in 1990, and used the phrase that '1990 was a bit of a fizzer'. I should have guessed that there might be a reporter in the audience; and to my horror I opened the newspaper the next day to see a headline 'NZ's 1990 year called "a fizzer"' and quoting the words of the government's chief historian. The Department of Internal Affairs was responsible for the 1990 commemoration and that very week Graeme Lee had managed to obtain some additional money from Cabinet for that purpose. I heard about his fury while still in Christchurch. I scurried to the airport to catch a plane for Wellington and summoned Raewyn Dalziel as chair of the advisory committee, and together we visited the minister to give my apologies, assert that I had been quoted out of context, and outline the work of the branch.

My apologies paid off. Nine months later, in August 1991, I was confronted by what was called 'a scoping review'. This had been established by the new government's Cabinet Expenditure Control Committee to direct officials of the Treasury and State Services Commission to examine all businesses in the department and recommend whether their outputs should continue or be discontinued – specifically, whether government still required those outputs, whether they were best produced by a government department, and, if so, whether there was scope for reducing expenditure. The review recommended that all funding to the Historical Branch should cease and that if the operations of the branch survived then this must be on the basis of full cost recovery. This would mean the end of employment for the branch historians, including myself. I was not averse to some cost recovery. Indeed, on taking up the chief historian's position, I had decided that if under the Cabinet minute we were tasked with monitoring histories of other government departments, then it was only fair and reasonable that those departments should pay for our services. I had various ambitions which could only be fulfilled if we could start earning money, and this seemed a fair way of doing so. We began to charge departments $15,000 for our monitoring role.

So when the committee argued that all our costs should be earned, I was prepared with a compromise. I suggested that all departmental histories

Graeme Lee, in the centre, after launching the guides to oral history and women's history in 1993. Also present were, from left, Megan Hutching (author of the oral history guide), myself, Raewyn Dalziel (chair of the Historical Branch advisory committee) and Bronwyn Labrum (author of the women's history guide).
MANATŪ TAONGA MINISTRY FOR CULTURE AND HERITAGE

should be conducted on a cost-recovery mode, but other history work, such as the projects of the branch members, should continue to be funded. This would save our core staff and the heart of our operation. The officials opposed this alternative and I could see that it would be a close-run thing. Once more the advisory committee stepped into the fight, passing supportive motions and sending letters to the minister. I visited my friends in the new Ministry for Cultural Affairs, who proceeded to brief their minister, Doug Graham. I also decided to go and see Graeme Lee. When I turned up at the minister's office, the departmental chief executive, Perry Cameron, was already there. He wanted to get rid of the Historical Branch, and wanted to brief the minister himself. Cameron was in the process of telling me to leave the office when Graeme Lee walked in. He immediately said, 'No, let him stay. I would like to hear Jock's point of view.' I was just briefing him when the phone rang. It was Doug Graham, arguing for the survival of the Historical Branch. So Graeme Lee went in to fight for us and we survived in Cabinet by one vote.

From that point on, Graeme Lee was our most enthusiastic defender. He loved launching our books, when he would refer to me as 'my chief historian

Jock'. When he left the role as minister he wrote to the advisory committee that 'I was very proud of our achievements of the Historical Branch, particularly in the United States-New Zealand 50th year celebrations and suffrage year.' The last two are a later story, and indeed the crisis over the branch's funding was not the last time I came to depend on the independent support of the advisory committee against the department's chief executive, Perry Cameron.

The heart of the activities of the Historical Branch was the writing of official histories. In an earlier meeting before my arrival a paper to the advisory committee had summed up the projects the branch was undertaking. There were five – a history of the State Services Commission; a history of female immigration to New Zealand, which was simply a write-up of Charlotte Macdonald's thesis; two volumes on the history of the police; and Ian McGibbon's work on New Zealand in the Korean War. It was a very thin menu. I set out to attract more work, in part to justify our existence, in part to enrich New Zealanders' understanding of history. This meant that we had to write books about government activity which would appeal to readers and please those who commissioned them. The Williams report had warned against huge volumes of documents, and had recommended histories that were reasonably short and readable. I fully agreed and decided that we had to start working on different kinds of official history – not long, exhaustive histories of departments as institutions. Instead we should have histories which told of the impact of government activity on New Zealand life and so involved much social history. Or we could have histories which treated the development of government policy and became of real value for policy-makers in the future. In proposing at my first meeting with the advisory committee a new series on 'Government and the people', I noted that few people would read books on the institutional history of a government department such as Internal Affairs. But they would read history about what such departments regulated, such as the history of gambling or censorship or the treatment of children. For example, when I visited the Ministry of Transport to discuss a history, I wrote back to the ministry with three possibilities, none of them institutional histories of the Ministry of Transport. The first was a three-year project on transport and New Zealand society, which would be less a history of changes in modes of transport than an examination of how those changes shaped New Zealand society; the second was a two-year project on the history of the car – its social impact and how government had regulated car transport; and the third was a one-year project of photographs and oral histories about lighthouses and lighthouse keepers.[9] In the end the ministry chose the first, which was eventually published as an excellent book by James Watson, *Links*.

Similarly, after talking to the governor-general's office about a history, I submitted a proposal which said:

> the theme of the publication should be the changing social, political and constitutional role of the Governor. This is not intended to be a detailed blow-by-blow account of events, nor a narrow legal treatise. Rather it is intended to be an overview which describes the evolution of the Governor's position in New Zealand. The individual personalities and contributions of particular Governors will be highlighted.[10]

Eventually this book too appeared, as Gavin McLean's *Governors*.

I insisted that the books had to be attractive to readers – reasonably short, written with some literary grace and clarity, and well illustrated, with thoroughly researched photographs. Not that popular appeal was given a higher priority than scholarly accuracy. I included in my recommendation on the governor-general proposal the sentence: 'To satisfy an audience of policy-makers and constitutional experts the publication will need to be an accurate and scholarly work based on thorough research.'

Armed with this vision and backed by the Cabinet minute, which gave us a formal overview of all departmental history projects, I then set out to attract clients. I wrote to every government department offering our services in any historical project. We prepared a glossy corporate profile which I could hand out on my subsequent visits, and we held an open day. In my proposals for departments I offered them assistance in defining the project, drawing up the job specifications, selecting the historian; and then, once selected, I promised the close supervision of one of the branch historians, the requirement of a detailed report on progress every four months to ensure requirements of length and timetable were met, editing of the final manuscript and supervision of the publishing process. I also offered to house the contracted historians in the Historical Branch, both because I believed this would make the supervision easier and also because I was keen to develop a lively community of

The cover of a Historical Branch strategic plan, featuring the covers of some of the branch's publications.

engaged historians. I set up a monthly seminar where the historians could present their work publicly and gain valuable feedback and encouragement. For all these services we initially charged $15,000 plus the salary of the contracted historian; but after the scoping review in 1991 when we were committed to charge on a full cost-recovery basis, our charges became $10,000 a year.

We were remarkably successful in attracting new work. Here again the timing was highly fortuitous. The radical changes in the public sector brought about by the Fourth Labour Government meant that quite a number of institutions went out of existence. As they disappeared from the scene there were often residual funds left, or former members agitating to have their story documented. The history of the Electricity Department was one such project, with the new state-owned enterprise, Electricorp, keen to show their faith with the old department. Here too the book that eventuated focused not on the department itself but upon the much more dramatic story of building the nation's dams.

There were also two environmental bodies that disappeared in the reorganisation that created the Department of Conservation and Ministry for the Environment. One was the Water and Soil Conservation Authority, and the second was the old Wildlife Service. Ross Galbreath did a magnificent job telling the fascinating story of Wildlife's efforts to save the country's flora and fauna, with the high point being Don Merton's work on the Chatham Islands black robin. We then hired Ross to write a history when the DSIR was abolished. In drawing up a proposal for the DSIR, my suggestions were characteristic of my ambitions for state history. I dismissed the need for an administrative history which would 'not make for exciting reading' and was unnecessary because a fifty-year-anniversary history already existed; I examined the idea of an economic history which would look at the impact of DSIR work on New Zealand productivity but dismissed that because it would ignore the department's contribution to pure science; then I suggested an intellectual history, which would not be organised around the institutional divisions of the department but rather would focus on 'perhaps ten to a dozen research problems', and in which each chapter 'would be an interesting story in which the drama of discovery could be explained'. They accepted this suggestion and Ross followed it to the letter to produce a second fascinating book.

The timing was also perfect because the 1990s were a hundred years after the great reforming Liberal government of the 1890s. A number of government departments wished to mark their centenaries with a publication. The Housing Corporation asked for a series of essays to commemorate the centennial of State Advances in 1894, which we managed to convert into a full history of state housing policy. The Department of Agriculture gave us eighteen months to complete a history of the state and agriculture in time for its centenary in 1992; and John Martin's history of the Labour Department was also timed for that department's anniversary. I had hoped to convince my own department to join in the anniversary party by commemorating 150 years since the Colonial Secretary's Office (the predecessor of Internal Affairs) was created in 1840. Initially my powers of persuasion failed with my colleagues; but as a result of these efforts the section of the department which regulated gambling suggested I approach the Lotteries Commission, then in the full flood of success with the early years of Instant Kiwi and Lotto. The chief executive, David Bale, was enthusiastic, and David Grant was hired to pen a lively history of lotteries and gambling in New Zealand society. The Ministry for Civil Defence, another part of Internal Affairs, also hired us to revise and complete a draft history of their organisation. Eventually the department did agree to a full history, which was completed by an ex-minister, Michael Bassett himself.

Two national anniversaries also helped the cause. One was the sesquicentenary of the Treaty of Waitangi in 1990, which heightened public awareness of history. The second was the centenary of women's suffrage in 1993. After a meeting with the National Council of Women and the Ministry of Women's Affairs in July 1990, Melanie Nolan and I promoted our services to government departments to mark the anniversary with historical publications. No fewer than six departmental projects eventuated, usually as a result of agitation by women within these departments who wished to have their predecessors remembered. There were small publications about women in the Valuation Department, the Ministry of Commerce, Inland Revenue and the health system, and booklets on the treatment of women in social welfare and income support. In addition the Historical Branch marked the anniversary with our own efforts. Melanie Nolan organised a major international conference on the history of suffrage and began work on her own book about women and the welfare state.

However, I wanted to mark 1993 with a more ambitious work. So when in 1990 I heard that Michael Bassett had offered us $200,000 from the Lottery Grants Board for a new encyclopedia, I decided to use some of the funds for an encyclopedia of women's organisations. I established a committee of the country's leading women historians, led by Margaret Tennant from Massey. Anne Else was appointed as editor, ably assisted by Fiona McKergow as researcher, Tania Rei researching Māori organisations and Alison Carew as copy-editor. The book was not intended as a complete encyclopedia of all organisations, which would have been an impossible job. Instead the committee suggested that the publication be divided into different types of organisation (thirteen as it turned out). Each section would have an introduction edited by a specialist, followed by entries on the most significant past and current organisations in that field. Anne did a brilliant job cajoling the contributors into delivering on time and seeing the whole project through to completion, with Alison's able assistance. Fiona unearthed forgotten histories and collected excellent images. All was going swimmingly until one day in December 1991 I received a call from the chief executive of the department, Perry Cameron. He said that he was unhappy with the presence of a section on lesbian organisations in the book and suggested that lesbians be included in a new section on 'feminism'. He suggested that I consult with the advisory committee and that I wear a skirt when I met with them.

Perry Cameron had won fame as the first person to swim Cook Strait from south to north, and had subsequently entered management in Canada, but I had never got on well with him and we had already had that contretemps when he had tried to exclude me from meeting the minister. I suspect that his concern was less his own prejudices than a desire to keep on side with the minister, Graeme Lee. Lee had won some notoriety as an opponent of gay relationships, although he had actually appointed a gay woman, and very helpful member, to the Historical Branch advisory committee. When I discussed the issue with Anne Else she was clear that she saw the issue as censorship and could not continue in the project if the section was removed. She agreed that most of the women writing for the project would also refuse to participate. I tried to have Margaret Tennant, who chaired the book's advisory committee, and Raewyn Dalziel as chair of the branch advisory committee come to see the chief executive. Perry Cameron refused to meet with them and claimed that he was not seeking the removal of the section, but 'a broader

Anne Else proudly displaying Women Together *soon after the launch in 1993.* ANNE ELSE, PRIVATE COLLECTION

mandate for its inclusion'. In response I gained endorsement for the lesbian chapter from the project's committee and from both the Ministry of Women's Affairs and Dame Miriam Dell, chair of the 1993 Suffrage Centennial Trust. Eventually we made a symbolic concession by using a quote to name each section on the contents page, rather than stating the types of organisations they covered. Perry Cameron was not happy. Six months later, when my performance review came up, he wrote to the general manager, 'Please ensure my assessment of poor performance is passed on to Jock Phillips.'[11]

There were two interesting follow-up incidents. The launch of *Women Together*, as the book came to be titled, by Governor-General Silvia Cartwright, was a glittering occasion at Government House. Just before the speeches were due to begin, I received a note to come and see the minister, Graeme Lee, urgently in a side room. My heart fell. Presumably he had seen the chapter on lesbian organisations and wished to express his displeasure. I walked into the room and the minister greeted me enthusiastically. 'Thank heavens you are here, Jock. Can you tell me what I should say in my speech?' I could feel the relaxation flooding my body. Some time later Warren Cooper became minister. He was not a man with much instinctive sympathy for the historical work of the department, but he had even less time for Perry Cameron. I recall the sense of exaltation when, as a result of a dispute between the two men over an appointment, Perry Cameron was forced to resign. At the impromptu drinks session later that day I was not alone in smiling broadly.

Anniversaries, energetic lobbying and promotion, professional performance and good luck meant the number of projects in the Historical Branch increased fast. The five projects in place when I started in March 1989 had become twenty-two by November 1991 and twenty-six by July 1997. In that year we earned $440,000, built up from nothing in 1989. The vast majority were completed. In retrospect it was a halcyon time. From 1981 to 1988 the branch had seen six books published – fewer than one a year. Between 1990 and 2000 we produced sixty-seven books, averaging over six a year. That level was not sustained. Over the next sixteen years another sixty-five were published, about four a year, and in the five years to 2017 the figure dropped to three.[12]

Not all of these books were official histories of government activity. We also supervised work for voluntary organisations such as Margaret Tennant's history of the children's health camps, and for a time we provided a service auditing historical publications, such as a local history for the Nelson City Council. I was also committed to continuing the proud tradition of official war histories, since that had long been a fundamental role of the branch and one with political support. Indeed, within months of my appointment I found myself vehemently defending the intellectual value of the war histories when we discovered that a former National Party minister, Eric Halstead, had shamelessly plagiarised the war histories for a potboiler on the New Zealand forces in World War II. We succeeded in getting the volumes pulped. So work continued on war histories – Ian McGibbon worked on his fine two-volume history of New Zealand in the Korean War; Roberto Rabel prepared a volume on the domestic story of the Vietnam War; Chris Pugsley wrote a history on the New Zealand involvement in the Indonesia–Malaysia Confrontation and the Malayan Emergency; and we supported Laurie Brocklebank, a Massey graduate student, to complete a history of Jayforce, the soldiers who occupied Japan in a peacekeeping role after World War II. With funding from the Ministry of Defence, Ian put together an exhaustive *Companion to New Zealand Military History*, which was a model reference work likely to be of value for years to come. We also planned a series of volumes to mark the projected hundredth anniversary of World War I, twenty years ahead. I had learnt from tough experience that it was never too early to plan for an anniversary.

As chief historian I was keen to contribute personally to war history – not that I was interested in the story of battles and bombs, but I remained intrigued by the cultural meaning of war to New Zealanders. Again anniversaries were a significant inspiration. So in 1990, on the seventy-fifth anniversary of Gallipoli and within a year of becoming chief historian, my book with Chris Maclean on war memorials was published. I also delivered a published lecture on the meaning of Gallipoli which challenged the idea that it was the birth of New Zealand national identity. In March of that year I travelled to Turkey to present the paper at a gathering of international historians, timed in March for the seventy-fifth anniversary of the beginning of the naval attack. After the conference we headed to Gallipoli Peninsula, where I spent an unforgettable day walking the terrain with a very short Chris Pugsley and a very tall Bill Gammage, the two sniping at each other as to whether the New Zealanders or Australians were really the finest soldiers on these shores. I will never forget one moment when one of us slipped coming down an old trench wall and dislodged a large bone. Chris picked it up, put it against my thigh and said 'That must be a Kiwi – too big for a Turk.' We carried the bone to one of the war cemeteries and buried it as we recited a karakia. I also went across the Tasman twice in 1990 to talk about war memorials and national identity and contributed an essay to a catalogue on war art.

Then in late 1991 Graeme Lee contacted me and asked if the Historical Branch could prepare a publication to mark the fiftieth anniversary of the arrival of the US marines in the country in June 1942. I read Nancy Taylor's book on the home front, and realised this was a fascinating topic which combined official history duties with my own interests in both American and New Zealand history. I decided that we would prepare a short illustrated booklet on the 'American invasion'. In February of that year I went to the United States on a Fulbright travelling fellowship to give lectures, and while in Washington I decided to see if there were any official US photographs of their New Zealand sojourn. In the National Archives I came across a shoebox of

Scenes from my trip to Gallipoli in April 1990 – the conference in Ankara with the Turkish red flag dominating proceedings (top), while Chris Pugsley speaks, watched by Ahmet Mete Tuncoku, Bill Gammage and, of course, Kemal Ataturk. With Bill Gammage (centre) and Chris Pugsley (above) I spent a memorable day walking the battlefields of Anzac.

images compiled by the marines' public-relations section, which was intended to illustrate the warm relationships between US marines and New Zealand civilians, especially women. The images were good, but the Hollywood-style captions telling of marines 'doing a mean line' with local women were irresistible. There was a problem. Some days before I had broken my glasses. I could not see without them so rushed in to an optician for an emergency replacement pair. The new glasses cost more than US$1000, which maxed out my credit card. When I visited the US National Archives I had about $50 in cash in my pockets. So I had to be very selective indeed when choosing which images to be photocopied at 20 cents a go. I returned with enough to add considerable spice to the short history, which we entitled *Brief Encounter*. The book itself was enthusiastically received by the minister and American veterans, and the print run of 900 quickly sold out. A few weeks after its release I received a call from a Māori woman in Gisborne, Peggy Kaua. The book contained a photo, sourced in the Washington archives, of a marine dressed in a piupiu dancing with a local Māori woman. Peggy was the woman in the photo and she politely asked if I could possibly contact the marine in question. She had never forgotten him. About a month later I received a letter from an American marine, Norman Hatch, who said he was the individual in that same photo and would I by any chance know how to contact Peggy. I duly exchanged the addresses and telephone numbers, but whatever happened subsequently I never found out.

In 1992 I was determined that the awful cost of the Passchendaele battle of 12 October 1917 not be forgotten. Within two hours, 843 New Zealand men had died in the largest loss of life on one day in New Zealand's recorded history. But the story was almost unknown in 1990s New Zealand. So I arranged a seventy-fifth-anniversary service at the National War Memorial Hall of Memories, where we read Leonard Hart's unforgettable description of that day. I also published an account in the country's main newspapers.

If histories of government and war provided important reasons for our existence, the original centennial Historical Branch had established a precedent for a role in contributing to New Zealanders' sense of nationhood. We kicked off a number of big projects designed with this in mind. The first and biggest was the *New Zealand Historical Atlas*. Work had begun on a historical atlas for the country as part of the 1940 centennial, but the project had dragged and was eventually killed in the early 1950s. Even before my arrival as chief historian, plans for a new project were under way. The Department of Survey

Peggy Kaua teaches Norman Hatch how to dance in Gisborne in 1942.
U.S. NATIONAL ARCHIVES & RECORDS ADMINISTRATION

and Land Information (DOSLI) had begun to plan a commemorative atlas for the 1990 sesquicentenary. Ian McGibbon, as acting chief historian, had met with DOSLI and convinced them of the value of a joint DOSLI/Historical Branch historical atlas. A seminar had been suggested, but funding had yet to be found. Michael Bassett obviously heard about these plans and within weeks of my appointment the Lottery Grants Board provided the money. I also organised a seminar involving the editor of the Australian historical atlas and scholars from around the country to thrash out the timetable and approaches. The seminar enthusiastically endorsed the project, recommended a six-year time frame, and pushed for extensive coverage of social history, the biological and geological history of the country, and strong Māori representation. Māori perspectives were fluently presented by Jim Milroy, Sydney Melbourne, Te Aue Davis and Miria Simpson. Soon after, I met with DOSLI and gained their agreement for the use of a cartographic team with no payment for copyright on existing maps or mapping resources. I asked Ian McGibbon to take on the role of the managing editor, and we then were delighted to be able to appoint Malcolm McKinnon as the general editor. I had worked with Malcolm at the Victoria University history department, where we had frequently been fellow stirrers. Malcolm had trained as a geographer as well as a historian, and had a lifelong fascination with maps. He was a most creative, thoughtful historian with high scholarly standards, and he had a superb manner in welding together an effective team.

Having set up the project, I stood back to watch Malcolm, with the assistance of a highly original deputy, Russell Kirkpatrick, and a fine lead cartographer, Barry Bradley, put together the atlas. Early on Malcolm decided to use one room as 'the map room', with a space for each of the hundred plates. Over the next six years we all watched entranced as the plates gradually took shape. As hoped, science and social history were well represented, and the presentation of Māori perspectives was stunning. Following the lead of the Dictionary of New Zealand Biography, Malcolm set up a Māori committee, in which Miria Simpson, Charles Royal and Bruce Biggs played leading roles, and with their help he presented Māori history in new ways. Māori mapping was oral rather than visual, so the atlas used three-dimensional 'Papatūānuku' maps to clothe the landscape in oral traditions. Rather than create conflict by trying to map tribal boundaries, Malcolm and his team concentrated on place names. Russell Kirkpatrick was very much a postmodern map-maker, so with Malcolm's enthusiastic support he devised intriguing ways to highlight historical points of view through appropriate visual perspectives. For example, in a page on the history of transportation there was a map centred on Nelson. Thick blue lines emanating out from Nelson showed the tonnage of shipping over a forty-day period in the 1880s, while the jagged relief map of the land illustrated the problem of building a rail link to the city. Nelson's peculiar transport problem was illustrated without a word being written. The *Atlas* ran highly successfully with very little input from me. I contributed two plates – on the domestic history of the two world wars – which I found a fascinating challenge and which brought home just how much careful

Malcolm McKinnon in the map room at work on the New Zealand Historical Atlas *(above); and Jim Bolger launching the finished volume on the evening of the day that he had been replaced as prime minister in 1997 (below). This political crisis, rather than the appeal of the atlas, explains the barrage of television cameras at the launch. Miria Simpson looks on, while I seem singularly unimpressed.*
MANATŪ TAONGA MINISTRY FOR CULTURE AND HERITAGE

gathering of statistical material was required to put together one plate. Malcolm was insistent, and quite rightly so, that every line on the page had to be scrupulously documented.

The launch of the atlas in 1997 was a dramatic affair. Jim Bolger was due to launch the volume. But the event occurred late in the very afternoon when Bolger was rolled as prime minister and replaced by Jenny Shipley. As we arrived for the launch it was unclear who would actually do the honours, and I recall a rather harassed deputy prime minister, Don McKinnon (Malcolm's brother), sidling up to us and warning that Bolger might not appear. But to his very great credit, the ex-prime minister fronted up and launched the atlas with appropriate grace and enthusiasm.

Another contribution to national identity was a project I initiated on the peopling of New Zealand. In 1989 Judith Binney had invited me to write an overview of New Zealand historiography. I jumped at the opportunity, since it gave me an excuse to brush up on my knowledge of New Zealand historical writing. The article was published as 'Of Verandahs and Fish and Chips and Footie on Saturday Afternoon'. I argued that New Zealand historians had singularly failed to explore the history of New Zealand culture 'in all its richness – its smells, its tastes, its fashions, its rituals, its words'.[13] I also suggested that if historians were really to explore such culture then they needed to examine where that culture came from. They had to examine the peopling of New Zealand. I wrote: 'We cannot understand what made New Zealand different unless we understand the habits and the values of those who came here. We need to trace who those people were and where they came from; and we need to question that naive frontier hypothesis, which simply assumes that it is the frontier that creates a new people.'[14] That challenge to the profession became a challenge to myself and I was keen to find some way to discover the regional and cultural origins of the Pākehā who had peopled New Zealand.

My initial hope had been to develop such a project at the Museum of New Zealand, but that did not eventuate. Instead in 1995 I realised that the new Foundation for Research, Science and Technology, set up to fund research projects in the Crown research institutes which had replaced the DSIR, was also open to others. So I applied for two years' funding for a pair of researchers to begin investigating this issue. We succeeded in getting the money. One of the researchers, Terry Hearn, began using a scientific sample of death registers to determine the characteristics of those who had migrated to New Zealand

– their age, gender, family situation, occupational background, country and region of origin. The other researcher, Paul Hudson, and then Nicholas Bayley, examined the cultural characteristics of these places of origin. In 1997 we obtained funding for another two years. For some time I was not able to spend as much time as I wanted on the project, and in the end we decided that the drafts produced by Terry and Nicholas were simply too long to be published. So instead we put them up on the web, and then I sat down and put together a much shorter summary of the findings. The manuscript was eventually published in 2008 as *Settlers*. As I had hoped, the book has been widely used as a starting point for many types of investigation of New Zealand culture, from the origins of New Zealand English to explaining patterns of religion and drinking.

There were two other forms of history, Māori and oral history, which the Williams report had emphasised and which occupied much creative energy in my early years as chief historian. Of Māori history, Williams wrote that the chief historian needs to 'seek means by which the writing and publishing of Maori history may be advanced'. In considering this matter, Ian McGibbon as acting chief historian had suggested some financial assistance for historians 'in this field' but nothing had been done for lack of funding.[15] In addition, as I took over there were discussions about a possible cross-government Māori History and Archival Council to assist iwi to maintain archives and train researchers, but the officials involved felt that this raised expectations which could not be fulfilled, and nothing eventuated.[16] The only ongoing project was an oral-history programme for Ngāti Awa, which had been funded through the Lottery Grants Board after Michael Bassett met with Professor Sid Mead. I spent a fascinating day in Whakatāne being shown around by local kuia, but it was clear that this did not offer a precedent for other tribal histories.

Still aware of my own failures in involving Māori at the Stout Centre, I was determined to achieve something, and it quickly became clear to me that what was really needed was a Māori historian in the branch. At that time none of the university history departments had a historian with a Māori cultural background, and I thought we could provide a lead. But how? Within my first month on the job I applied for additional funding to provide for such a position, but this was turned down.[17] The only option was to use the money we were beginning to earn for our services to support a position. The trouble with this was that since the earning of revenue varied from year to year we could only guarantee an appointment for one year, rather than a permanent position. Learning from past failures, I decided to consult. I began with Miria Simpson, Māori editor at the Dictionary, who as a forthright woman had run into some difficulties at the Dictionary. I quickly befriended her. She never forgot my early support, and provided me with a valuable source of advice for the next five years. I then talked to Jim Milroy of Ngāi Tūhoe; Irihapeti Ramsden, a good friend whom I had met through Phillida; and Bill Cooper, the department's Māori adviser. They all pointed out that to make a permanent appointment of a Māori historian from one iwi could create tensions with other iwi. So, faced with guaranteed funding for only one year, I decided to make a virtue of that fact and turn the position into a fellowship. This would allow Māori from different iwi to receive support in turn, provided we earned sufficient revenue.

At the end of 1989 a committee comprising the same people who had given me advice interviewed candidates. The interviews were largely conducted in te reo Māori and each began with formal mihi with whānau present. There

Members of the Historical Branch and Dictionary of New Zealand Biography teams at the Ruapani hui at Rongopai in 1990.

were two outstanding candidates, Joe Pere from Te Aitanga-a-Māhaki and Rongowhakaata in the Gisborne area, who was a published historian, and a young and recent graduate, Te Ahukaramū Charles Royal, from Ngāti Raukawa. It was a very difficult choice. In the end we appointed Joe Pere. But I was so impressed with Charles that I managed to scrape together some money to hire him to write a guide to researching tribal histories, and the next year he became the fellow in Māori history.

Joe Pere set to work researching the history of Ruapani, a famous Tūranganui-a-Kiwa ancestor. A year later his findings were presented at a hui on Rongopai marae. This was another powerful occasion. At the pōwhiri at Rongopai I was expected to speak and to present a large koha to the hosts. I endlessly rehearsed my opening words of te reo and positioned myself in the front row of the manuhiri paepae. Charles Royal was sitting behind me. As the oratory flowed over me from the tangata whenua, Charles whispered, 'They don't want you to speak. English has never been spoken on this marae. Let me speak first.' So when it came my turn, Charles stood up and explained in te reo Māori that I was bringing a fat koha and unless I was allowed to speak in English, the koha would return to Wellington. I eventually stood and spoke. For the next few days it was a joy to sit in the whare looking at the magnificent painted kōwhaiwhai of Rongopai, listening to the fluent words about Ruapani roll around me. We broke these sessions with memorable trips to local landmarks and pā sites important to the Ruapani story. Although Joe Pere's work was not published, it was an inspiration to the local community in reviving the memory of Ruapani.

Two of the later fellows in Māori history never completed their projects, but some significant iwi history did emerge from the scheme – Charles Royal completed a beautiful book on the waiata of Ngāti Raukawa, Tip Reedy published a fine collection of the writings of Pita Kapiti, and Brad Haami put together a fascinating volume on the writings of his ancestors at Waimārama in Hawke's Bay, published as *Pūtea Whakairo: Māori and the Written Word*. The fellowship did not last after I had left the job, partly because the branch historians felt, quite fairly, that a one-year fellowship was too short to allow for the completion of a major work.

While the fellowship was my major initiative in Māori history, I tried to support Māori history and culture in other ways. We placed a priority on Māori subjects in our various awards schemes, and I decided that we also needed a Māori name. After a number of options were put forward by Māori supporters of the branch, Bruce Biggs' suggestion, Te Puna Kōrero Tuku Iho (the source of stories handed down), was adopted and appeared on our letterhead. In November 1992 a hui was proposed to establish an association of Māori historians. I agreed that the branch would provide Charles Royal's time, and assistance with transport and accommodation expenses. The result was the formation of Te Pouhere Kōrero, which has subsequently played a major role in the revival of writing by Māori historians. To help educate the Pākehā in the branch, I arranged a Māori immersion course which provided some understanding of te reo, if not fluency or full comfort with the language.

The other form of history emphasised in the Williams report was oral history. Williams wrote that the advent of the Official Information Act meant that people now had more caution about the written record, so oral history became a crucial tool for recording history. But when I became chief historian the branch had no oral historian and did not undertake oral history; its only interest in the area was supervising the annual grant to the New Zealand Oral History Association run by Judith Fyfe and Hugo Manson, which really meant that the department simply handed over the money. I realised that what we needed was an oral historian to undertake projects and give advice, and some funds to assist oral historians in the community. Unbelievably, with some more of that extraordinary run of luck which befell me in those early years, both problems were solved within eighteen months. First, while on holiday in early January 1990 and about to kayak down the Ōtaki River with my kids, I was rung by the Prime Minister's Department to say that the Australian government wished to give the New Zealand people A$1 million as a sesquicentennial gift. $100,000 was to be used for sporting trophies between the two countries; the remainder was 'for the support of oral history'. It was a hugely imaginative gift, and I suspect that the idea came from Don Watson, an Australian historian who was in Paul Keating's office. The Prime Minister's Department wanted ideas as to how the money might be used. I finished my kayaking and rushed home to suggest that the gift be put into a trust fund, with the earnings to be used for publicly contestable awards in oral history. The National Library also suggested that the funds be used to support a new oral history centre at the Alexander Turnbull Library. Our proposal received favour, and I was able to mend any hard feelings with the Turnbull by promising that all recordings funded by the awards would be deposited in the library.

At their inaugural meeting, members of the Australian Sesquicentennial Gift Trust for Oral History meet Robert Laurie, the Australian high commissioner (third from left) in 1990. The members are (from left) myself, Tamati Reedy, Judith Binney, Judith Fyfe and Ata Malifa.
MANATŪ TAONGA MINISTRY FOR CULTURE AND HERITAGE

So by mid-year the Australian Sesquicentennial Gift Trust in Oral History had been established, chaired by Judith Binney, and including two Māori (Te Aue Davis and Tamati Reedy), a Pacific Island advisor (Ata Malifa), an archivist (Sharon Dell), an academic historian (David Hamer) and Judith Fyfe from the Oral History Archive (our first resident at the Stout Centre). We were able to give out about $80,000 a year and the first call for applications in early 1991 attracted no fewer than 118 responses. Of course the creation of this award made the need for an oral historian even more urgent. But how to fund this? Once more a solution fell from the air. In June 1990 I was called to a meeting with the trustees of the New Zealand Oral History Archive and learnt that they were intending to cease operations from the end of the year. Immediately I realised that this left $50,000 in Vote Internal Affairs which was allocated as a grant to the archive. The money could be used to provide for an oral historian. In December 1990 Cabinet agreed that the funds would be transferred to the Historical Branch for an oral historian, that the branch would monitor all departmental oral-history projects and supervise the oral-history grants, and that new funds would go to the National Library for an Oral History Centre.

Before long we appointed Megan Hutching as the branch oral historian, and she did an outstanding job overseeing the early years of the awards in oral history and ensuring professional standards of recording. In addition we wrote to government departments offering our services to record oral histories; immediately the Statistics Department commissioned us to undertake six recordings. The next year I went to Australia and recorded a number of radio interviews about the scheme. I had seen this as a way of thanking the Australian people for their imaginative gift; I discovered, belatedly, that all it did was create resentment among some Australians that their government was funding New Zealand oral histories, but not recordings in their own country! As for New Zealand, the scheme has produced over 300 collections of oral history since 1991, all safely lodged in the Turnbull Library and all completed, under the guidance of the branch oral historian, to the highest standards of technical expertise and ethics. Megan went on to complete a fascinating book based on oral histories about the 'ten pound Poms' who came to New Zealand after World War II, while her successor Alison Parr also made a major contribution with a series of impressive oral-history volumes, largely about the war.

This encouragement of oral history within the community was but part of a larger mission to heighten research, writing and public awareness about New Zealand history in the broader society. Here again Robin Williams had been prescient. He wrote of 'the importance of encouraging local, often voluntary, effort, so that the broad basis of historical studies can be increased at least cost to central government'.[18] This was a cause close to my own heart. From the time in the 1970s when I had been involved in writing for the *Listener*, I had taken seriously the obligation of historians to speak to the wider community. My work at the Stout Centre indicated this; and in 1991 I published at the invitation of Warwick Roger an article in *Metro* magazine in which I argued that there were promising signs of a growing public interest in New Zealand history. The article concluded: 'Compared with the situation in the fifties, New Zealand has now become a country with a visible history; a history which can be located in our bookshops if not in our pubs. The past in New Zealand has at last got a future.'[19] This was a development which I believed in passionately and was keen to encourage. By 1993 when we were asked, like all government institutions at that time ruled by 'corporate speak', to come up with a 'mission statement', the words I penned were 'to contribute to an enhanced awareness and knowledge of New Zealand history among government, policy-makers and the New Zealand people'.

Yet again luck and timing were on my side. When I became chief historian Michael Bassett had just arranged for the Lottery Grants Board to give $1 million to a New Zealand History Research Trust Fund. Its aims were simply 'to encourage and support research into, and the writing and publication of, the history of New Zealand'. One of my very first tasks was to work out how to spend this fund. Quickly I made several crucial decisions. The value of the fund would have to be maintained, so some of the earnings needed to be reinvested to keep pace with inflation and ensure that its value in real terms was maintained. At the time I estimated that we were likely to earn $100,000 a year, but the reinvestments would reduce this to $50,000 for any grants, not a huge amount. We had to determine how the funds were spent very carefully. Initially it had been anticipated by the minister and the advisory committee that the funds could be used to support student bursaries in the branch plus publication subsidies for books. I believed that if we did this there would be very little left to support researchers and writers. So they were excluded and I determined to find other ways to meet these demands. Instead, all the available earnings were made available for awards in history to support writing and research. We decided to omit university historians, so all applicants would have to be freelance community historians. I suggested grants of $1000 to $12,000, and in the brochure the areas of support suggested were: 'political, social, cultural and labour history, community history, oral history, women's history and Māori history', with preference given 'to those projects which have a wide significance for understanding New Zealand's past.'

We were staggered at the response. The first call for applications in 1990 brought in 85 responses, requesting over $870,000; and the quality was impressive. After five years in 1994 we undertook a review and found that the awards had provided support for seventy-one projects, of which eighteen were in Māori history, sixteen were biographies, six were in local history and four about migrant groups. By that stage, twenty-two of the projects had been completed and made publicly available through publication or preparation of a manuscript deposited in a library. This was hugely cheering. There can be no question that these awards made a difference in facilitating freelance work in New Zealand history and they brought the branch in touch with history out-of-doors.

I also quickly acknowledged the need for support to publishers for significant works of New Zealand history. Although Creative New Zealand did provide assistance for the publication of non-fiction, few of their grants went to scholarly history books as distinct from works of creative writing. In the past the Historical Branch had provided some assistance, but in an ad hoc way and with, in my view, clear favoritism towards certain publishers. I was keen on a formal scheme of assistance open to all. I talked to publishers and realised that grants of no more than $5000 could make a huge difference to the viability of serious works of New Zealand history, where the print runs were likely to be small and the sales insignificant. It would allow books to appear that would make a difference to public understanding of the past. Then, when I looked at the branch budget, I discovered that we could fairly set aside $40,000 each year for this purpose. A grants to publishers scheme was established, which called for suitable manuscripts twice a year. Members of the branch then read the manuscripts and recommended up to about eight grants each year.

The branch bursary scheme to assist graduate students doing theses in New Zealand history had its origins in an initiative by Jim Holt during his short stint as chief historian. Through his support, Philippa Mein Smith received support to turn her thesis on the history of maternity services into a book. It was a good precedent, and in 1988 through the Lottery Grants Board Michael Bassett provided funds for eight to twelve bursaries each year. A total of fifty-two students were supported, each receiving about $4000. But in 1993 the funding ceased. I replaced this with a scheme whereby students were appointed as 'research apprentices' during their summer vacation. They spent half the time on their own work, half working as a research assistant for a branch historian. It was a worthwhile initiative while it lasted and we had several very promising students. Eventually financial stringency ended the scheme.

With the establishment of the two awards, we became increasingly aware of the numbers of people doing research in the community, but also of the deficiencies of some of the work that was being done. Two areas particularly concerned me. One was the low quality of the applications we received in the area of local history; and the second was the urgent need to increase both the quality and quantity of community research in Māori history. Out of this emerged an idea to develop a series of useful guidebooks to doing history. We commissioned Gavin McLean to prepare a guide to local history, and I invited Charles Royal to create a guide to writing tribal history. They were relatively short books of forty to sixty pages, intended to provide helpful clear advice, and were taken on for publication by Bridget Williams. Both were highly successful, with the local-history one selling over 1000 copies and *Te Haurapa*, the Māori history guide, being reprinted. Encouraged by this response, I invited Bronwyn Labrum to write a guide to doing women's history, timed for women's suffrage year, and Megan Hutching wrote a guide to oral history, which has become over the years a standard text.

My interest in awakening public interest in New Zealand's past was reflected in several other initiatives. In 1988 Michael Bassett had sponsored a series of cultural presentations at Parliament under the rubric 'Art in the House'. Keen to strengthen our political support, I came up with the idea of a companion series of 'History in the House'. The next year was the sesquicentennial of the Treaty, and the 1990 Commission, keen to broaden its mandate, had identified another six significant anniversaries. So under the title 'Towards 1990' I invited leading historians Atholl Anderson, Judith Binney, Raewyn Dalziel, Erik Olssen, Bill Oliver and David Hamer to examine each of these in turn. They delivered their lectures in the Beehive theatrette, and I concluded the series with one on '75 years since Gallipoli'. The series was not a roaring success. The attendances were not huge and members of Parliament were notable for their absence. We did not repeat the experiment. But the lectures made an interesting book.

I also started a monthly seminar in the branch, intended primarily to provide an opportunity for branch and contract historians to trial their ideas before a critical audience, but they increasingly served to attract a wider public to our work. I established a regular Historical Branch newsletter, which we distributed to academics, historians in the community who applied for our grants, and libraries. I came up with the name *People's History*, in the attempt to signal that we were involved in more than institutional histories of government departments; we wished to encourage the history of all New Zealand's peoples.

As part of a commitment to 'people's history', I found myself serving on the committee of the Trade Union History Project. This group had also been the recipient of largesse from Michael Bassett, and the branch was tasked with overseeing its spending of government grants. Richard Hill had been the branch representative on the committee but when he left I replaced him. I found it a very congenial task. The committee attracted some energetic and committed labour historians, such as Peter Franks, Kerry Taylor and Pat Walsh, and interested union leaders such as Colin Hicks; it was led at the time by a brilliant entrepreneur, Francis Wevers. Our major effort when I first joined the committee was to commemorate the centenary of the first Labour Day, in 1990. I became active on the committee, being responsible for a labour-history film festival, inviting my old University of Sussex colleague Alun Howkins to a major conference, and delivering a paper at that conference on 'Burying the Labour dead', about the memorials to Harry Holland and Michael Joseph Savage. In later years I helped organise a memorable day on the life of Rona Bailey under the theme of 'Dissenting New Zealand', and I delivered a paper on the 1951 lockout at a labour-history conference in Melbourne in 1991.

All these initiatives towards making history more meaningful to the community were reflected in my decision to advise the minister to change the composition of our advisory committee. Originally the committee had six academics – one from each of the universities – along with a librarian and publisher. But as our community responsibilities grew, I suggested in 1992 that the academic representation be reduced to four, and replaced by two Māori historians and two non-academic historians.

Not that I was hostile to academic history. I had grown up and worked for sixteen years in a university history department and I had huge respect for scholarly standards of history. I continued to mark theses and serve as an editorial adviser to the *New Zealand Journal of History*. As chief historian I was keen to involve university historians in our work. In 1989 I visited five of the six university history departments to present a seminar spelling out my vision for the Historical Branch and inviting their help and participation. Yet the more that I oversaw the work of contract historians, the more frustrated I became at the lack of professional skills shown by successful graduates of history departments.

By 1993 my frustration reached such a level that I went up to the Victoria University history department to deliver a paper to staff and senior students on 'University History Departments and Public History: Why are they failing us?' I argued that increasingly graduates were finding jobs in public history – working on Waitangi Tribunal claims, in museums, on conservation reports, not to mention the Dictionary of New Zealand Biography or contracts for the Historical Branch. For such tasks, students needed to be taught a fierce respect for accuracy backed by documentary evidence; they needed skills in interpreting photographs and conducting oral history; they should know the Māori language; and above all they had to be able to plan and complete a project to an assigned length and within an agreed time. In part reflecting on my own difficulties in completing my thesis, I argued that these skills were too often poorly taught or enforced within the classroom, and that I had become very frustrated at the sloppy research and disregard for timetables shown by recent graduates who had taken up contract positions. At the time the talk caused some stir, but remarkably, the history departments were very responsive. The presentation was published in the New Zealand Historical Association bulletin, and one academic colleague generously wrote to me that the essay was 'constructively provocative'. I was invited to talk to several other university history departments about this issue subsequently. More impressively the universities responded by introducing courses in public history. Later in the decade I worked with Bronwyn Dalley to prepare a collection of essays on public history in New Zealand to provide a text for such courses.

During the early and mid-1990s, I was also determined to continue my own writing and presenting. I feared becoming no more than a public servant and administrator. I wrote a paper on the 1950 Empire Games in Auckland, which I delivered at the 1990 Auckland Commonwealth Games. Also in sports history I wrote a paper looking at patterns of leisure among men and women in the post-war years, and another examining the story of Australia and New Zealand sporting rivalries, entitled 'Watching Big Brother'. I wrote six biographies for the *Dictionary of New Zealand Biography,* mostly on subjects who had emerged in my war-memorial research, and I delivered another overview talk to the Institute of Landscape Architects, who rewarded me by making me an honorary fellow of the Institute. I organised a conference and put together a volume looking at New Zealand and the United States as 'new societies' for the Fulbright programme.

Within the branch, I was supposed to be researching and writing a history of New Zealand since 1940. My argument was that from 1940 to 1990 there was a revolution in the New Zealand value system over issues such as race, gender, the environment, the nature of the economy and foreign allegiances, and that the transformation could be shown through a series of public

The cover of my short book on the royal tour of 1953–54. The book was superbly designed by Sarah Maxey for Daphne Brasell Associates Press.

occasions when people went into the streets, either to applaud or protest. I worked away at this project steadily until 1994. It was never completed, but I did manage to publish pieces along the way, with essays on the 1940 centennial, the celebration of VE and VJ days, the 1951 waterfront lockout and finally the royal tour of 1953–54. I managed to complete the last in time for the fortieth anniversary of the tour and it appeared as a nicely produced and well-illustrated booklet called *Royal Summer*.

None of these publications was a major contribution to New Zealand history, but they kept my identity as a working historian alive. Most of my energy in the first half of the 1990s had gone into turning around and building up the Historical Branch, and endeavouring to use the resources of that position to facilitate a boom in New Zealand history. I began to feel that I was achieving something in that respect and others too were taking note. After we had survived the battle over the scoping study of the Historical Branch, advisory committee chair Raewyn Dalziel wrote me a very generous letter which pleased me hugely:

> Now that at least some of the heat and dust has died down, I thought I should just say what a splendid job I think you are doing. 1991 must have been an awful year in many ways... However you have made the branch into something we all hoped for and I certainly hope you will be there for a long time yet.[20]

Two weeks later, on returning from holiday, I formally resigned from the university staff, ending my leave-without-pay status. But this did not signal any cooling of my relationship with the university. In June that year (1992), I received a letter which told me, 'An Interdepartmental Conference of History Departments meeting in May noted with considerable pleasure the revival of the fortunes of the Historical Branch since our last meeting in February 1987. The delegates were impressed by the great vitality of the Branch as well as the quality of the work emerging from it. We acknowledge and welcome its significant contribution to historical scholarship in this country. It was felt that the great improvement in its situation was due in no small measure to your leadership.'[21] But there was no time to rest on my laurels. Another opportunity was about to call – at the new Museum of New Zealand.

8
Exhibitionist

For four years, from late 1993 to late 1997, I walked several times a week along the Wellington waterfront from the Museum of New Zealand project office, across the road from the new museum building, to the Historical Branch in Waring Taylor Street. As I gazed out at the waters of Wellington harbour, always different, sometimes shimmering with colour, at other times grey and stormy, I would try to compose myself and adjust to moving from the adrenalin rush, the highs and lows, of Te Papa to the ordered calm of the branch. It was a considerable culture clash. I used to say that working at Te Papa was three days of despair and frustration followed by two of ecstasy. You would have to deal with prima donnas – some developers, some designers – and you had to have a stomach for arbitrary decision-making and authoritarian project managers. I had given up drinking coffee before I joined the museum, but then it became a cup every hour! The Historical Branch, where I had my own empire, seemed to have a quiet efficiency by comparison. And there was a huge difference in the way the two places treated history. At Te Papa it meant presenting our past to diverse audiences, young and old,

Shaking the hand of Dr Well-and-Strong from Exhibiting Ourselves.
DOMINION, 11 FEBRUARY 1998

Māori and Pākehā, locals and overseas tourists, using film and sounds and images and objects and computer games. Going back to the branch and the linear progress of typing words on a computer seemed easy. Yet those years at Te Papa were among the most exciting (along with the most frustrating) of my life, and through the friends I made there and the lessons I learnt, they changed my life and my approach to New Zealand history.

How did I find myself involved in the greatest museum project the country had ever seen? As a young boy in Christchurch, I often popped into the Canterbury Museum while waiting for my father to finish work across the road. I would gaze entranced and somewhat terrified at the model of a cabin on one of the 'first four ships' with the huge seas rolling outside the porthole, and I always made a beeline for the dioramas of seabirds upstairs. I loved the sense of being above Shag Rock looking at their nests. Then, when in London and Europe in 1963, the museums had always been at the top of the family's list, so I spent much time looking at ancient treasures. But the real breakthrough came in 1978 when we went off to Boston on refresher leave with two children under three. It was the snowiest winter on record, so Phillida and I spent much time with our two toddlers enjoying the children's museums and the facilities for kids in adult museums. I became convinced of the value of interactive experiences. After returning to New Zealand I wrote a piece for the *Listener*, 'A Great Place to Bring Up Children', in which I suggested that winter in snowy Boston was a better experience for children than a Kiwi summer on the beach because they were exposed to such a range of interactive museums, creative playthings and progressive childcare centres. This piece prompted some fierce letters suggesting that I had been captured by American capitalism, but it also attracted the interest of the museum community. I was invited to spell out my thoughts at the next Museums Aotearoa conference; the chair of the session was Cheryll Sotheran, at the time director of the Govett-Brewster Art Gallery in New Plymouth. She was enthusiastic, and presumably kept tabs on me. Meanwhile, during a year I spent on the Board of the Historic Places Trust, I had got to know and like Ken Gorbey, who was then in charge of the Waikato Museum. So in 1989, during the earliest stages of planning the new national museum, and before Cheryll's appointment as the inaugural chief executive, I was invited to take part in a residential 'Exhibitions Brainstorming Workshop' at the Gear Homestead in Porirua. The aim was to come up with a conceptual plan for the new museum's

Cheryll Sotheran (left), and (right) Ken Gorbey (with Geoff Knox in the background), the two geniuses behind Te Papa. MUSEUM OF NEW ZEALAND TE PAPA TONGAREWA; KEN GORBEY COLLECTION

exhibitions. I vividly remember a couple of very powerful presentations from two Māori women, Rose Pere and Ngapare Hopa, but I have no recollection of anything I contributed at all.

The challenge of that workshop stayed with me, however. I made it the inspiration for my article 'Fish and Chips and Verandahs and Footie on Saturday Afternoon' in the *New Zealand Journal of History* later that year, and eighteen months later, in 1991, I sent a paper to Rose Young, who was working with Ken on planning the new museum. The paper suggests what attracted me to the possibilities of Te Papa. It begins with the view that Te Papa offered the chance to go beyond the book and evoke New Zealand's history in new ways. I wrote that 'a museum has the possibility of calling upon other bodily movements than the rather passive act of reading words on a page. It can use all the senses.' I gave the examples of tactile feelings – 'the sensation of churning butter, the effort of clipping shears'; sight – 'old newsreels and photographs'; and sound – 'the songs, the accents, the radio announcers, the political speakers, the street sounds, the bar-room stories and jokes of past periods'. Then I suggested that Te Papa allowed old disciplines and boundaries to be broken – 'between art and craft, between popular and elite culture', and in particular between Pākehā and Māori, so that you might treat Pākehā ideas of Māori but also Māori ideas of Pākehā; you might compare the ways of life of 'early 19th century Scottish crofters... with that of 19th century Maori and the similarities would become as obvious as the differences'.[1]

Much of my previous work had been interdisciplinary – from my books on stained-glass windows and war memorials to the Stout Centre conferences 'Te Whenua, Te Iwi' and 'The Body/Te Tinana'. I had begun tentatively, with false starts but with determination, to think about Māori participation in national cultural enterprises. Te Papa promised to be a great bicultural experiment. Clearly by 1991 I was already itching to have the chance to tackle some of these issues.

One day in 1993 the new chief executive, Cheryll Sotheran, and her senior institutional planner, Ken Gorbey, took me out to lunch and invited me to apply for a position heading the history team. At that stage I was in the full flow of creating the Historical Branch and was loath to leave a flourishing enterprise. But the chance of helping to create a hugely significant new national institution was too good an opportunity to spurn. The constant focus of my research and writing had been the attempt to define Pākehā culture, and I had begun to argue, as in my 'Fish and Chips' article, that what New Zealand history urgently needed was the exploration of material objects and popular culture.[2] I put in an application, was duly interviewed on a grey Saturday afternoon in the old museum building, and was offered the job.

The offer was not quite what I had expected. My official position was to be 'concept leader: tangata tiriti history and cultural development'. My role was simply to come up with the ideas for the history exhibitions, and not to have any staff, budgetary or management responsibilities. This was not what I had imagined. In my application letter I had described myself as 'an institution builder' and, citing the examples of the Stout Centre and the Historical Branch, I promised to create a major centre for the study of Pākehā culture, and noted that 'I enjoy building a team, seizing opportunities, empowering people, attracting both financial and popular support'.[3] I envisaged a role where the exhibitions we planned would be based on appropriately skilled staff, a relevant policy of purchasing and acquiring new objects, and a sustained research programme. I saw it as one large enterprise, all operating out of a coherent history department which I managed. But the concept leaders had no ability to appoint staff, control money or attract the long-term relationships on which a sustained research programme might be built. I wrote Ken a long letter spelling out my frustration and asking for the powers and position that would allow me to do the job properly: 'To fight for the ideas and exhibitions which excite me, I must be where the important decisions are made. If not, I will simply suffer frustration and resentment.'[4] I turned down the offer. Ken and Cheryl were not to be put off. They refused to change their staff structures, but they wanted my input. We came to an agreement. The Historical Branch would provide contractual services to Te Papa. The museum would pay for my input at the level of fifteen hours a week, and they would receive, as a bonus, the added value of the historians in the branch to check and provide advice into the development of the exhibitions. I circulated everything, from conceptual schema to the smallest label, around the branch, and the staff always improved them. In the end it worked well – I enjoyed the challenge of coming up with the history exhibitions, while being able to hold at a distance the inevitable 'madhouse' of a team dedicated to opening a whole museum in a mere four years. And I was able to continue my exciting work at the branch. My walk along the waterfront was a way of keeping the two worlds in balance.

In mid-December 1993, just as we entered the crazy Christmas season, I joined the team of concept leaders to begin planning the new museum. We would sit around a table and the ideas would flow. They were a stimulating group of people. Ken Gorbey was the leader, wise, experienced and totally committed to producing a museum that would pull in the punters. In arguing for the primacy of the visitor experience he was backed by two wonderful individuals – Neil Anderson and Karen Mason. Both articulated the claims of children, and of visitors from all social classes and backgrounds. They were committed to a series of children's discovery stations, as had already been trialled at the old Buckle Street building. They insisted that everything we talked about had to work well for the first-time visitor as well as for the expert. Then there was Ian Wedde, an old friend from the Stout Centre, one of the country's most distinguished poets, hugely well read, a real intellectual. Ian always wanted to evoke exhibition ideas that would shock and surprise, that were fresh and challenging. There would be no simple regurgitation of national myths for him. Arguing for the natural-environment exhibitions was Geoff Hicks. He had the advantage on the rest of us since he had been at Te Papa for some years and had been thinking about the exhibitions for a long time. Most of the scientists at the old museum had looked on the Te Papa initiative with horror, as the replacement of a scholarly institution by a theme park. But Geoff had embraced the new museology, and had already come up with the brilliant idea of a living forest on the waterfront, which eventually became 'Bush City'. His enthusiasm and combination of scholarly commitment with fun ideas was infectious. Stuart Park had been poached from Auckland Museum, where he had been director. He had the hardest task of all, to come up with exhibitions which spanned the disciplines. He went about his task with a careful, consultative style and a huge admiration for scholarship. He had a genuine and warm commitment to bicultural processes, but in the end somewhat lacked the combination of inspiration and stubbornness needed for truly interdisciplinary exhibitions. There was Janet Davidson, eminent archaeologist, whose work on early New Zealand 'prehistory', as it was called at the time, I knew well. She was a formidable scholar and was tasked with leading the Pacific exhibitions. I liked her, enjoyed her slightly devilish wit, but realised that she too had a tough row to hoe against plans to limit the floor space devoted to the Pacific. An exhibition about canoes, on which she had set her heart, was already under threat.

Finally, presiding over us with an extraordinary good humour and wisdom, was Cliff Whiting, the museum's kaihautū, who officially partnered Cheryll in the chief executive role. From Te Whānau-a-Apanui, born and raised in Te Kaha, he brought not only his wonderful artistic skills as a carver, and experience as both a teacher in schools and an art administrator, but also a rich knowledge of Māori traditions and stories. He had a real feel for what would work on an exhibition floor. Cliff never spoke loudly, was never assertive, but always made his point with a twinkle in his eye. One of the real privileges of my life was to work with him planning the Pākehā pou that came to adorn the magnificent new marae at Te Papa, designed by Cliff, who then supervised its carving and construction. Often he came to the meetings with other members of the Māori team, such as the irrepressible Hinemoa Hilliard or the more serious but highly informed Arapata Hakiwai. It was a lively, opinionated, immensely stimulating team. As we threw ideas around, trialled things and then rejected them, the discussions were often captured on film, as Anna Cottrell set up the cameras collecting material which eventually went into Gaylene Preston's documentary *Getting to Our Place*.

We were faced with quite a challenge. For a start it was a crazy timetable. By early March 1994 we had to come up with the major exhibition ideas to be presented to an international peer group. There would be no long days lounging on the beach that summer. More significantly the opening of the museum itself with all its exhibitions had been promised for early 1998, to fit

Cliff Whiting, the inspirational kaihautū and master carver at Te Papa.
MUSEUM OF NEW ZEALAND TE PAPA TONGAREWA

in with the New Zealand Festival. It was a mere four years to devise all the exhibitions from start to installation. The pressure was intense and it was also high-profile. This was by far the largest New Zealand museum development ever undertaken, and it involved a huge amount of public money. There were very high expectations that we had to deliver a museum experience which went to the heart of New Zealand identity, and there was already a heavy pall of suspicion around the project. There were legitimate concerns about housing all the nation's treasures in a waterfront building, exposed to tsunamis and earthquakes. That did not concern me.

What did concern me was the political and cultural environment of the country at that moment. The sesquicentenary of the Treaty of Waitangi in 1990 had shown that New Zealand was far from settled in terms of who it was. The country was going through a kind of post-colonial identity crisis, as the old sense of New Zealand as the British Empire's most loyal child became untenable but we had yet to feel comfortable with a multicultural identity located in the Pacific (or even a bicultural one). The emergence of Māori protest about their status, the revival of Māori culture and language, and the creation of a Waitangi Tribunal to explore Māori grievances under the Treaty had induced a dangerous combination of guilt, defensiveness and anger among some Pākehā. Many were suspicious of the new museum. Because of its ethnographic origins, the museum was naturally stronger in Māori artefacts than in the objects of popular Pākehā culture, and it was feared that Māori culture would be overly represented. Suspicions were strengthened when the museum gave itself a Māori name, Te Papa Tongarewa, and it had already announced its major conceptual structure – on the ground floor would be Papatūānuku, the land on which we stood, and the exhibits above would be divided between the cultures of tangata whenua (the people of the land) and tangata tiriti (the people who were in the country by virtue of the Treaty). There was widespread suspicion that the museum would be 'politically correct', overly sympathetic to Māori, and that while the Māori exhibitions would be celebratory, the non-Māori exhibitions would be cynical and questioning. A clamour had begun in the newspapers for a museum which highlighted Pākehā achievement. Walls of white pioneering and sporting heroes seemed to be the required recipe. There were some on the museum's board sympathetic to such views.

There were also of course pressures from another side – the hope from many minority groups that they might be represented in the museum. This included ethnic groups, and also other groupings, the different regions of the country, diverse occupations, gay and lesbian people and of course the female majority. Representation in a national museum was a symbol of membership in, and recognition by, the nation.

In the concept leaders' early meetings, we discussed many issues that cut across the museum – methods of wayfinding, large ideas which might unify the experience ('journeys' became a potent concept), the shared interdisciplinary spaces, the positioning of a café, the tone and language of the exhibitions. It was all fascinating stuff. My particular responsibility was to come up with a large schema for the 'tangata tiriti' history exhibitions. I made a couple of immediate decisions. The existing history team in the museum had trialled in the old museum building a chronological walk-through of

New Zealand history. I was not interested in such an approach. It seemed predictable and boring; given the space available, I felt we had to do instead sharply focused, engaging exhibitions about particular themes. And I decided to respond to the public clamour, and confront head-on the question of national identity. The country wanted answers to that issue and a national museum seemed an appropriate place to begin providing them. But whose identity were we dealing with? 'Tangata tiriti' included all non-Māori people; but it was highly questionable whether all non-Māori had a collective identity. It was even dubious that there was such a thing as Pākehā identity. People talked instead about national or New Zealand identity. So I decided to accept that point and to focus on New Zealand identity. This was not a racist way of expanding a Pākehā definition into a nationalist whole, but rather a recognition that for most New Zealanders, New Zealand identity did include Māori aspects, from the haka to Air New Zealand's koru. I therefore decided to include Māori elements within the exhibitions where they were appropriate.

How to respond to the clamour for simple nationalist affirmations? I was an academic historian, occupationally suspicious of slogans and unquestioned certainties. I wanted to engender debate, not offer comfort. I recognised the urgency of the identity issue and was interested in exploring the question asked most famously in the great play of the 1980s, Greg McGee's *Foreskin's Lament*: 'Whaddarya?' But I wished to offer a number of answers so that museum visitors might get different angles on the question. I structured the history exhibitions around three possible ways of explaining New Zealand identity. They derived in part from insights I had gained while studying United States history, and in part from the larger conceptual device we had come up with of 'journeys'.

One possible answer to the question was that New Zealand identity came from the types of people who settled this land. This was the 'cultural baggage' view of the American historian Lewis Hartz. He had argued that the culture of the United States and Australia reflected the values and traditions carried to the New World by the people who settled the country. So the first exhibition explored the journey *to* New Zealand and sought to explore the experiences and cultures of those who migrated here. The theme was 'New Zealand – nation of immigrants'. Eventually the finished exhibition, which came to be called *Passports*, included a kiwiana trail in which visitors could discover that certain Kiwi icons were in fact brought in the luggage of immigrants – the beer

WHO ARE NEW ZEALANDERS?	EXHIBITIONS	JOURNEYS/ IDENTITIES
Inherited Culture?	"The Peopling of New Zealand"	Journeys from the Old World
A New Environment?	"Life in New Zealand"	Identities in the New World
An Image?	"Exhibiting Ourselves"	Journeys to the Old World

The conceptual diagram which I used to explain the history exhibitions to the visiting peer group in March 1994.

from Germany, health stamps from Denmark, fish and chips from northern England, the word 'sheila' from Ireland.

The second set of exhibitions took the opposite hypothesis. Here the major historian was Frederick Jackson Turner, who in 1893 presented a famous paper, 'The Significance of the Frontier in American History'. He suggested that what had made American democracy was not the values the new settlers inherited from the Old World, but their interaction with the frontier, with the environment of the New World. This approach assumed that New Zealand identity was formed after the journey here and as a result of journeys *in* the country. I gave this exhibition the large title *Life in New Zealand*, and originally proposed that it have three elements based on the classic eight-hour division of the day: a section on work, a section on recreation and a section on home life and relationships

The third exhibition, which we entitled *Exhibiting Ourselves*, offered a different perspective. It focused upon the history of the *idea* of national identity and explored the way that the country had presented itself to the world. The theoretical inspiration here was postmodernism, which suggested that identity was no more nor less than what we imagined it to be. It was a product of the mind, a deliberate construction. To the extent that this construct of identity was aimed at overseas audiences, it represented a journey *from* New Zealand towards the outside world. So we had three approaches – identity was the sum of immigrant cultures, identity was a result of the interaction with a distinct environment, and identity was simply a mental construct. My hope was that this would invite debate and open up perceptions, not close them down.

This conceptual structure was approved by the visiting peer group and by the board; so now I had to make it happen. Here the real challenges began. I was a trained and published historian with ways of working which were comfortable to me. I worked largely by myself, and when I wrote I determined the order and pace of how I delivered the news. It was in many ways an egotistical, authoritarian experience. I usually had an audience of other historians in mind. Now I had to work in a different way. The great sin of the exhibition developer was to attempt to put a book upon the wall. I learnt very quickly that I was not a single omnipotent author proclaiming one vision. I was part of a team. For each exhibition there was a core team – a developer to further develop the ideas; an interpreter, who was essentially an audience advocate and who focused on the emotional and intellectual impact of the

Some of the detailed documents we prepared for the Peopling exhibition.

exhibition upon visitors; a designer; and, keeping us all on track and on time, a team coordinator. But that was just the start. As the exhibitions developed, there would be graphic designers to prepare the labels, a conservator to look after objects, researchers to assist in finding content or identifying relevant images, writers to prepare labels, film-makers to put together moving images, a team to clear copyright, and an exhibitions evaluator to conduct user-testing. I had never worked with such a wide-ranging group of experts. This was both difficult and inspiring.

There was constant highly detailed reporting to the museum's larger exhibition-management team, to the overall project manager and to the museum board. We had to present detailed documents at various stages – a concept development report, then further reports at 30 per cent, 90 per cent and 100 per cent of concept design. Every stage required responding to issues. The bureaucracy and endless meetings could be frustrating, but they did ensure that everything was done professionally, and I was very lucky with the quality of the people in the core team. Alison Preston, as the team coordinator, was both firm and extraordinarily diplomatic and was one of the sanest people on the planet. She kept us all grounded and managed to turn mornings of clenched fists and teeth-grinding into afternoons of laughter and celebration. The interpreters in the team were hugely valuable. One was Jean-Marie O'Donnell, who had worked with us as a student in the Historical Branch, and the second was Jane Martin, with a background in primary education. Both insisted that every element of an exhibition, every label, every interactive device was comprehensible and engaging for a wide range of audiences. They were scrupulous at testing with a range of users. For someone who had been used to writing purely for other academics or at least highly literate adults, this was a shock, but one that I came to treasure. Often critics considered that we were 'dumbing down' information. I never accepted that, and came to believe that the real trick of a good exhibition was to 'layer' the experience – so that it would work for the twelve-year-old, but also for the professional historian. We constantly thought about the range of audiences – literate scholars, families, schoolchildren, overseas visitors and locals, Māori and Pākehā. We thought about those who interacted with exhibitions in diverse ways – the ones who read every word and pushed every button, but also those who skimmed quickly. We thought about the fact that people would enter exhibitions in a different sequence – some from the back, some from the side, some from the main entrance. The experience had to work for all of them. This focus on exciting and informing diverse audiences was a huge learning curve for me but one that I came to respect.

It was a particular privilege to work with the writing team, which included some of the country's most talented writers, such as novelist Nigel Cox; playwright Dave Armstrong; Michael Keith, an old friend from schooldays and a brilliant writer for children; and a fine imaginative writer, Johanna Knox. Their success in turning our bald meat-and-potatoes briefs of facts and figures into labels which were both accurate and informative, yet also through clever analogies and wit captured the imagination, was one of the joys of Te Papa and, in my view, one of its great achievements.

For a historian like myself it was a new experience to begin building the story not primarily through a sequence of words, but in other ways. I always gravitated to using theatrical sets to evoke the larger metaphor of an exhibition. We did this in *Passports* by presenting the experience as a journey to the new land, and in *Exhibiting Ourselves* where we reconstructed international exhibitions and world fairs. Obviously objects were a key since museums traditionally were showplaces of significant artefacts. Early on I spent hours exploring the museum's collection of objects, held in a cold warehouse in Miramar. There was always something intriguing that I was determined to fit in somewhere, but I usually came away disappointed at the quality of the collection. For a national museum it seemed thin indeed. I realised that we had two options: we could purchase relevant objects, or borrow them from better collections such as the Auckland or Otago museums; or we could use other ways of telling the story. Initially I gravitated to oral histories because of my long interest in capturing people's words, but I quickly found that it was not easy presenting extensive oral histories in a museum. If you had the oral histories playing loud, there was inevitable sound bleed and disturbance to other museum visitors, and if you provided headphones people had to sit down stationary for a length of time, which those with a family or group are loath to do. Some visitors were also uncomfortable, for hygiene reasons, with putting on previously used headphones. So while we collected a lot of oral history, especially for *Passports*, we preferred to use them in short, bold extracts displayed as words on the wall. We found that oral history worked better in film, and helping to make short films or putting together extracts from old movies and newsreels was one of the new skills I was forced, not always successfully, to acquire while at Te Papa.

Equally challenging were interactives. My enthusiasm for communicating history through encouraging visitors to touch or move physical devices had been one of the museum techniques that had first attracted Cheryll and Ken to me, and it was one of the aspects that attracted me in turn to the Te Papa opportunity. So I put huge amounts of energy into conceiving these devices. There were originally no fewer than seventeen in *Passports*, including drawers that you pulled, flaps you lifted and buttons that you pressed.

Finally I found myself, to my surprise, developing computer games. In about 1996 the museum came to us and said that we could have three such games for the history exhibitions. Would I like to come up with some ideas? This was a wonderfully inviting challenge. In the end I prepared three games. One imagined that you were a new migrant to New Zealand at a particular time and place – perhaps the Otago gold rushes, or Auckland city at the turn of the twentieth century. You were presented with a series of life choices, such as where you would live, what groups you might join, what job you took up. You were then told whether your selections were likely to make your adjustment easier or more difficult – for instance, a woman migrating from Scotland who chose to live in Dunedin rather than Christchurch or Wellington would have the support of many more compatriots to ease her life in a new world. Another I devised was used in the Treaty of Waitangi exhibition. The user was invited to imagine that they were on the Waitangi Tribunal and had to decide on appropriate remedies for particular grievances. The results did not tell you whether your decision was right or wrong, but simply how your choices compared with those of other users of the game.

But the most successful computer game and, as it turned out, the most problematic, concerned the nineteenth-century voyage out to New Zealand, part of *Passports*. In the game, you were a ship's captain who had to get as many live immigrants to New Zealand as possible in the shortest possible time. Along the journey you were faced with a series of problems – an outbreak of measles, or the ship encountered huge seas in the Southern Ocean – and you had to choose a response from a series of four options. Some options meant a loss of days or of passengers; others brought a quicker journey. Every so often a wild-card event, such as fire breaking out, would interrupt the game. Although it was a game and one beautifully presented with excellent graphics, I was insistent that the incidents be as accurate as possible. I went down to the Turnbull Library and read various shipboard diaries, and since

Scenes from the 'Voyage Out' computer game in the Passports *exhibition.*

one of my students at Victoria University had written the draft of a thesis on 'the voyage out', we asked her to provide material. I was chuffed with the game and thought that it had worked well, until I received a note from Cheryll to say that the mayor of Christchurch and a member of the Te Papa board, Sir Hamish Hay, had complained that in the game Lyttelton was not one of the choices as to ports of landing in New Zealand. Both Cheryll and Ken got onto the case and considered reworking the game. But I wrote an obsequious letter to Sir Hamish explaining that programming allowed only four choices for any segment, that I wanted two North Island ports and two South Island ports, and that I had come across two interesting stories, one about a group of passengers who had left their ship when it called at Nelson because it was harvest time and workers were needed, and another about several ships kept from entering Otago Harbour on account of strong winds. So for historical accuracy I had chosen Nelson and Dunedin as the two South Island options and Lyttelton missed out. I also went on to detail the other Christchurch elements in the history exhibitions, and concluded, 'As one brought up with stories of the "First Four Ships"', I understood his disappointment but had been equally determined that the experiences of Christchurch people would have good representation in the history exhibitions as a whole.[5] Sir Hamish replied very graciously.

Issues were not always so easily resolved. Undoubtedly the hardest challenge was dealing with the internal politics of Te Papa.[6] In this respect the least problematic was the exhibition we finished first, *Exhibiting Ourselves*. The idea had been to represent New Zealand identity as a construct by looking at the ways the country's image had been projected overseas. Initially I had proposed three sections: one on symbols of nationhood such as stamps, coins and flags; one on significant moments of national definition such as women's suffrage, the 1905 All Blacks tour, the landing on Gallipoli, the passage of social security, Hillary's ascent of Everest, the Māori land march, 1981 Springbok tour, the *Rainbow Warrior*, etc.; and one on New Zealand's presentation of the country at international exhibitions. It rapidly became clear that we could not do all three, and that the collection was comparatively strong in objects from the international exhibitions. So we decided to reconstruct the displays at four of them – the New Zealand Court at the world's first international exhibition in the Crystal Palace in London in 1851, the international exhibition held in Christchurch in 1906, the centennial exhibition held in Rongotai, Wellington, in 1940, and the New Zealand display at the 1992 Expo in Seville, Spain.

There were many advantages to this structure. It gave us a bead on national identity approximately every half-century since European settlement; it offered the opportunity to create theatrical sets evoking the spirit and aesthetics of each period; and we uncovered some wonderful objects – such as the mock crown jewels and kitsch souvenir pottery from 1940 and the splendid glass works, already in the museum's collection, from the Seville expo. The concept developer, Paul Thompson, was an inventive exhibition developer who always had his eyes on entertaining and informing the audience. He was also a highly efficient producer who inevitably got things done. Paul helped develop some imaginative interactives which kept the story entertaining – such as the phalanx of little boxes standing for the government departments represented at the centennial exhibition, which you could open to find an intriguing object symbolic of that department. We also came across an amazing amateur film of that exhibition showing off the amusement park at Rongotai. I had to do a great deal of fascinating research to uncover the details of the exhibitions and eventually ended up contributing papers on the 1906 and 1940 exhibitions to two books on those events. The museum regarded the group which produced this exhibit as 'a dream team', and we managed to get the exhibition prepared so efficiently and smoothly that it was the first in the museum to reach sign-off.

Exhibiting Ourselves was implicitly slightly subversive, particularly in a national museum where the demand was for nationalist affirmation. It made obvious that each generation's interpretation of New Zealand identity was a deliberate construction, an act of puffery and propaganda intended to achieve political purposes at home or economic benefits abroad. The 1851 display was obviously designed to sell goods, mostly flax as it turned out, in Britain, and to attract both immigrants and investors. The 1940 centennial exhibition was intended to trumpet the Labour Government's success in turning the country into a progressive welfare state and a modern electricity-driven economy; the image at Seville was of a go-getting nation of entrepreneurs living in a green land and producing organic wine, cheese and apples which it could sell to the European market. Identity, we learn, reflects the needs of certain groups with particular ends in mind. But the exhibition was only mildly subversive because it also affirmed certain consistencies over time. One was the theme of New Zealand as Maoriland – the appropriation of Māori culture to express national identity. In 1851 this was articulated through a model pā which expressed a pride in the Māori as a fierce warrior; by 1906 the abundant use of Māori motifs and the model pā made Māori into an exotic and picturesque element of the country. By 1992 Māori were entertainers, either as singers or dancers. So the search for identity through Māori remained constant. Similarly the idea of New Zealand as 'the most beautiful country in the world' – the 'wonderland' of 1906 was a constant theme. Visitors were invited to ask, ever so gently, whether these images were true or just constructions. But these questions were as much affirmations as serious challenges. Further, there were plenty of heart-throbbing moments in the exhibition – images of beautiful New Zealand, the glorious sounds of Kiri Te Kanawa singing at Seville. Indeed I worried that visitors would take the propaganda as truth, and not see the four exhibitions as time-bound puffery. This fear proved groundless because the re-creations were carried out with attention to the style of each period and executed with a degree of humour so visitors were necessarily distanced and did see them as products of their time. When they entered the 1940 court and saw the robot, Dr Well-and-Strong, proclaiming the wonders of the health system and the welfare state, people smiled in a way that implied both fond recognition yet wondering detachment. *Exhibiting Ourselves* was able to tread a fine line between affirming certain consistent strands of national identity and inviting a questioning of those myths.

Somewhat more difficult was the second exhibition we completed, *Passports*. From my earliest interest in being involved in Te Papa I had wanted to do an exhibition about the peopling of New Zealand. Ever since writing my article on 'Verandahs and Fish and Chips . . .' I had been convinced that we needed to think more about the cultural contribution of the various peoples who had settled New Zealand. So the very first task was to hire several researchers to go out and collect oral histories with migrants from different parts of the world. We had decided early that we would tell the narrative through personal stories as a way of giving it a human face. The oral histories would document such stories and hopefully also bring in additional photographs and objects, for the museum collection was not strong in the objects of the Asian or south European communities. I realised that this approach had real political advantages. It would allow us to represent some of the different ethnic groups who had migrated to New Zealand, which would fulfil the museum's obligation to represent the diversity of the country. Furthermore, when I had first presented the ideas of the history exhibitions to the museum board, one member, Anne Salmond, had been insistent that the museum had to recognise the heritage from the Old World. At the time she was writing her magnificent series of books about the early Pākehā discovery and exploration of New Zealand, and in order to understand the world view of people like James Cook and Marion du Fresne she had steeped herself in the intellectual life of eighteenth-century Europe. She was convinced, quite correctly, that New Zealand could not be understood without its Old World heritage. I was asked to fly up to Auckland to brief her. Over an enjoyable lunch I managed to convince her that the peopling exhibition would focus on the cultural heritage brought by migrants, colonial and more recent. She was happy and became a stalwart supporter.

But the focus on the diverse cultural origins of New Zealand also brought problems. The exhibition itself had three main sections: leaving, voyaging and arriving. Knowing that it would be a long-term exhibition, I wanted to leave the fourth section as a changing community gallery where different immigrant groups might tell their story. For opening day the concept developer Lyndon Fraser and I decided that the first story to be told would be that of the Chinese migrants to New Zealand. This was a fascinating history, involving the Otago gold rushes, cruel discrimination with the introduction of the poll tax and a vicious murder by Lionel Terry in 1905, tales of opium dens and gambling, of market gardening and service in World War II, and of course the huge recent immigration of people of Chinese ethnicity. Given the growing proportion of the New Zealand population of Asian background and the number of visitors from that part of the world, a small temporary gallery about the Chinese was the least we could do. News of this idea seeped out to the newspapers early on, at a time when suspicions were rife that Pākehā culture would be short-changed in the new national museum. There were complaints about the 'political correctness' of the 'Pākehā' exhibits. Letters to the newspaper alleged that we had deliberately chosen a group who had suffered most from New Zealand society. The British inheritance was being ignored, and Pākehā New Zealanders were being made to look bad. Well, we just knuckled down, and set up a Chinese community committee who were a huge asset and a delight to work with as we planned the display. They added individual stories and objects, and were proud to be the first group represented.

At other times we did lose out. One was when the Chinese government presented the museum with a large Chinese dragon, as used in dragon-dancing. It seemed to be the perfect object to hang above the community gallery and advertise the story of the New Zealand Chinese. But the museum managers wanted to give it a more prominent site.

Second, I lost the battle of the de Surville anchor. In sympathy with Anne Salmond's sense of the importance of the early explorers, I had always wanted to have at the entrance to all the non-Māori history exhibitions and to *Passports* in particular the huge metal anchor which had been lost by de Surville's expedition and had been recovered from Doubtless Bay some years before. Jean François Marie de Surville was a French explorer who had reached New Zealand in early December 1769, two months after James Cook had arrived at these shores. At the end of December de Surville was on the east coast of Northland, and Cook on the west coast. In their logs both record getting caught in a fierce north-westerly storm. Cook's *Endeavour* rode it out. De Surville put down two anchors, but his ship started to drift towards the shore. He put down a third. That too did not hold the ship, so he cut the anchors. He decided to abandon this god-forsaken place and head eastwards to South America. James Cook was left to 'discover' New Zealand and claim it for the British Crown.

The three anchors were therefore the first European objects left in New Zealand waters. Two were recovered, one of them given to Te Papa. It was an icon of early European discovery. What could be more appropriate at the entrance to the non-Māori exhibitions? Also, within the collection was 'Kupe's stone', a large rock said to have been used by Kupe, the Māori discoverer of Aotearoa, when he had anchored his waka on arrival in the country. It seemed a perfect symbolism to have Kupe's stone welcoming people to the Māori exhibitions and de Surville's anchor to the Pākehā ones. But the museum authorities decided that neither was sufficiently 'celebratory' or 'reverential' to our origins. People should enter the non-Māori area beneath a sculpture or arch which paid tribute to non-Māori civilisation. It seemed to me that a huge block of cast iron (the anchor was very large) was a stunning expression of the industrial creativity of the West. I screamed, but to no avail. The anchor was eventually positioned on a high wall at the entrance to the museum, where it is dwarfed by the surrounding architecture and is almost wholly ignored by the visitors who walk beneath. The celebratory arch, meanwhile, was quietly dropped.

Inevitably in a project of this size and complexity, you win some and lose others, and generally we won most of our dreams for *Passports*. As had worked well in *Exhibiting Ourselves*, we created a theatrical experience in which the visitors acted out the story that unfolded – the choice to leave the Old World; the trauma of the voyage; and the arrival at the promised land, signalled by a sculpture of the Southern Cross. As you entered the exhibition, like anyone going on a journey, you picked up a passport. Each one was a printed account of a real immigrant's life, and at each stage of the exhibition, leaving, voyaging and arriving, you could stamp your passport and learn what happened to that individual – that is, if you were able to journey at all, because before setting off on the nineteenth-century voyage you had to answer some questions: were you under the age of forty, were you an unmarried woman, or if male, a rural labourer or a builder? If you answered 'yes', then you would receive a free passage. Then when you came to the twentieth-century journey, you once again had to answer questions which determined if you would be allowed in at all.

The section on leaving was dominated by a large graph showing the ups and downs of immigration, and each period was associated with certain objects – gold nuggets for the gold rushes, for example. I modelled this on a wonderful graph which I had seen at the Ellis Island immigration museum in New York Harbour. Similarly, a visit to the Museum of Sydney led to a set of pull-out drawers which told the story through objects of individual migrants. Some were positive stories of migration, such as Edward Mroczek, a Polish resistance fighter imprisoned in a Nazi concentration camp, who

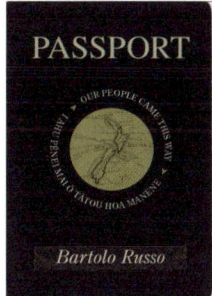

The first four pages of a Passports *passport.*

after release fell in love with a New Zealand woman and came to the new land. For him New Zealand was truly 'godzone', a place of freedom and peace and love. But pull out the next drawer and you came across Ingeborg Stuckenberg. Ingeborg was a Danish writer who fled to New Zealand in the 1890s, partly to escape the social embarrassment of falling in love with the gardener of her lodge and partly because she was attracted to New Zealand as the social laboratory of the world. Disillusionment followed. She wrote:

> New Zealand – the land of blue mountains and blue skies, the land which flows with milk and honey; where land is cheap and work well paid! . . . yes, the mountains are blue, just as the sky is blue, but the sun shines down on thousands of mute, frustrated hopes . . . All who think of New Zealand as the promised land should see the madhouses and read the death list in the newspapers . . . [7]

Prophetic words – within fifteen months Ingeborg was dead, a revolver at her head. We were determined that the exhibition would not be a banal presentation of the immigrant experience as a triumph and a journey to a promised land. Individual stories showed complexity and variety.

Yet I was always conscious of the need, both for reasons of politics and historical accuracy, to acknowledge the British and Irish majority. We tried to respond by making sure that stories from that part of the world were well represented throughout the exhibition, and in the 'leaving' gallery we gave the background of the British and Irish a particular emphasis. In that part

Scenes from our trip around Britain and Ireland in 1997: Mark Derby videoing the squire's estate at Chilham in Kent (left); and a woman in Wychwoods, Oxfordshire, holding a painting of the Cospatrick, *aboard which seventeen locals died when it caught fire on a migrant voyage to New Zealand in 1874 (right). The fountain behind was put up in 1878 as a memorial to those lost.*

of the display we had suggested that the people who came to New Zealand derived from very precise locations – the Dalmatians from just south of Split, the Indians from the Gujarat area, many Italians from Stromboli. So we applied this to those who came from the United Kingdom and presented their regional origins in detail through a continuously playing film. This came about in 1997, towards the end of my time at Te Papa. I managed to convince the British Council to pay for me and a cameraman, Mark Derby, to travel around Britain and Ireland, to eight particular locations which had sent large groups of people to New Zealand. Through my own reading and the peopling project which I had kicked off in the Historical Branch, I knew a fair bit about the regional and class origins of New Zealand's immigrants from Britain and Ireland. Mark and I spent about five days in each place filming characteristic activities in that region and interviewing locals about why their ancestors might have left for New Zealand. It was a fascinating trip around the British Isles, which was both exhausting and immensely stimulating. In the finished piece, you visit hop pickers in Kent, miners in Cornwall, rural labourers in Oxfordshire, peat farmers in the Shetlands, linen workers in Belfast, potato farmers in Tralee. You hear different accents, see different scenery, understand local rituals and ways of life. The message is that the culture inherited from Britain and Ireland was not just from well-educated gentlemen speaking a BBC English. The British inheritance consisted of many distinct minority cultures. New Zealand's immigrant world was always multicultural, so there was never a disjuncture between the British migration and other migrations. All were people from difficult economic situations who brought their distinctive traditions to the New World.

We still needed more to satisfy the museum board and our outside critics that we were doing justice to the European inheritance. The museum board especially were uneasy that the loving presentation of taonga in the Māori exhibitions would not be balanced by similar treatment of European culture. One way of allaying the concerns was to present the visitor as he she entered the 'new country' with a wall of treasures showing some of the objects and traditions brought to New Zealand by non-Māori. There was a huge photograph, which I commissioned from Ans Westra, of some distinctive ethnic foods; there were musical instruments, such as a piano landed on Petone beach in 1840, an Italian violin and a bagpipe said to have been played at the battle of Culloden; and there were some beautiful religious objects – a huge Jewish prayer curtain, a Catholic Bishop's cope, some Hindu and Greek Orthodox icons. Yet even here I was determined that it would not all be just stories of success and heroism. Among the personal stories was one about the Guard family, drawing on an existing Te Papa collection. We told the story of John Guard's whaling ventures in the Marlborough Sounds, but also recounted the capture of Guard's wife and children by Māori on the south Taranaki coast and the terrible fire-bombing of the tangata whenua by the British navy in retribution. There was nothing much to be proud of in that. In the next cases we find the story of the Babich family, four brothers who came from Dalmatia to dig for kauri gum and eventually built up a very successful business making wine, and the story of the Mene family, migrants from Samoa whose daughter Bernice became one of the country's great netball stars. Variety, complexity, richness of both culture and experiences was what we strove for. If people came wanting an unvarnished picture of New Zealand culture they would be disappointed. But hopefully they would get a sense of the range of human experiences among New Zealand's non-Māori migrants by becoming absorbed in the personal accounts.

The exhibition which we developed last, *Life in New Zealand*, became another battleground. The original idea was that the exhibition would focus on the development of a distinctive New Zealand way of life through the interaction with the local environment. We suggested that the exhibition might have three elements – work, for which we proposed an exploration of the wool industry; leisure, and here we wanted to develop a show on gambling; and a piece on home life and relationships, with an exhibit on patterns of love in New Zealand. The idea was that these would be relatively short-term shows with frequent changes, which was why we positioned them beside the goods lift. The first casualty was the gambling exhibit. We had promoted this idea partly because it was a way of contextualising the skeleton of Phar Lap, the famous racehorse from the 1930s, which had always been a crowd favourite, and also because there was at the time a proposal for a casino next door to the museum. We were intending to treat the opposition to gambling, as well as its practice, and this would have allowed us to unpick male and female cultures in New Zealand and also the huge role of religion. From the beginning the museum board expressed nervousness about the gambling concept, since it was feared the museum might be seen to endorse the pursuit. I agreed to drop that part of the show.

We proceeded to develop the shows *Love* and *Woollen Yarns* – but the museum then requested each team to sacrifice some floor space to ensure that the Day One exhibitions were completed on time and budget. We would be allowed only one exhibit and the whole history team argued strongly for the *Love* show. It seemed an exciting and novel idea, which might particularly appeal to teenagers who were not well served elsewhere in the museum. It would also be the one place where gay experience was acknowledged and we hoped to explore inter-racial relationships. We had uncovered some intriguing objects, including a marvellous group of Valentine's Day cards, a comprehensive run of contraceptives since the 1930s and a lovely collection of wedding dresses. We also had some interesting ideas such as short clips from New Zealand films of 'love at first sight', the 'New Zealand kiss', 'fond farewells' etc. But the board decided that *Love* too was a little dangerous – the chair, Sir Ron Trotter, noted that 'it would appeal to young people who do not know the difference between love and sex'.

As a former chief executive of a stock and station agency, Sir Ron was, however, keen on the wool show. It was given the go-ahead. Many in the museum were disappointed. They considered *Woollen Yarns* to be an unexciting subject – and would frequently endow it with the adjective 'baaaaa-ring'. But there were real advantages in the subject even without the chair's personal endorsement. An oft-mentioned symbol of the museum's alleged insensitivity to European culture and Pākehā treasures had been the fact that the collection of seventeenth- and eighteenth-century British antique furniture given to the museum in the 1920s by Ellen Elgar was not planned for display. There was much correspondence about this. I did some digging and discovered that Ellen Elgar was from a family of Wairarapa run-holders. Indeed her grandfather had brought sheep into the Wairarapa in 1845. All of Mrs Elgar's furniture had been purchased with wool profits earned during the Great War. So we could tell the story of the wool barons by focusing on Mrs Elgar's drawing room, and through the windows you could see a wool press. Her furniture was 'on the sheep's back'. The show would also offer a recognisable place for family groups from the provinces, who were not well catered for elsewhere, and it built on the foreign-tourist image of 'a nation of 60 million sheep'. There were other relevant pieces in the museum's collection – an antique wool press; some amazing woollen suits placed in barrels on the subantarctic islands in the 1880s for castaways; some unique craft work using the distinctive style of Kiwicraft (where Māori women in shearing gangs pick up bits of wool, which they roll on their knees and knit using number-eight fencing wire). We developed the idea of four settings – the world of the run-holders, where the Elgar collection was found; a reconstructed shearing shed, in which of course Māori had played a full role; the city and the industrial experience of the wool factory; and the domestic circle with its traditions of weaving and knitting in wool. Important social divisions were explored – rich and poor, country and city, Māori and Pākehā, men and women.

Then in July 1996, with about eighteen months to go before opening, and just as the exhibition started to capture our enthusiasm, a bombshell landed. The museum had decided that despite our best efforts, the Pākehā exhibitions were not sufficiently 'celebratory', and *Woollen Yarns* should be replaced by a 'feel-good' multimedia experience. The cancellation in Washington of the Enola Gay exhibition about the atomic bomb dropped on Nagasaki had shown that there was a right-wing reaction in the museum world, and the museum did not want exhibits that asked too many troubling questions. I was furious. I wrote an ill-mannered letter to Cheryll, arguing that none of the history exhibitions denigrated New Zealand culture, that where there was criticism it was 'a gentle questioning', and that 'All is done with affection – but also with scholarship and integrity'. There was no need for a strident celebratory theatre. And I stood on my dignity: 'I have spent three years and a lot of museum money thinking about the history exhibitions. I do not appreciate being ignored and given non-negotiable orders by a group who have not been acquainted with the facts.'[8] My fury must have had some effect, because the next I heard was that the available space would be shared. Both *Woollen Yarns* and *Golden Days*, as the feel-good show was called, would proceed. In the long run I was forced to eat humble pie. *Golden Days* turned out to be a very successful and highly popular account of 'magic moments' of the previous forty years, all set in a junk shop. It worked well, but was unashamed nostalgia, something which I was proud the other history exhibitions had avoided.

So *Woollen Yarns*, or *On the Sheep's Back* as it came to be called, went back on track. We had a great team working on the exhibition, including two young women, Bronwyn Labrum and the interpreter Jean-Marie O'Donnell, and the more we developed the show the more interesting it became. I went down to Alexandra to look at the merino shearing championships. There I met Des Williams, a fine journalist of shearing, and through him we managed to get some hand-pieces from some of the country's champion shearers. I began to realise how distinctive was the culture and language of shearing – and before long we had devised a little interactive where you had to match shearing terms such as 'jingling johnnies' with definitions.

A couple of us visited the woollen mills in Mosgiel and did oral histories with some of those who had worked in the factories, which we were able to turn into short, evocative accounts. We met Mary-Annette Hay, who had been a promoter for the Wool Board in the Godfrey Bowen era. Through her we located some amazing wool fashion clothes from the 1950s, and this led us to explore more recent fashions by younger designers using wool. We also decided that the Swanndri was an archetypal use of New Zealand wool that called for promotion, so we made a public call for stories about Swanndris and managed to get the results onto the Paul Holmes show. Some classic Kiwi tales came in, including one from an old hard-bitten farmer who, when one

A turn-of-the-century woollen suit, one of those left in barrels for possible use by castaways stranded on the subantarctic islands one of the nice woollen objects in Te Papa's collection which we used in the On the Sheep's Back *exhibition (left). Here (right) I promote the collection of Swanndri yarns for the exhibition in late 1996.*
MUSEUM OF NEW ZEALAND TE PAPA TONGAREWA FIELD COLLECTION 1947; *DOMINION POST* COLLECTION, ALEXANDER TURNBULL LIBRARY

of his sheepdogs died, would wrap them in a Swanndri and bury them at the bottom of his garden. It was fun collecting items to furnish the woolshed – we had a pair of shearer's moccasins made by a shearer from a wool sack, to go along with the 'Jacky Howe' black singlets; and a new friend of mine, Frida Susan Harper, went home to the sheep farm in Geraldine and ransacked the place for relevant equipment such as stencils once used on wool bales.

Our problems were not entirely over. The exhibition had always been seen as fertile grounds for sponsorship. We went courting Wools New Zealand. They came part of the way, and then stopped. They were trying to position wool as a modern fibre developed with the latest technical expertise. A backward look at the culture of the wool industry was precisely the message they did not want to give. We came under pressure to change the focus of the show. But we had come too far and resisted, and to its credit the museum held firm. The exhibition went ahead without a sponsor.

I thought I was coming to the end of my work at Te Papa when I was summoned to a meeting with Ken Gorbey. He asked me if I would work with Paul Thompson, who had been the developer for *Exhibiting Ourselves*, and Haniko Te Kurapa from the Māori team to develop an exhibition on the Treaty of Waitangi. There had already been several different attempts at coming up with a plan for this exhibition, and because *Exhibiting Ourselves* had proceeded so smoothly we were considered a good bet to get the job done successfully. The previous teams had fallen short, after a convoluted, time-consuming and expensive journey. Under the leadership of Stuart Park and Hinemoa Hilliard, they had begun with a highly information-rich exhibition which told the history of the Treaty in all its detail. Then the museum, in an effort to attract additional funding from government ministers, had proposed that the Treaty exhibition might be one of the museum's key high-energy attractions. In response the team came up with the idea of a theatre of characters who debated the Treaty and told the story of its development and its very different reception among Māori and Pākehā. The museum decided however that the cast of characters was too historical and insufficiently populated with contemporary voices, and was weak on the Pākehā or tangata tiriti side. The team reverted to another information-rich and rather didactic approach positioned between two huge flags – the 1834 flag of an independent New Zealand and the New Zealand Ensign. Again this was rejected, and the team was dismissed.

This time four groups were invited to come up with concepts for the Treaty exhibition. The instructions were that the exhibition had to appeal to Pākehā because of a growing nervousness about a Pākehā backlash, and it had to appeal to teenagers because audience segmentation analysis had suggested a lack of teenage attractions. Not surprisingly this was a tough request, and none of the proposals were accepted. So it seemed that I was being handed a poisoned chalice. There was under two years to go, I did not know much about the Treaty of Waitangi, and the fear that the exhibition might accentuate Pākehā suspicions hung over us. The proposed exhibition was positioned at the centre of the museum, beneath the high, curved wooden ceiling which sat between the Māori and history exhibitions. It was a key site which could not be left vacant and would be observed by every visitor to the place. We were not allowed to fail. This seemed like a difficult and risky challenge. I accepted reluctantly.

There was a carrot in the offer. To help stimulate the creative juices Te Papa proposed to send the three of us on a two-week tour around museums in the United States. I was a little sceptical that the US would have many comparable exhibitions on treaties (although to my surprise we did find one in Warm Springs, Oregon), but was happy to go along on the ride. In the event we worked hard, visiting up to five museums a day in Los Angeles (including of course Disneyland), Washington, New York, Buffalo, Madison and Portland. There were some hairy moments, especially on the flight from New York to Buffalo. It was springtime and in New York a warm wind had brought temperatures into the mid-20s. But as we flew north-west we hit an Arctic storm. The plane veered terrifyingly while lightning flashed outside the windows. I was sitting with Haniko and before long he was chanting Tūhoe karakia. I did my best to join in, for the first and only time in my life finding greater trust in Māori spirituality than European technology. Eventually we landed on a snow-covered runway. It was freezing outside.

The trip paid off in a surprising way. Given the fact that we had a short time to develop the exhibition, and the space already had a rather sacred feel because of its curving roof, Paul Thompson came up with the brilliant idea of enhancing that impression and producing an experience which would not be object-rich and have numerous large panels of information (which would be time-consuming to produce), but rather one that would provide a quiet, sacred, contemplative space, as if you were in a cathedral. We would honour the Treaty and explain it without being too didactic. There were plenty of wordy object-laden exhibitions on either side. We wanted a different kind of experience, a place to sit and think. Quickly realising that we were not likely to get the actual Treaty itself from the National Archives, where it properly belonged, Paul suggested that the cathedral-like ambience might be accentuated by a huge glass panel of the treaty, functioning rather like a rose window. That was a good start, but the American trip gave us a further important inspiration. One afternoon in Washington, feeling exhausted from a morning taking in the Museum of American History and the Holocaust Museum, we decided to take some time out by following my passion and looking at some of Washington's memorials and monuments. We visited the Vietnam memorial, with its long sombre black wall of names, and we started to think about words on stone. Then we moved on to the memorial to Abraham Lincoln. It was a high, elegant room and there were only two elements – a strong and very large statue of

The Lincoln memorial, Washington, in April 1996 (left); Haniko Te Kurapa standing in front of the Gettysburg address carved into the walls of the memorial (right).

Abraham Lincoln and the words of the Gettysburg address on one side and Lincoln's second inaugural on the other. We quickly realised that here was a model. We could have two large panels of the words of the Treaty of Waitangi high up on either side of the exhibition space. The words carved in stone on the Vietnam memorial and in the Lincoln memorial had an extraordinary power and impelled a silent and respectful contemplation. You could not fail to read the Gettysburg address as you sat there. So we measured the size of the type, thought about its height from the floor and worked out how the words of the Treaty, in English on one side and in Māori on the other, might look against the walls of Te Papa. I wrote in our report that 'individual letters need to be 3 to 4 inches high with double space between the lines, and with good visual contrast'. And concluded: 'Words have a power in themselves. Dramatic roof and verticality is important.' By the time we returned the major conceptual work for the exhibition had been done – and inspired not by museums, but by memorials.

There were of course many more details to work out. Paul, after seeing a similar display at the Museum of Sydney, came up with the idea of talking pou at the entrance to the exhibition, and we spent much time working out, and recording, suitable oral histories. The aim was to acknowledge the debate about the Treaty, while suggesting that above the different perspectives the words should stand supreme. Later I enjoyed researching the more instructional panels upstairs, where there was a timeline, and also preparing the computer game based on imagined Waitangi Tribunal cases. Before the Treaty exhibition finally appeared, there were inevitably further political battles to be won as we steered a tricky course between our own vision and intellectual integrity, and the nervousness of the board and management team about the exhibition. One of those moments of approval was captured permanently in Gaylene Preston's documentary *Getting to Our Place*.

In February 1998 Te Papa opened with appropriate ceremony. On the eve of the opening Paul Holmes hosted his 7 p.m. television show from the site. He had been working on it all day and in early afternoon I received an urgent call from Te Papa. Holmes was in a furious temper and complaining about the lack of knowledge about the exhibitions among those who had been put up to be interviewed. Could I come down to the museum and be available in case Holmes wanted accurate answers? I headed off to the museum and hung around watching Holmes film an interview. He saw me watching and came up: 'What are you doing. I hate being watched while I am filming. Who are you anyway?' I explained that I was Jock Phillips, concept leader for the history exhibitions. 'Jock Phillips,' Holmes replied. 'You must be Cathy's brother. How is Cathy – the love of my life?' My younger sister, Catherine, had had a relationship with Paul Holmes when they were both at Victoria University in the early 1970s. Holmes was desperate to hear news about her. 'Stop the filming,' he shouted to the crew, as we sat down and proceeded to chat. I filled him in with details of her life since Victoria days, and disappointed him by telling him that she was now happily married. We ended with him asking for her address. My sister had saved the day for Te Papa. From that point on Paul Holmes was a different man. He insisted on interviewing me, gave me a charmed run, and was suitably enthusiastic about the history exhibitions.

As I had hoped, the exhibitions were generally well-received. Thousands flocked in, and *Exhibiting Ourselves* especially won praise. Denis Dutton, in a much-publicised piece, attacked Te Papa as a theme park aimed at nine-year-olds; but when I wrote to him he replied that he was not including the history exhibitions.[9] I remained disappointed that apart from publicity on the day there were almost no probing reviews, and the exhibitions were largely ignored in print by the community of historians. My hope that the exhibitions might have some impact on serious history was a vain self-promotion.

I was also disappointed that much of the work we as concept leaders had put into thinking about the shared spaces had come to nought. I had always been attracted to the museum because I wanted to work in an interdisciplinary way, and the museum had originally planned a number of shared spaces for art and history, tangata whenua and tangata tiriti, and science and culture. But none of these eventuated. We never found a space for an art/history exhibit; and the science/culture space, which had been set aside for the third floor of the museum, was retained for later development. Most serious was the absence of a shared tangata whenua/tangata tiriti area. True, we eventually did get a Treaty exhibition, but the other space was taken over by a coffee bar, which was thought to have higher value. The result was that Te Papa never dealt with issues about relations between Māori and Pākehā which were central to New Zealand identity. We did much talking about this space. I always wanted exploration of some of the sites where the two peoples had interacted – marriage, sport, music and war, to cite four good examples. This never happened, so relations between Māori and Pākehā, including such major events as the New Zealand Wars, were not treated at all in Te Papa. Even our Treaty exhibition, because it became primarily an evocative spiritual site rather than a didactic information-rich exhibition, did not address such matters. This was a huge gap, which many others have noted. I share their disappointment.

But I was proud of what we had achieved in the history exhibitions. Getting to opening had been four years of hard work, and many days of anguish and frustration. Yet 90 per cent of what I had dreamed did appear on the exhibition floor. The history exhibitions were popular, and they escaped the torrent of criticism which everyone had once feared. Although I found myself repeatedly seething with anger at the authoritarian way in which decisions that affected us descended from on high, I have come to recognise that Cheryll and Ken had a really tough task. They had to mediate between our dreams and huge public expectations, a board that was very nervous of a Pākehā backlash, and a government wary about money. Their treatment of us was one way of protecting our integrity from these direct political pressures. Despite the constant need to win approval from higher authorities, we were able to produce exhibitions that satisfied political masters while retaining a degree of intellectual and scholarly integrity.

After Te Papa I continued for a time to dabble in museum matters. I was asked to prepare a conceptual plan for a projected museum at Taupō, and I journeyed to Edinburgh to speak at the Museum of Scotland about objects and images pertaining to New Zealand and Scotland. But I had little contact with Te Papa after 1998, and, was horrified to find one day when I was visiting that *Exhibiting Ourselves*, an exhibition that had been successful and was my personal favourite, had disappeared without warning and with no farewell.

In the long run the impact for me of the four years at Te Papa was not a future career as an exhibition developer, but rather that I learned a series of hugely important skills as a historian. I was further educated in working in a bicultural institution – the shared responsibility of Cliff Whiting and Cheryl Sotheran and the strong input from a Māori advisory committee were models I would not forget. I learnt, in a way that I had never previously experienced, the value and the challenge of working in a team. The satisfaction that came from a group of four or five all owning a collective task was a key lesson. The Gantt charts and detailed planning at Te Papa were often a target for ribald sarcasm, yet they really paid off, and I came to recognise the essential value of planning and reporting. Without these methods we would never have delivered on time and on budget. I began to think much more about interdisciplinary approaches, despite the failure of the shared exhibitions; and I relished the multimedia ways of communicating history. Discovering that you did not need to tell history through lines of text, but could do it through photographs, or paintings, or films, or interactive devices, or even computer games, was an exciting insight. Combining these modes with the latest research-based scholarship gave me enormous pleasure. Above all I learnt for the first time to think constantly about the audience, about the different needs of young and old, locals and tourists, readers and scanners. And I learnt that you could never second-guess audience reactions – everything needed to be checked through user testing. All these were lessons which I did not forget, and when I came to my next major project, preparing an encyclopedia of New Zealand on the web, they would come into their own.

9
A sojourn on the dark side

On 31 July 1997 I put in an application to become general manager heritage in the Department of Internal Affairs. In my application I spelled out my experience in starting institutions and delivering exciting results at the Stout Centre, the Historical Branch and Te Papa, and I concluded with this statement:

> My whole creative career – from the books I have written, to the exhibitions I have curated, to the computer games I have authored, to the institutions I have established – has been driven by a belief that the history and heritage of New Zealand is central to our national sense of well-being and must be fostered. I wish New Zealanders to regard their own history with as much affection and awe as Americans do of their history and heritage.[1]

Exactly three months later I was offered the job – or at least in an acting capacity.

This photo appeared in the Sunday Star-Times *on 9 January 2000. At the time I was acting general manager heritage, but on this occasion I was also being a historian and indeed prophet of the digital age.*

Why would I aspire to become a senior public servant and manager in pursuit of history? After all, during my time at the university I had regarded administration as the dark side, a refuge for failed academics (a judgement my father's experience did not challenge), and once I became chief historian, I had contempt for the chief executive under whom I had served longest, Perry Cameron. Yet, like it or not, I had actually become quite experienced as an administrator and manager. At the Stout Centre I had established and created a new institution and built a collegial environment which I had enjoyed. In the Historical Branch I was as much a manager as a historian, and found that the challenge of turning around a dormant institution was immensely satisfying. I liked creating a congenial high-performing team, and I prided myself on my abilities to balance the budget and grow the revenue. I had also joined the board of the Fulbright Foundation and in 1996 found myself as its chair; and had been president of the National Library Society. The whole question of how to choose and motivate talented people to work together for common goals had become interesting to me. While I scoffed at much of the language of business planning – the outputs, the indicators, the measures of improvement – I was interested in sharing with people a sense of direction.

The opportunity came about because when Perry Cameron left the Department of Internal Affairs his position was taken by Roger Blakeley. Roger was a breath of fresh air. Young, bubbling with energy, he had huge ambitions for the department which, despite its age as the very first government department (the Colonial Secretary's Office), had a very low status within government circles. Roger had established his reputation by orchestrating an agreement between conservationists and foresters on the West Coast, and had then moved to the Ministry for the Environment, where he had helped design the Resource Management Act. Roger could be a bit 'new agey', most notably when in 1996 he brought in an American guru to conduct a major cultural transformation of the department, called 'Focus Change'. We were given branded 'Focus Change' T-shirts, and were sent away on residential workshops where, in a manner akin to a religious revival meeting, we were encouraged to learn new high-performing values and come up with innovative ideas. However, I liked Roger, and I was stimulated by his commitment to high standards. And at my particular 'Focus Change' session we had developed an exciting proposal called 'Whakapapa 2000'. The idea was that the department would establish a website aimed at family historians in which we would bring together the shipping records from the National Archives, the database of 15,000 historical New Zealanders from the Dictionary of New Zealand Biography, and the births, deaths and marriages records which were also administered by the department. We aimed to integrate all these sources to provide a way for New Zealanders to uncover the story of their ancestors. The experience got me thinking of the possibilities of combining different units in the department, especially using the new digital technology.

As part of his vision to raise the ambitions of the department and to get different sections working coherently, Roger Blakeley decided, as all chief executives eventually do, to restructure the department. He proposed to put into one unit, which he called Heritage New Zealand, four separate groups – the Historical Branch, the Dictionary of New Zealand Biography, the Heritage Property Unit, which looked after war graves and national monuments and memorials, and the National Archives, which held all government records. As the manager of the Historical Branch I spent a week with the other managers thinking about how such a grouping might work and whether it had advantages. From the very start the fiercest opposition came from the National Archives, where the chief archivist, Kathryn Patterson, articulated a view, widely shared within the archives community, that the National Archives was too important, and had too significant a constitutional role as the keeper of the government record, to be subsumed within a larger grouping. She strongly resented being downgraded to a third-tier position within the department, not reporting directly to the chief executive. To a considerable extent I shared her anxieties, but I could also see that Roger Blakeley was determined that a Heritage Group would be established and it might be able to accomplish interesting projects by working together. I began to think that if the group went ahead, then I wanted to lead it. I knew the business of the Historical Branch well and did not want its work hamstrung by an unsympathetic general manager. I knew the Dictionary well too, having written some half-dozen entries for the project and having served on its advisory committee since becoming chief historian. I had not worked closely with the Heritage Property Unit, but of course I was passionate about monuments and memorials and was keen to help promote them as a way of encouraging a nationwide interest in history. As for the National Archives, ever since I had begun work on *A Man's Country?*, I had been convinced of the extraordinary unexplored wealth of historical information to be found within

From 1997 to 2000 I was a member of this Department of Internal Affairs Executive Management Team, from left: Alwyn Clement, Brenda Tahi, Janice Calvert, Roger Blakeley, Paul Curry (in front), Pam Madgwick, Helen Algar, Annette Offenberger, me and Anne O'Shaunessy.

its walls. I had got to know the previous chief archivist, Ray Grover, well and had worked with him on a number of initiatives. The more we talked in our week-long sessions about the possibilities of bringing these units together, the more I believed the venture was worth doing. I came to believe that the best way I could promote the growth of New Zealand history was to take on a full-time management role.

So for almost three years, from October 1997 to June 2000, I found myself a second-tier manager, a general manager no less, in a department of over 1000 employees. The Executive Management Team (EMT) would gather every Monday afternoon for formal meetings. Consistent with Roger's idea of expanding our skills, we each took turns in chairing the sessions; the papers were prepared in a rigorous format – always with full costings, a risk analysis and a survey of options. After any event there would be time set aside for us to share our 'learnings'. I used to laugh inwardly at the jargon and the overly self-conscious process, but I also came to appreciate the value in making decisions explicit and spending fully transparent. The more I participated in senior management the more acculturated I became. Roger was excellent in providing advice and encouragement and we had extensive performance reviews every six months, not to mention psychological assessments and 360-degree evaluations in which stakeholders, peers (other members of the senior management team) and staff commented on your strengths and weaknesses. I usually did well in these exercises and before long Roger was encouraging me to think in terms of becoming a chief executive in a cultural agency. As training for this, I even applied (unsuccessfully) for a fellowship to travel overseas and upskill my management abilities. Of course it was not all fun. I often found myself involved in other parts of the ministry which did not really interest me – spending many hours on a staff remuneration committee; serving on a committee to oversee the introduction of a new computerised register for death records; and, most onerous of all, chairing a working group responsible for 'Y2K' – remember that? Y2K was the fear that at one minute past midnight on 1 January 2000 the world's computers would go awry. Our role was to check every system in the department to ensure that at least in DIA we were safe. This was decidedly not how I wanted to occupy my time and creative energy.

The trials of being a general manager were greatly alleviated in those years by the early years of my relationship with Frida Susan Harper. After the end of my marriage to Phillida and a tumultuous period of relationships, most notably with Jan Bassett and Kim Walker, I encountered Frida again on the occasion of my fiftieth birthday celebration in May 1997. We had first met some years before on a couple of social occasions, but then my old friend and former Karori neighbour, Jeff Kennedy, invited Frida along to my fiftieth. Her own marriage had collapsed and Jeff decided that Frida should meet a wider circle. I was immediately attracted. From a Canterbury farming family, Frida had a background similar to my own. She was warm, funny and highly intelligent, and had taught English literature and history in schools, most notably Onslow College, where both my children had met her. We also shared a love of the outdoors, and over successive summers during these years we tramped South Island trans-alpine passes – the Whitcombe, the Dennistoun and the Three Passes trips. Within a year of re-meeting we had bought a lovely 1896 house in Mt Cook, a walk of ten minutes to Cuba Street and half an hour to Courtenay Place. The urban life of Wellington was on our doorstep. A happy domestic life, where we had much contact with both my two children and

Setting out to climb up and over the Dennistoun Pass with Frida Harper in December 2000.

Frida's four beautiful daughters, provided an inner security which made the tribulations of being a public-sector manager very much easier.

As the general manager of the Heritage Group, my first initial challenge was to try to end the 'acting' role. This came about because the moment Heritage New Zealand had been announced, the Archives and Record Association (ARANZ) had lodged a legal challenge. They argued that demoting the position of chief archivist from a second-tier role, reporting to the department's chief executive, to a third-tier role reporting to me was contrary to the Archives Act. Because my role was under legal challenge, I could not be formally appointed. In the end this did not make much difference operationally, except that I was not able to formally resign as chief historian, which in the long term worked to my advantage.

On the substantive issue I had much sympathy with the ARANZ point of view. I had been a member of the association for over twenty years. Their argument was that the National Archives had a very significant constitutional role since, by preserving the official record of government, archives kept government accountable to the people. I agreed with this and indeed had actually written to the minister of internal affairs in the 1970s suggesting that Archives become a separate government department or Crown entity. I always thought that placing Archives within the Department of Internal Affairs made the operation of its constitutional role very conflicted when it came to overseeing DIA records. However, given that Archives *was* within the department, it did not seem to me to make much difference whether the role was second or third tier. Further, while I respected Archives' constitutional role, I was also very aware of the enormous richness of historical material within the archives and was keen to make that material more accessible. I could see things that urgently needed doing.

Initially, dealing with Archives was very difficult. There was the constant irritation that I was involved in a court case and spent a lot of time briefing lawyers, and trying not to allow the legal situation to affect my personal dealings with Archives staff. I was constantly aware that anything I communicated could be passed immediately to those appearing for ARANZ, so I had to be scrupulous about what I said or wrote. I lost old friends in the process, which was personally painful. We did win the case in the High Court, but it was immediately appealed, so I remained in limbo as the acting GM. Then within a few months Roger Blakeley decided that he wanted to replace the chief archivist, Kathryn Patterson, and of course I had to be the bearer of the awful news. When she left, one of the top managers of Archives began to deluge me with the most personally offensive emails I have ever received. I became more stressed and lost more sleep over these confrontations than I had ever experienced. I realised that senior management was not a bed of roses and I began to wonder why I had ever taken it on. Oh for the quiet self-directed life of the researching historian! Yet I worked hard to visit and speak to the various groups involved – especially genealogists, archivists and the Archives staff. I quickly found that most of the staff were amazingly supportive and professional. I liked them.

Together with the astute advice of the Archives finance officer, Lindsay Ferguson, and a brilliant project manager, Pam Madgwick, we accomplished much of what I had hoped. On two separate occasions in the previous years Archives had failed in budget bids to get a new floor in their Mulgrave Street building to shelve the growing quantity of government files. I was determined to succeed. So we invited the Treasury boffins along to our meetings. We did not succeed in convincing them, but at least we heard their contrary arguments – that keeping all this stuff was unnecessary; that the papers should all be digitised; that Archives could be moved to cheaper storage in the provinces. I knew that we had to answer all these options in the paper that went up to ministers. Finally there was a meeting in the office of the minister of finance, Bill English. Treasury had recommended against funding, but English, listening to our arguments, rejected their advice and we won a new floor, plus, in the following year, additional baseline funding. Then I discovered that the roof of the Archives building suffered from leaks – in a bad northerly storm (not unknown in Wellington) there would be buckets everywhere. This was not at all a good look for a repository of the nation's treasures, including the Treaty of Waitangi. Again Kathryn Patterson had failed to convince the department to fund a new roof. I argued the case passionately to my colleagues on the Executive Management Team, and once more I got the money. In all I was able to obtain over $5 million in capital investment and over $2 million in baseline funding for the National Archives. In addition I tried to show my commitment to the constitutional role of Archives by pressing hard for a new Archives Act. This was finally achieved after my time (in 2005), but we had all put a huge amount of thought and energy into it.

Nor was this all. I was determined to make the point that while the constitutional role of the National Archives was important, the archivists had also to recognise that by far the greatest number of its users were genealogists and historians. This was especially important now that the Treaty of Waitangi claims process was in full gear. When I had worked at the Archives as a historian, it had been a frustration that the finding aids were so difficult. They were in large black folders, and you had to have a detailed understanding of the institutional history of government departments and agencies to find your way around. You also had to go along to the Archives building itself to accomplish this. There was no possibility of ordering material from your base in Auckland or Invercargill. Surely now was the time to digitise the finding aids and make them searchable for anyone with a computer. Once more I went in to battle and once more came back with a small amount of funding so that we could begin the process on an instalment plan. The huge project of digitising Archives finding aids was begun.

Another frustration, which went back to my time researching there, had been the total inaccessibility of the photograph collection. The images were not properly catalogued and were rarely used. But dipping into some files I realised that, as would be expected, government departments had many fascinating images hidden away. It was too big a job to index all of these images, but I did encourage Bronwyn Dalley in the Historical Branch to begin looking at the photographs and to prepare a book drawn from them on life in the twentieth century as a millennium project.[2] When launched in 2000 it was a very fine achievement, which I hope served to awaken interest in the Archives collection.

I enjoyed my work with the Heritage Property Unit in encouraging and supporting the use of memorials to heighten awareness of New Zealand history. There were inevitable difficulties. When the New Zealand dollar fell we had a battle with Treasury to assist in the funding of New Zealand's contribution to the Commonwealth War Graves Commission, which looks after all the cemeteries where New Zealand servicepeople are buried. They turned us down and we had to skimp on other places to fulfil the obligation. We were more successful in getting funds to help maintain the National War Memorial. I had always loved the carillon and enjoyed the playing of the bells on Saturday afternoon, which I could hear while working in the garden in our Mt Cook house. I was fascinated by the repair work, which involved running an electric current through the concrete to prevent rusting of the metal reinforcement.

It was also a fascinating experience to be involved in the design and building of a New Zealand memorial at Canberra. The design itself, by Kingsley Baird, was a brilliant concept – two soaring bronze handles of a kete placed on either side of Anzac Parade and symbolising the two nations sharing the load. There were some lovely details, such as Aboriginal and Māori designs on the pavements beneath each arch, and a superb poem by Jenny Bornholdt. There were some tricky moments here too, when we discovered that the cost of the bronze construction was likely to be way beyond the budget. Treasury asked stern questions and we had to come up with an alternative and much less satisfactory design using a hollow shell with a bronze-coloured covering. Fortunately once more a minister, this time Helen Clark, the prime minister, came to our defence, and overruled Treasury advice with the view

As general manager heritage I encouraged efforts to remember New Zealanders' sacrifice in war. In October 1999 I helped organise an event to commemorate the departure of New Zealanders to the South African War. Here Jack Cromie throws a wreath into the sea at Queen's Wharf, marking the place from where his grandfather had set sail exactly a hundred years before. Governor-General Sir Michael Hardie-Boys assists (left). DOMINION POST COLLECTION, ALEXANDER TURNBULL LIBRARY. *One of the two kete handles on either side of Anzac Parade, Canberra, the New Zealand memorial in Australia, which was opened in April 2001 (right).*

that if we were going to do an international memorial it should be done to the highest standards.

I also worked with the Heritage Property Unit and Ian McGibbon in the Historical Branch to publish a guide to the battlefields of the Western Front and to organise a suite of activities for the hundredth anniversary of the departure of New Zealand soldiers to the South African War in 1899. We held a conference on the war, published a new illustrated history of the New Zealanders' involvement in South Africa, and on 21 October, the exact anniversary of the departure of the first contingent, we held a re-enactment of the march of the men from their camp at Ben Burn Park in Karori down to Queen's Wharf. There was excellent press and television coverage. I was pleased at our success in using novel means to awaken public interest in the nation's past.

As general manager I continued to have a close involvement in the activities of the Historical Branch. I remained comparatively hands-on, and delegated Claudia Orange, then general editor of the Dictionary of New Zealand Biography, to take over the formal management. This was a major mistake which I came to rue later. The members of the branch, understandably, resented the fact that I had not trusted one of them to take on the role. However, their output continued at a good level. In terms of historical publication, the initiatives that were most exciting to me were those in digital history. The Te Papa experience had awakened an interest in computer-based learning; and as the world wide web took off with extraordinary speed in the late 1990s, the possibilities for web history became evident. The most important project was the launching at the National Archives of a New Zealand History website by the minister of internal affairs, Jack Elder, in March 1999. This was a project involving people across the group, especially those in the Historical Branch and the Dictionary of New Zealand Biography, and was effectively led by a researcher in the Dictionary unit, Jamie Mackay. It began very much as a shop window for the Historical Branch and DNZB publications; but Jamie and his team had larger ambitions, and increasingly saw the site as New Zealand's premier resource for information about New Zealand's past. Jamie had a real talent for understanding what would work on the web, and before long the site was attracting what seemed like huge numbers – about 50,000 visitors a month. I was not much involved in the day-to-day running of this site; but I wrote a number of essays for it, and looked with wonderment and admiration at its runaway success.

I was more directly involved in a project to digitise the Dictionary of New Zealand Biography as a millennium project. We could not obtain the money for this from departmental funds, so I made an agreement with the New Zealand Historical Association that they would formally publish the site, which allowed them, as a voluntary organisation, to seek funds from the Lottery Grants Board. A grant was duly forthcoming, and we worked hard to have the site launched in early 2001. Along with the complete text of all the dictionary biographies, we added portraits of the individuals where possible, and associated the site with a series of overview essays about New Zealand's past which drew heavily on maps from the *Historical Atlas*. The digital world increasingly captured my enthusiasms and I came up with various other schemes, including a proposal that the British Council fund a digital guide to the immigrants from the British Isles. This emerged naturally from the ongoing project to provide a solid statistical basis for the peopling of New Zealand from the British Isles. Sadly the funding never came through.

The other form of history which interested me in the late 1990s was television history. I had always enjoyed history on television, relishing such BBC productions as the twenty-six-part documentary *The Great War* from the mid-1960s, Sir Kenneth Clark's *Civilisation* or Ken Burns' wonderful story of the American Civil War. At home an interesting start had been made by Kenneth Cumberland's programme *Landmarks*, which had been produced by George Andrews. One day in the early 1990s Andrews had contacted me and invited me to take part in a five-part history of rugby, *The Game of Our Lives*. I was duly interviewed, and was impressed by how effectively the medium had told the historical story of rugby. Towards the end of this project, George asked whether I would be interested in writing a television series on the history of New Zealand. He wanted a six-part venture – a kind of *Landmarks* for a new generation. I spent several weeks looking at various options and came up with the idea that people often act to prevent pain they have suffered. I suggested that this might be a good route into exploring New Zealand history – for example, the migration of settlers to the New World came about partly to escape the poverty and uncertainty of life in rural Britain, where population growth and industrialisation had undermined the opportunities for work and created starvation and misery. Similarly, the creation of the welfare state in the 1890s and 1930s was a reaction against the distress which people had suffered in the two big depressions just preceding these years. The cultural revolts of the 1970s were a generational rebellion against the conformity and smugness of the 1950s – and so on. I became quite excited about the series, but sadly it was stillborn. The funds never eventuated. Several years later the Historical Branch was invited to provide background information for a series being produced by Ninox Films about the history of the twentieth century, told through the story of particular families. Our role here was no more than providing contextual information, but it did serve to awaken my interest further. At the time James Belich was fronting his magnificent series on the New Zealand Wars, so it looked as if television was becoming a promising outlet for communicating the serious history of New Zealand to a wider audience.

Then, about 2000, we were approached by Ray Waru to see if the Historical Branch would like to provide the background scripts for a proposed thirteen-part television history of New Zealand. Obviously we accepted. My initial idea was that the overarching theme should be New Zealand dreams and New Zealand realities. I was convinced that as a new society, New Zealand had always been a place where people had dreamed of a better life. Where the dreams came from and how they worked out would make a fascinating story. In the end the only thing which remained from this idea was a title, *Frontier of Dreams*. Instead both Ray Waru and his associate producer Vincent Burke, plus the other historians in the branch, felt that a more conventional and comprehensive narrative of New Zealand history was what was needed. So I then commissioned twelve historians (besides myself) to prepare overviews of each period – they included major contributors to the profession like Judith Binney, Miles Fairburn, Ranginui Walker, Erik Olssen, Charlotte Macdonald and Claudia Orange, alongside some of the branch historians such as Gavin McLean and Bronwyn Dalley. We each scripted a story and then brainstormed them in a fascinating day-long seminar. Eventually the programme was produced, and aired successfully in 2005. After I left the Historical Branch, Bronwyn Dalley and Gavin McLean edited a book of the series. I authored a chapter on the years 1965–84, which was a hangover from my previous project on New Zealand from 1940 to 1990. The book too was phenomenally successful.

These experiences ensured I did a lot of thinking about television history. It was a different challenge from exhibition or digital history. On television you could control the order and pace in which your audience heard the story, and

Appearing in George Andrews' television programme The Game of Our Lives *in 1996.*

the real challenge was how to enrich the narration with visual interest – site locations, reconstructions, old photographs, music and sounds. This was interesting, and it sharpened my appreciation of the multimedia communication of history; but unlike book or exhibition history, even digital history, the control lay in the hands of the directors. You as historian had little influence on what bits of your interview were included and what bits hit the cutting-room floor. Meanings could be distorted, nuances lost. This television experience sat alongside my thinking on digital history, and I began to ponder the challenges for historians in communicating through new media. I was increasingly aware of the limitations of traditional academic manuscript-based history. The 1990s had seen a real boom in different forms of professional history outside the university – the research called for by the Treaty of Waitangi, the expanding production of the Historical Branch, the work by special publicly funded exercises like the Dictionary of New Zealand Biography and the Historical Atlas. I had already argued the need for universities to start preparing their students for these public-history careers. Now I decided that we should produce a text for their efforts. Bronwyn Dalley and I worked together to edit a collection, *Going Public: The Changing Face of New Zealand History*. I wrote a chapter on history in the new media, where I explored the challenges of preparing history for television and the web.

So despite my involvement in public administration, I continued to think about New Zealand history during these years. And I tried to use my historical skills to assist in various departmental initiatives. Roger Blakeley invited me to lead a project on national identity, and he also volunteered my services in a so-called Foresight project which set out to imagine various futures for New Zealand. I came up with three scenarios – a future New Zealand in which we were swallowed up by global forces; a stridently nationalist New Zealand; and a multicultural New Zealand. This was fun and it provoked some worthwhile discussion, but it did not really seem to add much to the country's historical knowledge. The reality was that most of my time was spent on budgets and business cases and delicate personnel problems. The question started to become more urgent – was my life as a historian at an end?

Two events brought this home to me. One day, about late 1998, Roger Blakeley invited me to sketch out a long-term future for the Heritage Group. Despite all the work that I had put into creating a united set of activities, I was not convinced that there *was* a long-term future in the group (especially since the legal appeal remained unresolved), and I remained wedded to the view that the ideal situation for the National Archives was as an independent entity. Further, I had become increasingly worried at the exposed position of historical pursuits within the Department of Internal Affairs. Whenever our activities were ranked by other members of the Executive Management Team, we would come out near the bottom. Managers involved in the regulation of gambling, or providing ministers with personal services like cars or accommodation, or giving Kiwis new passports and registering births, had little sympathy for serious works of history. So I suggested that in an ideal future the National Archives would become a separate institution – my suggestion was as a Crown entity responsible to Parliament – and the historical and heritage property functions would transfer to the Ministry for Cultural Affairs, a very small ministry which had been established in 1991. My paper caused some discussion among the EMT, whose members were amused that I should be so keen to do myself out of a job. Whether it was this think-piece, or an entirely different initiative, I am unsure, but soon after the State Services Commission began a project to investigate the status and future of the National Archives. I became involved in the discussions, which were tediously over-burdened with process, but the recommendations were much as I had suggested – a separate National Archives and a transfer of the history and heritage activities to Cultural Affairs.

At a function to celebrate the creation of Archives New Zealand as a separate institution in 2000. Some of those who helped take me to court seemed to have forgiven me. They are (fourth from left) Ian Wards, former chief historian and (far right) Ray Grover, former chief archivist. Others in the photo are (from left) Gavin McLean, myself, Claudia Orange, Richard Hill and Michael King. ARCHIVES NEW ZEALAND

Then, in May 1999, the position of chief executive of the Ministry for Cultural Affairs was advertised. I decided to put in an application. I was shortlisted and went for an interview. The interview panel included the former president of the National Party, Sue Wood. When it came her turn to ask questions she began by saying, 'You are a successful and distinguished New Zealand writer and historian. Why would someone who had your skills and track record want to throw them away to become a government chief executive?' The question caught me by surprise and I mumbled an answer to the effect that administering cultural affairs would allow me to promote New Zealand history in a more direct way. But even I was not convinced and the question kept eating away at me. When I was invited to ask questions I turned to Michael Wintringham, the state services commissioner, and asked why the position was being advertised and an appointment made at this point when the future of the ministry was under review. Would it not be better to find a new chief executive after that review was completed and we knew exactly the nature of the ministry – whether it would just deal with the creative arts or whether it would also include heritage activities? Wintringham was quite clear that this did not matter. About three weeks later, when I was on holiday in Fiji, I received a call from Wintringham, which implied that I was the preferred candidate. He was seeking permission to follow up with referees. I breathed hard. About ten days later, on my return, I was summoned to Wintringham's office. He congratulated me on my application and interview, and then said that the commission had decided that because of the review process, the appointment of a new chief executive would wait until after the review had reached its conclusion. I made no comment and left.

In November 1999 a Labour Government was elected, and one of its earliest decisions, pushed eloquently by a former historian, Michael Cullen, now minister of finance, was that the National Archives would become a separate institution – not a Crown entity, but a fully fledged department called Archives New Zealand. The history and heritage units would transfer to the Ministry for Cultural Affairs, which would be renamed the Ministry for Culture and Heritage. I spent until 30 June 2000 working on the transfer agreement. On 1 July 2000 I gave up being a general manager, and, because I had served simply in an acting role, I was restored to my old position as chief historian in the Ministry for Culture and Heritage. The minister for the portfolio was the prime minister, Helen Clark.

It was a relief to get back to the branch, or History Group as it became, and before long we had some interesting new initiatives on the boil. Helen Clark had returned from visiting Gallipoli on Anzac Day 2000, having read Maurice Shadbolt's gripping set of oral histories with Gallipoli veterans, *Voices from Gallipoli*. I had met with her several times in her Beehive office, and one day she approached me in the corridors of parliament and suggested that we begin an effort to capture in oral-history form the memories of the veterans who were still remaining from World War II. It was a great idea and before long, the oral historian Megan Hutching, a member of the pacifist Women's International League for Peace and Freedom, was heavily involved in recording the memories of those who had served in Crete in 1941. Historical projects attracted me once more, and Sue Wood's question would not disappear from my consciousness. Several months after the transfer, the State Services Commission decided, once more, to advertise the position of chief executive of the Ministry for Culture and Heritage. The experience of being a government bureaucrat had not been all bad. Indeed, in a letter to a friend at the end of 1998 I wrote, 'Despite all the difficulties I have found that I actually quite enjoy the administration and have worn it much easier than I had expected.' But I then continued, 'I won't be doing it for ever.'[3] I had learnt much – how to create a team that pulls together, how to extract money from ministers. But I was itching for a more hands-on involvement in New Zealand history. I never thought for a moment about applying for the chief-executive role. Immediately I went to Martin Matthews, who was the acting head, telling him that I would not apply and giving him my enthusiastic support. The lure of power had palled. In 2001, nine months after stepping down as general manager, I spent two months in Belfast lecturing to Northern Ireland students about New Zealand history. It was stimulating to be back in an academic environment discussing ideas about the past. Once more New Zealand history was calling – and it came this time in the form of a national encyclopedia on the web.

10
Encyclopedist

The new millennium brought change. Within six months I was married to my new love, Frida Susan Harper, and just days later I had ceased to be a top government bureaucrat and moved with the renamed History Group (the former Historical Branch) to the renamed Ministry for Culture and Heritage. Within twelve months I was elected to the Victoria University Council and was to spend much time and intellectual energy over the following twelve years on the governance of that august institution. Within eighteen months my father was dead. I happened to be driving to a conference in Northern Ireland when my mother rang with the news. I had visited him just days before. To compose myself I went for a walk in the wind on the high moors between Belfast and Derry. There I came across a collection of stones which spelled out the words 'God is Dad'. I could not have put it better myself.

But the real theme of my life for the next few years was spelled out nine days after the new millennium arrived. I was asked by the *Sunday Star-Times* to contribute to a series on the meaning of the next thousand years. I suggested that while the previous millennium had seen 'the Gutenberg revolution', the

Speaking at the launch of the last theme of Te Ara, in October 2014.
MANATŪ TAONGA MINISTRY FOR CULTURE AND HERITAGE

'God is Dad' spelled out in stones on a misty moor between Belfast and Derry on the day that my father died.

emergence of the printing press which had opened up understanding of the world, the next thousand years would be digital. The internet would transform all our lives. I did not realise at the time how quickly this would happen, or how rapidly my own intellectual life would be consumed by attempting to create the world's first born-digital national encyclopedia on the web.

From 2002 until 2014 most of my creative juices went into this task; and it proved the most exciting and enjoyable period of my life. Much of my previous experience paid off in this work – my experience of managing a small team; my training in how to budget and project-manage; my growing enthusiasm from the time at Te Papa and in television work about the value of multimedia communication; the insights I had gained at Te Papa about the benefits of user-testing; my hard-won lessons about developing bicultural projects; my growing fascination with computer games and digital communication; and my love of exploring New Zealand. I was well prepared. There were many aspects which made those years so enjoyable – the privilege of learning about every aspect of New Zealand science, culture, society and history; the challenge of writing about subjects which were intriguing and new to me; the

excitement of working on a cutting-edge project; the public recognition and acclaim. But the real joy was working with others who were as enthusiastic about what we were doing as I was. Whether expert writers, holders of images or professional designers, hardly a person turned us down. People could recognise that the project was important and bent over backwards to give us a hand. Most important of all, we built up a magnificent team who were passionate about Te Ara, proud of what we were doing, got on well with one another and knew how to celebrate our achievements.

The story of Te Ara begins long before the millennium. Encyclopedias of knowledge were originally a product of the Enlightenment, but by the early twentieth century they were hawked from house to house by travelling salespeople. My parents purchased an *Oxford Junior Encyclopaedia*, which I would spend hours browsing and occasionally using for school projects. There was not much about New Zealand. The first New Zealand encyclopedia, the *Cyclopaedia of New Zealand*, came out in six regional volumes at the turn of the twentieth century and was primarily an outlet for colonial boosters who wanted to trumpet their achievements. People paid to contribute entries about themselves or their businesses. Then in the early 1960s A. H. McLintock, the parliamentary historian, put together a scholarly *Encyclopaedia of New Zealand*. It was a fine achievement. With its distinctive blue covers, it was published in three volumes, organised A–Z, in 1966. The volumes were produced by the Government Printer, sold 31,000 copies in two months, and when the full run of 34,000 was sold within eighteen months the volumes were never reprinted. The Government Printer was not at that stage governed by any commercial imperative. My father, who had contributed a biography of James Hight, purchased a set for the house, and I must have flicked through it. But at the time I was not interested in New Zealand, so I never gave the volumes close study, and not until much later was I aware of a more racy and less comprehensive encyclopedia of New Zealand, published in 1984 by David Bateman under the editorship of the journalist Gordon McLauchlan.

It was not until 1990 that I reluctantly turned my attention to a New Zealand encyclopedia. As one of his last gestures to encourage New Zealand history, my old patron and minister of internal affairs, Michael Bassett, presented the Historical Branch with $200,000 from the Lottery Grants Board towards a new encyclopedia of New Zealand. I realised there were indeed good arguments for a new encyclopedia. The existing texts were clearly unsatisfactory. Bateman's was a once-over-lightly, good for the glovebox of the car, but not for serious students of New Zealand. McLintock's volume was impressive and was still used as a reference work by scholars for the details of such subjects as sheep breeds or natural disasters. But, produced by a committee of government officials, it was heavily institutional, with much attention to government activities and little to the wider culture. Further, there had been a revolution in New Zealand's research culture since 1966. There had been a huge expansion in serious research as the country began to produce its own PhDs and academics were expected to advance scholarship rather than just teach. A substantial body of new material needed to be distilled for general use. Social attitudes on such matters as race and gender had changed dramatically. An interest in social history and 'history from below' had emerged which made many McLintock entries look very dated. There were striking absences – nothing about New Zealand foods or childbirth, no coverage of the country's iwi.

So I could see why Bassett thought it was time for a new encyclopedia. I discovered that an earlier chief historian, Ian Wards, had actually prepared a scoping study for a new encyclopedia in 1983. But in 1990 I was not convinced that the need was urgent. The first volume of the *Dictionary of New Zealand Biography* had yet to appear and another four were planned; and we had only just begun the process of preparing a historical atlas of New Zealand. With these two major reference works in full swing, I did not believe that the country had the intellectual capacity to begin a third major reference work. There were also personal concerns. I was just starting my time as chief historian and had a large agenda of other projects. Frankly I could not get myself excited about a conventional print encyclopedia. I was interested in exploring new aspects of New Zealand history in depth. The task of writing potted summaries of other people's researches seemed distinctly boring. In any case $200,000 was clearly insufficient to get the job done and I was not convinced that once Michael Bassett was gone there would be further funds forthcoming. We used the $200,000 for an encyclopedia of women's organisations, *Women Together*, for the suffrage centennial, and I largely forgot about a new encyclopedia of New Zealand.

It was almost eight years before once again I was forced, still reluctant, to think about a new encyclopedia of New Zealand. The pressure came from two directions. Paul Bateman and Tracey Borgfeldt from Bateman Publishing had won the contract to publish the *Historical Atlas* in 1997, so we saw quite a lot of them. Reasonably often either Paul or Tracey would raise the subject of a new encyclopedia. Their own encyclopedia had been highly successful commercially, running to about five editions, but they realised that the content had become outdated and was superficial. They were keen to publish a new encyclopedia but knew that if the task was to be done properly it had to be done by a public institution. No publisher could possibly cover the research and writing costs for a fully researched new encyclopedia. Second, by 1998 the *Historical Atlas* had been launched, and the *Dictionary of New Zealand Biography* had published four volumes and was looking to complete its task in 2000. This meant that the earlier argument about the lack of scholarly capacity no longer applied. The reverse was the case. There were academics now trained in preparing material for a government reference work, and the staff involved in the *Dictionary* were eager to find a new project to which they could turn their energies and editing experience. They were looking for jobs. As general manager of the Heritage Group I had an obligation to listen to their concerns.

In mid-1998 I submitted a paper to Cabinet, which did not request new money but simply the use of the funds ($700,000 per year) already in the baseline dedicated to the Dictionary of New Zealand Biography for a period of seven years. Since the Dictionary only covered people who were dead, and the volume due for publication in 2000 covered those who had flourished in the period 1941–60, I suggested that there were not enough significant people who had died from the next period (1961–80), so it was appropriate to have a pause in the preparation of biographies. This would provide a seven-year moratorium while the encyclopedia could be produced. The justifications for the encyclopedia were that it would strengthen 'national identity', which was a government priority and also 'lift educational standards and deepen the knowledge base', which was a second priority. Although I mentioned the possibility of a CD-ROM, the project was conceived primarily as a series of print volumes totalling 1.5 million words. It was really an updated McLintock encyclopedia.[1] Cabinet was not impressed. We were turned down. The project stalled, and although I ran various other options past the minister, such as confining the project to cultural and social matters by excluding scientific knowledge, and presenting the encyclopedia as a millennium project, there was no green light from on high. I was not upset – an encyclopedia was still not a project which fired me.

Then I became interested in the web. It was not until the later 1990s that the world wide web became a viable technology. In June 1993 there had been a mere 130 websites in the world. Two years later there were over 20,000. In the next few years the new technology took off. By 1997 there were over 100 million sites and everyone was talking about the internet. I began to surf the web. I discovered some wonderful historical sites. There was The Valley of the Shadow, produced by the University of Virginia, which was a collection of historical materials – letters, diaries, newspapers, church and census records, and images – from two communities, one in the north of the United States and one in the south, in the years either side of the American Civil War.[2] And there was a fascinating essay about the great Chicago fire of 1871 produced by the Chicago Historical Society.[3]

Several aspects of such sites attracted me immediately. One was their multimedia quality – photographs, interactive maps, documents in their original format, films. It took me back to my days designing exhibitions at Te Papa. History really did come alive. There was an immediacy of impact. And as a user I loved the freedom to explore at my own pace and in any direction. I could flit from one object to another using links or through searches. I realised that by comparison with reading a book, or even watching a historical television production or wandering through an exhibition, a historical website gave enormous control to the user. Instead of the authoritarian book historian who held you in thrall as an argument was unfolded in the order and pace that he or she chose, a website reversed the power balance. The user became king or queen and the historian a mere facilitator. I also realised that preparing such a site was necessarily a team endeavour – you needed writers, yes, but also archivists to source documents, designers to optimise images and provide a look and feel, even people to clear copyright. Compared with the lonely world of the academic historian ploughing away silently, pen in hand or in front of the computer screen, preparing websites seemed like an exciting new cooperative way of doing history, much more akin to preparing exhibitions or films. I wanted to get beyond the one-man-voice of book history.

Before long we started to explore web ventures ourselves, such as the New Zealand History website, nzhistory.net.nz. Its phenomenal success convinced me of the future of the medium. In addition we began planning a web version of the *Dictionary of New Zealand Biography* as a millennium project, and I spent many hours talking through how this would work with the developers Click Suite. As I became more acquainted with examples of web history, both overseas and with our own ventures, I decided that there were three forms of history which seemed to work well on the web. One was mediated collections of primary materials such as The Valley of the Shadow. A second was short multimedia essays, such as the Great Chicago Fire. But a third form which had real potential was reference sites. I came across a site of world history, hyperhistory.com, which worked well, and also Microsoft's encyclopedia on the web, Encarta. I realised that the web had many advantages for reference works, especially their searchability. I became both excited by digital history and convinced of its value for a future encyclopedia.

So in February 2000, while still acting general manager heritage, I sent a paper up to Judith Tizard, the associate minister (to Helen Clark) for arts, culture and heritage in the new Labour-led Government. The paper provided a number of alternatives, ranging from a six-volume encyclopedia of New Zealand taking twelve years to an encyclopedia of history taking three years. The recommendation was for a general encyclopedia in three volumes

Helen Clark launches the DNZB website at the National Library in early 2002.
MANATŪ TAONGA MINISTRY FOR CULTURE AND HERITAGE

taking seven years – in other words of the same scale as McLintock's 1966 volume. But the crucial steps forward in this paper were two aspects: 'The Encyclopaedia would appear at the end of seven years in printed book form, organised with entries from A to Z. However it would initially be produced in digital form on the internet, and it would be done in stages focusing on themes. There might also be subsidiary print publications along the way.' Secondly: 'Efforts would be made to enlist the cooperation of major repositories so that illustrated material and objects might be linked to the encyclopaedia entries. e.g. the essay on gold-mining might link to illustrations about gold-miners in the National Library and information about gold-mining objects in Te Papa.'[4] In early 2000 a budget bid for $945,000 a year was submitted for a new encyclopedia. Ranked fourth of five bids by the Department of Internal Affairs, it was rejected.

However, the proposal had caught the imagination of Judith Tizard, who proceeded to become our fairy godmother as Michael Bassett had once been my godfather in the Historical Branch. In May 2000 she suggested that

Three people who were crucial in the development of Te Ara: Martin Matthews (left), chief executive of the Ministry for Culture and Heritage; Judith Tizard (right), associate minister of arts, culture and heritage; and Bronwyn Dalley (second from right), who worked with me planning the encyclopedia. The fourth person is Lyn Provost, chief archivist. The occasion was the launch of Bronwyn's book based on National Archives photographs, Living in the 20th Century.
MANATŪ TAONGA MINISTRY FOR CULTURE AND HERITAGE

I prepare a work programme to develop the encyclopedia proposal, and then in December she set up a one-hour session with Michael Cullen, minister of finance. Cullen had been in the class ahead of me at Christ's College, and he subsequently became a lecturer in history at the University of Otago. So I knew him and, more importantly, he knew me. I prepared a PowerPoint demonstration. This presented the 'online Encyclopaedia of New Zealand', as I was now calling the venture, as 'the first port-of-call for reliable information about New Zealand', 'a gateway to the cultural treasures' of the country, which referred to the photographs and documents and films in the museums and libraries, 'an exciting multi-media project' which would be 'available progressively on-line and eventually in print'. I argued that the major reasoning for a new encyclopedia was that there had been huge advances in knowledge since the 1966 encyclopedia and a growing fascination by New Zealanders with their own society and history. I emphasised the value to tourism because of the international nature of the web and the use that would be made by schools, and I stressed the particular need to have accessible and accurate information about Māori history and culture, which had been poorly represented in 1966.

I realised too that Cullen was primarily a book-based academic by background. The web publication would have to be sold to him and to other ministers. So in my presentation, and in briefings prepared for other ministers including Helen Clark, I summed up the advantages of a digital encyclopedia over a book version. This was the argument: a digital work was hugely more searchable than the old print version. It made for a multimedia experience, using sounds, photos, paintings, maps, films and historical documents. A digital work would allow interactivity by the user, who could add stories or comments and so become personally involved. It would stimulate the digitising of the materials held by museums and galleries, giving exposure to their holdings and creating links across the nation. Equally, a digital encyclopedia would be far more accessible overseas, available wherever people had a computer and an internet connection. A digital encyclopedia was also less time-bound. A book encyclopedia became fossilised the moment of publication, but a digital one could be updated as new discoveries were made or new events unfolded. You could make instant corrections. Further, the encyclopedia could be produced on an instalment plan. Instead of waiting the seven years for a full A–Z print version, the encyclopedia could have a presence within a year or two – in a rather crude nod to political advantage I rashly promised the minister that something would appear 'before the next election'. Publication on the web by instalments would allow these parts to be thematically organised, which would make it easier to cluster the expertise required for the preparation and provide good opportunities to target particular interest groups with a series of regular launches. I ended by showing Cullen an example of an entry – a story about whaling with hyperlinks to biographies of whalers, maps of whaling sites, an oral history with a Ngāti Kahu kaumātua talking about whaling in the far north, historic photographs of whalers from the Turnbull Library and a film of the Perano family whalers from the Film Archive. I had practised this demonstration hard, and it did the trick. As I stood to leave, Michael Cullen walked over and said, 'Congratulations. You will get the money.' Judith Tizard beamed.

So the digital encyclopedia was a goer. But when the budget announcement arrived the next year, I discovered that Cullen had been cannier than I had realised. Rather than giving us the full budget straight away in the

Encyclopedist | 311

Follow the underlined links to read further about whales, whalers, or regions where whaling was important.

Shore Whaling

Whaling in New Zealand waters began with pelagic or off-shore whaling. From 1801 whalers from Australia, Britain and then New England visited New Zealand waters to hunt sperm whales. In 1828 Benjamin Turner and Captain Peter Williams established a shore whaling station at Rakituma, Preservation Inlet in Fiordland, followed by John Guard's station at Te Awaiti in Tory Channel, the Marlborough Sounds. On-shore whalers hunted the southern right whale, valuable not only for its oil but also for its baleen or whalebone. This was the bristle of the whaler's upper jaw and was used in such objects as umbrellas. The right whale made a seasonal migration from Antarctic waters to breed in the warmer New Zealand coastal waters during winter and early spring. There it became easy prey for on-shore whalers. They would post a sentry and when the first whales were sighted, the shout would go up, the longboats would be launched, and the hunt was on.

The success of such operations led to a rapid spread of on-shore whaling during the 1830s and 1840s. There were stations along the coasts of Southland and Otago, on Banks Peninsula, in Cook Strait from Port Underwood to Kapiti Island, and along the East Coast of the North Island. By the early 1840s almost 400 right whales were caught each year. Since the hunt was seasonal, the whalers often formed communities who farmed and made more permanent marks on the landscape. They frequently mixed with the local Māori, some of whom became whalers themselves while the women often intermarried into the community. The early shore whalers thus became important in pioneering later Pakeha settlement.

The ease of hunting right whales bore the seeds of the industry's decline as numbers caught plummeted. At the turn of the century, H.F. Cook and his family at Whangamumu, near the Bay of Islands and J.A. Perano in the Tory Channel, used launches and explosive harpoons to capture humpback whales. Because they were hard to catch and lacked commercially valuable baleen the whalers had largely ignored humpbacks. The Cooks and Peranos hunted the humpback for their oil and set up mechanised processing factories on shore. Both operations continued for some 50 years before the International Whaling Commission prohibited humpback whaling throughout the Southern Hemisphere in 1963. This marked the end of whaling in New Zealand, and the numbers of whales recovered slowly. Sperm whales appeared once more, giving birth to a new lucrative industry – whale watching at Kaikoura and in Northland.

Maps and Graphs

Location of whaling sites in the South Island of New Zealand before the 1840s. Click here to see North Island sites.

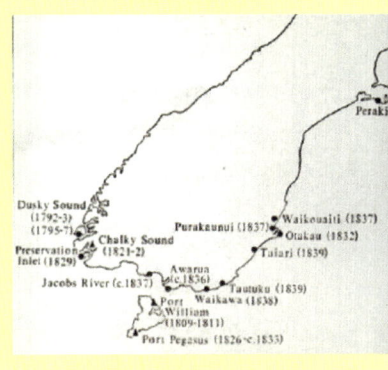

Images

This image comes from Timeframes, an on-line selection of images from the Alexander Turnbull Library in Wellington, New Zealand. Visit Timeframes on the National Library of New Zealand website and see more images of whales: http://timeframes1.natlib.govt.nz

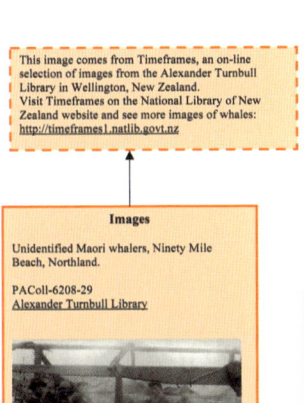

Unidentified Maori whalers, Ninety Mile Beach, Northland.

PAColl-6208-29
Alexander Turnbull Library

Documents

Read more from Edward Jerningham Wakefield's book and papers from the manuscripts at the Alexander Turnbull Library on www.tapuhi.natlib.govt.nz

A description of whaling around Kapiti Island in 1845 from Edward Jerningham Wakefield, *Adventure in New Zealand*.

'The quick obedience to his instant order of "starn all – lay off!" saves the boat from annihilation, as the whale swings round its huge tail out of the water, and brings it down with a tremendous report. She then "breaches", or leaps, and plunges in every direction; the headsman continues to direct his crew and boatsteerer, while he poises a new lance, and keeps just out of the vortex formed by her evolutions; the assistant boat and a third one have come up, and, being all of one party, watch outside the splashing for the best chance.'

Places in New Zealand

You can see whales today at Kaikoura, in the South Island, where you can go whalewatching: www.royaletours.co.nz/whalewatching

Tour the remains of a Maori pa which was visited by the first American whaling ship in 1792 at the Butler Point Whaling Museum, and see objects related to whaling.

Sounds

Click here to listen to a Ngati Kahu kaumatua talk about the meaning of whales for his people who live at Mangonui, in the northern part of New Zealand's North Island.

You need RealPlayer to listen to this. A free download is available here.

A sample entry on shore whaling which I used to convince Michael Cullen, minister of finance, of the value of an online encyclopedia of New Zealand in December 2000.

2001–2 year, he promised that the money would come on stream in the following year – in July 2002. This gave us a year to plan the venture. It was a brilliant idea. It was agreed that Bronwyn Dalley, a highly talented historian in the Historical Branch who was interested in the web, would join me in planning the initiative. Bronwyn made a large contribution, not least in deciding that to signal the innovative nature of the venture we should spell the name without the Latin diphthong. The 'encyclopedia' it became, and not once in the twelve years I managed the project did anyone object to this 'Americanism'. It was really valuable having Bronwyn at my side to talk through issues as we did the planning, and I also set up regular sessions with a former Te Papa colleague, Jean-Marie O'Donnell, who asked probing questions and provided a sounding board for our ideas.

Bronwyn and I set off on a number of paths. The first was working out what the unit of production would look like. Plucking a number out of mid-air, I had promised Michael Cullen that the encyclopedia would contain about two million words, about the same length as the 1966 three-volume set. But how would these words be organised? Traditionally encyclopedia entries varied from the very short – perhaps 100 words – to the very long, perhaps 10,000. I quickly realised that on the web each 'entry' would be a relatively complex beast with a number of different elements – from images and other resources to bibliography – so very short entries would be uneconomical. Instead I proposed about 1000 entries which might range from a minimum of 200 words to a maximum of about 10,000, averaging about 2000 words, giving us the two million total. Later as we trialled these entries, both the minimum and maximum became unworkable. In the end a range of 1000 to 5000 became the rule.

What would an entry look like? Bronwyn and I spent hours exploring the web, looking at examples and trying to deduce some principles about what worked and did not work on the web. We realised from experience, and from consulting web specialists, that people find it harder to read on the web than on the printed page. We knew to avoid large screeds of text. We decided that each 'page' or screen should be no more than about 500 words. Any entry of more than this would be divided up into different sections, each with a title. This in turn meant that there would be a home page listing each of these different pages and hosting what we came to call a 'hero image'. We found from experience that blocks of text of 500 words should be broken up, and readers given pointers. Many web-users skimmed rather than reading word by word. So sentences should be short, and the text broken into brief paragraphs with a bolded heading. The page had to look lively and inviting. From the start I was keen that we include 'topic boxes', as we came to call them – short (under a hundred words) anecdotes or details to enliven the text. Originally I had ambitions that these might be colour-coded along different themes – 'Uniquely New Zealand', 'Did you know?', 'Kiwi words', 'A bit of a dag' and 'Whakataukī' were the suggestions. In the end we abandoned this scheme as too confining, but the topic boxes remained. The other element to add colour and visual richness to the page was the multimedia resources – images, films, maps and the like. Here we learnt from overseas examples that the best way to present these was through a column of thumbnails on the right-hand side of the page. We decided after trialling various options that about one such resource for every hundred words of text was the right proportion.

There were two other significant decisions. They both derived from my Te Papa experience that people took in information in different ways. Some people were attracted to visual stimuli, rather than to the written word. We decided that entries could also be read by moving from one image or movie file to the next. I argued that if the captions provided the context as well as the precise details of each image then users on this 'resource trail' would quickly get a sense of the overall argument of the entry. I had also been very impressed by the junior encyclopedia that was part of the Canadian encyclopedia – originally a print work that had been subsequently digitised. So I was committed to having a short-story version of each entry prepared, which would provide the essence of the story for primary-age children. This could also be an entry point for foreign-language speakers and a useful summary for all users.

When I look back now at these decisions, a decade and a half later, they still seem robust. Users continue to say they find Te Ara easy and enjoyable. However, I now think that, with my background in the book world, I envisaged each entry as a complete package, with a coherent argument. I anticipated that people would read each entry from start to finish, either on the web or by printing out the text. This was probably naïve, for all the statistics on usage suggest that most people go to Te Ara to check small facts. The average time spent on the site is well under five minutes. People rarely sit down to read a whole entry. So we made a mistake in not disaggregating the text into even smaller units than the 500-word page. If we had broken it down into more discrete bits, even if these were presented on the one page, the content would have become more usable by other sites and search engines. I also now think that we should have done more to combine the 'short story' and the contents page. If the short story had been more rigorously a summary of each page, rather than a summary of the whole entry, it would have proved a more useful entranceway.

Once Bronwyn and I had worked out the way an entry was structured and looked, we trialled a couple of examples. I wrote an entry on the Irish in New Zealand; Bronwyn wrote one on wine. Then these were put up on nzhistory.net.nz so that users could critique the format. I knew that the language and level of generalisation was about right when I discovered that the whole of the Irish entry had been plagiarised word-for-word in a magazine without acknowledgement or permission!

Having developed a unit of production, Bronwyn and I then set out to visit people and get them interested and involved in the encyclopedia. We went to every university, delivering a seminar about the new venture and having individual sessions with academics whom I thought might provide valuable input – either by serving on an advisory committee or by writing entries. I was also keen to find out what kind of encyclopedia would be most useful for the universities, since it was obvious they would be significant users. Hamish Campbell, whom I had met at Te Papa, set up an opportunity for me to address the Institute for Geological and Nuclear Sciences (GNS). This really paid off, both because it got GNS on board providing images and information, and also because the talk attracted the interest of Simon Nathan, who subsequently became our science editor. We also visited museums and libraries to begin awakening their interest in providing visual resources.

In some ways the most important step was to hold two hui for the Māori community. I realised that the success or failure of the project would in considerable part rest on our being able to gain the enthusiasm of Māori scholars and experts. Mason Durie set up one hui at Massey, and then on the day after 9/11, in September 2001, we held a second at Auckland courtesy of Manuka Henare. Both gatherings were hugely beneficial in shaping my ideas and developing a real commitment to the encyclopedia within the Māori community.

Early the next year, in 2002, with several months before the money came on stream, the ministry advertised the position of general editor. Without a moment of hesitation I put in an application, and without a moment of hesitation (or so the chief executive, Martin Matthews, told me afterwards) I was offered the job. There had been other applicants, but Martin had rung a couple of prominent academics and Māori leaders and received their backing for my appointment. I was offered the position, a nine-year contract, without an interview. Martin set me up reporting to him, and on the ministry's management team. He continued to back the endeavour consistently and generously for the next few years.

I began just days after my fifty-fifth birthday, in May 2002. I remember walking into my room, staring at the wall and thinking 'what the heck do I do now? The dreaming has finished; I actually have to deliver!' I was without the support of Bronwyn, who was quickly appointed my replacement as chief historian, and had plenty to do without thinking further about the encyclopedia. On that first morning, I began by pulling out the three volumes of McLintock's 1966 encyclopedia to analyse it in detail – the length of entries, and the larger themes within which they fell. My idea was that we could use McLintock's entry list, supplemented by new subjects that I considered obviously missing, to ensure that any thematic structure we devised had about the same number of subjects per theme. If the digital encyclopedia was to be prepared in instalments, by themes, then devising a thematic structure was a key place to start. There had already been much work on this. When the digital encyclopedia was just an exciting glint in the eye, I had asked Malcolm McKinnon, fresh from the launch of the *Historical Atlas*, to prepare a paper on possible thematic structures. This provided a starting point. Then while Bronwyn and I had worked together we held regular meetings to progress our thinking. Whiteboards became filled with possible schema, and I spent a lot of time while in Ireland looking at printed encyclopedias and exploring how they organised their material.

We made a number of key decisions. One was that although most national encyclopedias included biographies of notable people, the existence of over 3000 outstanding biographies in the *Dictionary of New Zealand Biography* made this unnecessary, especially since we were in the process of digitising the *Dictionary* volumes. We could make the DNZB part of the new encyclopedia. Second, most encyclopedias had many geographical entries covering particular townships and beauty spots, and also regional overviews. It seemed to me that we should prepare two large entries for each region, one providing

```
   A              Ba                 Bb                        C
① Getting started  ① Land + sea      islands/moutere          ① Whakapapa (origins)
② Establishing     ② Nature          habitats/kainga          ② Governance
③ Changing         ③ Settlement      journeys/hekenga         ③ Daily life
④ Growing          ④ Demography      identities/tohutanga     ④ Identity (what did they do?)
⑤ Challenging      ⑤ Community + Civil Society  Connections/Nga Hononga  ⑤ Economy
⑥ Enjoying         ⑥ Politics/govt   power, conflict, crises/Tu-ka-riri  ⑥ Natural Environment / Mana Whenua
⑦ Expressing Ourselves  ⑦ Economy/commerce  trade + exchange/tauhokohoko  ⑦ Resource Management / Kaitiakitanga
                   ⑧ Culture + sport Creations/Whakaaturanga  ⑧ Health + Welfare
```

Whiteboard jottings showing some of the options for a thematic structure of the encyclopedia, which Bronwyn Dalley and I explored while planning the project in 2001.

an overview which dealt with the natural and social history of the region, and one with short paragraphs on particular locations. Third, after trialling various schemes that involved a separate Māori section, I became convinced that we should include Māori perspectives in every theme. This was not an attempt to co-opt Māori and make Māori entries invisible, but rather to have a Māori team working on Māori subjects throughout the project, and by treating general cultural matters from both a Māori and Pākehā perspective interesting questions might arise. The encyclopedia would explore the Rātana Church and Ringatū alongside denominations like Anglicanism and Catholicism; we would explore haka and waiata at the same time as we treated hip hop and popular music. We also came to believe that scientific and cultural questions should where possible be treated together. For example, while the entries on native trees were being prepared, we should also cover those on the history of botanical exploration or the cultural meaning of the bush. Here my long-standing interest in interdisciplinary approaches came to the fore. In the end of course the themes would largely disappear into a searchable A–Z; but it would be valuable intellectually and socially to prepare them at the same time, and so it proved.

The larger scheme remained very much an open question. We decided on eight or nine themes, about one a year. But what would those nine themes consist of? We tried metaphorical and poetic concepts – islands and habitats; journeys, identities and creations. We tried active concepts – establishing, growing, enjoying, challenging and expressing ourselves. Slowly we came to realise that the web needed simple, direct categories. Eventually I built the sequence on both intellectual and pragmatic grounds. We would begin with a theme on the peoples of New Zealand: about half would be on the major iwi of the country, and half on the major immigrant groups who had settled New Zealand after 1769. This would allow me to draw on my knowledge and interest in the history of immigration, and would also necessarily involve large numbers of Māori in preparing the very first theme. It would give Māori a powerful stake in the project from the start and build their confidence in our bicultural intentions. In a wider sense this first theme might work as a mihi, a welcome, to the people of New Zealand. We were providing a story for everyone in the country and recognising all New Zealanders' whakapapa.

Having welcomed the peoples, we would then explore the land to which they came. Here again I wanted to be able to cluster scientific expertise, so we had three themes which drew on natural-history knowledge – one on the shaping forces of the land (the geology, the climate and the seas around us), which came to be called 'Earth, Sea and Sky'; one on the indigenous flora and fauna, 'The Bush'; and one on 'The Settled Landscape', involving introduced plants and animals and the farming of New Zealand. There followed another three themes looking at the development of New Zealand society – a theme on the economy and life of the city; another, 'Social Connections', about family and other social groupings; and one about government and national identity. Finally there were two themes on culture – one on sport and popular culture, and a final theme, which I hoped would be a joyful way to go out with a bang, on creative life, from the arts through to intellectual life. My hidden motive was to keep these goodies to the end in order to entice the staff to stay on until everything was done. It might have been a real problem if members of the team deserted us before the whole job was done. When I scattered the McLintock entries plus additions into these themes, the numbers of entries per theme worked out almost perfectly.

There was a final decision that followed from the instalment-plan model of preparing the encyclopedia. If the content was to be drip-fed, I was worried that people might come to the site with false expectations. They would expect a full encyclopedia of New Zealand from the very beginning. There were two ways to satisfy this yearning – at least partially. One was to recognise the quality of the 1966 *Encyclopaedia* and position ourselves as its successor, by digitising the three volumes. This would provide a complete, if outdated, encyclopedia on the web; and in the long run provide a fascinating time warp which would allow users to compare the 1966 view of New Zealand with the view from the new millennium. When we started to explore how this digitising might happen, we teamed up with the Electronic Text Centre at Victoria University. They sent three copies of the volumes to India, where the text was typed out three times to ensure accuracy. The cost was about $20,000, which seemed like exploitation of third-world labour for a text of over two million words, but it proved to be an extraordinarily accurate version. The second way to deal with the instalment plan was to prepare some short entries providing overviews of New Zealand. Under the rubric 'New Zealand in Brief', we prepared succinct summaries of New Zealand's history, natural environment, creative life, economy, society, government, sports and leisure, and one on Māori.

There was much detailed reshaping and fine-tuning before we arrived at these decisions and this structure; an essential stage was consultation with our advisory committees. Setting up these committees was another task that occupied my first few months. Helen Clark decided that she wanted someone appropriate to lead the committee so she appointed the former prime minister Sir Geoffrey Palmer to chair the major advisory committee. He was a brilliant choice – consistently enthusiastic about the project, a fine chair of a meeting, respectful of scholarly standards, and possessing a very wide knowledge of New Zealand history and culture. The rest of the committee was left in my hands; and my choices were largely based on my discussions as Bronwyn and I visited the universities. These included Roger Horrocks, literary and arts critic and teacher of film, whom I had first known at American Studies conferences; Paul Spoonley, a distinguished professor of sociology from Massey in Albany; Lloyd Davis, an expert on penguins who taught an innovative course in science communication at Otago; Eric Pawson, professor of geography from Canterbury, who had done an excellent job chairing the Historical Atlas Committee; Lydia Wevers, director of the Stout Centre and a fine writer on New Zealand literature; Geoff Hicks, whom I had got to know well when he was the concept leader of the natural sciences

Ranginui Walker, chair of Te Ara Wānanga, speaking at the launch of Māori Peoples of New Zealand: Ngā Iwi o Aotearoa, *a book based on Te Ara's 'Māori New Zealanders' theme.* MANATŪ TAONGA MINISTRY FOR CULTURE AND HERITAGE

exhibitions at Te Papa; Margaret Tennant, professor of history from Massey in Palmerston North, who was an old friend and had chaired the Women Together committee when I had been chief historian; Alison Dobbie, who managed the Auckland Public Libraries and chaired our resources or Pātaka committee; Ranginui Walker, who chaired the Māori committee; Murray Brown from the Ministry of Education, whose support I was hoping to attract; and Bronwyn Dalley as chief historian. It was a hugely talented group of people, enthusiastic about what we were doing and keen for it to succeed. There was an excellent mix of disciplines, approaches and geographical backgrounds. Whenever I had a major issue, I would run the matter past the committee, which inevitably added value. The committee met three times in the first year as we worked out the general structure and the way the site would work; then we usually met once or twice a year thereafter.

Alongside the general committee there was a committee responsible for Māori approaches which came to call itself Te Ara Wānanga. The chair was Ranginui Walker, once regarded as a young radical, whose columns in the *New Zealand Listener* would get tongues talking. He became a highly distinguished historian of Māori, an acknowledged leader among the Māori academic world, and deeply respected by his own iwi, Te Whakatōhea in the Bay of Plenty. The rest of the committee was largely chosen in consultation with the ministry's kaihautū, Martin Wikaira. We looked for a combination of scholarly experience and iwi representation. So from Ngāpuhi in the far north came Hone Sadler and a young, enthusiastic historian, Rawiri Taonui. From Tainui there was Ngapare Hopa, whom I had first met and been hugely impressed by at a hui planning Te Papa in 1990. She had become professor of Māori at Auckland. From the east coast came Mere Whaanga (Ngāti Rongomaiwahine), who, as a fellow in Māori history in the Historical Branch, had steeled my determination for deep Māori involvement in the encyclopedia, and Piri Sciascia from Ngāti Kahungunu, whom I knew well because he was the Māori pro-vice-chancellor at Victoria University. My early supporter Mason Durie brought his wisdom and knowledge of the Māori academic world, while the young historian who had so impressed me in the early 1990s, Te Ahukaramū Charles Royal from Ngāti Raukawa, spoke for a newer generation. Finally, Edward Ellison from Ōtākou carried the support of Ngāi Tahu. It was a brilliant group, who gave enormous intellectual energy to Te Ara. The hui of Te Ara Wānanga were a real privilege for me. Everything about the site passed before their eyes, but I particularly enjoyed the annual meeting when we turned to the group for input into the Māori entries and writers for a particular theme. Often the discussion was in te reo Māori so my comprehension was at times vague, but it was always fascinating listening as the kōrero flowed. There was laughter, great stories, and always wise and considered advice. Those hui remain one of the highlights of my time at Te Ara.

I also set up a third committee, the Pātaka committee, to deal with issues arising from the display of visual and moving-image resources. Early in the project I spent much time visiting and negotiating agreements with those who held resources that could be useful. Some were special-interest collections, such as the geological material held by GNS, or the extraordinary library of natural-history photographs – insects, trees, birds – held by the Department of Conservation. We also needed contemporary photographs, so we managed to develop an excellent working relationship with the *New Zealand Herald*. Their images immensely enriched the site although they required us to display them with a watermark. Many museums and libraries, especially Te Papa, the Hocken Library in Dunedin, Puke Ariki in New Plymouth, Auckland Art Gallery and the Auckland Museum came on board. So did Archives New Zealand. I managed to get access at a reasonable cost to Television New Zealand archives, and short clips from their collection added much-needed moving footage to our stories – much needed because we were notably less successful in our relations with the (then) Film Archive. On the other hand the Sound Archives in Christchurch were extremely helpful, until the earthquake of February 2011 put them out of commission temporarily. But the greatest source of material was the Alexander Turnbull Library, which provided thousands of photographs, documents and ephemera for the site at a very reasonable reduced cost.

In order to establish effective relationships with these repositories, the Pātaka committee met about every six months in the early years of the project. Alison Dobbie from Auckland Public Libraries was a fine chair, and there were also representatives from some of the other collecting institutions. There was also another spin-off of long-term significance. In 2001, before I had even become general editor, I visited Christopher Blake, then the national librarian. I was keen to get his support in attracting the collecting institutions to the encyclopedia, and at the time I believed that the project might help significantly to bring the sector into the digital age. Christopher was receptive. Together we came up with the idea of holding a major conference at the National Library about digital communication and display. I managed to get Helen Clark's agreement to open the conference. There was an impressive attendance. I presented my vision of the encyclopedia and at the end of the two days it was decided to make the gathering an annual event and to establish the National Digital Forum. The forum has continued to hold highly successful meetings ever since.

Having established the people who were going to advise us, the most important task was selecting the people who were going to make it happen in-house. The more we planned the project, the more I realised that I had slightly underestimated the numbers of staff that we would need. It was a bigger job than I had imagined. Fortunately there were three people remaining from the Dictionary of New Zealand Biography project in its wind-down; and since the Dictionary would become part of the encyclopedia I had little compunction about incorporating them into the team. They had long experience running a major reference work and this would prove invaluable. So the general editor of the Dictionary, Claudia Orange, took on a role planning the regional entries. Nancy Swarbrick, who had been in charge of managing the day-to-day scheduling of staff work, became managing editor. She had the dual responsibility of managing the writing team and retaining an overview of the detailed schedule. Using her famous whiteboard, Nancy would chart the progress of every entry from commissioning, writing, checking, resourcing, designing, returning to author for approval to finally publishing. Keeping the sausage-machine churning effectively was a key to making sure the project remained on track. Nancy did a brilliant job. She had amazing mastery of detail, was polite but firm in her insistence on keeping to schedule, and proved to be an outstanding manager of the writers. I have never been the most proficient manager of schedules, so Nancy's skills compensated for my own weakness.

The third Dictionary person was Shirley Williams. She had been responsible for collecting the photographs for the digital DNZB. I quickly appointed her to lead the team which would hunt out and collect the images, sounds and film clips for the encyclopedia. Finally I needed a person who could help plan the technology and the IT systems. We advertised, and I appointed Ross Somerville who had managed the editing team for the Dictionary and was leading the project to digitise it. So in the early days I had a team entirely drawn from people who had led the DNZB. They were enthusiastic about having new jobs, and brought their years of experience of running a collective team to the task. In the first years we had regular meetings planning the new project.

Before long we began appointing people who could do the detailed work of preparing the content. We advertised, and I was amazed at the numbers and quality of the people who applied. When we called for five writers to begin preparing the text, we received over 250 applicants. Realising that the quality of the staff would make or break the whole project, we put much thought into choosing people. We consistently looked for two major qualities. First, we wanted people who could work with others, and make for a happy team. Therefore we put much emphasis upon our instinctive response to their personalities and relied heavily on recommendations from referees. I would

Encyclopedist | 323

Four people from the DNZB who joined the Te Ara team are shown in 2002 (top): Nancy Swarbrick, Shirley Williams, Ross Somerville and Claudia Orange. Here Nancy Swarbrick talks through progress on Te Ara with Janine Faulknor, with the aid of her famous whiteboard (middle). A meeting in 2008 to choose images and other media for a Te Ara entry (bottom). From left are researcher Emma Dewson, resource researcher Leanne Tamaki, resources team leader Shirley Williams and writer Carl Walrond. MANATŪ TAONGA MINISTRY FOR CULTURE AND HERITAGE

spend a long time on the phone getting detailed insight into how individuals related to others. Nancy Swarbrick, presumably from long experience managing the Dictionary team, had a real nose for who would fit in well and who would not. I came to respect her instincts. Second, we needed people who could do the tasks required. We devised tests which replicated that work, and at the end of the interview would set them up with a computer and ask candidates to carry out the sample work. For writers we provided background information and documents and asked them to write a 400-word essay. For resourcers we would give them a piece of text and invite them to use the web to find suitable images, oral histories or films, etc. Then we would mark the exercises blind. We never appointed anyone who had not shown their abilities in such exercises.

This process proved its worth. The aspect of preparing Te Ara of which I remain most proud was putting together such a highly performing and happy group of people. Over the eleven years of the project, only twice did we have to suggest gently to people that it was time to move on. The rest were without exception enormously talented and devoted to the project. They got on extraordinarily well with one another, and had great fun together. Morning coffees and Christmas lunches were a laugh a minute. In my performance review in July 2008 I wrote, 'To be honest this is the most productive and congenial group of people I have worked with in 35 years of employment', and I was not alone in feeling this. The various in-house surveys of staff conducted each year consistently showed the Te Ara people were more content than any other group in the ministry. At the end of the project I felt so privileged to have had such a dedicated and high-performing team that I presented each team member with a ceramic Māori taonga nestling in flax as a permanent memento.

Although preparing the content of a new encyclopedia would prove a challenge, I was always confident about my skills and ability to accomplish this. I had infinitely less confidence in my ability or knowledge to plan a workable technology platform for the site. We needed a site that would deliver a seamless web experience with all the films and sound clips operating smoothly, and that looked inviting and handsome. Behind this we needed ways of organising the content – not only the texts, but also all the resources, with details about their location, copyright status and so forth. In setting out to develop such a site Ross Somerville was my right-hand person. We did not actually need to understand the technology itself. What we had to do was specify in the greatest possible detail exactly what we wanted the technology to deliver. Much of my first year as general editor was spent working with Ross defining the user requirements. This meant specifying the dimensions of the site – the number of words, of images, of sound files, of film clips. It meant working through exactly what was needed on a page of the site. Then there was laying down what was needed for our back end – the kinds of information needed by those collecting resources, such as copyright information, any time restrictions on use of materials, etc.

Towards the end of 2002 we had prepared these requirements and went out to tender. We drew up a shortlist, and then asked the five shortlisted teams to prepare a mock-up. We gave them the task just before Christmas, and asked for a response by mid-January. It was a devilish timetable, so to make the job more appealing I prepared an entry on 'The Beach', which was full of enticing film clips of Kiwis having fun in the surf. I consoled the developers by telling them that though they may have been missing out on their Christmas holidays they could enjoy a virtual frolic in the waves. We were hugely impressed in the end by the design and the ideas presented by a Wellington firm, Shift. Their designs were beautiful and easy to use, and they were presented by an engaging American, Brian Smith. We agreed that they were the people to work with. They came backed by a Microsoft content management system supplied by a firm called Optimation. Early in 2003 Helen Clark, showing her commitment to the project, took time out to come along to Shift's offices and sign an agreement with Shift and Optimation. The design work by Shift and Brian Smith in particular made a fine contribution to the success of Te Ara. The backgrounds of bright colour gave the site a unique look and the navigation and movement around the site proved intuitive for users. Not that this came easily. Shift spent many hours testing mock-ups with a range of users, chosen from a selection of ages and cultures. As we prepared each theme Brian devised a distinct palette of colours so that the new entries consistently looked bold and fresh.

In the long run the technology proved less satisfactory. Making changes was extremely expensive and I was forced to go back to Cabinet and obtain an extra $200,000 annually to cover these technology costs. Eventually even more money was not the solution. When faced with continual costly updates, we decided to learn from the experience of nzhistory.net.nz and migrate the whole site onto an open-source Drupal platform. This finally allowed us to dispense with outside consultants and appoint a number of developers in-house.

I never really mastered the intricacies of the technology, but I did get heavily involved in the look and feel of the site. As Shift developed their design they correctly emphasised the need for a distinctive brand. They prepared mood boards which gave us a sense of the look and colour palettes. But we also needed a distinctive name and a logo. The name came quickly. I had been keen from the start that we have a Māori name, in part to signal our bicultural commitment. I took the problem to the Māori committee. There was a fascinating and highly engaged discussion which lasted much of a morning. There were some ingenious suggestions. They included Ngā Wētā (wētā), Tātai Hikohiko (digital genealogies), Rarauhe Hiriwa (silver fern), Te Mātāpuna (the source) and Te Kura Nui (the great treasure). In the end the choice came down to three: Ngā Pakiaka (the roots), Te Awa Kōrero (river of discourse) and Te Ara Rau (the many paths). Eventually the wānanga decided on the last, shortening it just to Te Ara (the pathway). I was delighted – it was short and memorable and the meaning was highly appropriate for a site full of links and different journeys. But my enthusiasm took a hit when I was approached by Paul Tapsell, very annoyed that we had chosen the same name as the journal of Museums Aotearoa. There were concerned letters and meetings with chief executives, and I took the issue back to Te Ara Wānanga. When they confirmed Te Ara, Paul graciously accepted the decision and became in time one of our best writers and a strong supporter.

Having a name was just the first step. We also needed a brand. The start of this process was a fascinating all-day workshop at the Royal Port Nicholson Yacht Club, where we worked with a former Saatchi and Saatchi chief executive, Kim Wicksteed, to devise a list of brand values. Then we took this to a design firm, Designworks, to develop a logo and a strapline. Designworks were at first not comfortable with a Māori name and urged us to reconsider. But I held firm and before long they had taken the bicultural message on board. A young designer, Paul Johnson, began to think about Māori mythology. He came up with various versions of the words Te Ara, which gave a sense of the letters pushing at top and bottom, in an expression of the sky father Ranginui and earth mother Papatūānuku and the separation of the earth from the heavens. Johnson also noted his debt to the paintings of Colin McCahon and the crude do-it-yourself culture of New Zealanders. The logo subsequently became a

Versions of the Te Ara logo developed by a brilliant young designer from Designworks, Paul Johnson. TE ARA

prize-winner at the New Zealand design awards, and in its various forms served the site brilliantly over the years. The Designworks teams also gave us a slogan, 'What's the story?', a classic Kiwi expression which encouraged us to call our entries 'stories'.

Just as we had dispensed with outside developers, so eventually we moved away from Shift for the overall design, largely for financial reasons. Instead Heath Sadlier, a brilliant young designer who had joined us part-time straight out of design school, took over refining the look and feel and the way people moved around the site. He drew on findings from another exhaustive series of tests with users to make significant improvements to the navigation and presentation. The distinctive colours and style of the site remained but its operation became much more intuitive and easy.

Once we had a name, a logo, a look and feel and an operational technology we had the shell of a site. But it had to be filled with high-quality content, for, as we all learned, on the web 'content is king'. This began with preparing entries. The first task was drawing up an entry list for each theme. For the first theme on the people of New Zealand I drew on my own knowledge of immigration to draw up the list of non-Māori subjects. For Māori subjects we had appointed Rangi McGarvey as Māori editor, and he drew up the list of iwi and the choice of authors in consultation with Te Ara Wānanga. In every case except for the entry on the Whanganui iwi we were able to find a really knowledgeable member of the iwi to write the entry. They usually passed the draft around other iwi members, and as a result the level of accuracy was astonishingly high – especially in comparison with the stories about non-Māori immigrants which we were preparing at the same time. Subsequently Rangi, whose real interests were in te reo, decided to move on and was replaced as the Māori editor for all the later themes by Basil Keane, who brought a great combination of an interest in web technology with an excellent knowledge of Māori history. Apart from the first theme, consistently about 15 per cent of the entries were on Māori subjects.

All themes but the first and last had a theme editor, who would come on board for a fixed term to oversee the development of content alongside me. It was a great comfort to have a specialist with disciplinary knowledge looking consistently at the entries. Simon Nathan, a former employee of GNS and with a wide historical interest based on his research into the lives of Harold Wellman and James Hector, served as editor for the two natural-science themes. I loved working on those themes, partly because, with no scientific training, it was all so new to me. I was amazed at the diversity – and weirdness – of much of New Zealand's plant and bird life, not to mention the great story of the New Zealand bats. After a memorable trip to Stewart Island, when I looked out of the tent at dusk and realised that we were pitched on the dinner table of the forest's resident kiwi, I took on the challenge of writing the entry about our most extraordinary bird. I was really impressed with the skills and accuracy of those who contributed to the natural-science subjects, whether it was on glaciers or spiders.

For the 'Settled Landscape' section I had real difficulty finding a person who knew about the farming sector. After writing to all my acquaintances I finally managed to get the name of Allan Gillingham, then working as a freelance consultant and with excellent contacts with both Lincoln and Massey. I drove up to Allan's home outside Palmerston North and managed to persuade him to take on the task. He took it up with alacrity and due efficiency. For 'Economy and the City', two good friends who had worked together on the *Historical Atlas*, Malcolm McKinnon and Ben Schrader, shared the role, with Malcolm taking charge of the economic side and Ben able to express his passion for the history of the city. There were some really new stories from Ben, such as his classic on street life. Rosemary Du Plessis, a distinguished sociologist from Canterbury, took on the task of theme editor

Rosemary Du Plessis (left) was the 'Social Connections' theme editor, while Stephen Levine and Nigel Roberts (right) shared that responsibility for the 'Government and Nation' theme. They are shown speaking at its launch in 2012.
MANATŪ TAONGA MINISTRY FOR CULTURE AND HERITAGE

for 'Social Connections', where her knowledge of the sociology community was a huge asset. This was probably the theme where we had the greatest difficulty turning in-house jargon into easily understood prose. The theme editors for 'Government and Nation' were Nigel Roberts and Stephen Levine, whose experience in researching and writing on New Zealand politics was irreplaceable. With funding drying up I once again took over the full theme-editor role for the last theme, 'Creative Life', and David Green helped on the sports section of 'Daily Life, Sport and Recreation'.

The first task of the theme editor was always to draw up a draft entry list with assigned word lengths. Then we would call together a committee of subject specialists. They would suggest modifications and additions to the list and also recommend authors. Occasionally when a tricky entry came in which was beyond our expertise to judge, we would send it off for review to one of these committee members. I always enjoyed the meetings of these groups – the ideas flew, and the enthusiasm for the project was infectious.

The 'Places' theme was a different process. Initially Claudia Orange took on the role as theme editor, and she helped draw up the list of twenty-one regions (plus one on offshore islands). Each region had an overview entry plus a detailed gazetteer. We decided that these twenty-two regional sections would be prepared alongside the other themes, at the rate of three to four a year. Claudia prepared the first section on Northland before she took up a leadership job at Te Papa. However, just at that point, Malcolm McKinnon returned to Wellington after time overseas following his magnificent work on the *Historical Atlas*. With a training in geography as well as history, and impeccable standards of scholarship, he was the perfect person to take on the task, and he did an outstanding job. We tried to choose authors for each regional entry who were locals with a personal passion for their area. Malcolm wrote five himself.

About two-thirds of the entries of Te Ara were written by specialists in universities or Crown research institutes, or freelance authors. We gave them a detailed writing guide and paid them 40 cents a word. But there was often some distance between the way authors – especially academics – prepared their material and the way we wanted it to work on the site for users of a great variety of backgrounds. We also had to ensure that everything was accurate and up-to-date. I knew that major errors would undermine our credibility. So once an entry was received and the theme editor and I had looked at it and made recommendations for improvement, the in-house writers sat down and checked all the facts and reshaped the essays to ensure they were the right length and format and in accessible language. They also captioned the resources and prepared a bibliography. I was always aware that it could be a bit soul-destroying for the writers just working on other people's masterpieces, so from the beginning I was keen that the writing team be able to express themselves by preparing entries under their own name. It usually worked out that about a third of the entries in each theme were written in-house – normally about five or six entries a writer. Writing for the web did not always come naturally. The language could not be too abstract or technical; the sentences needed to be short, pithy and direct, and to avoid long, hanging subordinate clauses. The tense should be active. 'Plain English' was the goal. Every year we would have a course for our writers, both to teach any new members of the team how to write for the web and to refresh those already doing it.

Personally I found this education in web writing hugely beneficial. Every theme I took on my quota of five or six entries. It was the general editor's privilege to be able to choose first! Sometimes I wrote up subjects I knew well – my 'History of Immigration' in the first theme became consistently Te Ara's most popular story. But I also used the task to research and write about subjects which had always interested me but I had never had time to pursue. Some were weighty subjects which gave me the chance to get on top of a historiography, such as a long entry on class, one on the South African War and entries on sealing and whaling. Some were new subjects, where few had gone before – I think of a fascinating story on the history of advertising, and one on anniversaries. Some were intriguing and explored fresh questions – stories on light and on timekeeping. I even wrote a piece on waterfalls which combined geology with mythology. For the theme on daily life I pursued a series on New Zealanders' vices, with stories on smoking, alcohol and drugs. The longest entry I wrote, and one which took me from complete ignorance to some knowledge, was an entry for the 'Places' theme on the subantarctic islands. I became so fascinated by their unusual history of castaways and failed colonies, and also by the amazing megaherbs with their huge leaves and brightly coloured flowers, that I decided, having finished the entry, I just had to go south and visit – which I did over Christmas in 2013. Apart from greatly enriching my knowledge, I discovered that writing for Te Ara improved my literary style. Several people noted at the time how much less ponderous my writing had become.

Once a draft entry was prepared, it was time to choose what we called the resources to illustrate the entry. They could be a historic image, a cartoon, a short film clip, an interactive graph, a modern photo, a relevant historical document, a map. A team of five, led initially by Shirley Williams, and when she left Janine Faulknor, carried out the resourcing task. The researchers, most notably Melanie Lovell-Smith, Marguerite Hill and Emily Tutaki, did an outstanding job, drawing on their knowledge of the various museums, archives and libraries. They would come to a meeting with folders of possible resources, and then we would sit around the table – myself, the theme editor, the leader of the resource team, the writer, or, if it was an externally written story, the checker, and the resource person. This was the most enjoyable stage of the whole process. There was always a rich choice, and there would be intense, but never fierce, discussions as we explored the options. We wanted resources which illustrated the story appropriately, and which gave a range of different experiences for the user. I had a large library of my own photographs, collected on tramps and road trips over the years, and since these were available and cost nothing, many (about 500 in all) were used on the site. I also thoroughly enjoyed helping to resource the various regional entries for the 'Places' theme. For many places I would do a road trip after the entry had been written and drive around, camera in hand, trying to illustrate the words on the page. This also provided an excellent way to reality-test the text of the entry. After the first theme, where we had become overly ambitious and had far too many series of images, we became more disciplined, with a fixed quota. I was always impressed by the ingenuity of the resourcing team and the richness of the images or film clips they unearthed. Once they were chosen, it was time for the ordering and copyright clearance, while the writer went to work captioning the images.

Now we were getting there with an entry – but still two vital stages remained. The editing team took over. Led by Ross Somerville, they gave the entry a close scrub-up, seeking out inconsistencies or meanings that were not clear, brushing up the text to ensure that plain-English principles were upheld, preparing a short story for younger users, adding links. It was partly the training we gave the writers and partly the rigorous work of the editing team that won Te Ara a Writemark award for the best use of plain English in the public sector in 2008.

The second stage was the in-house design: preparing the resources for the site by optimising images, cutting films and preparing graphs and maps. When we began the project I had allowed for one full-time designer. We appointed a young graduate of the Wanganui School of Design, Helene Coulson, to carry out this job. She had a fine eye and established a visual language for graphs, diagrams, maps and interactives which sat nicely within the colour scheme laid down by Brian Smith of Shift. It rapidly became clear that one person could simply not do all the work. We began hiring students on a part-time basis but eventually graduated to a full team of three. As technology developed so their ambitions flowered, and the ways film clips or images were displayed became much more interesting and interactive – for example, certain images could be magnified and displayed full-screen. If the round-table meetings to choose the images for an entry were one high-point in the progression of an entry, the gathering around the computer screen to choose a colour and a hero image for each story was the other. This was a moment of celebration, as the entry finally appeared in all its glossy freshness on the screen. Choices were rarely made without laughter and teasing, and a profound sense of satisfaction about a story which the whole team had improved.

The entry was now up on the web, but only available to view through a password. This allowed the original author to look at the entry in all its illustrated glory, check it and give their approval. For me this was another special moment because, almost without exception, it led to an enthusiastic response from the author, thrilled to see their work in its finery, embellished with images and films and shaped into clear prose. Some would occasionally find an error to be corrected, but more often the response was one of undisguised enthusiasm and pride.

If the entry was about a Māori subject, we also needed a translation. My original hope had been that the whole site might be made available in te reo Māori, but we were unable to get funding for this. Instead we followed the lead of the Dictionary project and simply translated those stories with substantial Māori content. For the first theme, which included no fewer than forty-five stories about the major iwi of the country and about Māori voyaging and arrivals, the task of translation was a huge enterprise. Rangi McGarvey took charge and set up an excellent process whereby Te Taura Whiri (the Māori Language Commission) reviewed all the translations. Even then it was not always clear-cut. Tamati Reedy, who wrote the story about Ngāti Porou, insisted that the translation be in Ngāti Porou dialect, which he very generously provided. For the later themes, covering about fifteen Māori stories apiece, the task was less onerous, but we had to keep up the momentum, and of course nothing, even a freshly minted translation, could go up on the site without an edit. In all Te Ara has some 170 stories in the Māori language, which have made a considerable difference for kura kaupapa.

Two other elements needed work before a theme was complete. We had to link our stories to biographies contained within the Dictionary of New Zealand Biography, which we had just digitised. Tracking down relevant biographies was always fun, and often added a personal richness and meaning to the story. Until 2006 the links took users to a separate website, the eDNZB, but from 2006 we integrated the 3000 biographies into the site for seamless linking. Undoubtedly these links added real human value to the stories, but sadly I was never able to achieve the reverse linking – from biographies to relevant Te Ara entries. I still believe that this would have helped to put the DNZB biographies into a useful wider context.

The other element I was keen to include was a degree of input from our audience. As Bronwyn and I had surfed the web looking at historical websites, I was impressed with those sites, such as those on the New Orleans floods and the New York blackout, which attracted stories from users. So as we planned the first theme about immigrants to New Zealand, I decided to issue a call for people to contribute stories of voyages to New Zealand. We issued press releases and did radio interviews and the response was staggering. Some two hundred and fifty stories flooded in and I spent several fascinating weekends reading them and choosing the best twenty-five. Some were from family historians, describing the voyage out of their ancestors from letters and diaries; others were accounts of British immigrants from the 1950s; and a few came from more recent third-world migrants. Once the stories were chosen, we asked their authors for photographs and used them at relevant points through the site. The next year for the 'Earth, Sea and Sky' theme we called for stories about disasters. Again the response was gratifying, with some powerful accounts of harrowing experiences, such as the 1968 *Wahine* storm. We had enough good stories about earthquakes that we even added two sub-entries about survivors' stories in the 'Historic Earthquakes' entry. Then in 2006 we called for stories about the bush.

By then the days of calling for stories through press releases, with responses arriving by mail or email, were coming to an end. Technology was changing. In the early 2000s Web 2.0 hit the world. The buzzword became the 'social web', in which users could contribute instantly. Sites like Flickr and Facebook began their inexorable march towards digital dominance. From our perspective the most dramatic expression of this came with Wikipedia, which I had first come across as a proposal during my early research into digital encyclopedias. When the first theme of Te Ara was launched, David Farrar suggested that the encyclopedia was a waste of money, and a much better solution would have been to subsidise people to contribute New Zealand stories to Wikipedia. I did not agree with this, believing that in a country with such a small population there was real value in having contributions from experts, illustrated richly in a way that Wikipedia has never done. But the arrival of social media did put pressure on us to allow a greater level of user interactivity. Following advice from two web gurus, Deb Sidelinger and Nat Torkington, we added several interactive aspects to the site. We set up a Te Ara page on Flickr asking for contributions on the stories we were researching. Before long we had a devoted set of followers keen to contribute their images. We invited people to submit 'What's Your Story?' accounts to any page of Te Ara, and also allowed users to add comments to images. The response to these initiatives was disappointing and only occasionally added real value.

We also set up a blog, 'Signposts' – named in recognition of Te Ara, the pathway. This proved a great outlet for people to reflect on Te Ara happenings and link events in the world to the site content. All writers were expected to contribute to 'Signposts'. I found myself writing regularly, and thoroughly enjoyed the experience, in all contributing over 100 blog posts. Seven of these were a daily journal from my trip to the subantarctic islands. Writing blog posts also helped to tighten my writing, and felt like a rekindling of that journalist aptitude which I had first learnt while working for the *Listener* in the 1970s. Later came other Web 2.0 initiatives. We set up a Facebook page and established a Twitter feed in which we provided links to relevant Te Ara resources. We set up a team of five members who took turns to manage the Twitter desk, one week in five. I found it a challenging if worthwhile experience; but frustrating because it was so hard getting complex ideas across in 140 characters. Gradually Te Ara was dragged into the twenty-first-century web. I never felt that this was our strongest aspect, and to some extent we were unfortunate in planning the site just before the Web 2.0 revolution hit.

Once we had written, checked, resourced, edited and designed entries and enriched them with biographies and user contributions, then it was time for the launch of a theme. I already had much experience of launches from my time as chief historian, but Te Ara launches were always both more exciting and also testing, largely because there was technology involved. For the launch of the very first theme, on the peoples of New Zealand, I made the task unnecessarily difficult. At that stage a senior manager of the Ministry of Education, Murray Brown, was on the advisory committee, and he offered to set up links to schools. The idea was that as I led a walk-through of different parts of the site, moving from one immigrant group or iwi to another, we would cross via the internet to cameras set up in six schools, where the pupils would do a short performance relevant to the story. After talking about the Scots entry we crossed to Southland Boys' for a taste of bagpipes, after talking about the Ngāti Porou one we crossed to a powerful mihi from Ruatōria, and after presenting the Pacific peoples entries there was a kava ceremony from Papakura. This took a lot of setting up and the technology was distinctly shaky. The launch was at Te Papa in the late morning. The prime minister was there to launch the site, and there was as much press and television presence as we could attract. As I set off to begin the presentation, it looked as though the links had collapsed, but three seconds before we were due to cross to the first school,

I saw the producer with thumbs up frantically waving at me. We made the link. I had never felt so nervous before any launch in my life – I had not slept for days beforehand. I have never felt so relieved as I did afterwards. We retired to a rollicking party at Frida's and my Mt Cook house.

We tried to make later theme launches as interesting and relevant as possible. 'Earth, Sea and Sky' was held in Wellington's Embassy Theatre, where we summoned people to their seats with the sound of a conch shell. For 'The Bush' theme in the Opera House, we furnished the stage with large images and greenery to replicate a forest environment. We took 'The Settled Landscape' launch to the agricultural centre of Massey University, where the launcher was Frank Torley, long-time producer of *Country Calendar*. For 'Economy and the City', the obvious site was Auckland, where Steven Joyce did the honours, following a fiery mihi from Ranginui Walker. The launch of the final 'Creative Life' theme was at the capital's Paramount Theatre. I called on an old school acquaintance, Sam Neill, who without a moment's hesitation agreed to fly from Sydney to launch the theme and proceeded to deliver a magnificent talk surveying New Zealand creativity. The images and sound clips always looked wonderful on the big screen at these launches, and although there was inevitably some performance anxiety, the launches passed without disaster and to warm applause.

We decided that it would be valuable to launch the different regional entries in the secondary towns of the country – the Northland one in Whāngārei, South Canterbury in Timaru, Waikato at Hamilton, Hawke's Bay in Napier. I hoped that this would be a way of introducing Te Ara to the provinces and attracting local publicity. We almost abandoned this strategy after the second launch, the Bay of Plenty entry, in Tauranga. We had catered for about fifty people, but when chief executive Martin Matthews and I walked into the hall to begin proceedings there were no more than twelve of us there. There were mountains of uneaten sandwiches. I was just relieved that the minister who had been scheduled to actually launch the entries had to pull out at the last moment, and that I had bought the booze on a sale-or-return basis. Thereafter we prepared better, and for nearly all the later 'Places' launches we attracted full houses. Usually a minister or the local MP would do the honours; and this proved an excellent way for getting such people onside with the project. The local press were usually fulsome in their coverage. They were always gratified that a national Wellington-based project was

The cartoon by Allan Hawkey which appeared in the Waikato Times *the day after the launch of the Waikato entry.* ALEXANDER TURNBULL LIBRARY, DCDL-0014490

telling their story; and on quite a number of occasions, such as in Timaru and Invercargill, we received front-page billing in the local paper and coverage on local radio stations. In Hamilton the *Waikato Times* cartoonist even made the local entry the subject of his daily cartoon.

The reception by the media in the regions was in striking contrast with our reception nationally. The launch of our first theme did lead to a brief interview on breakfast television, but the national press ignored us. I had anticipated in-depth reviews as people explored the site. But there was a deafening silence and the only review we received came from the *New Zealand Journal of History*. At the time I was bitterly disappointed that all our work and creativity had been so ignored. What made this especially galling was the contrast when we published books from the Te Ara content. The original proposal had been that once all the themes were completed there would be a printed A–Z like the old 1966 *Encyclopaedia*. But once the first theme was published Bateman, who had so encouraged the encyclopedia project in the first place, came up with a proposal to publish the themes as they emerged. We prepared two books, one on the immigrant peoples of New Zealand, one on the major iwi. Both were handsome volumes, the first launched by the prime minister at parliament, the second by Ranginui Walker at Te Papa's marae. What interested me was that these volumes were widely reviewed despite the fact that they lacked much of the richness of the website, especially the moving footage, the interactives and the links. It was as if a print publication could be accepted by the print media while a digital publication was simply a threat. The iwi book sold well, and eventually we published a spin-off volume of the short-story summaries, which has become a standby in tourist shops around the country. Subsequently Bateman published two books from the 'Earth, Sea and Sky' theme, *Life on the Edge: New Zealand's Natural Hazards and Disasters* and a very handsome volume on *New Zealanders and the Sea*. Finally 'The Bush' theme led to a beautifully presented book, *Te Taiao – Māori and the Natural World*, which won a prize for the best Māori non-fiction book for 2009. We then sat down and prepared the text from 'The Settled Landscape' theme on the subject of New Zealanders and rural life. It came together well, but sadly Bateman decided that with the notable exception of the Māori volumes these spin-offs were not economically viable. A printed A–Z has never appeared and is not likely to do so. Te Ara would have to live on the digital world.

Well, not entirely. Another spin-off from our work came when Gibson Films approached me and said that they wanted to pitch a television series about the immigrant experience, basing the content on Te Ara's immigrant entries. I sat down with the producers and, once their pitch was successful, with their writers to prepare a series under the title *Here to Stay*. A number of our writers, including me, were interviewed for the series. Unfortunately no one had the zeal to prepare a similar series on the iwi of the country, despite our suggesting that.

Radio New Zealand also took note of our efforts. Bryan Crump on Nights invited us to talk about Te Ara entries, and I arranged for a number of our writers to take up the challenge. But the next year Bryan felt that he would prefer just me to do the job, which I continued to do, on the first Monday of the month, for the next few years. I found this an interesting way to communicate history. I would prepare a brief beforehand, and Bryan was scrupulous in following the suggestions. This gave the illusion of a free-flowing, engaged conversation, but in fact I was fully prepared for the direction the chat would take. Radio required me to cultivate a fluency of expression and a clarity of exposition which was invaluable. You had to also be very careful to be as accurate as possible, or some listener would promptly pick you up. Afterwards it was gratifying to find that people had listened and emails and telephone calls would often follow from these sessions. So did visits to the relevant pages of Te Ara.

If the press took no notice of Te Ara and the books were not bestsellers, users certainly flocked to the site. With long experience of the print world, I had come to think of 2000 sales of a book as highly successful. *A Man's Country?* had sold about 7500 in its lifetime. But within the first few months of launching Te Ara, when there was only one theme up on the web, we were attracting over 50,000 visitors a month; within a year that reached 100,000. Visitors steadily grew, and by the time the project was completed in 2014, over 600,000 people visited each month – over 20,000 a day. At any hour during the day there would be over 2000 people on the site. These were figures way beyond our wildest dreams. True, many visitors stayed on the site under five minutes; but at least they were there and using the material. Before too long we found that for many New Zealand subjects our stories would top the Google rankings. Beyond these cold statistics, warm comments flooded in. With the launch of the entries about immigrant groups, some members of those groups wrote about their thrill in having their community given recognition within the nation. The author of the Vietnamese entry, Trung Tran, wrote to me:

> As a child growing up in Kihikihi (a small rural town of 400 odd in the early 1980s), my family used to receive boxes of used clothes, toys, pots, pans etc from very thoughtful and generous people from the local church and wider community. I remember receiving a dark red 15 volume encyclopedia set. I recall them being quite dated for the time ... Anyway I used to spend hours, just looking through the pictures, the acetate plates, and kind of reading through basic facts. ... For me, this was just this fantastic source of information and 'imagination' ... Anyway, I just want to say thank-you for giving me the opportunity to be immortalised into New Zealand

history (well kind of anyway). Being able to write about and share my heritage (and for me, where I came from and how I got to where I am now) is very rewarding.[5]

It was also gratifying that there was an impressive uptake overseas. Consistently about 40 per cent of Te Ara's users came from outside New Zealand. They took notice of what we were doing. Not surprisingly, there was interest from across the Tasman. Soon after we launched, several Australians invited Ross Somerville and me to a gathering of what came to be called ANZDEG or the Australia and New Zealand Digital Encyclopaedia Group. In 2005, and again in 2006, we gave papers and led discussion about the Te Ara experience, and encouraged similar ventures in Australia. At that time the online Dictionary of Sydney was just beginning their work, and they invited me to come across and give a series of presentations on how we had organised and structured Te Ara. We continued to exchange information with the Dictionary for the next couple of years. There were also enquiries from the American Endowment for the Humanities, which had sponsored a series of state-wide digital encyclopedias in the United States. Here too I provided detailed information on our systems and planning. From Guam came letters from the Guampedia, a digital encyclopedia of Guam, which openly acknowledged its debt to Te Ara. Then in 2008 I was invited to travel to Taipei to talk about Te Ara at an international Culturemondo group, which was a gathering of digital reference sites from around the world. It was a fascinating experience, if in large part because of my encounter with this highly capitalist Chinese community. The following year Culturemondo came to Wellington. Periodically, out of the blue would come gratifying letters of appreciation. Let me cite just one: 'I am a TV documentary director working mainly for French & UK & USA broadcasters (mainly science topics). I just want to say how impressed I am with your site – I trawl through thousands of web pages for research each year so I have some experience. You are doing a fantastic job – congratulations.'[6]

Despite such encouragement and support, by 2011, with three years to go before our last theme would be launched, I was becoming exhausted. I was sixty-four, and alongside managing the Te Ara team and writing my full quota of entries and blog posts, I continued to keep up scholarly publication. Every Saturday morning I would work away at my own projects. I finished writing the study of British and Irish immigration to New Zealand, which was published in 2008 as *Settlers*. And there was a constant stream of smaller pieces – a chapter on the years 1965 to 1984 for the *Frontier of Dreams* book; a talk on New Zealand's 'Quiet War', about the Great War in New Zealand memory, which I first gave at an international conference in Sydney and which was then published in a volume by Oxford University Press; various papers on memorials – one on French memorials in New Zealand for a conference in Paris, and one entitled 'War Memorial Capital of the World' about Whanganui's memorials, for the book *Heartlands*. I also produced several publications about Ulster's migrants to New Zealand, a history of New Zealand in the twentieth century for an international encyclopedia, a well-received presentation to the Rising Dragons, Soaring Bananas conference in Auckland about the history of treatment of the Chinese in New Zealand, and an essay about a fascinating post-World War I mural which had once hung in a Palmerston North department store. There was even a short speculative essay for a photographic catalogue on the caravan in New Zealand culture.

I was also involved in outside administrative work as a member of the Victoria University Council and the Fulbright Board. And in 2008 I was given responsibility for also managing another ministry website, NZLive, which had been established by Helen Clark as a digital guide to New Zealand cultural events. The site was extremely lively, as you would expect from the name, and the staff were energetically committed to the work. But unfortunately a private company, Eventfinda, had also come on the scene and was providing a highly efficient guide to cultural events. The Eventfinda site did not have any additional high-quality background information but they did have an efficient catalogue of events and ticket-ordering service. The ministry wanted to save money; the government had changed, and this seemed to be a place where there was little argument for public investment. I was given the unfortunate role of integrating NZLive and Eventfinda at the cost of several jobs. The task was an unpleasant one, and although I never lost the loyalty of Jackie Hay, who managed NZLive, there was pain and anguish all round.

So I had been extremely busy. I wanted to keep writing, but I could not do everything. In 2011 I decided to retire from my role as general editor, and become simply the managing editor of content. Fortunately Janine Faulknor had shown herself to be a superb manager in charge of the resource team. She was intelligent, had total integrity, was universally admired and was totally committed to Te Ara. She was willing to take on the job of managing the whole team. I was lucky indeed.

The timing was once again fortuitous. In 2011 the Rugby World Cup was held in New Zealand, and I was involved quite early on planning a digital presence for visitors. I came up with the idea that we might provide them with an audio guide to places along the main routes of New Zealand. They could listen to stories about those sites as they drove from game to game. Initially we had envisaged audio tapes which they put into their car audio systems, but distributing these seemed expensive and logistically difficult. So gradually the project morphed into a web resource, drawing on stories from Te Ara and repackaging them in an interesting way for World Cup visitors. I was able to get some money from Tourism New Zealand, and hired several researchers, one of whom was my old friend Chris Maclean, to prepare briefs. Then Dave Armstrong, whom I had known as a writer at Te Papa, turned these briefs into lively four-to-five-minute scripts, and used actors to record the stories at Radio New Zealand's studios, supplementing the spoken words with historical sound clips from Radio New Zealand's Sound Archives. I spent a lot of time travelling round the country taking photographs to supplement the stories, which then went up on the web and were eventually available as an app. In the end we completed 140 of these 'Roadside Stories', many of which we also included in Te Ara. They were not entirely satisfactory. Originally conceived as primarily sound files, they became visual experiences for the web, but the imagery was simply not strong enough to carry all the messages. But the stories did prove quite popular and were played over the following summer on National Radio.

Preparing this project for the Rugby World Cup led me into a close relationship with the people organising the Real New Zealand cultural festival, designed to sit alongside the World Cup. My friend from NZLive, Jackie Hay, had joined the Real New Zealand team. So I came up with the idea of travelling round the country and writing a blog for the festival about how the cultural events were panning out. Real New Zealand agreed to pay my petrol money and accommodation. Immediately on giving up the general editorship of Te Ara, I set off to explore the cultural side of the World Cup. Of course this also allowed me to see a few of the games in provincial centres. It was an immensely stimulating experience. I wrote a blog post a day – in all some forty posts, which ranged from pieces on Ralph Hotere and Len Lye to

Scenes from my Rugby World Cup trip – Jock the reluctant fan, Dunedin nude rugby, Whanganui floral sculptures, Nelson rugby models, Irish supporters, Wellington lighting.

musings on the artistic use of the colour black. The most disturbing stop was in my old home-town of Christchurch, still hugely wounded by the February earthquake and missing out on World Cup games. The exercise was a great way to mark my send-off from carrying the full load of Te Ara.

When I returned, the work preparing Te Ara content was as stimulating as ever. But a long fight began, which blighted my last years in employment, to save the soul of Te Ara. From the beginning of the project I had argued that one of the great virtues of digital publication was that updating and correction could occur easily. The encyclopedia would not become fossilised at one point in time. But in my focus on getting the site completed, I did not emphasise this point sufficiently or hammer home continually the fact that Te Ara would continue to grow and change even once we had completed all the themes. I also tried to inspire a sense of an exciting future by suggesting interesting ways forward. An obvious suggestion was that work on the biographies be revived. It had become increasingly absurd that very important people who had died since the last *DNZB* volume was published, such as Edmund Hillary, Robert Muldoon or Janet Frame, did not have major biographies. So alongside preparing Te Ara, we had published twelve new biographies.

Building on this success, I came up with the idea that the ministry should embark on a major project, 'The Making of Modern New Zealand'. I argued that New Zealand had undergone a revolution in values since the 1960s; and that the next set of biographies might be researched and written alongside overview entries about this revolution. Thus biographies about some of the major Māori leaders, people like Mat Rata, Sid Jackson, Eva Rickard and Ranginui Walker, might be prepared along with an entry about Māori protest. Biographies of Sonja Davies and Margaret Shields would sit beside essays on the modern feminist movement. The idea was received warmly by ministers but was never funded. We also began a project to prepare short 'War Stories' for the web as part of the centenary of the Great War. One of these, about George Bollinger, was created and posted online. This was well received, and coincided with a very similar initiative by the film-maker Anna Cottrell. We worked with Anna on two series of these short films, which were played on TV3 as *Great War Stories*, but once I had left, the ministry's involvement faded and eventually lapsed.

Eventually the efforts to give a new life and direction to Te Ara fell on fallow ground. The ministry was running short of funds, and although the

Sam Neill, Lewis Holden (Ministry for Culture and Heritage chief executive), Maggie Barry (minister of arts, culture and heritage) and myself at the final launch of Te Ara, in 2014. MANATŪ TAONGA MINISTRY FOR CULTURE AND HERITAGE

money we had gained from Michael Cullen became a permanent addition to the ministry's budget, and so, one might argue, should have continued to fund digital initiatives, the finance officer repeatedly referred to the windfall which would follow 'the end of Te Ara' and get the ministry out of its financial hole. We tried to dispute this viewpoint and press the claims that Te Ara, widely regarded as 'the ministry's flagship', should continue steaming forward. We put together a detailed business case and suggested that, with five people employed, the site could review a theme every nine years, make adjustments when a new census was done or a major event occurred, update the technology and keep up with social media. It was an unpleasant fight. Initially we thought we had made progress, when it was decided that five people should be appointed for one year after the rest of us said our farewells. But this turned out to be purely a defensive measure to quieten the fires while the team was still intact. When the year was up, all five people, despite doing outstanding work during that time, lost their jobs.

The ministry continued to maintain that Te Ara was being revised and updated; but to anyone like myself who knew the site well, these were largely empty protestations. Gradually elements began to wither and die – the blog ceased to be published; Te Ara's newsletter was transformed into a newsletter about all ministry publications and then stopped completely; no new entries appeared; and it took a long time before major events such as the Kaikōura earthquake appeared on the site. For a time I joined a group of concerned people writing to the minister and the ministry's chief executive. Bland reassurances came back. In the end I came to believe that since Te Ara had been in large part my baby, it was not really my task to fight for its survival. If the site was of value to New Zealanders then it was up to the community of interested users to ensure that it was kept alive. This was the right response, for once our grumblings fell away signs began to appear of a modest revival. Rosemary Du Plessis was contracted to oversee the updating of the 'Social Connections' theme, taking into account the results of the 2013 census, and in September 2018 twenty-five new biographies of women were published for Suffrage 125. Whether these hopeful signs portend a continuing life for Te Ara, only the future will tell.

Epilogue
NZ HistoryJock

Although my last months at Te Ara were a strange mixture of triumph about a job completed and sadness that the site might not be maintained, retirement brought much personal recognition. I found myself showered with honours. In 2011 I had received the Pou Aronui Award for service to the humanities from the Royal Society. Now I received an ONZM from the Queen, from Victoria University a Hunter Fellowship for my work on the university's council and then an honorary degree for services to scholarship, life membership of the Professional Historians' Association (PHANZA), and, most surprising and humbling of all, the Prime Minister's Award for Literary Achievement in non-fiction. I was deeply flattered and only too aware that so much of what had been achieved was as a result of a magnificent Te Ara team, who, because they so enjoyed each other's company, continued to meet regularly. The recognition inspired me to keep working.

I still believed that the digital revolution had not yet been fully grasped by humanities scholars. Researchers were using the web for research – the National Library's Papers Past website became a major source for all New Zealand historians. But few were using the web to publish their findings. Articles and books continued to be the avenue of publication. In an article in the *New Zealand Journal of History* I called for historians to begin doing web exhibitions, or at the very least to supplement their printed publications with digital collections of the documents and images they had uncovered in their research. I gave the example of the database which we had collected while undertaking research on war memorials in the late 1980s. After *The Sorrow and the Pride* was published, Jamie Mackay agreed to put this database up on nzhistory.net.nz. Over the subsequent years a large number of additional memorials and further information about those already there were posted by readers online. I realised that this web resource, collectively put together, made the old publication out of date. This allowed me to sit down in 2015 and completely rewrite the book, drawing on the additional digital material. The new version, *To the Memory*, came out as part of the World War I centenary commemorations. This time the publishers, Potton and Burton, did full justice to the images, and the book was well received, winning a prize as the best book on New Zealand heritage. A new book did not mean abandoning the web. I signalled my continuing interest in digital outlets by establishing a website, NZHistoryJock, where I could promote my own writing and host a blog.

I was also keen to try other forms of history. I had once dismissed family history as of no interest to serious historians, but I began to realise that it could be a route into wider stories. One day I was staying at the Geraldine farm where my wife Frida grew up. Her brother, Philip, went to a bottom drawer and pulled out a series of photo albums. They recorded the story of their grandfather and great-uncle, members of the Canterbury Mounted Rifles, who had fought at Gallipoli and in the Sinai desert in World War I. Soon after, Philip led me up a ladder into the roof of his garage, and began to dig out some amazing objects – a machine gun, which one brother had used throughout the campaign until his death, a Turkish machine gun which they had captured at Gallipoli, a prayer book with a bullet through it, some remarkable maps and compasses. I was hooked, and immediately looked at the collection of letters which their great-uncle Gordon Harper had written to his parents and which I vaguely remembered reading in the 1980s when I was researching World War I. They had been published as a scruffy, cheap volume. On reacquainting myself with the letters, I realised that they were a powerfully expressed story of two brothers at war, and that by putting together the photographs and images of the objects with the letters, we could produce a moving centenary publication. I set myself up as a publisher under the title of, what else, NZHistoryJock. The book was launched on the eve of Anzac Day 2015 by Maggie Barry at Te Papa, where the Gallipoli exhibition *The Scale of Our War* included the Harper brothers' guns and told their story. It was my hope that this book was more than family history. By inspiring a sympathy for the two brothers, it hopefully revealed both the motivations which took young New Zealanders to war and the tragedy and disillusionment once they faced its awful reality.

Nor was this my only exploration of family history. I found myself examining the story of my father and realising that his life and career had a wider significance. His story said much about the role of history in a British colony in the first half of the twentieth century. For my father, studying history was a way of paying honour to the British imperial tradition. History was something that evoked the richer world across the seas in Europe. It took my years in the United States from the late 1960s to develop an interest in my own New World origins and slowly conceive a different sense of being a historian. I became a committed cultural nationalist, at times embarrassingly strident, dedicated to the proposition that New Zealand had a rich historical story which had to inform the way New Zealanders went about their lives. I abandoned the pursuit of American history and turned my creative energies to illuminating New Zealand's past, presenting it in ways that would capture people's attention – in lively books, in photographic essays, in exhibitions, in journalism, on television and radio and through the web. And I tried to encourage other forms of history which would awaken public interest – oral histories, Māori history, official histories of government which would focus interest on policy and social impacts, a historical atlas.

A younger generation of historians is not quite so sure about this nationalist mission or my enthusiasm for communicating to a wider audience. For them history is an international discipline, where other historians are the primary audience; they are wary of nationalist historians becoming apologists for their own society and claiming an unwarranted uniqueness for New Zealand. I have some sympathy for this last viewpoint. New Zealand history in the Keith Sinclair years did focus on internally driven change; and it is obviously banal to keep recounting a story of New Zealand as a young country gradually growing to maturity. The New Zealand experience must be located within an international perspective. I have always seen New Zealand as an example of a New World society, created by an Old World people invading and colonising the lands of an indigenous people, and slowly developing its own traditions. It therefore bears obvious comparisons with the history of Australia, the United States, Canada and Latin America. I have tried

Robin Harper's prayer book, which was damaged when a bullet passed through it in Palestine in 1917.

to draw on the historiography of these societies. The experience of working on Te Ara also convinced me that there is extraordinary regional variation and distinctive cultures within New Zealand, which we tried to reveal, above all, in the 'Places' section of the site. Pasifika South Auckland is culturally a long way from Scottish Invercargill. My study of war memorials also threw up much regional variety. The nation is never a unitary cultural entity.

But for a country that is as geographically isolated as any country on earth, and that has, since 1876, been governed by a very powerful unitary state whose laws have drastically shaped the society, and where there is one indigenous people who speak one indigenous language, the nation is an excellent place to start. We are not unique, but we are sufficiently different from other societies to be worth serious examination. I have always believed that unless historians in New Zealand study the story of their own society honestly and fearlessly, no one else will. To study the myths of New Zealand nationalism is not to endorse them uncritically. Rather, to understand how the nation developed those myths is the first step in freeing the community from their dominance. Unpicking the myth of *A Man's Country?* was a contribution to becoming a diverse and free society. I firmly believe that unless historians recount accurately and with elegance the history of this country, then the society will be much the poorer.

And they must learn to communicate their ideas to a wide audience, not just to other professionals. Ever since I returned from the United States in 1973 and rediscovered my own country, I have endeavoured to make New Zealand's past meaningful to other New Zealanders as much as to other historians. New Zealanders are interested in their own history, which is why a book like Michael King's history of New Zealand sold in such huge numbers. Serious works such as Vincent O'Malley's study of the Waikato War or Barbara Brookes' history of New Zealand women are read because New Zealanders want explanations for the world around them. I believe passionately that we cannot improve this society unless we understand what caused the pains and what brought about the pleasures of the past, and we will never appreciate the richness of our immediate environment unless we clothe it with stories from our history. Historians are needed to add their insights in answering big questions – what is the nature of the relations between Māori and Pākehā; have we ever been egalitarian, and why are we not today; what impact has the rise of the city and especially Auckland had on our society; how is the immigration of diverse peoples to this country changing it; how has the revolution in government since 1984 transformed New Zealand; and how have our values and traditions been shaped by our distinctive physical environment? These are big and urgent questions, and our historians can make a major contribution to answering them in ways that can, and should, be grasped by many New Zealanders. It is my hope that in a small way I have made some contribution, through different ways of presenting history, to New Zealanders' understanding of themselves.

Notes

Introduction

1 Keith Sinclair, *Halfway Round the Harbour*, Penguin Books, Auckland, 1993, p. 5.
2 W. H. Oliver, *Looking for the Phoenix: A Memoir*, Bridget Williams Books, Wellington, 2002; Michael King, *Being Pakeha: An Encounter with New Zealand and the Maori Renaissance*, Hodder and Stoughton, Auckland, 1985.

Chapter 1

1 On the history of Jews in the East End see Gerry Black, *Jewish London: An Illustrated History,* Breedon, Derby, 2003; Todd M. Endelman, *The Jews of Britain 1656 to 2000*, University of California Press, Berkeley, 2002.
2 Birth certificate of Sam Phillips, Mile End Old Town, 1887. Some documents such as the UK census and his death certificate give his name as Samuel; but both his birth and marriage certificates, where the information would have come from his mother and himself, give 'Sam'.
3 UK census 1891.
4 UK census 1901.
5 Lazarus Morris Goldman, *The History of the Jews in New Zealand*, Reed, Wellington, 1958, pp. 132–36.
6 Neville Phillips (NP), oral history interview by Catherine Phillips, 1995; Elizabeth Winifred Rathgen, notes written for Jock Phillips (JP), 1987.
7 NP, oral history interview by JP, 12 February 1997; Goldman, *The History of the Jews*, pp. 180–81; on the van Staverens as his employer see *Hawera and Normanby Star*, 10 December 1923, p. 7.
8 Rathgen, notes.
9 'Phillips, Samuel – WW1 92917 – Army', army base record, http://ndhadeliver.natlib.govt.nz/delivery/DeliveryManagerServlet?dps_pid=IE19520165
10 Electoral rolls, 1908, 1911, 1914, 1919, 1922; Wise's street directory, 1905–24.
11 'Phillips, Samuel – WW1 92917 – Army'.
12 NP, oral history interview by Catherine Phillips.
13 Death certificate for Samuel Phillips, 9 December 1923; Rathgen notes; Coronial Inquest file for Samuel Phillips, Archives New Zealand (Wellington), Records of the Department of Justice, J46, 1923/1146.
14 Rathgen, notes.
15 *The New Zealand Traveller*, 5 February 1924, p. 14; 5 June 1924, p. 13.
16 Rathgen, notes; NP, oral history interview by JP, 12 February 1997.
17 NP, oral history interview by JP, 12 February 1997.

18 Bruce Hamilton, *Palmerston North Boys' High School, 1902–2001*, Palmerston North Boys' High School, Palmerston North, 2002, p. 137.
19 Ibid., p. 120.
20 A. C. Zohrab, undated letter, Phillips papers.
21 See Michael E. Parrish, *Felix Frankfurter and his Times: The Reform Years*, Free Press, New York, 1982, pp. 5, 6–7, 240–41.
22 NP, oral history interview by JP, 12 February 1997.
23 NP, oral history interview by JP, 13 February 1997.
24 N. C. Phillips, 'Hight, James', from the Dictionary of New Zealand Biography, Te Ara – the Encyclopedia of New Zealand, http://www.TeAra.govt.nz/en/biographies/3h23/hight-james
25 'Home No More Home', *Sun*, 24 March 1934.
26 NP, oral history interview by JP, 12 and 13 February 1997.
27 P. H. N. Freeth, reference letter, 27 March 1938; H. W. Vincent, reference letter, 27 May 1935.
28 See Peter Simpson, *Bloomsbury South: the Arts in Christchurch 1933–1953*, Auckland University Press, Auckland, 2016.
29 'Our Relief Camps', *Sun*, 10 September 1932.
30 'Ode to Herr Hitler', *Sun*, 1 December 1934.
31 Christopher Hilliard, *The Bookmen's Dominion: Cultural Life in New Zealand 1920–1950*, Auckland University Press, Auckland, 2006, p. 87.
32 Neville Phillips, 'New Zealand's relations with Great Britain, 1868–1901', MA thesis, Canterbury University College, 1937, p. 34.
33 Ibid., p. 10.
34 Ibid., p. 30.
35 Examiners' comments; Letter from J. Hight, 5 May 1938, both in Phillips papers.
36 T. H. Beaglehole, *A Life of J. C. Beaglehole – New Zealand Scholar*, Victoria University Press, Wellington, 2006, p. 84.
37 Phillips, 'New Zealand's relations', p. 264.
38 Toggers were the so-called 'Torpid' races among college rowing crews but excluding those who had been in the college eight the previous year.
39 NP to Patricia and Jim Nelson (P and JN), 5 March 1939.
40 NP to P and JN, 29 January 1939.
41 NP to P and JN, 20 November 1938.
42 NP to P and JN, 30 May 1939.
43 NP to P and JN, 11 July 1939. These abbreviations refer to forms of Gothic architecture viz. Norman and Early English; Decorated Gothic and Perpendicular Gothic.
44 *The Raleigh Club – Christmas 1938*, Phillips papers.
45 NP to P and JN, 20 May 1939.
46 NP to P and JN, 11 July 1939.
47 NP to P and JN, 30 May 1939.
48 NP to P and JN, 29 January 1939.
49 NP to P and JN, 5 March 1939.
50 NP to P and JN, 3 November 1939.
51 NP, oral history interview by JP, 15 February 1997.
52 NP to P and JN, 4 December 1939.
53 NP, oral history interview by JP, 15 February 1997; NP to P and JN, 21 May 1943.
54 NP to P and JN, 21 May 1943.
55 NP to P and JN, 2 January 1941.
56 Joe Berry, *Unwillingly to War*, University Texts, Hull, 1996, p. 8.
57 Ibid., p. 100.
58 Ibid., pp. 17–18.
59 NP, oral history interview by JP, 15 February 1997.
60 NP to P and JN, 3 May 1940.
61 NP to P and JN, 3 May 1940.

62 NP to P and JN, 13 March 1940.
63 NP to P and JN, 26 November 1944.
64 See for example Edmund Bohan's experience recounted in *Singing Historian: A Memoir*, Canterbury University Press, Christchurch, 2012, p. 47.
65 Mervyn Thompson, *All My Lives*, Whitcoulls, Christchurch, 1980, p. 70.
66 Pauline O'Regan, *A Changing Order*, Allen & Unwin; Port Nicholson Press, Wellington, 1986, p. 83.
67 Tony Simpson, *Along for the Ride – A Political Memoir*, Blythswood Press, Wellington, 2017, p. 60.
68 Bohan, *Singing Historian*, p. 35.
69 N. C. Phillips, 'Collectivism and the British Commonwealth', *Landfall*, September 1947, pp. 174–85.
70 N. C. Phillips, 'Referendum: A Retrospect', *Landfall*, December 1949, pp. 307–20.
71 N. C. Phillips, 'Burke and Paine – the Conservative and Radical Minds', *Landfall*, March 1954, pp. 36–46.
72 N. C. Phillips, *Italy. Volume 1: The Sangro to Cassino*, War History Branch, Dept. of Internal Affairs, Wellington, 1957, pp. 24–25.
73 Ibid., p. 30.
74 Ibid., p. 211.
75 Ibid., p. 217.
76 Ibid., pp. 353–54.
77 N. C. Phillips, 'Edmund Burke and the County Movement, 1779–1780', *English Historical Review*, vol. 76, no. 254, 1961, pp. 254–78.
78 N. C. Phillips, *Yorkshire and English National Politics, 1783–1784*, University of Canterbury, Christchurch, 1961; N. C. Phillips, 'The British General Election of 1780: a vortex of politics', *Political Science*, vol. 11, no. 2, 1959, pp. 3–22; N. C. Phillips, 'Namier and his method', *Political Science*, vol. 14, no. 2, 1962, pp. 16–26.
79 N. C. Phillips, 'Review of *A History of New Zealand*', *Landfall*, June 1959, pp. 181–85.

Chapter 2

1 Quoted in Geoffrey Dutton, *Founder of a City: The Story of Colonel Light*, Cheshire, Melbourne, 1960, p. 148.
2 See Dean Jaensch, ed., *The Flinders History of South Australia – Political History*, Wakefield Press, Netley, 1986, pp. 1–8; Douglas Pike, *Paradise of Dissent: South Australia 1829–1857*, Melbourne University, Melbourne, 1957, p. 96.
3 Quoted in Pike, *Paradise of Dissent*, p. 105.
4 Dutton, *Founder of a City*, pp. 194–95.
5 Pike, *Paradise of Dissent*, p. 222.
6 A. Grenfell Price, *The Foundation and Settlement of South Australia, 1829–1845*, F. W. Preece, Adelaide, 1924, pp. 98–103.
7 Quoted in Dutton, *Founder of a City*, p. 154.
8 Pike, *Paradise of Dissent*, p. 228.
9 Jaensch, *Flinders History of South Australia*, p. 41; Shaun Berg, ed., *Coming to Terms: Aboriginal Title in South Australia*, Wakefield Press, Adelaide, 2010.
10 Quoted in Price, *Foundation and Settlement of South Australia*, p. 121.
11 R. Cockburn, *Pastoral Pioneers of South Australia*, vol. 1, Publishers Limited, Adelaide, 1925, pp. 16–17.
12 Jaensch, *Flinders History of South Australia*, pp. 395–97.
13 G. D. Combe, *Responsible Government in South Australia*, vol. 1, Government Printer, Adelaide, 1957, p. 211.
14 *South Australia Register*, 29 January 1875, p. 4.; 'Fisher, Sir James Hurtle (1790–1875)', Australian Dictionary of Biography, http://adb.anu.edu.au/biography/fisher-sir-james-hurtle-2045/text2531

15 *South Australia Register*, 29 January 1875, p. 4.
16 Pike, *Paradise of Dissent*, pp. 499, 501.
17 *The Argus*, 1 July 1875, p. 15; 'CN Fisher Plate', Wikipedia, https://en.wikipedia.org/wiki/CB_Fisher_Plate
18 *Press*, 17 August 1910.
19 UK census 1841.
20 *Cyclopedia of New Zealand*, vol. 3, p. 262.
21 UK24a, Union Bank, 'Officers and their Sureties', Australia and New Zealand Banking Group Archives.
22 UK24a, Australia and New Zealand Banking Group Archives.
23 ACC 830, Australia and New Zealand Banking Group Archives.
24 G. R. MacDonald, 'Joseph Palmer', Dictionary of Canterbury Biographies, Canterbury Museum, https://collection.canterburymuseum.com/objects/715948. See also James Hight and C. R. Straubel, (eds), *A History of Canterbury*, vol. II, Whitcombe and Tombs, Christchurch, 1957–71, p. 89.
25 *Lyttelton Times*, 19 October 1861.
26 See Jock Phillips, 'Palmer, Joseph', from the Dictionary of New Zealand Biography, Te Ara – the Encyclopedia of New Zealand, http://www.TeAra.govt.nz/en/biographies/1p2/palmer-joseph
27 S. J. Butlin, *Australia and New Zealand Bank: the Bank of Australasia and the Union Bank of Australia Limited, 1828-1951*, Longmans, London, 1961, p. 218.
28 G. R. MacDonald, 'Joseph Palmer'.
29 Quoted in Gordon Ogilvie, *The Shagroons' Palace: A History of the Christchurch Club, 1856–2006*, Henry Elworthy for the Christchurch Club, Christchurch, 2005, p. 13.
30 Jill Lloyd, 'Woodford Historical Notes', unpublished manuscript, 2004.
31 G. R. MacDonald, 'Joseph Palmer'.
32 Selby Palmer, unpublished memoir.
33 'Edwin Palmer', ESPNcricinfo, http://www.espncricinfo.com/newzealand/content/player/38157.html; 'New South Wales tour of New Zealand at Christchurch, Feb 15–17 1894, ESPNcricinfo, http://www.espncricinfo.com/ci/engine/current/match/861965.html
34 Selby Palmer, unpublished memoir.
35 Mary McHardy, unpublished memoir in author's possession.
36 *Dominion*, 30 April 1908; *Manawatu Times*, 30 April 1908.
37 Selby Palmer, unpublished memoir.
38 Ibid.
39 Geoffrey W. Rice, 'Gould, George', from the Dictionary of New Zealand Biography, Te Ara – the Encyclopedia of New Zealand, http://www.TeAra.govt.nz/en/biographies/4g16/gould-george
40 Derived from Mary McHardy, unpublished memoir; Mrs Charles Wells obituary, *Press*, 7 October 1943.
41 Selby Palmer, unpublished memoir.
42 Mary McHardy, unpublished memoir.
43 Ibid.
44 See Ray Fargher, *The Best Man Who Ever Served the Crown? A Life of Donald McLean*, Victoria University Press, Wellington, 2007; Alan Ward, *A Show of Justice*, Auckland University Press, Auckland, 1973; Alan Ward, 'McLean, Donald', from the Dictionary of New Zealand Biography, Te Ara – the Encyclopedia of New Zealand, http://www.TeAra.govt.nz/en/biographies/1m38/mclean-donald
45 Pauline Palmer, 'The Native Ministry of Donald McLean, 1869–76', MA thesis, University of New Zealand, 1937, p. 29.
46 Ibid., p. 26.
47 Ibid., p. 123.

Chapter 3

1. Geoffrey W. Rice, 'Averill, Leslie Cecil Lloyd', from the Dictionary of New Zealand Biography, Te Ara – the Encyclopedia of New Zealand, http://www.TeAra.govt.nz/en/biographies/5a25/averill-leslie-cecil-lloyd
2. W. J. Gardner, 'Candy, Alice Muriel Flora', from the Dictionary of New Zealand Biography, Te Ara – the Encyclopedia of New Zealand, http://www.TeAra.govt.nz/en/biographies/4c5/candy-alice-muriel-flora
3. *New Zealand Official Yearbook*, 1958, https://www3.stats.govt.nz/New_Zealand_Official_Yearbooks/1958/NZOYB_1958.html
4. Jock Phillips (JP) to Pauline Phillips (PP), undated, 1965.
5. PP to Dorothy Palmer (DP), 13 December 1962.
6. Neville Phillips (NP) to Mr and Mrs D. G. McHardy, 17 January 1963.
7. Family diary, 6 January 1963.
8. PP to DP, 18 September 1963.
9. NP to DP, 17 January 1964.
10. JP to DP, 16 January 1964.

Chapter 4

1. Jock Phillips (JP) to Pauline Phillips (PP), 25 July 1965.
2. JP to PP, 2 June 1965.
3. JP to PP, 25 July 1965.
4. JP to PP, 3 January 1967.
5. JP to Pauline and Neville Phillips, 1 September 1968.
6. JP to Jane McCartney (JM), 6 September 1968.
7. JP to PP, 5 September 1968.
8. JP to PP, 14 September 1968.
9. Ibid.
10. Ibid.
11. JP to PP, 22 September 1968.
12. JP to PP, 6 October 1968.
13. JP to JM, 31 October 1968
14. JP to PP, 20 April 1969.
15. JP to JM, 23 April 1969.
16. JP to JM, 16 October 1969.
17. JP to PP, 15 April 1970.
18. JP to PP, 5 September 1968.
19. JP to PP, 25 March 1969.
20. JP to PP, 18 May 1969.
21. JP to JM, 31 May 1969.
22. JP to JM, 23 April 1969.
23. JP to PP, 18 November 1970.
24. JP to JM, 7 October 1968.
25. JP to PP, 1 December 1970.
26. JP to JM, 6 September 1968.
27. JP to JM, 9 June 1969.
28. JP to PP, 4 July 1970.
29. *Press*, 23 December 1970, p. 1.
30. JP to PP, 25 January 1971.
31. JP to PP, 26 January 1969.
32. JP to PP, 26 November 1969.
33. JP to PP, 26 January 1969.

34 JP to JM, 6 November 1968.
35 JP to JM, 12 January 1969.
36 JP to PP, 16 January 1969.
37 JP to JM, 18 May 1969.
38 JP to PP, 14 September 1968.
39 JP to PP, 27 August 1969.
40 JP to PP, 6 July 1969.
41 JP to JM, 22 July 1969.
42 JP to JM, 31 August 1969.
43 JP to PP, 31 August 1970.
44 JP to PP, 10 September 1970.
45 JP to PP, 11 August 1971.
46 JP to PP, 16 October 1969.
47 Henry David Thoreau, *Walden*, Signet Classic, New American Library, New York, 1960, p. 276.
48 Ibid., p. 137.
49 Ibid., p. 213.
50 JP to JM, 14 October 1968.
51 JP to PP, 6 October 1969.
52 JP to PP, 30 December 1968.
53 JP to JM, 31 May 1969.
54 JP to PP, 27 May 1971.
55 JP to JM, 25 October 1969.
56 JP to PP, 8 November 1970.
57 JP to PP, 6 October 1968.
58 JP to JM, 12 December 1968.
59 JP to JM, 2 July 1969.
60 JP to PP, 25 March 1969.
61 JP to JM, 2 July 1969.
62 JP to JM, 23 April 1969.

Chapter 5

1 Jock Phillips (JP) to Pauline and Neville Phillips (P and NP), 28 December 1978.
2 Jock Phillips, letter to the editor, *NZ Listener*, 19 April 1975, p. 9.
3 Jock Phillips, 'The Class of '21', *NZ Listener*, 28 April 1979, p. 6.
4 Jock Phillips, letter to the editor, *Truth*, 17 May 1979.
5 Jock Phillips, 'A Dying State?', *NZ Listener*, 17 April 1976, p. 6; 'Egalitarian Society', *NZ Listener*, 26 June 1976, p. 10; 'Unordinary Blokes', *NZ Listener*, 11 September 1976, p. 10.
6 Jock Phillips, 'A Kiwi Myth', *NZ Listener*, 15 January 1977, p. 6.
7 Jock Phillips, 'Truxtun Fall-out', *NZ Listener*, 16 October 1976, p. 10.
8 Jock Phillips, 'The Repressed', *NZ Listener*, 1 May 1976, p. 6.
9 Jock Phillips, 'Towards the Bush Garden', *NZ Listener*, 12 April 1980, p. 10.
10 Jock Phillips, 'Fear and Loathing in the New Zealand Landscape', in *New Zealand Where are You?: Proceedings of the New Zealand Institute of Landscape Architects' 1981 conference, 20–21 February, Victoria University*, Wellington, 1981.
11 Jock Phillips, 'Gold Medals or Movies?', *NZ Listener*, 9 April 1977, p. 6.
12 Letter from Chris Wainwright and Jock Phillips to university staff, 4 June 1974.
13 Jock Phillips, 'Celebration …', *NZ Listener*, 24 July 1976, p. 14.
14 JP to Pauline Phillips, 21 November 1977.
15 Jock Phillips, 'Come into my Parlour, said the 70s to the 60s', *NZ Listener*, 27 January 1979, pp. 18–19.
16 JP to P and NP, 4 February 1978.

17 JP to Jim Holt, 21 May 1980.
18 J. O. C. Phillips, 'Musings in Maoriland – or was there a *Bulletin* school in New Zealand?', *Historical Studies*, vol. 20, no. 81, October 1983, pp. 520–35.
19 E. H. McCormick to JP, 17 February 1984.
20 David Mackay, Malcolm McKinnon, Peter McPhee, Jock Phillips, (eds), *Counting the Cost: The 1981 Springbok Tour in Wellington*, Victoria University of Wellington History Department, Wellington, 1982.
21 *Counting the Cost*, p. 12.
22 FOR*MEN, Men in Transition registration form, October 1983, p. 2.
23 Dr Herbert Green at Auckland's National Women's Hospital had since 1966 been monitoring patients with abnormal cells in the cervix but without treating them and without informing the women they were part of an experiment. Phillida and Sandra Coney's article on 'An Unfortunate Experiment' was published in *Metro* magazine in June 1987. The resulting inquiry, headed by Judge Silvia Cartwright, condemned the experiment and proposed new steps to protect patients' rights.

Chapter 6

1 Jock Phillips (JP) to Pauline Phillips and Neville Phillips, 20 May 1983.
2 Jock Phillips, submission to Professor Les Holborow, 8 March 1987.
3 Jock Phillips, undated submission, 1987.
4 *VUW News*, 1986, p. 9; see also JP to Bryce Harland, 24 January 1986.
5 Peter Beatson, leave report to Massey University, 1986.
6 Colin Davis to JP, 30 July 1984.
7 Geoff Park to Patricia Evans, reviews administrator, 19 October 1994.
8 Christine Cheyne to JP, 6 July 1987.
9 Jock Phillips, 'New Zealand and the ANZUS Alliance: Changing National Self-Perceptions, 1945–88', in Richard W. Baker (ed.), *Australia, New Zealand, and the United States: Internal Change and Alliance Relations in the ANZUS States*, Praeger, New York, 1991, p. 201.
10 I ended a letter to my parents on 27 February 1987: 'Forgot to tell you the most important event of my life – I got roped into a cricket match yesterday, scored 98 and took four wickets including the last which tied the game! A good way to end my career!'

Chapter 7

1 Robin Williams, *Report on a Ministerial Review of the Historical Publications Branch*, Department of Internal Affairs, Wellington, August 1986, p. 1.
2 Jock Phillips, 'Of Verandahs and Fish and Chips and Footie on Saturday Afternoon: Reflections on 100 Years of New Zealand Historiography', *NZ Journal of History*, vol. 24, no. 2, October 1990, pp. 118–34.
3 Rowan Saker, typescript of article for Capital Community Newspapers, c. May 1989.
4 'Branch staffing', Historical Branch Advisory Committee (HBAC), 19 May 1989, item 4, Archives New Zealand.
5 John E. Martin, People, Politics and Power Stations: Electric P*ower Generation in New Zealand 1880–1990*, Bridget Williams Books, Wellington, 1991.
6 John E. Martin: *Holding the Balance: A History of New Zealand's Department of Labour 1891–1995*, Canterbury University Press, Christchurch, 1996.
7 Williams, *Report on a Ministerial Review*, p. i.
8 Ibid., p. 15.
9 'Departmental histories', HBAC, 25 August 1989, item 9.
10 'Departmental histories', HBAC, 25 August 1994.

11 Perry Cameron to Joel George, 18 June 1992.
12 Based on lists on the Ministry for Culture and Heritage website.
13 Phillips, 'Of Verandahs and Fish and Chips', p. 131.
14 Ibid., p. 133.
15 'Maori history', HBAC, 24 March 1988, item 3 (b) (i), Archives New Zealand.
16 HBAC, 25 August 1989.
17 Memorandum to Bill Buxton, 7 April 1989.
18 Williams, *Report on a Ministerial Review*, p. 14.
19 Jock Phillips, 'A past worth exploring', *Metro*, 128, February 1992, pp. 114–19.
20 Raewyn Dalziel to Jock Phillips, 23 December 1991.
21 David Mackay to Jock Phillips, 10 June 1992.

Chapter 8

1 Jock Phillips (JP) to Rose Young, 24 July 1991.
2 See JP to Cheryll Sotheran, 21 October 1993.
3 Ibid.
4 JP to Ken Gorbey, 5 November 1993.
5 JP to Hamish Hay, 8 December 1997.
6 On this issue see my article, 'The Politics of Pakeha History in a Bicultural Museum: Te Papa, the Museum of New Zealand, 1993–98', in Darryl McIntyre and Kirsten Wehner (eds), *National Museums, Negotiating Histories*, National Museum of Australia, Canberra, 2001, pp. 146–55.
7 Quoted in John Kousgard Sorenson, 'Ingeborg Stuckenberg in New Zealand', in Henning Bender and Birgit Larson (eds), *Danish Emigration to New Zealand*, Danes Worldwide Archives, Aarlborg, 1990, p. 49.
8 JP to Cheryll Sotheran, 8 July 1996.
9 Denis Dutton, 'State Treasure or Dog's Breakfast', *Evening Post*, 24 May 1998; Denis Dutton to JP, 26 May 1998.

Chapter 9

1 Jock Phillips (JP) to Jacqui Oldham, 31 July 1997.
2 Bronwyn Dalley, *Living in the 20th Century: New Zealand History in Photographs, 1900–1980*, Bridget Williams Books, Wellington, 2000.
3 JP to Peter McPhee and Charlotte Allen, 21 December 1998.

Chapter 10

1 Encyclopedia Of New Zealand Proposal, 1998.
2 The Valley of the Shadow, http://valley.lib.virginia.edu
3 The Great Chicago Fire, http://www.greatchicagofire.org/great-chicago-fire
4 Briefing to Judith Tizard, 'Encyclopaedia of New Zealand – Work programme 2000–2001', 19 May 2000.
5 Trung Tran to Jock Phillips, 23 June 2004.
6 Chris Hooke to Te Ara, 3 February 2010.

Index

Page numbers in **bold** refer to images.

1990 Commission 241

Aboriginal people, South Australia 47
Adelaide 43–44, 48, 50, 51
Adshead, Sam 32
Agar, Helen **284**
Akenson, Don 186, 192
Albers, Josef, *Variant IV* 125, **125**
Alexander Turnbull Library 161, 163, 170, 175, 183, 194, 197, 236, 238, 260, 310, 321
Alpers, Antony 189
Anderson, Atholl 241
Anderson, Neil 251–52
Andrews, George 292
ANZDEG (Australia and New Zealand Digital Encyclopedia Group) 340
ANZUS 191, 200–2
Aramoana aluminium smelter 149–50, **150**
Aramona, McHardy family home, Hawke's Bay 80–81, 84, 86
Archives and Records Association (ARANZ) 287
Archives New Zealand **296**, 297, 321; *see also* National Archives
Arlott, John 76
Armstrong, Dave 259, 342
Arnold, Rollo 190
art, New Zealand 73–75, 101
Auckland 100–1
Austin, Margaret 215

Australia 95, 151, 159, 198, 215, 243, 255, 290, 340, 351; *see also* ANZUS; South Australia
Australian Sesquicentennial Gift Trust for Oral History 236–37, **237**, 238
Averill, Leslie 67
Axford, Ian 179

Babich family 269
Bailyn, Bernard 112, 133–34, 135, 137
Baker, Garth 167
Bale, David 222
Barrowman, Rachel 161
Barry, Maggie **345**, 350
Bassett, Jan 209–10, 285
Bassett, Michael 95, 103, 205–6, **212**, 212–13, 214, 215, 222, 223, 229, 233, 239, 241, 304, 305
Bateman, Paul 305
Bateman Publishing 305, 338
Bayley, Nicholas 233
Beaglehole, John 21, 72, 98, 146–47, 207
Beaglehole, Robert 167
Beaglehole, Tim 97–98, 140, 144, 147, 183
Beatson, Peter 187, 188
Beauchamp family 58
Belich, James 2, 162, 192, 293
Berry, Joe, *Unwillingly to War* 29–30
Besser, Jonathon 169
Biggs, Bruce 230, 236
Binney, Judith 2, 185, **185**, 192, 232, 237, **237**, 241, 293

Index | 363

Bird, Crompton 17
Bird, Edward Punjab 12–13
Bird, Helen (née Stewart) 13, 17
Blake, Christopher 321
Blakeley, Roger 282, 283, 284, **284**, 285, 287–88, 295
Bloomfield, Ocean **13**
Boag, Peter **212**
Bogle, A. G. 24
Bohan, Edmund 34
Bolger, Jim **231**, 232
Bollinger, George 195–96, 344
Bolton, Joe 198
Bonita, Ruth 167
Borgfeldt, Tracey 305
Bornholdt, Jenny 290
Boyack, Nicholas 185–86, 194–97
Bradley, Barry 230
Brancovan, Constantine 127
Brasch, Charles 34, 35, 75
Brauer, Carl 127
Brickell, Barry 144
Briggs, Asa 72
Britain, New Zealand connections and views 70, 78, 152, 201, 254; Museum of New Zealand Te Papa Tongarewa 263, 265, 267–69; Phillips family and family background 1, 18, 19–21, 25, 26, 28, 35, 38, 41, 43, 58, 62, 71, 75–76, 78, 79, 81–82, 86–95, 351
British Commonwealth 35
British Empire: Jews 10; Neville Phillips' thesis 19–21; New Zealand membership and relations 20–21, 22, 78; Raleigh Club, Oxford University 24–25
Brocklebank, Laurie 225–26
Brookes, Barbara 353
Broughton, Ruka 189
Brown, Murray 319, 335
Buffalo 44–45
Bulletin school of writers and creative artists 159, 160
Bunkle, Phillida 119–22, 127, 128, 129, **142**, 143, 144, 156, 193, 194, 234; children 144–45, 203, 248; end of marriage to Jock Phillips 209, 285; feminism 119, 144, 166–67; National Women's Hospital 'unfortunate experiment' 168; Victoria University lecturing 140, 152–53, **153**; wedding to Jock Phillips 119, **120,** 121
Burke, Edmund 21, 35, 38
Burke, Vincent 293
Butler, Samuel 53

Caffin, David 86, 89, 103, 165
Caffin, Elizabeth (née Phillips) 28, **28**, 31, 71, 73, 75, 78, 86, 88, **99,** 165
Callaghan, Paul 102
Calvert, Janice **284**
Cameron, Perry 217, 218, 223–24, 225, 282
Campbell, Hamish 314
Candy, Alice 68
Canterbury centenary 67–68
Canterbury Club 53, 58
Canterbury Historical Association 73
Canterbury University College
  see University of Canterbury (formerly Canterbury University College)
Carew, Alison 223
Carrigafoyle, Wellington 166, **166**
Carter, Ian 190–91
Cassino, battle for 29, 35–36, 37, **39**
Cathedral Grammar School 66, 68, 70, **77**
Caxton Press 19, 35
Chadwyck-Healey, Edward 30–31
Cheyne, Christine 191
Christchurch 10, 12, 17, 19, 51–52, 53–56, 58, 67–68, 73–75, 76, 78, 81, 86, 95, 104, 248, 261; synagogue **11**; *see also* University of Canterbury
Christ's College, Christchurch 22, 56–57, 68, 70, 71, 85, 91, 93, 95, 97, 104
Churchill, Winston 36–37
civil-rights movement 108, 111, 113, 116
Clark, Bob 197
Clark, Fiona 189
Clark, Helen 290–91, 297, 307, **308**, 310, 318, 321, 325, 335, 341
Clement, Alwyn **284**
Cleveland, Les 169
Cole, G. D. H. 26
Coleman, Peter 186

Collinge, Jim 183, 192
Coney, Sandra 168
Cook, James 7, 8, **9**, 72, 146, 264, 265
Cook, Walter 165
Cooper, Bill 234
Cooper, Warren 225
Corner, Frank 98
Cottrell, Anna 252, 344
Coulson, Helene 332
counterculture 121–22, 130, 144, 158
Cowan, James 22, 160, 183, 199, 207
Cox, Nigel 259
Cripps, Stafford 26
Cromie, Jack **290**
Cross, Ian 3, 147, 148
Crump, Bryan 338–39
Cullen, Michael 297, 309–12, 345
cultural nationalism: Australia 159, 160; New Zealand 5, 22, 35–36, 38, 152, 160–61, 186, 201–2, 351
Curnow, Allen 18, 22, 187
Curnow, Wystan 155, 190
Curry, Paul **284**
Curti, Merle 72

Daley, Caroline 162
Dalley, Bronwyn 211, 243, 289, 293, **309**, 312, 314, 316, 318, 319, 333
Dalziel, Raewyn **212**, 214, 216, **217**, 223, 241, 245
Davidson, Janet 252
Davis, Colin 155, 189
Davis, Leigh 190
Davis, Lloyd 318
Davis, Te Aue 237
Dell, Dame Miriam 224
Dell, Sharon 237
Department of Internal Affairs **284**, 284–85; *see also* Heritage Group; Historical Branch Te Puna Kōrero Tuku Iho
Derby, Mark 268, **268**
Designworks 326–27
Dewey, John 3, 138–39, 140, 146, 147, 155, 156, 157, 160
Dewson, Emma **323**
Dictionary of American Biography 135–36

Dictionary of New Zealand Biography 17–18, 211, 213, 230, 234, **234**, 243, 283, 291, 294, 305; included in Te Ara 315–16, 321–22, 333, 344, 346; W. H. Oliver's editorship 32, 183, 189, 190, 208; website 292, 307, **308**, 322
Dobbie, Alison 319, 321
Douglas, Ken 154
Dreaver, Tony 187
Du Plessis, Rosemary 328–29, **329**, 346
Dulwich College, London 86–88, **91**, 93–94
Durie, Eddie 189–90
Durie, Mason 314, 320
Dutton, Denis 277

East–West Centre 201
Edmond, Lauris 183
Edwards, Brian 167
Elder, Jack 291
Eldred-Grigg, Stevan 187, 192
Elgar, Ellen 271
Ellison, Edward 320
Else, Anne 223, **224**
Encyclopedia of New Zealand 304, 315, 317, 318; *see also* Te Ara – The Encyclopedia of New Zealand
England 24, 30–31, 41, 75, 88–89, 94–95, 108, 127; *see also* London
Eventfinda 341

Fairburn, Miles 155, 176, 293
family history 350–51
Farrar, David 334
Faulknor, Janine **323**, 331, 341–42
feminism 118–19, 121, 144, 153, 166–67, 168
Ferguson, Lindsay 288
Fieldhouse, David 32, 72
Fisher, Charles 47, 48
Fisher, Elizabeth 44
Fisher, Hurtle 48
Fisher, James 47
Fisher, Sir James Hurtle 43–48, **46**, 50, 57
Fishman, Bob 127
Fitzgerald, Gay 156
Fleming, Donald 134, 137–38
FOR*MEN collective 167–68
Fox, Charles 58

Foxwell, Roland 30
Frame, Janet 131
France 41, 90, 91, 93, 109, 127, 128; see also Paris
Frank Knox Fellowship 109–10
Franks, Peter 187, 242
Fraser, Lyndon 264
Fraser, Robert 163, 165
Frontier of Dreams 293, 341
Frost, Lucy 156
Fyfe, Judith 184, **185**, 187, 235, 237, **237**

Galbreath, Ross 221
Gallipoli campaign 195–96, 226, **227**, 262, 297, 350–51
Gammage, Bill 226, **227**
Gardner, Jim 32, 72, 73
generational revolt, 1960s–70s 112–19, 121–23, 139, 143–44
Gibbons, Peter 182
Gillespie, Christine 167
Gillingham, Allan 328
Glover, Denis 19, 22, 131
Glover, Felicity 144
Goldington, Bedfordshire 43, 49, 50
Gorbey, Ken 248, 249, **249**, 250–51, 260, 261, 274, 275
Gould, George 58
Gould, John 107
Gould, Nell (née Lane) 58
Graham, Doug 217
Grant, A. J. 21
Grant, David 222
Gray, Alison 189
Gray, Ken 169
The Great Adventure (Jock Phillips) 194–97, **195**
Great War Stories 344
Green, Anna 192
Green, David 208, 209, 211, 329
Grey, George 47, 48
Gross, Richard 200
Grover, Ray 183, 284, **296**
Guard family 269
Guthrie-Smith, Herbert: *Sorrows and Joys of a New Zealand Naturalist* 82; *Tutira* 131, 159

Haami, Brad 235
Hakiwai, Arapata 252
Hamer, David 237, 241
Hamley, Robin 196–97
Hancock, W. K. 21
Handlin, Oscar 112, 135
Hangaroa 57, 58, **59**
Hardie-Boys, Sir Michael **290**
Harland, Bryce 188
Harper, Frida Susan 273, 285, **286**, 287, 301, 336, 350
Harper, Gordon 350–51
Harper, Philip 350
Harper, Robin 350–51, 352
Hart, Leonard 196, 228
Harton, Jean **185**
Harvard University 3, 108, 109–27, **113**, 131–35, 136–40, 156–57, 176; Charles Warren Center for American History 175
Hatch, Norman 228, **229**
Havelock North primary school 84, 86
Hay, Jackie 341, 342
Hay, Mary-Annette 272
Hay, Sir Hamish 261
Hearn, Terry 232–33
Hector, James 328
Heenan, Joe **206**, 207
Henare, Manuka 314
Henderson, Kennaway 19
Henry Adams History Club 135
Herbert, A. P. 18, 71
Here to Stay television series 338
Heritage Group, Department of Internal Affairs **280**, 281–98, 305–6
Heritage Property Unit 283, 289–91
Hicks, Colin 242
Hicks, Geoff 251–52, 318–19
Highet, Alan 180, 183
Hight, James 17–18, 19, 21, 31, 65
Hill, Marguerite 331
Hill, Michael 183
Hill, Richard 192, 208, 209, 210, 241–42, **296**
Hilliard, Hinemoa 252, 274
Hindmarsh, John 45–47, 48
Hipango Park, Whanganui River 12, **13**

Historical Branch Te Puna Kōrero Tuku Iho (later History Group) 205–45, **217, 220,** 247–48, 282, 283, 291, 293, 304; advisory committee 214–15, 216, 217, 223, 245; Branch history **206,** 207–8; contractual services to Te Papa 251; Māori history 214, 230, 233–36, **234,** 240, 241; official histories 218–19, 221–22, 351; *People's History* newsletter 241; support to publishers 240; war histories 225–28, 226, 227

history 2, 133; New Zealand history 1–2, 3–4, 20, 137, 145, 146, 175, 178–79, 183–84, 351–53 (*see also* Māori – history; oral history, New Zealand; Stout Research Centre); teaching 135; *see also* family history

'History in the House' presentations 241
Hoffman, Paul 106
Holcroft, Monte 146
Holland, Sid 103
Holmes, Paul 272, 277
Holt, Jim 155, 175, 208, 240
Holyoake, Keith 103
Hopa, Ngapare 249, 320
Hornsby, Harry 70
Horrocks, Roger 155, 190, 318
Hosking, Peter 168
Hotere, Ralph, anti-Aramoana sculpture 150, **150**
Housman, A. E. 24; *A Shropshire Lad* 15, **16**
Howden, Peter 196
Howkins, Alun 193, 242
Hudson, Paul 233
Hulme, Keri 187, 190
Humphrey, Hubert 112, 113
Hutching, Megan **217,** 238, 241, 297

In Light of the Past (Jock Phillips) 162–67
Inglis, Ken 198
Italy 29, 31, 35–36, 41, 79, 90–91, 127–28; official history of New Zealand soldiers, World War II 36–38

Jackson, Moana 102
James, Edward 136

Jeffcoat, Sir John 46
Jews: Christchurch synagogue 11; France 128; London 7–9, 93; New Zealand 10, 15, 17, 22, 30, 35, 107; United States 111–12, 127
Johnson, Lyndon and Lady Bird 103–4, 105
Johnson, Paul 326–27
Joplin, Janis 122
Joyce, Steven 336

Kaua, Peggy 228, **229**
Keane, Basil 328
Keith, Gerry 167
Keith, Ken 197
Keith, Michael 159, 167, 259
Kennedy, Edward 118
Kennedy, Jeff 285
Kennedy, Robert 111, 112
Kent, Dave 169, 190, 191
King, Martin Luther 108, 111, 116, 122, 123
King, Michael 2, 5, 104, 171, 180, 181, 184, 185, 189, **296,** 353
King, Peter 162
Kippenberger, Howard 35–36, **206,** 207
Kirk, Norman 143–44, 147
Kirkpatrick, Russell 230
Knox, Geoff 249
Knox, Joanna 259

Labrum, Bronwyn **217,** 241, 272
land: Canterbury 53, 57; Hawke's Bay 57, 62–63; Māori land 62–65, 151, 189–90; Pākehā approaches compared to Māori 189–90; South Australia 43, 47
Landfall 34–36, 38, 131, 168, 186
landscape architects 149, 151, 186, 189, 200, 243
Lane, Beauchamp 58
Lane, William Hannibal 58
Lange, David 183, 205
Laurie, Robert **237**
Leach, Helen 190
Lealand, Geoffrey 187
Lee, Graeme 209, 215–16, **217,** 217–18, 223, 224–25, 226
Levine, Stephen 329, **329**
Liddle, Peter 170

Lilburn, Douglas 186, 190
Little Akaloa, Banks Peninsula 80
London 21, 24, 49–50, 86–88, 89–90, 93–95, 127, 146, 248; East End 7–10, **9,** 12
Longman Paul 101, 168
Lovell-Smith, Melanie 331
Lyttelton 50–51

Macdonald, Charlotte 162, 189, 208, 210, 211, 218, 293
Mack, James 166
Mackay, David 161
Mackay, Jamie 291, 350
Maclean, Chris 145, 150, 162–63, **164,** 165, 166, 167, 181–82, 197–98, 200, 226, 342
Madgwick, Pam **284,** 288
Mahuta, Robert 190
Main, William 190
Malifa, Ata 237, **237**
Malone, E. P. 195
Malone, William 195
A Man's Country (Jock Phillips) 4, 167–73, **172,** 178, 192, 194, 200, 209, 339, 352
Mansfield, Katherine 58, 189, 192
Manson, Hugo 184, **185,** 187, 236
Māori: Hawke's Bay 84, 86; history 3, 214, 230, 233–36, **234,** 240, 241, 242, 249–50, 351; influence 202; land 62–65, 151, 189–90; Museum of New Zealand Te Papa Tongarewa 252, 254, 255, 263, 269, 271, 274–77, 278, 279; population 78, 202; revival of culture and language 254; Te Ara – The Encyclopedia of New Zealand 310, 314, 316, 317, 318, 319, 320, 326, 327–28, 333, 344; university lecturers and scholars 178, 181, 184; *see also* Treaty of Waitangi; Waitangi Tribunal
Māori Peoples of New Zealand: Ngā Iwi o Aotearoa 319, 338
'Maoriland' culture 160, 263
Martin, John 187, 211, 222, 258
Mason, Karen 251
Matthews, Jill 191
Matthews, Martin 298, **309,** 315, 336
May, Philip Ross 32, 38, 72

McCahon, Colin 101; 'Painting' 74–75, **74**
McCarthy, Eugene 111, 113, 118
McCartney, Jane **100,** 101, 110, 114, 116, 119, 122–23
McCormick, E. H. 160, **206,** 207
McDonald, Geraldine 183
McGarvey, Rangi 327, 328, 333
McGee, Greg, *Foreskin's Lament* 255
McGibbon, Ian 208, 209, 210–11, 218, 225, 226, 229, 230, 233, 291
McGovern, George 115, 118
McHardy, Douglas 81, 82, 95
McHardy, Mary (née Palmer) **59,** 61, 62, 80–81, 82, 83, 145
McKenzie, Don 106, 183
McKergow, Fiona 223
McKinnon, Malcolm 161, 176, **177,** 230, **231,** 232, 328, 329–30
McLauchlan, Gordon 148, 304
McLean, Donald 62–65
McLean, Gavin 219, 241, 293, **296**
McLintock, A. H. 31, 304, 317
McPhee, Peter 161, 176, **177**
Mead, George 139, 157
Mead, Sidney 180–81, 184, 189, 233
Meade, Anne 189
Meikle, Phoebe 168
Mein Smith, Philippa 240
Melhuish, Molly 150
Mene family 269
Middleton, Sue 189
Milford Track 84
Milroy, Jim 230, 234
Ministry for Culture and Heritage 295, 296–98, 344–45; NZLive website 341
Monk, W. F. 24
Moorhouse, William 51, 52
Morrell, W. P. 21
Muldoon, Robert 148, 161, 183, 344
Mulgan, John 22, 36, 106
Munz, Peter 106
Museum of New Zealand Te Papa Tongarewa 246, 247–79, **257, 261, 267, 273,** 302, 306–7, 313, 321; *Exhibiting Ourselves* exhibition 256–57, 259, 261–74, 277, 279; *Getting to Our Place* (documentary film) 252, 277;

Golden Days show 272; *Life in New Zealand* exhibition 256, 270–74; *Passports* exhibition 255–56, **257**, 259, 260–61, **261**, 263–70, **267, 268**; Treaty of Waitangi exhibition 274–77, 278; *Woollen Yarns (On the Sheep's Back)* exhibition 270, 271–74, **273**

Nash, Walter 26
Nathan, Simon 314, 328
National Archives 170, **174**, 175, 183, 198, 226, 228, 275, 283–84, 287–89, 295; *see also* Archives New Zealand
National Digital Forum 321
national identity, New Zealand 5, 35–36, 38, 131, 148–49, 151, 161, 162, 168, 201–2, 213–14, 226, 228, 232, 295; cultural and regional origins of Pākehā 232–33; Museum of New Zealand Te Papa Tongarewa 253, 255, 256–57, 261–63, 278; post-colonial crisis 253–54
National Library of New Zealand 236, 237, 282, 308, **308**, 321, 349
National Oral History Association of New Zealand (NOHANZ) 185
nationalism, New Zealand 22, 35, 194, 200, 352; *see also* cultural nationalism, New Zealand
Neill, Sam 336, **345**
Nelson, Bill 83–84
Nelson, Christine **81**
Nelson, James **81**, 83–84
Nelson, Jim 22, 24, 26, 31, 80, **81**, 83, 84
Nelson, Patricia (née Palmer) 22, 24, 31, 60, 80, 81, 83, 84
New Caledonia 108–9, **109**
New Zealand Historical Association 243, 292
New Zealand Historical Atlas 228–30, **231**, 232, 292, 305, 330, 351
New Zealand History Research Trust Fund 212, 213, 239
New Zealand History website 291, 307
New Zealand Journal of History 171, 178, 208, 242, 249, 337, 349–50
New Zealand Listener 3, 146–52, 154–55, 158, 173, 181, 187, 201, 238, 248, 320, 335

New Zealand Oral History Archive 184, 185, 237
New Zealand Oral History Association 236
New Zealand Trust and Loan Company 53
New Zealand Wars 20, 198, 199, 200, 278
Newton, Douglas **177**
Nicholls, Rex 166
Nixon, Richard 113, 118, 140, 143
Nolan, Melanie 211, 222
NZHistoryJock website 350
NZLive website 341

O'Connor, Peter 211
O'Donnell, Jean-Marie 258, 272, 312
Offenberger, Annette **284**
'Old World' culture 1, 3, 17–18, 19, 31, 41, 43, 44, 75–76, 78, 122–23, 146–47, 183, 185, 256, 264, 351
Oliver, W. H. (Bill) 5, 32, 72, 183, 189, **190**, 208, 241
Olssen, Erik 155, **156**, 189, 241, 293
O'Malley, Vincent 353
oral history, New Zealand 184–86, 214, 236–38, 259, 264, 277, 297, 351
Orange, Claudia 2, 192, 208, 291, 293, **296**, 322, **323**, 329
O'Regan, Pauline 33
O'Reilly, Ron 73
O'Shaunessy, Anne **284**
O'Sullivan, Vincent 192
Ouepoto, Hawke's Bay 81, 82, 145, **145**
Owen, Alwyn 185
Owen, John 31–32, 72
Oxford University 24–26; Labour Club 26; Merton College 22, 24, **25**; Pakeha Club 25; Raleigh Club 24–25

Paine, Thomas 35
Palmer, Dorothy (née Wells) 57–58, **59**, 60, **61**, 62, 94–95
Palmer, Emily (née Fisher) 49, 50, **52**, 54, 57
Palmer family 80–82, **81**
Palmer, George 55
Palmer, Jim 55
Palmer, John 60, 81
Palmer, Joseph 43, 48–55, **51, 52**, 56, 57, 58

Palmer, Miles 49–50
Palmer, Olive **55**, 56
Palmer Range 53
Palmer, Selby 49, 54–55, **55**, 56–58, **59**, 60, 61, 62, 80, 82–83
Palmer, Sir Geoffrey 318
Palmer, Ted 55, 56, 57
Palmerston North Boys' High School 14–16, 17
Paris 24
Park, Geoff 186–87, 191, 192
Park, Stuart 252, 274
Parr, Alison 238
Pascoe, Paul 68
Patterson, Kathryn 283, 288
Paul, Charlotte 101
Paul, Janet 101, 147, 168
Paul, Joanna, sketch of Hone Tuwhare 101, **101**
Pawson, Eric 318
Pere, Joe 189, 235
Pere, Rose 249
Perkins, Jack 185
Perry, Nick 190–91
Phillips, Catherine 71, **71**, 75, 86, 87, 89, 90, **99**, 123, 277
Phillips, Clara (known as Claire) (née Bird) 10, 12–13, **14**, 17
Phillips, David 12, 13, 14, 17
Phillips, Hester 144, 156, 157, 193, 203, 209, 248
Phillips, Jesse 144, 156, 157, 193, 203, 209, 248
Phillips, John (Jock)
  career *see* Heritage Group; Historical Branch Te Puna Kōrero Tuku Iho; Museum of New Zealand Te Papa Tongarewa; Stout Research Centre; Te Ara – The Encyclopedia of New Zealand; Victoria University of Wellington
  early years: childhood and upbringing 3, 67–68, **69**, 70–76, 77, 78–84, 203, 248; cricket 76, **77**, 90; family photograph, 1966 **99**; Hawke's Bay family and holidays **79**, 80–82, **81**, 82–84, 86, 94, 95; love of art 74–75, 90–91; 'My Obituary' school assignment 84, **85**; Queenstown holidays 86; schooling 66, 68, 70, **71**, 84, 86, 93–94, 95, 97, 104
  family background 1, 3, 5; *see also* Phillips, Neville; Phillips, Pauline (née Palmer); and names of other members of Phillips, Palmer, Bird, Fisher, McHardy and Nelson families
  honours and awards 349, 350
  personal interests: art 74–75, 90–91, 98, 101, 124–25, 134; music 98, 122, 125–26; New Zealand outdoors and landscape 3, 43, 82–83, 84, 86, 94, 131, 139, **142**, 144–46, 149, 151, 189, 200, 203, 285, **286**; photography 75, 109, 145, 203, 331–32, 342; politics 102–4, 112–19, 122, 123, 124; reading 73, 103, 107, 108, 112, 116–18, **117**, 119, 122–23, 131, 137; theatre 89, 100, **105**, 126, 203
  personal relationships *see* Bassett, Jan; Bunkle, Phillida; Harper, Frida Susan; McCartney, Jane; Walker, Kim
  travel: Britain, 1985 188; Britain and Ireland, 1997 **268**, 268–69; Edinburgh 279; England and Europe 86–91, **92**, 93–95, 127–28, 248; Northern Ireland 298, 301, **302–3**; passport **141**; Queensland, 1987 192; Sussex, 1985 **193**, 193–94; United States 128–31, **129**, 156–57, 248, 275–76, 276 (*see also* Harvard University)
  university studies, research and student life *see* Harvard University; University of Sussex; Victoria University of Wellington
  writing and lecturing: conference papers 155–56, 173, 201–2; early 2000s 340–41; *The Great Adventure* 194–97, **195**; letters from Harper brothers during World War I 350–51, **352**; *In Light of the Past* 162–67; *A Man's Country* 4, 167–73, **172**, 178, 192, 194, 200, 209, 339, 352; *To the Memory* 350; *Metro* magazine article on New Zealand history 238; 'Musings in Maoriland…' (article) 160; 'New Zealand and the ANZUS Alliance'

(paper) 201–2; *New Zealand Listener* contributions 3, 146–52, 154–55, 158, 173, 181, 187, 238, 248, 335; 'Of Verandahs and Fish and Chips and Footie on Saturday Afternoon' (article) 232, 249, 250, 264; 'Paradise by degrees' (lecture) 152; *Settlers* 233, 341; *The Sorrow and the Pride* 197–98, **199**, 200, **202,** 203, 226, 350; television and radio work 167, 192–93, 338–39; 'University History Departments and Public History' (paper) 242–43; 'War and National Identity' (essay) 194; 'Watching Big Brother' (paper) 243

Phillips, Morris 8

Phillips, Neville: career as historian 3, 7, 19–20, 31–38, **33,** 71–73; death 301, **302–3**; early years 12, 13–16; family background 7–12; interest in art 73–75, 90–91, 98, 125; interest in poetry 15, **16,** 18, 19, 71; as a parent 3, 71–72, 73, 76, 78, 86, 88, 90–91, 94, 122–24, 131; University of Canterbury, vice-chancellor **6,** 31, 38–39, **40,** 97, **99,** 123–24; university studies and thesis, Canterbury University College 16, 17–18, 19–22, 65; university studies, Oxford University 3, 22, 24–26; views on primacy of British, European and 'Old World' culture 1, 3, 18, 19–21, 25, 26, 31, 35, 38, 41, 75–76, 78, 122–23, 147, 351; visits to England and Europe, and retirement to England 83, 86–91, 93–95; war service 26, **27, 28,** 28–31; in Wellington, 1938 **23**; writing and radio talks 34–38, 76, 132, 207

Phillips, Pauline (née Palmer) 22, 28, 31, **99**; early years and education 60, **61,** 62–65, **63**; family background 43–58, 60; Hawkes Bay farm, Te Aratipi **42,** 60, 62, 80; interest in art and literature 73–75, 79, 98, 125; as a parent **28,** 78–81, **79,** 86, 90, 93, 122, 123, 131, 165; visits to England and Europe, and retirement to England 24, 36, 41, 79, 83, 86–91, 93–95, 165

Phillips, Sam 7, 8–10, 12, 13, 17

Phillips, Sarah (née Glock) 8
Pocock, Greville 72
Pocock, J. G. A. 32, 72
Pope, Diana and Jeremy, Mobil guides 165
Pound, Francis 190
Press newspaper 18, 20, 49
Preston, Alison 258
Preston, Gaylene 252, 277
Price, Hugh 182
Prior, Ian 183
Provost, Lyn **309**
Pugsley, Chris 225, 226, **227**
Punawaiti School, Hawke's Bay 84, 86

Queenstown 86

Rabel, Roberto 225
Ramsden, Irihapeti 234
Rearden, Steve 128
Reedy, Tamati 237, **237,** 333
Reedy, Tip 235
Rei, Tania 223
Reid, Tony 148
Renwick, Bill 152
Rigg, Bob 153
Roberts, Heather 187
Roberts, Nigel 329, **329**
Robinson, Roger 192
Roger, Warwick 171, 238
Ronnie, Mary 211
Ross, Angus 134
Rotoiti, Lake 83
Rouncil, Nelsons' house, Hawke's Bay 80, 83, 84
Rowling, Wallace 147
Royal, Te Ahukaramū Charles 230, 235, 241, 320
royal tour, 1953–54 78, 81–82, 244, **244**
Rugby World cup projects 342, **343,** 344

Sadler, Hone 320
Sadlier, Heath 327
Salkin, Barry 127
Salmond, Anne 264, 265
Salmond, John 107, 108, 144, 155
Sargeson, Frank 22
Saunders, J. J. 32

Savage, Roger 106
Schrader, Ben 162, 328
Sciascia, Piri 320
Scott, Tom 147, 167, 190
Seddon, Richard 22
Sedgwick, Charles 189
Settlers (Jock Phillips) 233, 341
Shadbolt, Maurice 297
Shaw, George Bernard 18
Shift 325, 326, 327, 332
Sidelinger, Deb 334
Simpson, Heather 150
Simpson, Miria 230, **231**, 234
Simpson, Tony 33–34, 185
Sinclair, Keith 2, 5, 72, 137, 147, 171, 173, 189, 351; *Penguin History of New Zealand* 38
Smallwood, Chris 126, 127
Smith, Athol 196
Smith, Brian 325, 332
Smith, Wilfred Collinson 196
Somerville, Ross 322, **323**, 324–25, 332, 340
The Sorrow and the Pride (Chris Maclean and Jock Phillips) 197–98, **199**, 200, **202**, 203, 226, 350
Sotheran, Cheryll 248, **249**, 250, 251, 252, 260, 261, 272, 278, 279
South African War 20, 170, 200, 290, 291, 331
South Australia 43–48; *see also* Adelaide
Spoonley, Paul 318
Springbok rugby tour, 1981 143–44, 153–54, 161–62, 262
Statham, Edith 198, 200
Stead, Edgar 56
Stead, G. G. 56
Stead, Noel 56
Stone, Frank 107, 110, 111, 121, 162, 163
Stout, Anna 164; stained glass windows from house 181–82, **182**
Stout, John David 180
Stout Literary Archive 187
Stout Research Centre 173, 175–76, 178–203; books written by researchers 192; conferences 188–92, **190**, 250

Stout, Robert 164, 180, 181; stained glass windows from house 181–82, **182**
Stout Trust 180, 181
Students for a Democratic Society (SDS) 112, 113–14
Sun newspaper 17, 18; 'Sunspots' column 18
Swarbrick, Nancy 322, **323**, 324

Tahi, Brenda **284**
Tamaki, Leanne **323**
Taonui, Rawiri 320
Tapsell, Peter 213
Taupō 60, **61**, 83, 279
Taylor, Aila 189
Taylor, Kerry 162, 242
Taylor, Nancy 207, 226
Te Ara – The Encyclopedia of New Zealand **300**, 301–46, **311**, **316**, 349, 352; advisory committee 318–19, 335; international interest 340; launches 335–37, **345**; logo **327**, 327–27; Pātaka committee 320–21; published books 337–38; Te Ara Wānanga 320, 326, 327
Te Aratipi, Hawke's Bay **42**, 60, 80–81, **81**
Te Awekotuku, Ngahuia 189
Te Kurapa, Haniko 274, 275, **276**
Te Papa *see* Museum of New Zealand Te Papa Tongarewa
Te Pouhere Kōrero 236
television history 292–94, **294**, 338
Temara, Pou 191
Tennant, Margaret 223, 225, 319
Thatcher, Margaret **40**
Thompson, Mervyn 33
Thompson, Paul 262, 274, 275, 276–77
Thomson, Alistair 194
Thomson, John 183, 186, 190, 191, 192
Thoreau, Henry David 130–31, 139, 144, 159
Tizard, Judith 307, 308–9, **309**, 310
To the Memory (Jock Phillips) 350
Tolerton, Jane 185–86, 187
Tomorrow 19
Torkington, Nat 334
Torley, Frank 336
Trade Union History Project 241–42

Tran, Trung 339–40
Traue, Jim 170, 175, 180, 183
Treaty of Waitangi 192, 260, 274, 276, 288, 289, 294; Museum of New Zealand Te Papa Tongarewa exhibition 274–77, 278; sesquicentenary 216, 222, 241, 253
Trethewey, Alan **199,** 200
Trethewey, William 200
Trotter, Sir Ron 270–71
Tutaki, Emily 331
Tuwhare, Hone 101, **101,** 187, 190

Union Bank 49, 50–52, 54, 55, 56, 60
United States 107–8, 191, 200–2, 215, 218, 243, 255, 256, 340; Jock Phillips' experiences and views 110–18, 121–22, 123, 124–27, 128–31, 133, 140, 275–76, **276,** 351; Marines in New Zealand, World War II 226, 228; see also ANZUS; Harvard University; Vietnam War and protests
University of Canterbury (formerly Canterbury University College): Neville Phillips' education and later career 3, **6, 7,** 16, 17, 19–22, 31–35, **33,** 38–39, **40,** 71–73, 97, **99,** 123–24; Pauline Palmer's education 62–65
University of Sussex 193–94
University of Waikato 153; winter lectures, 1979 151–52

Victoria University of Wellington 210; Council 301, 341; Electronic Text Centre 318; Jock Phillips' career 140, 146, 152–56, 158–61, 169, 176, 177, 178–79, 200, 206–7, 230, 245; Jock Phillips' studies and student life 97–98, 102–4, **105,** 106–8; see also Stout Research Centre
Vietnam War and protests 39, 103–4, **105,** 107–8, 114–15, 117, 143, 225, 275, 276
von Arnim, Elizabeth 58

Waimārama 60, 62, **79,** 80, 82, **83,** 235
Wainwright, Chris 152
Waitangi Tribunal 2, 63, 191, 242, 254, 260, 277

Wakefield, Edward Gibbon, *A Letter from Sydney* 44, 47
Walker, Geoff 167, 171
Walker, James 163
Walker, Kim 210, 285
Walker, Ranginui 190, 293, 319, **319,** 320, 336, 338, 344
Walrond, Carl **323**
Walsh, Pat 242
Wanganui Collegiate 57, 60
War Histories Branch **206,** 207
war memorials 197–98, **199,** 200, **202,** 203, 226, 289–91, **290,** 350, 352
Wards, Ian 208, **296,** 304–5
Waru, Ray 293
Watson, Don 236
Watson, James 219
Webster, Peter 155
Wedde, Ian 187, 251
Weir House, Victoria University 97–98, 100, **100,** 102–4, 107
Wellington 97, 100, 107, 144, 153, 154, 163, 285–86; see also names of organisations based in Wellington
Wellman, Harold 328
Wells, Charles 57–58, 60
Wells, Florence (née Lane) 58
Westra, Ans 269
Wevers, Francis 242
Wevers, Lydia 192, 318
Whaanga, Mere 320
Whanganui 12
Whiting, Cliff 252, **253,** 279
Wicksteed, Kim 326
Wikaira, Martin 320
Williams, Bridget 189, 241
Williams, Des 272
Williams, Robin 207, 213–14, 218, 233, 238
Williams, Shirley 322, **323,** 331
Wilson, Frank 127–28, 147
Wilson, Ormond 147
Winter, Jay 198
Wintringham, Michael 296–97
Women Together (encyclopedia of women's organisations) 213, 223–25, **224,** 305, 319
women's suffrage 222, 262, 346

Wood, Fred 72
Wood, Sue 296
Woodford, Christchurch 54, **55**
Woodford House, Havelock North 60, 62
World War I 12, 67, 170, 194–97, 198, 226, 271, 291, 344, 350, 352
World War II 26–31, 35–36, 170, 198, 200, 207, 225, 226, 228, 297; official history of New Zealand soldiers in Italy 36–38, 207
Wylie, David 180, 192

Young, David 186, 187
Young, Rose 249

Zohrab, A. C. 15, 17, 18